DATE			
JAN 19 '78			

THE OPEN AND CLOSED MIND

IN COLLABORATION WITH

Richard Bonier

Gloria Cheek

M. Ray Denny, Ph.D.

Richard I. Evans, Ph.D.

Franz Geierhaas

Leo Gladin

C. Gratton Kemp, Ph.D.

John J. Laffey

Jacques M. Levy

Figes Matheson

Warren C. McGovney

Bernard Mikol, Ph.D.

Alfred Oram

Frank Restle, Ph.D.

Theodore Rottman

Patricia W. Smith

Theodore S. Swanson

Hans H. Toch, Ph.D.

Don A. Trumbo, Ph.D.

Robert N. Vidulich, Ph.D.

Martin Zlotowski

Stephanie Zlotowski

THE
OPEN
AND
CLOSED
MIND

INVESTIGATIONS INTO
THE NATURE OF BELIEF SYSTEMS
AND
PERSONALITY SYSTEMS

by

MILTON ROKEACH

BASIC BOOKS, INC. · Publishers · NEW YORK

© 1960 by Basic Books, Inc.

Library of Congress Catalog Card Number 60-5888

Printed in the United States of America

DESIGNED BY PETER MARKS

74 75 76   20 19 18 17 16 15 14 13 12 11

To

Miriam, Ruth, and Martin

Preface

This book is addressed to all those who, for one reason or another, have had occasion to reflect on the nature of their own belief systems and that of others. I hope that the ideas and findings presented herein will provide such persons with a useful frame of reference to guide further reflection or research.

In preparing this work for publication, I have tried to keep in mind two sorts of audiences: my scientific and professional colleagues in psychology and related disciplines, and a larger audience of persons who for many reasons are likely to have strong investments in the ideological, social, and personal issues which are here raised and investigated. Both kinds of audiences, I am sure, will include persons concerned with the nature of ideology, philosophy, politics and religion, their relation to personality and the thought processes, and to the psychology and sociology of knowledge.

First and foremost, this work is intended as a monographic report of research on the nature of belief systems, and it should be evaluated as such. Nevertheless, it is my hope that despite the inclusion of technical material the basic ideas, findings, and conclusions presented herein will be communicated clearly to the larger audience for whom this work is also intended. To this end much of the technical material, which is primarily of a statistical nature, will appear in "Notes" at the end of the chapters. Whenever it is necessary to use a statistical notion in the text it will be explained in a special footnote addressed to the general reader. These devices will place a somewhat greater burden on the professional reader, but it is hoped that he will be compensated for this by the fact that the text as a whole is generally more readable than it would otherwise be.

It is often the case in psychology, and in other social sciences as well, that researchers select and formulate research problems because of their personal or ideological significance. This is undesirable to the extent that it leads to blind spots and to hidden value judgments, which detract from the scientific merit of the research. I have tried to be aware of the dangers involved and to avoid them, insofar as it was possible for me to do so. However, the reader will have to decide for himself to what extent this effort has been successful.

Formally, the research reported here was initiated in 1951. During this period, I was fortunate in receiving support from several sources and it is a pleasure to acknowledge my gratitude to them. From 1951 to 1954, the research was supported by a grant from the Social Science Research Council, which freed me, half-time, from teaching duties. During this time and also afterwards I received annual grants from the All University Research Fund of Michigan State University, which supported various aspects of the research in progress. The National Institute of Mental Health (M-1885) provided funds for the completion of the various research projects reported herein and for the completion of this book. For this support I am also very grateful.

Most of the material in this volume is published here for the first time. Portions of it have already appeared in modified form in various psychological journals. Parts of Chapters 1 and 2 appeared originally in "The Unity of Thought and Belief," *Journal of*

Personality, 1956, *25:* 224–250, and is reprinted here, with revisions, by permission of the editor, Edward E. Jones, and the Duke University Press. Chapter 2, a small part of Chapter 3, Chapters 4, 6, and 9 are reprinted, with modifications, from the following journal articles with permission of the managing editor, Arthur C. Hoffman, of the American Psychological Association:

"The Nature and Meaning of Dogmatism," *Psychological Review,* 1954, *61:* 194–204.

"A Distinction Between Dogmatic and Rigid Thinking" (with McGovney, W. C., and Denny, M. R.), *Journal of Abnormal and Social Psychology,* 1955, *51:* 87–93.

"Political and Religious Dogmatism: An Alternative to the Authoritarian Personality," *Psychological Monographs,* 1956, *70:* No. 18 (whole No. 425).

The F Scale is reproduced in Appendix B by permission of Harper & Brothers from T. W. Adorno, *et al., The Authoritarian Personality.* Harper & Brothers have also kindly granted permission to quote from D. Elton Trueblood's *The Logic of Belief.* The Gough-Sanford Rigidity Scale is reproduced in Appendix C with the permission of Consulting Psychologists Press.

"A Factorial Study of Dogmatism and Related Concepts" (with B. Fruchter), *Journal of Abnormal and Social Psychology,* 1956, *53:* 356–360.

"A Factorial Study of Dogmatism, Opinionation, and Related Scales," *Psychological Reports,* 1958, *4:* 19–22.

The former is reproduced with the permission of the managing editor of the American Psychological Association; the latter, with the permission of Robert Ammons, editor of *Psychological Reports.*

I would also like to thank the following publishers and individuals for permission to quote from the materials specified:

Addison-Wesley Publishing Co., Inc.: G. W. Allport, *The Nature of Prejudice,* 1954.

American Psychological Association: F. H. George and J. H. Handlon, "A Language for Perceptual Analysis," *Psychological Review,* 1957, *64:* 14–25.

Harper & Brothers, Inc.: H. A. Witkin, *et al., Personality through Perception,* 1954; J. Gunther, *Inside Africa,* 1955.

B. Herder Book Co.: H. J. Schroeder, *Disciplinary Decrees of the General Councils,* 1937.

Houghton Mifflin Co.: G. W. Allport and P. E. Vernon, *A Study of Values: A Scale for Measuring the Dominant Interests in Personality,* 1931.

The Journal of Aesthetics and Art Criticism: H. D. Aiken, "The Aesthetic Relevance of Belief," 1951, 9: 301–315.

Journal of Social Issues: I. Chein, "Research Needs," 1956, *12*: 57–66; R. Williams, "Religion, Value-orientations, and Inter-group Conflict," 1956, *12*: 12–20.

Longmans, Green & Co., Inc.: J. V. L. Casserly, *The Retreat from Christianity in the Modern World,* 1953.

Vassar Alumnae Magazine: R. Waelder, "Notes on Prejudice," 1949.

John Wiley & Sons, Inc.: M. B. Smith, J. S. Bruner, and R. W. White, *Opinions and Personality,* 1956.

It is with great pleasure that I acknowledge my indebtedness to many persons who contributed to the success of the present research effort. As can be seen from the Table of Contents, the various researches reported herein are the result of a collective labor of many individuals who, in one way or another, made significant contributions to the total effort. (As can also be seen from the Table of Contents, some chapters carry by-lines, whereas others do not. In the latter instances, I am the sole author of the chapter.) This collaborative effort is by far the most gratifying intellectual experience of my entire career. It developed spontaneously out of conversations with colleagues and students in graduate seminars and in many informal discussions outside the classroom. In this connection, I will always especially remember the pleasurable hours spent with my friend and colleague M. Ray Denny exploring together the strange world of Joe Doodlebug. I would also like to acknowledge my gratitude to many friends, colleagues and students who at one time or another during the past few years provided advice, constructive criticism, and intellectual stimulation. It would be impossible to name them all, but I would like to single out the following: Drs. Christian Bay, Donald T. Campbell, Al Eglash, Charles Hanley, Daniel J. Levinson, Frank Restle, the late Else Frenkel-Brunswik, R. Nevitt Sanford, Fillmore H. Sanford, Irving Sigel, Henry Clay

Smith, Bernard Taylor, H. A. Witkin, and Edith Weisskopf-Joelson. Drs. Ingram Olkin and Leo Katz of the Statistics Department at Michigan State University gave invaluable statistical advice on many aspects of the research.

The staff of the Psychology Department was always cooperative in obtaining subjects, in and out of class time. I am very grateful to them, as I am also to colleagues at New York University, Brooklyn College, and University College and Birkbeck College in London. The English worker sample was made available through the kind offices of Mr. R. R. Hopkins, Personnel and Welfare Manager at Vauxhall Motors in England. I wish to single out especially Miss Joan Ray of University College, who gave generously of her time and energy to collect the most important segments of the English data presented herein. I would also like to thank Dr. Cecily de Monchaux and Mr. Arthur Summerfield for their assistance in constructing the British version of the Opinionation Scale.

Dr. Robert N. Vidulich deserves special thanks for his critical reading of the entire manuscript, for his editorial suggestions and statistical help, and for assisting me in many other ways in connection with the preparation of the manuscript. I am also indebted to Mrs. Gloria Plath and to Mrs. Alice Lawrence for preparing the manuscript for publication and for relieving me of many burdensome details.

Finally, the person to whom I am most indebted is my wife, Muriel. Many of the ideas contained in this volume are hers. Some of the ideas which I might claim as my own took shape or were sharpened through conversations with her. This labor of love would not have been possible without her encouragement and help.

Contents

PART FIVE: On the Dynamics of Belief Systems

PART SIX: Summing Up

APPENDICES

THE OPEN AND CLOSED MIND

1

Introduction

There is a widely known story about two men who greet each other on the street in a small town in Poland. "Why have you not returned the pot I lent you?" one says to the other. "I did not borrow your pot," the other replies. "Besides, it was broken when you lent it to me and besides, I have already returned it to you intact."

There is a second story which is also said to have taken place in Poland. One day there came to visit the town Rabbi a man and wife who were in dispute over a marital problem. In accord with tradition, the Rabbi was to hear both sides of the argument and then decide who was right. He first heard the husband's side of the story and, when he was finished, the Rabbi said to him: "You are right." Then he heard the wife's side of the story. "You are right," the Rabbi said. When they both left, the Rabbi's wife stepped from her hiding place behind the draperies. She had overheard everything. "But how could they both be right?" she asked. The Rabbi answered: "You are right."

3

Both of these stories illustrate a closed system of beliefs. In the story of the pot, the borrower makes three separate statements, each of which contradicts the other two. In the story of the marital dispute, the Rabbi makes three identical statements, and again each one contradicts the other two. Nevertheless, despite their contradictory character, the three statements form a system, not a logical system, but a psychological one. The parts hang together (almost elegantly, we are tempted to say) because each statement seems to serve the same over-all purpose or to stem from the same underlying motive. In the case of the man who borrows the pot, the motive is to defend himself against the accusation that he is a dishonest man, that he doesn't return things he borrows. In the second story, the motive is to preserve somehow the illusion of infallibility.

Main Purposes of This Study

Our research into the nature of belief systems began with the analysis of ideological dogmatism. Over the years, we have had occasion to observe a number of persons, mostly intellectuals, who in real-life settings appeared to be characteristically dogmatic or closed in their modes of thought and belief. What they were dogmatic about varied from one person to another. They represented different political, religious, and scientific viewpoints. Included among them were liberals, middle-of-the-roaders, and conservatives; Jews, Catholics, and atheists; Freudians, behaviorists, and Gestaltists.

In the initial stage, we also found it helpful to study expressions of institutional dogmatism, as distinguished from individual dogmatism, in the writings of various ideologists and theorists, and in the mass media of communication. Other stimulating ideas came from such books as Orwell's *1984* (1951), Crossman's *The God That Failed* (1949), Blanshard's *Communism, Democracy and Catholic Power* (1951), and, most of all, Eric Hoffer's *The True Believer* (1951).

Long before we were able to define the phenomenon of ideological dogmatism explicitly, it seemed clear that it referred to a number of things: a closed way of thinking which could be associated with any ideology regardless of content, an authoritarian outlook on life, an intolerance toward those with opposing beliefs, and a sufferance of those with similar beliefs. To say that a person is dogmatic or that his belief system is closed is to say something about the way he believes and the way he thinks—not only about single issues but also about networks of issues. The closed mind, even though most people cannot define it precisely, can be observed in the "practical" world of political and religious *beliefs*, and in the more academic world of scientific, philosophic, and humanistic *thought*. In both of these worlds there is conflict among men about who is right and who wrong, who is rational and who rationalizing, and conflict over whose convictions are dogmatic and whose intellectual. In both sets of worlds ideas—and the people and authority figures responsible for them—are accepted and rejected.

The informal study of dogmatists proved very helpful in the early stages of our thinking. We asked ourselves: What precisely do these people do or say that gives the impression that they are closed in their mode of thought and belief? Authoritarian? Intolerant? What characteristic of the belief system seems to be involved? Is this characteristic unique to a particular ideological viewpoint or does it apply to other viewpoints as well? Is this property measurable?

It is now necessary to add that our original interest in persons with extremely closed belief systems was meant to be only a point of departure. We hoped to get a better understanding of the open mind no less than the closed mind. And, assuming that open and closed are but extremes along a continuum, we extended our investigation so that it became a broader inquiry into the general nature of all belief systems. In considering the properties of belief systems, it is necessary to keep this continuum in mind. We will employ the term "dogmatic" synonymously with "closed" and we will have frequent occasion to contrast the performance of high dogmatic (closed) and low dogmatic (open) groups. The reader should not construe such comparisons of extreme groups to mean that people can be classified simply into one or the other category. It is a convenience that we often employ in psychological research and that, in the present case, is designed to give us insight into the general nature of all belief systems rather than solely their open and closed extremes.

5

To study the organization of belief systems, we find it necessary to concern ourselves with the *structure* rather than the *content* of beliefs.* The relative openness or closedness of a mind cuts across specific content; that is, it is not uniquely restricted to any one particular ideology, or religion, or philosophy, or scientific viewpoint. A person may adhere to communism, existentialism, Freudianism, or the "new conservatism" in a relatively open or in a relatively closed manner. Thus, a basic requirement is that the concepts to be employed in the description of belief systems must not be tied to any one particular belief system; they must be constructed to apply equally to all belief systems.

In any investigation of belief and ideology there is the danger that the investigators' value judgments will bias the outcome of the research. In this respect we consider ourselves somewhat more fortunate than others who have concerned themselves with such problems. For if we focus on ideological structure rather than content, our own ideological biases become more irrelevant. If we do have an ax to grind, it will be with certain ways of adhering to a particular ideology. The ax we frankly grind is simply this: it is not so much *what* you believe that counts, but *how* you believe.

In Chapters 2 and 3, we will try to spell out a theory about the structural and formal characteristics of all belief systems. With this theory as a framework, we will deal with various problems of personality, ideology, and cognition, and with the interconnections that may exist among them. Each of these areas has been a matter of lively concern among psychologists. But typically different concepts and methods have been employed to study personality organization, ideological organization, and cognitive organization. For example, the personality theorist thinks in terms of the organization of id, ego, and superego, the self, personality syndromes and profiles, trait clusters, and personality types; the student of ideology can describe such configurations as fascism, anti-Semitism, fundamentalism, humanism, liberalism, and conservatism; cognitive theorists talk in terms of such con-

---

* A complete understanding of the nature of belief systems would include both the study of its structure and its content. For an analysis of the ways in which belief systems may vary in content, see the work of Charles Morris (1956) and also that of Elsa Whalley (1955).

cepts as cognitive styles, cognitive dissonance, frame of reference, the phenomenal field, and sign Gestalten. When connections are seen among these three types of concepts, we try to account for them with the help of a fourth set of concepts which are considered to be deeper, more underlying, more psychodynamic than the others. It is our opinion that a more powerful and simple way to proceed is to try to find a single set of concepts, a single language, that is equally appropriate to the analysis of personality, ideology, and cognitive behavior. During the course of our investigation we have come more and more to view a given personality as an organization of beliefs or expectancies having a definable and measurable structure. We have also come to conceive of ideology, insofar as it is represented within the psychological structure of the person, in exactly the same way, namely, as an organization of beliefs and expectancies. And, finally, we have come to conceive of man's cognitive activities—thinking, remembering, and perceiving—as processes and changes that take place within a person who has already formed a system of beliefs, which we can describe and measure.

Within this broad framework we will address ourselves to the relation between belief and thought and to the possibility that there is a basic unity between them. If we know something about the way a person believes, is it possible to predict how he will go about solving problems that have nothing to do with his ideology? What can we learn about a person's total belief system by observing his thought processes in the laboratory as he works on problems involving an imaginary bug that jumps around in an imaginary world? We will try to find out if belief and thought can be tied together because of certain structural properties they might have in common. If they can, then we should be able to predict, from a knowledge of a person's ideological orientation, his conceptual behavior when solving intellectual problems.

To go one step further: we may think of all persons as having not only ideological systems and conceptual systems but also perceptual and esthetic systems. To what extent would it be meaningful to speak of structural properties which tie together a person's ideological, conceptual, perceptual, and esthetic systems? Is it possible to say that the extent to which a person's belief system is open or closed is a generalized state of mind which will reveal itself in his politics and religion, the way he goes about solving intellectual problems, the way he works with perceptual materials, and the way he reacts to unorthodox musical compositions?

By extending the range of our investigation in this way, that is, to the study of esthetic systems, we come up against a distinction widely accepted by psychologists: the distinction between cognitive and emotional processes. In everyday discourse we often precede what we are about to say with the phrase "I think . . . ." "I believe . . ." or "I feel. . . ." We pause to wonder whether such phrases refer to underlying states or processes which are really distinguishable from each other. After all, we can often interchange these phrases without basically affecting what we mean to say. "I think segregation is wrong," "I believe segregation is wrong," and "I feel segregation is wrong" all say pretty much the same thing. The fact that these phrases are often (although not always) interchangeable suggests to us the assumption that every emotion has its cognitive counterpart, and every cognition its emotional counterpart. The implication of this assumption is that although our approach to belief systems, including esthetic ones, is a purely cognitive one we are not thereby abandoning our interest in the emotional side of man. Quite the contrary. If the assumption is correct that every emotion has its cognitive counterpart, then we should be able to reach down into the complexities of man's emotional life via a study of his cognitive processes.

Let us next consider another broad problem that will concern us. There are three types of acceptances and rejections which are ordinarily regarded as more or less distinct: the acceptance and rejection of *ideas*, of *people*, and of *authority*. The first is classified as a cognitive phenomenon, the second involves the phenomenon of prejudice or intolerance, and the third, authoritarianism. Is it not possible, however, that the way we accept or reject ideas, people, and authority all go together? Perhaps they are but different facets of the same thing, related to each other in a one-to-one fashion within the belief system. Thus, if we know something about the way a person relates himself to the world of ideas, we may also be able to say in what way he relates himself to the world of people, and to authority.

8

The problem of authoritarianism to which we have just referred has received a good deal of attention in recent years. Earlier attempts to define and measure this phenomenon will be considered and certain shortcomings will be pointed out. Then a way of thinking will be proposed which, it is hoped, will permit us to study and measure authoritarianism on a broader scope than has been the case in the past—in religious and antireligious movements, in communism and in fascism, and in fields of human endeavor far removed from the political and religious arenas, such as in the academic world and in the worlds of art and literature. Our goal, in other words, is to conceive of authoritarianism in an ahistorical way so that it will be equally applicable to all stages of history and to alternative forms of authoritarianism within a given historical stage.

In a similar vein, we will attempt within the present framework to arrive at a conception of intolerance and prejudice which is also ahistorical. How, for example, can we redefine and measure this phenomenon so that the bigots of the political left, center, and right all achieve a similar score on the same scale? While we are re-examining our definitions of intolerance, we will also want to examine some other implicit assumptions about it. For example, is liking someone necessarily indicative of tolerance and disliking someone, of intolerance? What about liking someone *because* he agrees with you? Is the bigot's attitude toward Negroes who agree him the same as that toward Negroes who disagree with him? What about his attitudes toward whites who agree and disagree with him? These are some questions we propose to raise and to investigate empirically.

The problem of intolerance leads us to another distinction which will interest us, the distinction between ingroup and outgroup. We usually talk about these in a black-white fashion, as if the outgroup were as homogeneous as the ingroup and as if it possessed attributes opposite to those possessed by the ingroup. Thus, we are said to derive our beliefs from the ingroup, and to resist those of the outgroup. We are said to glorify the ingroup, vilify the outgroup; we are supposed to identify positively with the ingroup, and to identify negatively with the outgroup.* We

---

* Similar dichotomous distinctions are made between positive and negative reference groups, positive and negative authority, and between beliefs and disbeliefs.

suspect that this way of talking about ingroups and outgroups is highly oversimplified. But in what way? The difficulty seems to lie in the fact that the outgroup is far from the homogeneous entity that the ingroup is; it is often composed of several or many groups that are all lumped together under the global concept "outgroup." We may be ignoring the possibility that in our daily lives we react differently to different outgroups. We hope to find out whether such differences in reactions do indeed exist, and if they are lawful. In this way, we hope to open for investigation a variety of phenomena which to our knowledge have not been studied before. For example, suppose a person of a given religious affiliation wants to leave his church to join another. Can one predict the relative probability of joining various other churches? What is the probability that persons of one denomination will marry persons of another denomination? What is the probability of marital conflict in such interfaith marriages? We will raise questions of this kind in the hope that our theory of belief systems will lead us to a richer conception of the ingroup-outgroup distinction.

Another distinction we will want to look at is the one between *change* and *resistance to change* in behavior, belief, or personality. There is a strong tendency in psychology to describe and account for change with the help of such concepts as flexibility, independence, nonconformity, open-mindedness, psychological health, reality-orientation, and so on. On the other hand, resistance to change is described or explained in terms of conformity, rigidity, fixation, compulsiveness, closed-mindedness, extremeness of belief, intolerance of ambiguity, etc. Such a way of thinking places a positive value on change and a negative value on nonchange. We do not think that this way of making the distinction is very helpful because it does not leave room for the possibility that there may be different varieties of change and of resistance to change. For example, there is a difference between rigidity and stability, between intellectual conviction and dogmatic conviction, between a party-line change and a more genuine change. But more of this later.

The first steps in the development of any science, physical or social, are to analyze and describe rather than to explain. We sometimes note among some of our colleagues a tendency to be impatient with careful analysis and description of psychological events and to be prematurely concerned with psychodynamics or other types of explanations of such events. Our own view is that before we can explain a phenomenon, we must first know what it is we want to explain. Accordingly, we will focus a good deal of attention on the formulation rather than the explanation of concepts. As already suggested, there are alternate ways of thinking about authoritarianism, intolerance, change and non-change, ingroup and outgroup. The particular way we think about such variables may involve implicit value judgments and may exert a profound influence upon the operational definitions employed, the nature of the hypotheses selected and omitted from investigation, the research findings, and their interpretation. For this reason, we will try to pay more attention to the way we formulate our variables and only afterwards, in the latter part of the book, will we try to explain what we have described.

In the course of exposition of the various issues to be raised herein it will be necessary to introduce some concepts that will be new to the psychological literature, such as belief-disbelief systems, the similarly matrix, dogmatism, opinionation, primitive beliefs, and peripheral beliefs. Let us assure the reader at the outset that we do not consider it justifiable to introduce new terms when old ones will do just as well. The burden is placed squarely on us to justify the introduction of each new concept, and to differentiate such concepts from others presently used which might appear to be synonymous. Wherever possible, we will try to perform "defining experiments" to demonstrate the discriminations we see among concepts that appear to be similar.

Points of Departure for the Present Inquiry

FROM THE STUDY OF RIGHT AUTHORITARIANISM TO THE STUDY OF GENERAL AUTHORITARIANISM

A major point of departure for the present research is the writings of Fromm (1941) and Maslow (1943) on the authoritarian character structure and, most particularly, the widely known investigation of the "authoritarian personality" by Adorno, Frenkel-Brunswik, Levinson, and Sanford (1950). This research began in 1943 at a time when the problem of anti-Semitism, particularly as it occurred in Nazi Germany, was of overriding concern to both social scientists and laymen.* It began as a research on anti-Semitism; the researchers analyzed the ideological content of anti-Semitism, devised quantitative methods for measuring it (Levinson and Sanford, 1944), and studied the personality characteristics associated with it (Frenkel-Brunswik and Sanford, 1945).

One of the questions raised early in this research had to do with how general or specific prejudice is—whether those who are anti-Semitic are also likely to express hostility toward other minority groups. In the course of investigation it became evident that this was indeed the case.[1] Those who scored high on the anti-Semitism Scale also tended to score high on other scales measuring attitudes toward other minority groups. It was on the basis of such findings that the Berkeley investigation, as it is sometimes called, branched out from the study of anti-Semitism to the broader study of ethnocentrism. An ethnocentric person is one who generally rejects and vilifies outgroups, and at the same time overly accepts and glorifies the ingroup (Levinson, 1949).

Attention next shifts to the F Scale, a widely known personality scale that since its publication in 1950 has been used in literally hundreds of investigations.[2] The F stands for fascism, and the F Scale had a twofold purpose when it was constructed: it was designed to be used as an indirect measure of prejudice without mentioning the names of any specific minority group; and it was designed to measure underlying personality predispositions toward a fascistic outlook on life.† It should be added that the originators' expectations about the F Scale were borne out in their own work, and have been confirmed many times since by others. Those who score high on the F Scale also tend to score high on measures of ethnocentrism, anti-Semitism, and anti-Negro feelings, and tend to be politically conservative. In addition, many personality differences are found to distinguish those who score high from those who score low on the F Scale.

The publication of the F Scale, along with the evidence for its validity, appeared in a book under the title, *The Authoritarian Personality*. As a result, the scale became known not only as the

* For a full historical account, see Sanford (1956).
† A copy of this scale will be found in Appendix B.

12

"fascism scale" but also as the "authoritarian personality scale." In our opinion, this gave rise to a certain amount of conceptual confusion, because in the shift from "fascism in the personality" to "the authoritarian personality" there is an unwitting leap from the particular to the general. The confusion begins when the F Scale is first used to measure "Fascist authoritarianism" and, later, "general authoritarianism." The difficulties become greater when we try to keep in mind the main ideological findings about high F scorers: they are generally more ethnocentric, anti-Semitic, and politically conservative. If we try to generalize from such findings, it becomes embarrassing to point to persons who seem to be authoritarian and intolerant but are not fascistic, or anti-Semitic, or politically conservative. Authoritarianism and intolerance in belief and interpersonal relations are surely not a monopoly of Fascists, anti-Semites, Ku Klux Klanners, and conservatives. We have observed these phenomena, as no doubt has the reader, among persons adhering to various positions along the total range of the political spectrum from left to right. We have observed them in religious circles and in antireligious circles; in the academic world where the main business at hand is the advancement of knowledge; in the fields of art and music, and so on. It is hard to generalize to such areas of behavior from the findings reported in *The Authoritarian Personality* because the theory that guided the research and its main measuring instruments focused on Fascist authoritarianism.

THE SPECIAL CASE OF LEFT AUTHORITARIANISM

What seems to be required, then, if we are to advance the study of authoritarianism, is a movement away from the conceptualization and measurement of rightist forms of authoritarianism. Indeed, a good deal of criticism has been directed at the Berkeley researchers, especially by Professor E. Shils, the sociologist (1954), on the ground that they studied only right authoritarians and neglected to study left authoritarians. With this criticism we agree, except that it does not go far enough. From the standpoint of a sociology of knowledge it is quite understandable why the Berkeley group was most concerned with Fascist authoritarianism. Their research owed its origins to the unprecedented anti-Semitic brutality of Fascist Germany. But from the standpoint of the

13

sociology of knowledge it becomes equally understandable why Professor Shils, writing in the middle 1950's, suggests a shift of attention from right to left authoritarianism. In doing so, however, he leaves himself open to exactly the same criticism at some future date, when some other form of authoritarianism may possibly preoccupy us. Also, the dichotomy of "left" and "right" authoritarianism is undesirable from a theoretical standpoint because it closes the door in advance to the possibility that there may be yet other forms of authoritarianism—in the political center or outside the realm of politics altogether—which may have properties in common and which therefore ought to be studied also. In other words, if our interest is in the scientific study of authoritarianism, we should proceed from right authoritarianism not to a re-focus on left authoritarianism but to the general properties held in common by all forms of authoritarianism. Authoritarianism can be observed at any one time in history in a variety of human activities, and we should think that it would have similar properties regardless of whether it is exhibited under Caesar, Napoleon, Hitler, Stalin, Khrushchev, Roosevelt, or Eisenhower. What is needed is therefore a deliberate turning away from a concern with the one or two kinds of authoritarianism that may happen to be predominant at a given time. Instead, we should pursue a more theoretical ahistorical analysis of the properties held in common by all forms of authoritarianism regardless of specific ideological, theological, philosophic, or scientific content. We would then be in a position to apply more powerfully the fruits of such analysis to any specific authoritarianism we might happen to be interested in now or in the future.

Now that we have reformulated the problem of authoritarianism in this way, the question arises of how to proceed. A first requirement, it seems to us, is to make a sharp distinction between the *structure* and the *content* of ideological systems. A person may espouse a set of beliefs that are democratic in content. He may take a militant stand against segregation; he may advocate permissiveness in parent-child relationships; he may regard McCarthy as a demagogue. Yet adherence to such beliefs, considered alone, is not necessarily a true guide of an anti-authoritarian outlook. For a person espousing such beliefs may still strike us, from the *way* he espouses his beliefs as authoritarian, intolerant of

14

those who disagree with him and closed in his mode of thought and belief. The discrepancy we may note between what is said and the way it is said is a discrepancy between content and structure. Our theoretical task, then, is to formulate the formal and structural properties of belief systems apart from specific content, and in such a way that they can be measured. We need some way to think about a person's belief system which will enable us to skirt around the content of the belief system and still reveal, intact, its structure. We will try to come to grips with this problem in Chapters 2 and 3.

FROM THE STUDY OF RIGHT INTOLERANCE TO THE STUDY OF GENERAL INTOLERANCE

Parallel to the emphasis in past research on rightist forms of authoritarianism is a similar emphasis on rightist forms of intolerance. Although social scientists have employed various *general* concepts in studying this phenomenon—concepts such as intolerance, discrimination, prejudice, bigotry, social distance, and ethnocentrism—it almost always turns out that in the measurement of these concepts the attitude statements constructed are directed primarily (not solely) at the bigots on the political right. The statements concern Jews, Negroes, foreigners, and the like. Here again, parallel to what has happened in the study of authoritarianism, there is a confusion between the generic and the particular. There are other forms of intolerance, based upon criteria other than ethnic or racial, which ought to be studied. For example, what about intolerance among Marxists, liberals, Freudians, Unitarians, academicians, and art critics, to name but a few? Here intolerance rarely takes the form of ethnic intolerance. It may have nothing to do with such issues. In fact, it is often in strong opposition to it. Current concepts and measures of intolerance seem to be woefully inadequate in addressing themselves to non-ethnic forms of intolerance.* As we have already pointed out

* In the past few years there have been a number of symposia sponsored by the American Psychological Association on the reduction of international tension and hostility. In such discussion there is heavy reliance on social-science findings concerning ethnic prejudice and ethnic stereotypes, and the suggestions made for reducing international conflict boil down to suggestions for reducing interethnic conflict and stereotypes. Without in any way trying to minimize the social importance of such conflict, it is our opinion that the major international conflicts confronting us today have very little to do with such things. They involve ideological conflicts

with regard to authoritarianism, what seems to be called for here too is an ahistorical, contentless way of thinking about intolerance, independent of the specific group discriminated against, equally applicable to different periods of history and to all kinds of intolerance within a given period of history.

ATTITUDES AND COGNITIVE BEHAVIOR

In recent years there have appeared a number of investigations on the relation between social attitudes and cognitive functioning (thinking, memory, and perception). In the great majority of these studies the specific social attitude under scrutiny was ethnic prejudice, or the authoritarianism conceived to underlie it (Adorno et al., 1950).[*] Some major findings that come out of such studies are that persons who are high in ethnic prejudice and/or authoritarianism, as compared with persons who are low, are more rigid in their problem-solving behavior, more concrete in their thinking, and more narrow in their grasp of a particular subject; they also have a greater tendency to premature closure in their perceptual processes and to distortions in memory, and a greater tendency to be intolerant of ambiguity.[3]

Until now the major attempt to account for such results has been by Frenkel-Brunswik, who has written extensively on the interrelations among personality, belief, and cognition under the general heading of "personality-centered" approaches to perception (1948b, 1949, 1951, 1954).[4] Her main thesis, derived from psychoanalysis, is that there exists a close correspondence between the cognitive spheres of behavior on the one hand and the emotional and social spheres on the other. Stated very briefly, she starts with the psychoanalytic concept of emotional ambivalence and the role it plays in the development of the personality structure of the child. She then develops the notion that as a result of early parent-child relations involving varying degrees of permissiveness or punitiveness there emerge individual differences in the ability to tolerate emotional ambivalence toward parents which, in turn, "spill over" into the social and cognitive spheres as well. Thus, a

---

primarily between communism and anticommunism; between colonialism and anti-colonialism.

[*] Most typically, these are measured by the F Scale and the Ethnocentrism Scale.

person who, through punishment, is not permitted to express his normal ambivalent feelings toward his parents develops a generalized need to structure his world rigidly, a pervasive tendency to premature closure and a general intolerance of cognitive ambiguity. This should become equally evident in stereotyped social attitudes toward minority groups and in restricted and ineffective cognitive functioning. In this way a bridge is built, via psychoanalytic concepts such as ambivalence and repression of hostility toward parents, to account for observed relations between social attitudes and cognitive behavior.

Investigations of the relation between personality on the one hand and ethnocentric-fascistic ideology and cognition on the other has enriched both social psychology and personality theory and has also led to considerable integration of these two fields. Despite methodological shortcomings,[5] we learned a good deal about anti-ethnic beliefs, their relation to the cognitive processes, and the psychodynamic determinants conceived to underlie both sets of variables. But, we will contend, the advances were achieved in depth at the expense of breadth. We advanced in knowledge and theory about one particular set of beliefs—at most, one particular ideology—and cognitive functioning. What was still lacking was a theory that could tie together in a more general way the organization of belief with the organization of cognition. One way to do this is to scrutinize more closely than has been done heretofore the general properties of all belief systems in order to see whether cognitive functioning could be also described in such terms. In other words, what is called for is a line of thought similar to that suggested earlier for the analysis of general authoritarianism and intolerance—an analysis of structural similarities between the way one believes and the way one cognizes.

Let us consider more specifically the relation between belief and thought. The idea that there may be some direct structural relation (in addition to a possibly indirect, dynamic relation) between thought and belief is not a new one. One can note numerous characterizations of thinking or believing in popular language that point in this direction. Thus, from a variety of ideological viewpoints one may hear thinking described as conventional, radical, subversive, communistic, reactionary, atheistic, orthodox, heretical, ritualistic, Calvinistic, and puritanical. The Marxist speaks of deviationist thinking, petty bourgeois thinking, and formalistic thinking. To some, a meaningful distinction is conveyed by the contrasting ideas: "Goyische Kopf" and "Yiddische Kopf." And one may note nowadays a good deal of interest in such things as "party-line" thinking and "brainwashing." All the illustrations have something in common. Each one points to behavior that is both ideological and cognitive.

Social scientists have also been attracted to the structural inseparability between thought and belief. This is seen in the sociologist's interest in the sociology of knowledge (Mannheim, 1946) and in references to such phenomena as ethnocentric thinking (Adorno *et al.*, 1950; Levinson, 1949), stereotyped thinking (Katz and Braly, 1952; Maslow, 1948), "narrow-minded" thinking (Rokeach, 1951a, 1951b), and middle-class thinking (Mills, 1951). These do no more than suggest that a systematic analysis of the properties common to both belief and thought may prove to be rewarding. We hope to do this in many places in this book, particularly in Part Three.

FROM THE STUDY OF BELIEFS TO THE STUDY OF BELIEF SYSTEMS

Present-day theory and research are typically focused on the properties, the determinants, and the measurement of single beliefs and attitudes rather than on belief systems and attitude systems. Similar emphasis is placed upon the study of single concepts, percepts, sets, *Aufgaben*, habits, expectancies, and hypotheses. For example, Bruner (1951) and Postman (1951) have written about the determinants of *a* hypothesis' strength; Asch (1952) and others have analyzed the attributes of *a* sentiment. Krech and Crutchfield (1948) talk about the precision, specificity, strength, saliency, and measurement of beliefs and attitudes. There is little theory and research about the nature, formation, learning, and change of attitude *systems*.

In the present investigation we will have very little to add to the study of beliefs considered as single units. Our focus will be on the belief system as a whole. This is not the place to say what we mean by a system. We will do so in Chapter 2. Let it suffice to say here that in our view much of man's social behavior can be better understood by relating such behavior to man's belief systems rather than to the elements of such systems. For example, if I say I like Japanese music, the referent is a system. If, on the other hand, I say that I like this particular melody, the referent is part of a system. Similarly, to accept Catholicism is to accept a system, but the belief that birth control is wrong is only a part of such a system. We have attempted herein to search out a set of variables, which we will call *system* variables. It is in this sense that we will talk about, try to measure, and present research findings on the organization of belief systems, the openness-closedness of a belief system, accepting and rejecting a system, entertaining a system, synthesizing beliefs into a new system, changing a system, and loyalty to and defection from a system.

An Over-All View

Some readers might find it helpful to have a bird's-eye view of what is to be found in the following chapters. We shall emphasize here the major problems, the concepts and the hypotheses to be put to test, and, in a general way, the methods that have been employed. The specifics of research design and methodology can be more appropriately discussed later on when we consider each of the specific investigations in turn.

PART ONE

In Part One we consider the theory of belief systems and its measurement.

Chapter 2. We propose here a detailed description of what we consider to be the general properties of all belief systems.

Chapter 3. Here we set the stage for studying individual differences in belief systems by describing how and why such systems may vary in the degree to which they are open or closed. The chapter also discusses the personal and social conditions that may lead to belief systems varying in openness-closedness.

Chapter 4. Two research instruments are presented, along with the theoretical considerations underlying their construction: (a) *The Dogmatism Scale*, designed to measure individual differences in the extent to which belief systems are open or closed,* and (b)

---

* Were it not so clumsy, we would have preferred to call this scale, "The Open-Closed Belief System Scale." The term *dogmatic* will be used throughout as

19

The Opinionation Scale, designed to measure individual differences in the extent to which we accept and reject others depending on whether they agree or disagree with us. We also present a few basic statistical characteristics of these scales, and norms for various groups tested in the Midwest, New York, and England.

The remainder of the book deals with various investigations that elaborate upon and test many of the theoretical notions discussed in Chapters 2 and 3. The two scales based on these notions are assessed for validity.

PART TWO

We consider here the validity of our theoretical formulations regarding the nature of general authoritarianism and general intolerance.

Chapter 5. One of the first things it is helpful to know about a new personality or attitude scale, assuming it is sufficiently reliable, is whether it actually identifies people who are known on other grounds to possess the characteristics being measured. Two studies are described. Persons judged to be extremely authoritarian and intolerant are given the Dogmatism and Opinionation Scales. In one study, extremely open and closed graduate students are "nominated" by their professors; in the second study, extremes are selected by peers.

Chapter 6. We then go on to examine more closely whether the Dogmatism Scale indeed measures general authoritarianism, and whether the Opinionation Scale measures general intolerance. We try to find this out in two ways:

1. We compare and contrast scores obtained on these two scales with those obtained on the California F Scale and the California Ethnocentrism Scale. It will be remembered that we have good reason to believe that the latter two scales probably measure rightist rather than general authoritarianism and intolerance. The extent to which these assumptions—about the Dogmatism and Opinionation Scales on the one hand and the F and Ethnocentrism Scales on the other —are correct may be partially

---

synonymous with *closed.* Persons scoring high on this scale will be assumed to have relatively closed systems, and persons scoring low will be assumed to have relatively open systems.

ascertained by studying the way scores on the two sets of scales are related to each other, and the way such scores are related to other measures of liberalism-conservatism in politics.

2. We then compare the relative degrees of authoritarianism and intolerance among various religious and political groups tested in America and in England. If our hypothesis is correct, we should expect to find that Catholics and Communists, even though they are poles apart ideologically, will on the average score higher than other groups on general authoritarianism and intolerance because of similar group pressures upon them.

Chapter 7. We then probe further into the general nature of intolerance from yet another direction. Suppose we were given the opportunity to discriminate between two persons who differ on both ethnic and belief criteria simultaneously. For example, would most people prefer friendship, other things being equal, with a white Communist or a Negro anti-Communist? A white segregationist or a Negro antisegregationist? We are thus led to ask whether social discrimination is jointly determined by both ethnic and belief characteristics, or whether one overrides the other in importance. If our theoretical analysis is valid, then we should expect to find that, basically, we organize and discriminate between people in terms of similarity-dissimilarity of belief rather than in terms of ethnic or racial group. In this chapter we report on several investigations in which the racial or ethnic characteristics of a person are systematically pitted against his beliefs, in order to assess the relative contributions of each as determinants of social discrimination. In one set of studies, northerners and southerners are compared in their reactions to belief vs. race; in a second study, we compare two groups of Jewish children of different ages with respect to belief vs. Jewishness as determinants of discrimination.

PART THREE

In this section on "experimental cosmology" we investigate the cognitive processes of persons with extremely open and closed systems. Our strategy is to observe in the laboratory how open and closed persons, as measured by the Dogmatism Scale, cope with new systems that contradict their everyday systems. We assume that the more difficulties a person encounters in dealing with new systems, the more closed must be his everyday system. To this end, we introduce our subjects to several kinds of new systems—tasks involving conceptual, perceptual, and musical material. Some of these new systems have been especially invented and are varied to suit our experimental and theoretical purposes; hence, the term "experimental cosmology."

Most of our attention is focused on the way relatively open and closed persons handle new conceptual systems. Our subjects are introduced to a mythical creature named Joe Doodlebug, who inhabits a strange, miniature world in which the rules governing his behavior contradict those we follow in everyday life. Within such a setting, various problems are posed to the subject on how Joe goes about getting to his food, and the subject is invited to solve these problems aloud. Do persons with open and closed systems, as measured by the Dogmatism Scale, approach new conceptual systems differently? In precisely what aspects of thinking do they differ? In what aspects of memory? Are persons with open and closed systems equally willing to "play along" or to entertain new belief systems? How is this capacity to "play along" related to what will happen in the thought and memory processes?

Chapter 8. The first chapter presents the details of this miniature cosmology in its several variations, along with an analysis of its psychological characteristics, and the experimental conditions under which it is given. We also discuss here various quantitative methods we have developed to study what happens in the thought processes, the memory processes, and related emotional processes. Guided by our theory and armed with our various techniques and instruments, we then examine experimentally various facets of thinking in open and closed persons.

Chapter 9. Here we propose an important distinction between rigid and dogmatic thinking. Rigidity refers to the resistance to change of single tasks or beliefs; dogmatism, to the resistance to change of a total system of beliefs. For example, we may perform a given chore rigidly, but we adhere to a given religion, political creed, or scientific theory dogmatically. We say that a rat behaves rigidly, but never dogmatically. A main feature of the Doodlebug Problem is that, in the course of solving it, it is possible to isolate and to measure separately these two processes: (1) the ability to analyze, to break down single beliefs, and to replace them with new ones; (2) the ability to synthesize, to overcome an old system of beliefs, and to replace it with a new system. How are these two thought processes handled by open and closed persons?

Chapter 10. We then inquire, in this and in succeeding chapters, about the various conditions that help and hinder the formation of new belief systems. In this way, we hope to gain a deeper insight into the workings of the relatively open and closed mind. We here consider the assumption that the closed mind, through fear of the new, is a passive mind. It achieves its systematic character "for free," through the external authority's efforts rather than its own. When left to its own devices, like a fish out of water, it cannot integrate new beliefs into a new system because it cannot remember them. The reason it cannot remember them is because there is a dynamic unwillingness to "play along," to "entertain" strange belief systems. What will happen, then, if we experimentally "short-circuit" such a person's reliance on memory? Will it facilitate or retard the acceptance of new belief systems?

Chapter 11. How can we tell whether a conceptual system is psychologically "new" or "old" to a particular person, and what differences does it make in the way he thinks? It is reasonable to assume that "newness" or "oldness" depends on whether the person has had previous experience with certain kinds of systems. For example, persons who play chess should find new "chesslike" problems not so "new" as compared with persons who do not play chess. In this chapter we compare the performance of open and closed persons, some of whom play chess and some of whom do not, on a chesslike variation of the Doodlebug Problem. If our hypothesis is correct, we should expect no difference in problem-solving between open-minded and closed-minded people if they play chess; but we do expect differences between them if they do not play chess.

Chapter 12. On August 24, 1939, the Soviet Union and Nazi Germany signed the famous nonaggression pact. Some Communists easily changed over to the new "party line." Others did so less easily. Yet others defected. Our purpose in this chapter is to try to analyze the psychological processes involved in "party-line" thinking. We do so by introducing certain sudden changes into the world of Joe Doodlebug, after the subject has been "indoctrinated" with the new "Doodlebug ideology." Our theory makes certain predictions about what will happen. We observe open and closed subjects to see how well their behavior lines up with these predictions.

If you wish to teach someone a new belief system, is it better to introduce him to it gradually or to hand it to him all at once, on a "silver platter"? This too is the subject of Chapter 12.

Chapter 13. With yet another variation of the Doodlebug world, we try to study certain thought processes that are meant to be analogous and, hopefully, to illuminate real-life processes of loyalty to and defection from a belief system. Suppose it is impossible to work within a particular system because there are inherent contradictions in it. Imagine, for example, what Euclidian geometry would be like if it had two axioms that contradicted each other. If our theory is a fruitful one, we should expect closed persons not to see the contradictions and to have a blind faith that solutions do in fact exist. Open persons should more frequently defect.

Chapter 14. In this and in the next chapter, we try to extend the generality of our findings to the realms of perceptual and esthetic behavior. We report here an experiment in which open and closed persons are compared in their ability to analyze and synthesize perceptual material. Our procedure here is analogous to the Doodlebug tasks, which are essentially conceptual in nature.

Chapter 15. Open and closed persons are asked to react to classical music of the conventional sort (e.g., Brahms) and to "new-system" music in the 12-tone scale (e.g., Schönberg). According to theory, we should expect open and closed persons equally to enjoy conventional, but not unconventional music.

PART FOUR

In this part we elaborate upon a basic characteristic of belief systems first advanced in Chapter 2. Each person is assumed to have not only a system he believes in, but also a system he disbelieves in. The latter is called a *disbelief system.* Each person's disbelief system is assumed to consist of a series of "negative isms" arranged along a continuum of similarity to his belief system.

Chapter 16. This chapter describes the belief-disbelief systems of half a dozen Christian denominational groups. It then considers various other questions: To what extent are the subjectively perceived similarity continua of various denominational groups a reflection of objective similarity? Is there basically a single continuum of similarity for persons occupying different positions along it? To what extent do we reject another person depending upon his position along the similarity continuum? Do open and closed persons differ in this respect?

Chapter 17. We consider here certain everyday manifestations of the organization of disbelief systems. One study has to do with the relative frequency of movements in and out of various Christian churches. Consider, for example, any Methodist church in any city. Is it possible to predict, on the basis of our theory, the probability with which persons of various denominations will join this church? The probability of leaving it to join another church? We have gathered such data for Catholic, Episcopalian, Lutheran, Presbyterian, Methodist, and Baptist churches, and these data are considered in relation to the similarity continuum that exists among them.

A second study concerns the relative rates of enrollment in various denominational colleges in the Midwest by persons of different denominations. Again, we are interested to see to what extent enrollment rates vary with similarity. Finally, in a third study, we inquire into the relative frequency of interfaith marriages, and premarital and marital conflict, among students at Michigan State University, and how such frequencies are related to interfaith similarity.

PART FIVE

This part considers various hypotheses regarding motivational, childhood, and situational conditions which lead to closed belief systems.

Chapter 18. First is reported a study of changes in personal values and in choice of career that take place over a six-year period in a group of religiously oriented college students. An obvious hypothesis is that those with relatively open systems will change more in their personal values than those with relatively closed systems. But such a hypothesis is opposed to our theory.

For reasons to be stated later, we instead hypothesize that both open and closed persons change, but in different ways.

Chapter 19. Here we test the hypothesis that closed belief systems represent a defense against anxiety. To do so, we first consider some evidence on the relation between scores obtained on the Dogmatism Scale and on a test of anxiety. Then we compare various political and religious groups tested in America and in England to see if those groups which, in general, score highest on dogmatism also score highest on anxiety. Of particular interest are the findings for Catholics tested in America and for Communists tested in England. Finally, we trace dogmatism and anxiety to certain childhood experiences, particularly to attitudes toward parents, breadth of early identifications with persons outside the immediate family, and various childhood symptoms of anxiety and maladjustment.

Chapter 20. Open and closed persons are compared in time perspective, that is, their perceptions of the past, present, and future. Subjects tell imaginative stories to TAT pictures, and objective measures of time perspective are obtained. The stories are also judged for degree of anxiety manifested. To be discussed is the extent to which those with relatively open and closed systems differ in past, present, and future orientation and how such orientations are related to anxiety.

Chapter 21. This chapter deals with the effects of situational threat on the dogmatization of the Catholic Church. We have analyzed a dozen councils of the Catholic Church, which met in different periods of history. We should expect to find that the greater the situational threat to the Church immediately preceding the convening of a council, the greater the dogmatization of Catholicism, as reflected in the decrees issued by each council.

PART SIX

In the final part we present our summary and conclusions.

Chapter 22. We try to bring together the major findings of the research, consider how they bear on the theory of belief systems presented earlier, discuss various methodological issues, and raise some questions for the future.

Notes

1. In this connection see also Hartley (1946), and Campbell and McCandless (1951).

2. See Christie and Cook (1958) for a guide to these studies.

3. For example, see the investigations by Barron (1953); Becker (1954); Block and Block (1951); Brown (1953); Fisher (1951); Frenkel-Brunswik (1949, 1951, 1954); Kutner (1958); Levitt and Zelen (1953); Rokeach (1948, 1951a, 1951b, 1951c, 1952); Scodel and Mussen (1953); Solomon (1952a, 1952b, 1953).

4. See also Klein (1958), Levinson (1949), Smith, Bruner, and White (1956), Weisskopf-Joelson (1953), and Witkin (1954) who have worked on various aspects of the interrelations among belief, cognition, and personality.

5. See especially Hyman and Sheatsley (1954); Brown (1953); Christie, Havel, and Seidenberg (1958).

Part One

The Theory and Measurement of Belief Systems

Of course, all persons can be said to have belief systems. But what exactly is a "belief system"? How does it differ from an ideology? What are the basic elements which make it up, and how do such elements combine to form systems and subsystems? These questions will concern us in Chapter 2, and to answer them we will propose a set of attributes or properties held in common by all belief systems. These attributes will be structural or formal in conception, in order to equip us to look for underlying similarities among persons adhering to different belief systems and, conversely, to look for underlying differences among persons with similar belief systems.

The concepts to be employed in describing the organization of belief systems are not entirely new to psychology, as will be evident to those familiar with Kurt Lewin's concepts. What may seem new is the extension and application of Lewinian-like concepts to the theory and measurement of individual differences in belief systems and their relation to differences in personality and cognition. In Chapter 3 we describe how belief systems, with all their Lewinian-like attributes, can be conceived as varying along a single dimension ranging from open at one extreme to closed at the other; Chapter 4 deals with the measurement of individual differences along this dimension.

2

The Organization of
Belief-Disbelief Systems

What is a belief? To answer this question we can do no better than first to quote from Trueblood, a philosopher of religion. He writes:

> We have beliefs about history, beliefs about the structure of material aggregates, beliefs about the future, beliefs about God, beliefs about what is beautiful or what we ought to do. Most of these beliefs we state categorically. We say, "Columbus landed in the West Indies," "Water is composed of hydrogen and oxygen," "Rain is falling today," "There will be a snowstorm tomorrow," "God knows each individual," "Greek temples are more beautiful than Egyptian temples," "I ought to work rather than play tennis today." Each of these statements, similar to thousands we make every day, is elliptical in that the preliminary statement is omitted. We might reasonably preface each of these propositions by the words, "I believe," or "There

seems to be good evidence that." Every proposition becomes in fact a judgment, and man is a creature greatly concerned with his own judgments. We take our judgments seriously and, foolish as we are, we are deeply interested in the correctness of our judgments (1942, p. 24).

To all this let us add that every person also has countless other beliefs that he cannot verbalize. We infer them from his behavior, for example, from a slip of the tongue, a compulsive act, an expressive gesture. We infer a belief in God when we see a person in a prayerful position, a belief that it will not rain when we see him preparing for a picnic, a belief that the telephone transmits sound when we see him answering it. Any expectancy or implicit set is also a belief, which is also to say that it is a predisposition to action.

Also, let us not take at face value what a person says he believes. He may be deceiving us deliberately or he may be rationalizing. We do not necessarily take at face value a person's verbal endorsements of democracy, humanitarianism, or a particular brand of cigarettes. We have to infer what a person *really* believes from all the things he says and does. It is in this sense that we will use the term belief, and the total belief-disbelief system would thus be an organization of verbal and nonverbal, implicit and explicit beliefs, sets, or expectancies.

The reader may note our use of the term *belief-disbelief system,* and possibly object that it sounds somewhat academic. Is not the disbelief system merely the mirror-image of the belief system, and thus unnecessary? Our own observations lead us to propose that this may not be the case. We will put forward the idea that every system is asymmetrical rather than symmetrical; it includes on the one hand a system of beliefs that one accepts, and, on the other, a *series* of systems that one rejects. For example, the Freudian accepts one organized system of psychological beliefs and rejects a number of others, such as those advanced by Adler, Jung, and Horney, Gestalt and learning theory, and so forth. The Soviet Marxist accepts one particular system of beliefs and rejects Trotskyism, several varieties of socialism, Fascism, and so forth. The Catholic, the Unitarian, the Baptist, and the Jew each accepts one set of beliefs and rejects *several* others.

Furthermore, we cannot assume that the extent and the inten-

32

sity with which we reject each of the other systems is the same from one to the other. At first glance, it appears that rejection may depend upon how similar another system is to our own.

For this reason we will use the term belief-disbelief system. The *belief system* is conceived to represent all the beliefs, sets, expectancies, or hypotheses, conscious and unconscious, that a person at a given time accepts as true of the world he lives in. The *disbelief system* is composed of a series of subsystems rather than merely a single one, and contains all the disbeliefs, sets, expectancies, conscious and unconscious, that, to one degree or another, a person at a given time rejects as false.* Thus, our conception of the disbelief system is that it is far more than the mere opposite of the belief system. An analysis of its organization and properties should lead to insights over and above those to be obtained by studying only the belief system.

Consider now the concept *system*. When we say that a person has a belief system it brings forth the idea that it is a logical system, and that if it isn't logical, it isn't a system. We propose that logical systems, considered as human products, are but a subclass, a special kind of psychological system. In logical systems the parts are interrelated or in communication with each other according to the rules of logic. In psychological systems the parts may be interrelated without necessarily being logically interrelated. In fact, what may be of interest to the psychologist is that the parts are isolated or segregated from each other. It is precisely this isolation or segregation of parts which describes their relationship and makes possible certain predictions about behavior.

James G. Miller, in his discussion of "general behavior systems theory," defines a system as any organization ". . . surrounded by a single boundary . . . continuous in space-time," and having "recognizable functional interrelationships." ". . . When a typhoon hits the *Caine* and her sister destroyers, wiping out radio and radar contact, then the flotilla is no longer a system, because usual

---

* It may be asked, why not eliminate altogether the notion of disbeliefs and talk only of differing degrees of agreement with beliefs? We prefer not to do so for two reasons. First, there is an all-or-none sociological character to membership in one group or another. For example, a person *is* a Catholic, and *not* an Episcopalian, or Lutheran, or Baptist, etc. Second, it has led us into several fruitful lines of research (see Chapters 16 and 17).

functional interrelationships are impossible" (1955, p. 515). In our view, this flotilla is still a system. Surely there is a difference between a crippled flotilla with its communication system knocked out, and a string of ships randomly distributed across the Pacific Ocean. The randomly distributed ships are not a system; in the crippled flotilla, however, there is still a *potential* for communication and, undoubtedly, there will be efforts made to re-establish it. Thus, the disruption of communication does not destroy a system as such; disruption merely changes its state of "functional interrelationship."

In exactly the same way, a belief-disbelief system is conceived to be an organization of parts (wherein the rock-bottom units are single beliefs and disbeliefs) that may or may not be logically interrelated. If all belief-disbelief systems were logical ones, some people could be said to have them, most would not. Our assumption will be that *all* people have belief-disbelief systems that can be described in terms of the structural arrangement of their parts. Like Miller's crippled flotilla, some belief-disbelief systems may have little or no communication among parts, but the potential for communication is there.*

Having clarified the distinction between logical and psychological systems, we now go on to say that a belief-disbelief system is more than just a religious *or* a political *or* a scientific system. The words "religious," "political," and "scientific" are not psychological concepts. It is extremely unlikely that the mind, or the belief-disbelief system, is neatly subdivided into one or another of these compartments and that individual beliefs can be relegated to one or another compartment. Consider, for example, the Catholic's belief that communism is evil. It is not only a religious belief but also a political belief. At the time of writing, we believe that there exist several artificial satellites and planets in space. This has not only scientific implications but also political implications. For some, it also has philosophical and religious implications.

---

* Our definition of system is also broader than phenomenological definitions, such as the one advanced by Toch (1955), according to which a system of beliefs would include only those beliefs ". . . regarded by the believer himself . . . as forming part of the same ideational structure" (p. 57). When we speak of a system of beliefs, we include all of a person's beliefs, as inferred from all that he says and does, and regardless of whether they are so perceived by the person himself.

In the same way, a belief (or disbelief) in God, the infallibility of the Pope, desegregation, divorce, the separation of church and state, or federal aid to education cannot psychologically be relegated to one category of belief or another. Such categories are at best helpful logical or sociological conveniences. If carried over into the realm of psychological analysis, they convey an illusion of logical construction which the mind does not possess. Thus, in Krech and Crutchfield's (1948) terms, we commit the "logical error" when we speak psychologically of a person's political or religious belief systems. It would be more correct to say that a person's belief-disbelief system is really a political-religious-philosophic-scientific-*et cetera* system. We mean it to include each and every belief and disbelief of every sort the person may have built up about the physical and social universe he lives in. We mean it to represent each man's *total* framework for understanding his universe as best he can.

We would now like to draw a further distinction between belief-disbelief systems and ideology. Glazer writes: ". . . no study of the relation between attitude and personality has yet . . . solved the problem of distinguishing ideology—the views someone picks up—from character—the orientations that are basic to a person" (1954, p. 293). The concept of a belief-disbelief system tries to meet this conceptual problem. It includes *all* of a person's beliefs and therefore is meant to be more inclusive than what is normally meant by ideology. Ideology refers to a more or less institutionalized set of beliefs—"the views someone picks up." Belief-disbelief systems contain these too but, in addition, they contain highly personalized pre-ideological beliefs. The latter will be described shortly.

Organization Along a Belief-Disbelief Dimension

For reasons already discussed, we assume first that all of a person's beliefs are organized into two interdependent parts: a belief system and a disbelief system. The disbelief system is further conceived as being composed of several disbelief subsystems, which vary in degree of similarity to the belief system. It is hypothesized that disbelief subsystems that are similar to the belief system are more acceptable than less similar ones. For example, people with different beliefs often have to cooperate with each other, as in coalition governments, joint-service military operations, or interdenominational marriages. The success of such cooperation may depend, at least in part, on the similarity between the different belief systems. Similarly, suppose a person changes from one belief system to another. If our hypothesis is correct, he will more likely change to a system similar to than different from his own.

The belief-disbelief dimension is further assumed to have several additional properties. Not everybody will have these properties to the same extent.

ISOLATION

Suppose there are two beliefs that are intrinsically related to each other. To the extent that we are reluctant to see them as interrelated, the two beliefs are said to be isolated from each other (Krech, 1949; Lewin, 1951). They are potentially but not actually in communication. When a person says, "I do not see any connection between *a* and *b*," he is stating a relationship. The relationship is one of isolation. We shall take as indications of isolation such things as the following:

The coexistence of logically contradictory beliefs within the belief system. This is the well-known psychoanalytic mechanism of compartmentalization. It is designed to satisfy the person's need to see himself as consistent. Orwell, in his book *1984*, has more picturesquely called this "double-think." * In everyday life we note many examples of "double-think": expressing an abhorrence of violence and at the same time believing that it is justifiable under certain conditions; affirming a faith in the intelligence of the common man and at the same time believing that the masses are stupid; being for democracy but also advocating a government run by an intellectual elite; believing in freedom for all, but also believing that certain groups should be restricted; believing that science makes no value judgments, but also knowing a good theory from a bad theory and a good experiment from a bad experiment. Such expressions of clearly contradictory be-

* The two stories cited at the beginning of Chapter 1 may be considered as examples of "triple-think."

liefs will be taken as one indication of isolation in the belief system.

The accentuation of differences and minimization of similarities between belief and disbelief systems. No two persons have belief systems that are completely similar or completely different from each other. However, in a controversy among men who differ in belief systems we often hear strong denials of similarities between their respective systems and, instead, an overemphasis on differences. Thus, we have heard advocates of communism and Catholicism both insist that the two systems have absolutely nothing in common with each other. A similar accentuation of differences may also be noted in controversies between proponents of Catholicism and Protestantism, the United States and the Soviet Union, fascism and communism, psychoanalysis and behaviorism, science and religion, and so on. From a dynamic standpoint such accentuations of differences are viewed as attempts to ward off a threat to the validity of one's own system. From a structural standpoint it is viewed in terms of isolation between belief and disbelief systems.

The perception of irrelevance. A person sometimes judges as "irrelevant" what may well be relevant by objective standards. We have often observed in controversies among men that the argument boils down to a particular kind of disagreement between the disputants. Each accuses his opponent of bringing up irrelevant arguments. Each denies the other's accusation. Often enough, though not always, the judgment that something is irrelevant to something else points to a state of isolation between belief and disbelief systems. It is designed to ward off contradiction and, thus, to maintain intact one's own system.

Denial of contradiction. A final indicator of isolation is the outright denial of contradiction. Contradictory facts can be denied in several ways: on grounds of "face absurdity" ("It is absurd on the face of it"), chance, the "exception that proves the rule," the true facts are not accessible, and the only available sources of information are biased.

DIFFERENTIATION

Another way in which belief-disbelief systems may vary is in their degrees of differentiation or articulation or richness of detail. In studying a person's system, we would not only want to know about the degree of differentiation of the total system but also of the various parts within it. Thus, we can inquire separately into (1) the degree of differentiation of the belief system, (2) the disbelief system, and (3) each of the several disbelief subsystems. It would also be of interest to know if (4) the belief system is *more* differentiated than the disbelief system—and if so, how much more. Finally (5), is one disbelief subsystem *more* differentiated than another and, if so, does it have anything to do with its position along the similarity continuum?

We shall take as indications of differentiation such things as the following:

Relative amount of knowledge possessed. We have in mind here the sheer amount a person knows about things he believes in and disbelieves in. Intuitively, it would seem that most people know more facts, ideas, events, and interpretations consistent with their belief system than with their disbelief system. That is, the belief system is generally more differentiated than any one of the disbelief subsystems. Whether this is so, however, is a matter for investigation. Similarly, people probably vary in their relative knowledge about things believed and disbelieved. In some people the discrepancy in knowledge is great, in others less great. This discrepancy in knowledge may be taken as an index of the relative degree of differentiation of the belief as compared with the disbelief system. In the same way, the discrepancy in amount of knowledge possessed about each of the several disbelief subsystems may give us valuable information about the relative degree of differentiation in various parts of the disbelief system.

The perception of similarity between adjacent disbelief subsystems. Another index of differentiation within the disbelief system is the extent to which any two disbelief subsystems are perceived as "the same" or "different." For example, many Americans would say that communism and naziism differ in certain important respects, and this would suggest some differentiation between them. In contrast, the Hearst concept of "Communazi" implies no differentiation between them. At this stage of our thinking, we can suggest two possible principles that might govern the degrees of differentiation to be found in various parts of the disbelief system. One hypothesis is that two disbelief subsystems occupying adjacent positions on the similarity continuum will be seen as less differentiated than two subsystems occupying positions farther apart. A second hypothesis is that disbelief subsystems relatively close to the belief system will be relatively highly differentiated, while those farther away will be poorly differentiated. For example, most orthodox Freudians would probably have little difficulty distinguishing other brands of psychoanalysis from each other (Adler, Jung, Fromm, etc.). But they might have difficulty distinguishing various brands of behaviorism from each other (Pavlov, Watson, Hull, Skinner, etc.). The former occupy positions on the disbelief system that are relatively close in; the latter occupy positions relatively farther away from their own belief system.

But these are general hypotheses about where to expect high and low degrees of differentiation within everybody's disbelief system. It should not be overlooked that there are bound to be individual differences in this respect, as, for example, in the ability to differentiate at the far end of the disbelief system. Thus, Senator McCarthy was apparently unable to distinguish Communists from Socialists from liberals at the far end of his disbelief system. But other Republican senators could, to varying degrees, make better differentiations. Another example is that many Communists insist that both the Democrats and Republicans are the same; they are both run by Wall Street. But some Communists *can* see distinctions between them.

COMPREHENSIVENESS OR NARROWNESS OF THE SYSTEM

This refers simply to the total number or range of disbelief subsystems represented within a given belief-disbelief system (Bruner *et al.*, 1955; Pettigrew, 1958; Rokeach, 1951a; Tolman, 1948). Thus, to one person, Mohammedanism and Taoism may be represented in the belief-disbelief system. To another they may be meaningless words.

Organization Along a Central-Peripheral Dimension

To handle a number of complex theoretical issues it is necessary next to conceive of three layers organized along a central-peripheral dimension: (1) A *central* region represents what will be called the person's "primitive" beliefs. These refer to all the beliefs a person has acquired about the nature of the physical world he lives in, the nature of the "self" and of the "generalized other" (G. H. Mead, 1952). (2) An *intermediate* region represents the beliefs a person has in and about the nature of authority and the people who line up with authority, on whom he depends to help him form a picture of the world he lives in. (3) A *peripheral* region represents the beliefs derived from authority, such beliefs filling in the details of his world-map. We will discuss each of these regions in turn.

THE CENTRAL REGION

If we wish to understand something of the functional or dynamic aspects of belief-disbelief systems we must first look to the *content* of the central region which contains one's "primitive beliefs." Note that it is content rather than structure to which we refer here. What seems important to know about these primitive beliefs is their specific content about the physical and social world, the latter including the person's self-concept and his conception of others. Such content, it is assumed, will have much to do with the formal organization of the rest of the belief-disbelief system.

The concept "primitive belief" is meant to be roughly analogous to the primitive terms of an axiomatic system in mathematics or science. Every person may be assumed to have formed early in life some set of beliefs about the world he lives in, the validity of which he does not question and, in the ordinary course of events, is not prepared to question. Such beliefs are unstated but basic.* It is out of some such set of "pre-ideological" primitive beliefs that the total belief-disbelief system grows.

We will assume that such primitive beliefs have to do first with the nature of physical reality (color, form, sound, space, time), with the physical properties of the world we live in (its shape, its relation to the sun and the moon and the heavens), and

---

* The philosopher Black (1946) makes a distinction between basic and derived beliefs. Our primitive beliefs are roughly similar to Black's basic beliefs; our intermediate and peripheral beliefs are conceived to emerge from the basic, primitive beliefs and, hence, are similar to Black's derived beliefs.

with the world of numbers.* Second, all persons have primitive beliefs about the social world they live in—whether this world is basically a friendly or unfriendly place to live in, whether parental or authority figures are loving or punishing, whether people in general are characteristically to be trusted or feared, whether the future is to be regarded with security or apprehension. Third, there are the primitive beliefs about the self—beliefs about the way we orient ourselves in physical space,† beliefs about self-identity, beliefs about autonomy or dependence on others, about self-worth, etc.

Let us see if we cannot achieve a further conceptual clarification of primitive beliefs. Of all the thousands of beliefs a person has, how can we tell which ones are primitive and which ones are not? We will therefore press our analysis a bit further. Assume that for each belief a child or adult forms, there is formed also a second belief associated with it. The second belief is the person's estimate of how many others hold the first belief. If a person believes in God, he also has some idea about how many others believe in God. When a child first grasps that he belongs to a particular religion or race, he wants to know how many others are like him. The estimate can range from nobody to everybody. We assume that the same is true for every other belief a person may have. Attached to each one is some probability estimate regarding consensus. One definition of primitive belief is any belief that virtually everyone is believed to have also. For example, I believe that this object I write with is a pencil, and I believe that my name is so-and-so. I also believe that all persons in a position to know (this excludes infants, strangers, etc.) would agree with me on both counts. All such persons could be said to be external referents or authorities for these beliefs. When this is the case, my belief is primitive. It is rarely, if ever, challenged.

* The best description of how such primitive beliefs develop in the child will be found in the work of Piaget (1954). Asch's work on the effects of group pressures on the judgment of length of lines (1952) would also be relevant here. It involves the group violation of primitive beliefs about the physical world, and the cognitive and emotional effects of such group violation upon the individual.

† Relevant here is the important research by Witkin and his co-workers (1954) on the conditions influencing the perception of the vertical, on individual differences in the perception of the vertical, and on the personality correlates of such individual differences. This research seems to involve an approach to the experimental manipulation of variables affecting primitive beliefs about the orientation of the self in physical space and the personality correlates of such primitive beliefs.

If such a primitive belief could be seriously challenged, it would probably be extremely upsetting, because I have never expected it to be a subject for controversy.

A second kind of primitive belief is the converse of the above. Instead of virtually everyone serving as external referents or authorities, there is no one. Suppose I suffer from claustrophobia. I have been told many times that my fear is groundless, unrealistic. But it does not help. I go on believing that dreadful things will happen to me in closed rooms. The belief is a primitive one because there exist no external reference persons or authorities who can disconfirm it.*

The analysis and examples of primitive beliefs discussed above are not meant to be exhaustive. Rather, they are designed to point to what we have in mind when using this term. It is a task for future analyses to spell out in further detail the full content of the primitive belief region, its organization, the manner in which it is related to the intermediate and peripheral belief regions, and the conditions that give rise to certain primitive beliefs and to the intermediate and peripheral correlates thereof. It is to be stressed, furthermore, that primitive beliefs do not, strictly speaking, determine intermediate and peripheral beliefs, for only antecedent events can determine the formation of beliefs primitive, intermediate, or peripheral. We prefer to say that intermediate and peripheral beliefs *emerge* from primitive beliefs, as walking and running emerge from crawling.

THE INTERMEDIATE REGION

In functional relationship to primitive beliefs are nonprimitive beliefs represented within the intermediate region. Such beliefs are concerned with the nature of the positive and negative authority to be depended on to fill out a map of our world. For no person can hope to form such a picture all by himself. Authorities are the intermediaries to whom we turn for information to supplement what we can obtain for ourselves. In this connection, let us quote again some illuminating passages from Trueblood:

---

* Seen in this way, the purpose of psychotherapy is to "deprimitivize" such primitive beliefs. The psychotherapist's goal is to somehow become an external referent where there was none before. Perhaps this is what the psychoanalytic transference tries to accomplish.

Our dependence on facts turns out to be somewhat pathetic, since we do not know any facts at all except as they are involved in the experience of man. . . . When a man says "King Charles the First was executed," he means "I *believe* King Charles the First was executed." Our dependence appears to be on facts, but it is really a dependence on men. . . . Most of what we believe about the external world is received at second hand and rests on the prior belief that some men are more trustworthy reporters than others.

The area of immediate experience open to any individual is extremely slight—a mere slit in the world's expanse. Thus to say that we shall believe only what we know directly at first hand is to reduce our belief in a fantastic manner. All history would be thereby eliminated and we should be confined to the *specious present*. A life so ordered would be intellectually poverty-stricken, if, indeed, it were possible at all.

. . . The conclusion to be reached, in view of our individual mental poverty, is that we cannot avoid reliance on some sort of authority (1942, pp. 66-67).

Trueblood writes further that:

. . . popular error about authority which calls for correction is the notion that authority and reason are somehow rival ways of coming to know the truth. . . . The point is that when we rely on authority we are not, *for that reason,* guilty of credulity. *There is a reason for our reliance.* We trust the men and institutions presenting the most reason for being trusted. We must use reason to determine *which* authority to follow, just as we use reason to determine *which* faith to adopt (1942, p. 72).

In line with Trueblood's insights, we may now define authority as any source to whom we look for information about the universe, or to check information we already possess. Of course, people differ in the kind of authority they depend on for information. A person said to be high in authoritarianism does not differ from a person said to be low in authoritarianism because the first relies on authority and the second does not. Rather, they have different ideas about the *nature* of authority, different theories about the *way* to employ authority as a "cognitive liaison system" mediating between the person and the world this person is trying to understand.

How shall we conceive of variations in the *nature* of authority? Following Fromm (1941), we will assume it to range from rational, tentative reliance on authority at one extreme to arbitrary, absolute reliance on the other. It is easy to point to examples of the absolute kind. Some people believe that there exists a supernatural authority, or some absolute human authority. Some are convinced that there exists one true cause, one true bible, one elite, or one chosen people. Such absolute beliefs, by the way, do not qualify as primitive beliefs because the person who believes them knows that there are others who do not. Also, there exist authorities who could conceivably disconfirm them. For example, Khrushchev played exactly this role for Stalinists when he made his famous de-Stalinization speech in 1956.

Our conception of belief and disbelief systems seems to point to a negative as well as a positive side to authority. We are all assumed to have not only a set of beliefs about positive authority but also about negative authority. The former guides us to what is "true" about the world we live in; the latter "tips us off" to what is "false." Let us, by way of example, consider a person who wants to find out about the Soviet purges in the mid-thirties. What really happened, he wants to know? He is an admirer of Trotsky but distrusts Stalin. We suggest that in his search for an answer he will look not only to Trotskyist sources to learn what really happened but also to Stalinist sources (although perhaps not as closely and, perhaps, at second-hand) to learn what did *not* happen. To help him with his cognitive appraisal he relies on negative as well as positive authority. He "depends" on Stalin no less than Trotsky. The process need not be conscious, or deliberate, or rational. We can get to hear what the Devil advocates even if all the sources of information are in the hands of his enemies.

To all of the preceding it is now necessary to make three additional points. First, in the case of rational reliance on authority the psychological distinction between positive and negative authority is not nearly as great as in the case of arbitrary reliance on authority. Second, it will be recalled that in our description of disbelief systems we assumed a continuum of disbelief subsystems arranged in terms of similarity to the belief system. In the same way we also think it fruitful to assume a "pantheon" of negative authorities arranged along a continuum of similarity to positive authority.

Third, we have already pointed out in discussing the central region that our main interest is with the *specific content* of primitive beliefs. This is not so with the authority-beliefs we have represented in the intermediate region. What interests us most here is their *formal* content rather than specific content. For example, suppose there are two persons who adhere to opposing ideological positions. But they both believe in an absolute authority, one true cause, and so on. We will say that the specific content of their beliefs differs, but the formal content is the same. It is in this sense that we will here use the term *formal content*. The conception should guide us to look for similarities among persons in their orientations to authority even though they may adhere to different ones.

In our conceptualizations we have also found it convenient to imagine another set of beliefs within the intermediate region, beliefs about people in general. We suspect that the world of people is generally evaluated according to the authorities and belief systems they line up with. In other words, we have beliefs about people-who-have-beliefs. When authority is seen to be absolute, for example, it also leads to extreme cognitive distinctions between persons as faithful and unfaithful, orthodox and heretical, loyal and subversive, American and un-American, and friend and enemy. Those who disagree may be rejected as enemies of God, country, mankind, the working class, science, or art. And those who agree may be accepted, but only so long as, and on the condition that, they continue to agree. This sort of qualified acceptance is not much different psychologically from, and can easily turn into, unqualified rejection, as we hope to show later on. For the moment let us merely point to the harsh attitude often taken toward the renegade.

The connection just drawn is considered by us as important because it spotlights a possibly intimate connection between the way we accept and reject people and the way we accept and reject ideas stemming from authority. Perhaps the most clear-cut example of this linkage is to be found in the use of opinionated language. We will define an opinionated statement as any statement that gives us two kinds of information about the speaker. First, it tells us whether the speaker accepts or rejects a particular idea or belief. Second, it tells us whether the speaker accepts or rejects people depending on whether they agree or disagree with this idea.

Opinionated rejection refers to verbal phrases that imply rejection of a given belief and at the same time rejection of those persons who accept it. Some illustrations: "Only a simple-minded fool would think that. . . ." "A person must be pretty stupid to think that. . . ." "The idea that . . . is pure hogwash [poppycock, rubbish, drivel, muddleheaded, nonsense, silly, preposterous, absurd, crazy, ridiculous, insane, piddling, etc.]."

Opinionated acceptance refers to the acceptance of a belief and at the same time a qualified acceptance of those who agree with it. Some examples are: "Any intelligent person knows that. . . ." "Plain common sense tells you that. . . ."

Two persons may have opposing belief-disbelief systems. One may, for example, be for communism, the other against communism. Both persons may reject those who disagree with them, and accept those who agree. In both cases, the *formal content* of beliefs about people-who-hold-beliefs about communism is the same even though the specific content is diametrically opposed. Thus the frequency of use of opinionated language may provide us with an approach to measuring general intolerance that cuts across differences in ideological content.

Recall again that we conceive of the disbelief system as a similarity continuum. Recall also the parallel representation of a "pantheon" of negative authorities arranged in terms of similarity to one's positive authority. We will now add here the further suggestion that corresponding to these disbelief and negative-authority continua is also a disbeliever continuum. Adherents to various disbelief subsystems may also be seen by the person in terms of a continuum of similarity to adherents of his own belief system. In other words, the world of people is organized not merely in terms of ingroup and outgroups but in terms of ingroup and a continuum of outgroups.

THE PERIPHERAL REGION

A person still has many beliefs left which need to be brought into line with those already discussed. Represented within the peripheral region are each and every (nonprimitive) belief and disbelief emanating from positive and negative authority, regardless of whether such beliefs are perceived consciously as being thus derived by the person himself. For example, favorable or unfavorable beliefs about such things as birth control, the New Deal, and the theory of repression would be considered peripheral beliefs because they are derivable from the formal content of one's beliefs about the Catholic Church, Roosevelt, and Freud. The latter, according to our view, would be represented as part of the intermediate region rather than the peripheral region. If we know the specific nature of a person's intermediate beliefs about authority, it should be possible to deduce therefrom the content of many other beliefs, numbering perhaps in the thousands. In other words, not all of the thousands of beliefs held by a person are necessarily equally weighted. Some are more strategically placed than others. And this way of looking at a person can be scientifically exploited to predict a maximum number of his (peripheral) beliefs if we know where to look for the minimum number of (intermediate) beliefs which are assumed to give rise to them.

The *specific* content of peripheral beliefs and disbeliefs will, of course, again vary from one person to another. It is precisely this specific content to which we look when we wish to ascertain and identify another's ideological position. But what is of major concern here is not so much ideological content as the structural interconnections among peripheral beliefs and, in turn, their structural relations with those beliefs we have represented as being in the intermediate and central regions. Let us consider the possible structural interconnections more fully.

We will assume that all information impinging upon the person from the outside must be processed or coded in such a way that it is either rejected or somehow fitted into the belief-disbelief system. We call this processing-coding activity thinking. Our guess is

47

that it must be within some such context as the belief-disbelief system that thinking takes place.

It is far from clear how the processing-coding of new information proceeds. But as a first approximation—and in order to guide empirical research—we will assume that this operation begins with the person first screening the new information for compatibility with the primitive beliefs. The initial screening may lead to the rejection or narrowing out of this information so that nothing further need be done with it. For example, many people pay no attention to the current work on extrasensory perception because they are not prepared to accept it, no matter how good the evidence. For many, ESP violates the primitive belief that the world can only be known through the senses. To take another example: In the summer of 1958, I heard a terse radio bulletin announcing that the military had just perfected a camera that could take pictures of the past. I refused to believe it; it violated a primitive belief I have about what cameras are for. A few hours later there came another clarifying report that the camera was able to photograph the heat waves of cars on a parking lot, immediately after they had driven off. I accepted this; it no longer violated my primitive belief about the nature of cameras.

Even if the new information is compatible with primitive beliefs, it may not be compatible with one's intermediate (authority) beliefs. For this reason, people often selectively avoid contact with stimuli, people, events, books, etc., that threaten the validity of their ideology or proselyte for competing ideologies. Cognitive narrowing may be manifested at both the institutional and noninstitutional levels. At the institutional level, narrowing is achieved when the screening is done by one's authority rather than by the person himself; for example, by the publication of lists of taboo books, the removal and burning of books seen as dangerous, the liquidation of ideological enemies, the omission of news reports in the mass media unfavorable to the institutionalized belief system, and the conscious and unconscious rewriting of history.

At the noninstitutional level, narrowing may be achieved by the systematic restriction of one's activities in order to avoid contact with people, books and ideas, and social, religious, and political events that would threaten the validity of one's belief system or the "invalidity" of one's disbelief system. A person may expose himself only to one point of view in the press, selectively choose his friends and associates solely or primarily on the basis of compatibility of systems, selectively avoid social contact with those who adhere to different systems, and ostracize renegades.

In academic circles, cognitive narrowing over and above that demanded by the requirements of specialization may be evidenced by a selective association with and avoidance of certain colleagues and a selective subscription, purchase, and reading of professional publications so that one's belief system becomes increasingly differentiated at the expense of narrowing down or making less differentiated one's disbelief system.

But not all new information is handled in this way. Much new information does get through and need not be narrowed out if it can somehow be assimilated into the belief-disbelief system. This may require altering or rationalizing the new information, as by finding out what one's authority sources, positive and negative, have to say about it (intermediate belief region). The final step is to file this information, which now may or may not be new, into whatever world outlook one has come to call his own (peripheral belief region).

Let us look at one aspect of the filing process a bit more closely. In our conception, the new information is communicated from the central (primitive) region to the intermediate (authority) region and, in turn, to the peripheral region, where it becomes represented in its psychological form as a belief or disbelief. Such a belief or disbelief may or may not communicate with or be related to other peripheral beliefs in the system, depending upon the degree of isolation among such beliefs. The greater the isolation, the less direct effect will a change in one part (belief) of the peripheral region have upon adjacent parts (beliefs). But there can still be indirect communication among peripheral beliefs via the intermediate (authority) region. It is essentially in this way that we can now conceptualize what happens cognitively when one is said to undergo a "party-line" change. A "party-line" change is assumed to take place in a person if he changes a particular peripheral belief as a result of some instruction emanating from his authority figures. That is, there is high communication between peripheral and intermediate regions. But this is not enough. Such a change in peripheral belief should not affect other beliefs in the peripheral region, as the peripheral beliefs are isolated from each other in a "party-line" change. A more "genuine" change may be conceived of as taking place if a new belief or a change in an old belief, even though preceded by a communication from one's authority figures, sets off a sequence of autonomous activity that changes other peripheral beliefs, thereby changing the internal organization of the peripheral region and, possibly, of the intermediate and primitive regions as well.

It should be emphasized at this point that the processing-coding operation we have just tried to describe is not always to be conceived of as a "coercing operation." The extent to which information about the world is coerced into the system depends upon the degree to which the total belief-disbelief system is closed or open.* At the closed extreme, it is the new information that must be tampered with—by narrowing it out, altering it, or containing it within isolated bounds. In this way, the belief-disbelief system is left intact. At the open extreme, it is the other way around: New information is assimilated *as is* and, in the hard process of reconciling it with other beliefs, communicates with other peripheral, as well as intermediate beliefs, thereby producing "genuine" (as contrasted with "party-line") changes in the whole belief-disbelief system.

Regardless of whether a belief-disbelief system is open or closed, it forms a psychological system. As already pointed out, it may or may not be a logical system. A person may be "confused," "disorganized," or "chaotic" in his thinking but he still has his belief-disbelief system. In our view, it is the structural interconnections among central, intermediate, and peripheral beliefs that gives the total belief-disbelief system its integrated, holistic, and systematic character. Whatever characterizes the primitive region is assumed to be reflected within the intermediate region, and whatever characterizes the intermediate region will be further reflected in the peripheral region. Thus, the belief-disbelief system, however illogical, is still seen to be a highly organized system; that is, it has certain structural relations among its parts. In the language of the philosophy of science, it has a syntax of its

* In the next chapter we will consider in more detail what we mean by "closed" and "open."

own, a *psychological syntax,* as contrasted with the *logical syntax* of a scientific or mathematical system.*

A worthwhile task for the future is to discover and to make explicit all the syntactical rules governing psychological systems in the same way that it is the task of the philospher of science to discover and to make explicit all the syntactical rules governing that limiting case of psychological systems known as a logical system. We regard the present work as a beginning step in this direction. Further analysis in this direction would have as its point of departure the notion that the logical syntax of a scientific system includes primitive terms, defined terms, axioms, theorems, and the empirical testing of the validity of theorems. It also includes the rules of correspondence among the preceding items. In a parallel way, it is possible to conceive of every personality system as a psychological belief-disbelief system, composed of beliefs some of which are primitive, some defined, some axiomatic, etc.

Organization Along a Time-Perspective Dimension

We will now propose a third dimension of belief-disbelief systems: time perspective (Frank, 1939; Lewin, 1942). This refers to the person's beliefs about the past, present, and future and the manner in which they are related to each other. We conceive time perspectives to vary from narrow to broad. A broad time perspective is one in which the person's past, present, and future are all represented within the belief-disbelief system, and the person sees them as related to each other. A narrow time perspective is one in which the person overemphasizes or fixates on the past, or the present, or the future without appreciating the continuity and the connections that exist among them. Thus, in our view, persons who have a completely past-oriented, or present-oriented, or future-oriented time perspective are all seen to have equally narrow time perspectives even though their perceptions of the past or of the future may cover a very long time span.†

* A closely related view treated in more mathematical terms has been recently expressed by Abelson and Rosenberg (1958).

† It should be pointed out that broad and narrow time perspectives have not always been defined in this way. LeShan (1952), for example, measures breadth-narrowness in terms of the amount of time covered in telling a story, without pay-

What sorts of beliefs shall we take to be symptomatic of broad and narrow time perspectives? A person may be said to have a broad time perspective if his beliefs and anticipations about the future can be shown to be realistically based upon an awareness of the past and present. Such a person can appreciate and enjoy the present in its own right but, at the same time, believe and act as if it is the culmination of the past and a prelude to the future. In contrast, a person has a narrow time perspective if he is too much, relatively speaking, preoccupied with the past, present, or future. The old man who spends much of his time reminiscing about days gone by is one case in point. A similar example is found in ideological movements of the political right, which typically seek their models in the past. We are thinking here of German naziism and of Japanese and Italian fascism, whose goals are to reinstate the Aryan myth, or the medieval structure of Japanese society, or the grandeur that was Rome.

There are certain kinds of people whose narrow time perspectives are revealed in a relatively great preoccupation with the present, with little regard for the past or concern with the future. This is shown, for example, in the infant's behavior, or the behavior of the highly impulsive adult. A more pathological case in point is the psychopath who typically acts in a present-oriented manner because of an unrestraining superego. Another example that comes to mind is the "beat" generation, who act as if they are literally trapped in the present. Perhaps this is so because today's youth has turned its back on the past, and at the same time feels compelled to hold off the future with rear-guard actions.

However, it is the future-oriented variety of narrow time perspectives that will concern us most. For many people, it is primarily the future that counts. Throughout history, there have arisen many religious and political movements that have kept their eye on some future Utopia or heaven. The present is but a vestibule to the future, unimportant in its own right, full of injustice and human suffering. A belief in force may be condoned in order to get rid of the unhappy present. Another clue to a future-

---

ing attention to whether the action takes place in the past, present, or future. Wallace (1956), in his research, is concerned only with future time perspectives and measures its breadth or narrowness in terms of greater or lesser degrees of extension into the future.

oriented time perspective is the belief that one *knows* or *understands* the future. The person believing this often accuses others of not understanding. Such a person, guided by his belief-disbelief system, typically expresses *overtly* a greater confidence of what the future holds in store, and a greater readiness to make predictions about the future.*

Finally, the breadth or narrowness of a person's time perspective may perhaps be most simply gauged by noting the relative frequency with which he refers to past, present, and future in his daily actions and conversation.†

Let us now summarize briefly. We have tried to outline here a theory about the characteristics that may be usefully employed to describe all belief systems. We view all systems as having three major dimensions: a belief-disbelief dimension, a central-peripheral dimension, and a time-perspective dimension. Each of these dimensions, in turn, is seen to have additional attributes. In the following chapter we will consider how these various dimensions and attributes may be tied together theoretically to produce a mind which, in its totality, can be fruitfully described as varying in the degree to which it is an open or closed mind.

* In the scientific world, the future refers to scientific outcomes rather than to the historical future as such.

† Thus, Fink (1953) has shown in his study of the aged that those who are institutionalized use the past tense more frequently in the TAT stories they tell than an equated group of aged persons who are not institutionalized.

3

A Fundamental Distinction
Between Open and
Closed Systems

Milton Rokeach and Frank Restle

In this chapter we will try to lay bare the fundamental identity underlying various characteristics of open and closed systems. Our aim is theoretical—to show in what way the various dimensions and properties discussed in Chapter 2 may be tied together in the open and closed mind. What we hope to accomplish here is to develop a good working definition as well as a good conceptual definition, with as few assumptions and with as much clarity and logical rigor as we can manage.

Let us first propose that the three major dimensions of belief-disbelief systems and the several properties thereof, as put forward in Chapter 2, are not independent. We see a basic connection, a common psychological thread running through them all. This thread, which we hope to expose here to view, is what gives the total belief-disbelief system a unity, even with all its complexities. Our main thesis will be that the many characteristics of systems described in Chapter 2 are also, in the extreme, alternative, interrelated manifestations of the open and closed mind. It is these manifestations that we hope to exploit in our research—to measure the extent to which a person's mind is open or closed, and to test many hypotheses stemming from the theory.

Our first insight into the possible interdependence of the various characteristics of belief systems was an intuitive one, based on informal observations of persons who seemed to be characteristically closed in their ways of thought and belief. Almost all the variables mentioned in Chapter 2 were first observed to cluster together in an extreme form in such persons. From these observations we formed a general, detailed statement of the defining characteristics of open and closed systems. This is given in Definition I and will serve us in our research as a working definition. Then we will give Definition II, which is a more simple, more basic one.

Definition I: The Defining Characteristics of Open-Closed Systems

A Belief-Disbelief System Is

Open	*Closed*

A. *to the extent that, with respect to its organization along the belief-disbelief continuum,*

1. the magnitude of rejection of disbelief subsystems is relatively low at each point along the continuum;	1. the magnitude of rejection of disbelief subsystems is relatively high at each point along the disbelief continuum;
2. there is communication of parts within and between belief and disbelief systems;	2. there is isolation of parts within and between belief and disbelief systems;
3. there is relatively little discrepancy in the degree of differentiation between belief and disbelief systems;	3. there is relatively great discrepancy in the degree of differentiation between belief and disbelief systems;

Open	*Closed*
4. there is relatively high differentiation within the disbelief system;	4. there is relatively little differentiation within the disbelief system;

B. *to the extent that, with respect to the organization along the central-peripheral dimension,*

1. the *specific content* of primitive beliefs (central region) is to the effect that the world one lives in, or the situation one is in at a particular moment, is a friendly one;	1. the *specific content* of primitive beliefs (central region) is to the effect that the world one lives in, or the situation one is in at a particular moment, is a threatening one;
2. the *formal content* of beliefs about authority and about people who hold to systems of authority (intermediate region) is to the effect that authority is not absolute and that people are not to be evaluated (if they are to be evaluated at all) according to their agreement or disagreement with such authority;	2. the *formal content* of beliefs about authority and about people who hold to systems of authority (intermediate region) is to the effect that authority is absolute and that people are to be accepted and rejected according to their agreement or disagreement with such authority;
3. the *structure* of beliefs and disbeliefs perceived to emanate from authority (peripheral region) is such that its substructures are in relative communication with each other, and finally;	3. the *structure* of beliefs and disbeliefs perceived to emanate from authority (peripheral region) is such that its substructures are in relative isolation with each other, and finally;

C. *to the extent that, with respect to the time-perspective dimension, there is a*

1. relatively broad time perspective.	1. relatively narrow, future-oriented time perspective.

Definition I makes possible our research undertaking. For one thing, it provides us with a set of theoretical blueprints to guide the construction of many statements to be put to subjects for their endorsement or rejection. Agreement or disagreement with such statements, considered all together, should provide us with a single global measure of how open or closed a person's system is. For another thing, Definition I provides us with a large reservoir of hypotheses of two kinds: (1) hypotheses about the relations that may be expected to exist between each one of the structural characteristics of belief systems and each one of the others; (2) hypotheses about differences in cognitive and emotional behavior expected to exist between persons characterized as open and closed. Some of these will be tested in the present research. Others, we hope, will be tested in the future.

What will concern us now is whether there is a compelling theoretical reason for tying together in the way we have the different parts of Definition I.

Definition II: A More Basic Definition

We assume that, in any situation in which a person must act, there are certain characteristics of the situation that point to the appropriate action to be taken. If the person reacts in terms of such relevant characteristics, his response should be correct, or appropriate. The same situation also contains irrelevant factors, not related to the inner structure or requirements of the situation. To the extent that response depends on such irrelevant factors, it should be unintelligent or inappropriate. Every person, then, must be able to evaluate adequately both the relevant and irrelevant information he receives from every situation. This leads us to suggest a basic characteristic that defines the extent to which a person's system is open or closed; namely, the extent to which the person can receive, evaluate, and act on relevant information received from the outside on its own intrinsic merits, unencumbered by irrelevant factors in the situation arising from within the person or from the outside. Examples of irrelevant internal pressures that interfere with the realistic reception of information are unrelated habits, beliefs, and perceptual cues, irrational ego motives, power needs, the need for self-aggrandizement, the need to allay anxiety, and so forth. By irrelevant external pressures we have in mind most particularly the pressures of reward and punishment arising from external authority; for example, as exerted by parents, peers, other authority figures, reference groups, social and institutional norms, and cultural norms. Will the information received about a situation from such external sources be evaluated and acted on independently or in accord with expectations about how the external source wishes us to evaluate and act on this information? The more open one's belief system, the more should evaluating and acting on information proceed independently on its own merits, in accord with the inner structural requirements of the situation. Also, the more open the belief system, the more should the person be governed in his actions by internal self-actualizing forces and the less by irrational inner forces. Consequently, the more should he be able to resist pressures exerted by external sources to evaluate and to act in accord with their wishes. One important implication here is that the more open the person's belief system, the more strength should he have to resist externally imposed reinforcements, or rewards and punishments. These should be less effective as determinants of the way information will be evaluated and acted upon.

Conversely, the more closed the belief system, the more difficult should it be to distinguish between information received about the world and information received about the source. What the external source says is true about the world should become all mixed up with what the external source wants us to believe is true, and wants us to do about it. To the extent that a person cannot distinguish the two kinds of information received from the source, he should not be free to receive, evaluate, and act on information in terms of inner requiredness. He should be exposed to pressures, rewards and punishments, meted out by the source designed to make him evaluate and act on the information in the way the source wants him to.

An example may be helpful here. Suppose we are told by Secretary of State Herter in 1959 that the Russians are as stubborn as ever on the issue of disarmament. This piece of news contains two kinds of information which, in the open system, may give rise to two corresponding sets of beliefs, to guide two corresponding lines of action. First, the communication contains information about the Russians which, to the extent that we judge it to be factually correct, should give rise to or reinforce a corresponding cognitive belief about whether the Russians are indeed as stubborn as ever. This belief, in turn, should serve to guide our action with respect to Russia. For example, it should help us to decide whether we ought to support high expenditures for armaments and missiles, whether taxes should be increased, or whether we should advocate the exchange of scientific information with the Russians.

The communication also contains information about Secretary Herter himself, what he believes, what he wants us to believe, and what he wants us to do about it. This may give rise to, or reinforce, various cognitive beliefs about Herter and serve to guide *other* action—for example, to get rid of Herter (or not), to get rid of the Republicans at the next election (or not), and so on.

We assume that the more open the belief system, the more will the dual character of the communication received from Herter be appreciated and responded to with discernment, each piece of information being weighed on its own merits; and that the more closed the system, the less cognitive discrimination we will expect between the two sets of information, beliefs, and consequent actions.

We tentatively suggest that all information received has this dual character. This may be so even in extreme cases, such as in communications received from a scientific paper, or from the stark parade-ground command, "Attention!" Any scientific paper, no matter how carefully impersonal, contains not only substantive information but also information about the communicator— whether he believes that the research is important, carefully done, conclusive. It also contains information about action desired by the communicator—whether others should also busy themselves with the same interesting area and whether we should regard the communicator as competent, respectable, or original. The effect of such communications, to the extent that they are effective, is to reinforce agreement and respect, to arouse interest and further study, to inhibit criticism, scepticism, or indifference. To some mild and mannerly degree, such a scientific communication tries to control behavior directly, both with respect to what is being communicated and with respect to the communicator. The two aspects of the communication are indistinguishable to the closed system, but distinguishable to the open system.

Similarly, the command "Attention!" may also be said to contain the two aspects mentioned. It is mainly a signal issued by a superior intended to produce an uncomfortable posture in the soldier without enlightening him, so that the superior can better control his action on the spot. However, the soldier also gets substantive information from the command. It may herald the issuance of yet further orders, a new military activity, the beginning or end of a military ceremony, the arrival of an officer. Again, we see that there are two aspects to the communication, and in different people the dual aspects will be differentiated or fused together, according to the degree to which their systems are open or closed.

In attempting to formulate the basic defining characteristic of openness-closedness, we could have let the whole matter go by simply saying that the fundamental basis is the extent to which there is reliance on absolute authority. Using Fromm's terms (1941), we could have talked about rational versus arbitrary authority. Following Maslow (1951), we could have talked about individual differences in "resistance to acculturation." Other concepts we could have used are conformance vs. nonconformance (Jahoda, 1956), and independence vs. yielding (Asch, 1952).

It is obvious that all of these concepts are concerned with much the same issues. We could easily have defined openness-closedness in terms of any of the above. However, we have preferred to put the matter the way we have for good reason. Our primary concern and commitment is to try to describe what is going on, and not going on, at the cognitive level. Reliance on authority, yielding, conformance, and resistance to acculturation all may have a common cognitive basis, namely, the ability (or inability) to discriminate substantive information from information about the source, and to assess the two separately.

Reconciling Definitions I and II

Let us now see whether the several defining characteristics of open-closed systems, as presented under our more elaborate Definition I, each imply or may be seen to arise from the more fundamental distinction presented under Definition II.

WITH RESPECT TO THE ORGANIZATION OF THE BELIEF-DISBELIEF CONTINUUM

A system is defined to be closed to the extent that there is a high magnitude of rejection of all disbelief subsystems, an isolation of beliefs, a high discrepancy in degree of differentiation between belief and disbelief systems, and little differentiation within the disbelief system.

The more closed the system, the more is the acceptance of a particular belief assumed to depend on irrelevant internal drives and/or arbitrary reinforcements from external authority. The relation among beliefs should depend on such irrelevant considerations rather than on considerations of logical consistency. Isolation between parts reflects a tendency not to relate beliefs to the inner requirements of logical consistency, but to assimilate them wholesale, as fed by one's authority figure. On the other hand, the more open the system, the more should the person address himself to objective structural requirements—that is, logical relationships—and the more should he resist irrelevant motivational or reinforcement pressures. In this way, isolation is shown to be a defining characteristic of openness-closedness.

Furthermore, if a person were completely able to evaluate information on its own merits, he would seek information about a particular disbelief subsystem directly from the adherents or authorities of such a system. If a Stalinist wishes to learn about Trotsky's views, the best place to go is to Trotsky himself. If a Baptist wishes to learn about Catholicism, or Judaism, the best place to go is to Catholic or Jewish sources. But the more closed his system, the more sensitive should he be to communications, reinforcements, warnings, prohibitions, and promises issuing forth from his own group or authorities, and the more should he be dependent on such positive authorities for information he accumulates about a particular disbelief subsystem. Information about disbelief systems, if received at all, should come secondhand, spoon-fed by the person's positive authority. For example, the more closed a particular Stalinist is, the more likely it is that he will come into contact with Trotsky's views only through Stalinist sources. Similarly, the more closed a Baptist, the more likely it is that he will know what he knows about Catholicism or Judaism through Baptist sources.

Several consequences can now be seen to follow. The inability to distinguish the dual aspects of communications should in time lead not only to a stronger acceptance of the belief system but also to a stronger rejection of all disbelief subsystems. It should lead the person to have a greater discrepancy between what he knows about the belief system and what he knows about the disbelief system. It should also lead to less differentiation within the disbelief system as a whole, and to an increasing inability to distinguish among disbelief subsystems, the more dissimilar they are from the belief system. Thus, it follows from our basic distinction that the following will all be defining characteristics of openness-closedness: degree of rejection of disbelief subsystems, degree of differentiation of belief system as compared with disbelief system, and degree of differentiation within the disbelief system.

WITH RESPECT TO THE CENTRAL-PERIPHERAL DIMENSION

We assume that the more closed the system, the more will the world be seen as threatening, the greater will be the belief in absolute authority, the more will other persons be evaluated according to the authorities they line up with, and the more will peripheral beliefs be related to each other by virtue of their common origin in authority, rather than by virtue of intrinsic connections.

If a person feels strongly threatened or anxious in a given situation, he should above all be motivated to act so that the threat is reduced and the anxiety allayed. It is precisely because he is so motivated that the relatively closed person becomes highly attuned to irrelevant internal and external pressures and, accordingly, unable to evaluate information independent of source. Thus, primitive beliefs to the effect that the world is threatening is the very basis of the inability to distinguish information from source.

Consider now overreliance on authority. As has been said earlier, we all depend on authority for information, since we cannot inspect everything for ourselves. In the closed system, the power of authority does not depend on cognitive correctness, but on the ability of authority to mete out reward and punishment. Given a variety of information stemming from an external source, the relatively closed person is forced to accept all or reject all in a "package deal."

On the other hand, the world is seen to be a more friendly place by the relatively open person. He should thus be more free and more impervious to irrelevant pressures. For him, the power of authority is still there, but depends upon the authority's cognitive correctness, accuracy, and consistency with other information he has about the world. Authority that gives information in conflict with the information he possesses will be judged unreliable and will therefore be replaced by more reliable authority. Various peripheral beliefs derived from authority will be tested in application, and will thus be less likely to remain in relative isolation from each other.

Similarly, the more closed a person's belief system, the more he should evaluate others according to their agreement or disagreement with his own system; also, the more difficult should it be to discriminate between and separately evaluate a belief and the person holding the belief. Conversely, the more open the belief system, the less should beliefs held in common be a criterion for evaluating others, and the more should others be positively valued, regardless of their beliefs. In other words, the alternative to accepting and rejecting others on grounds of belief congruence is to accept others without evaluating them at all. Some extreme examples that come to mind are a mother's love of her child, a man's love of a woman, etc. This is also the ideal inherent in religions that preach the brotherhood of man (Judge not, lest ye be judged), and in psychotherapy.

WITH RESPECT TO THE TIME-PERSPECTIVE DIMENSION

To evaluate information on its own merits is necessarily to be oriented with both feet in the here and now. At the same time, this evaluative process implies a disciplined concern with the immediate, foreseeable future. For we continually make predictions and plans on the basis of information, and the way these predictions and plans turn out helps along the evaluative process. Similarly with postdiction, which implies a realistic evaluation or re-evaluation of our past in terms of the present. In either case, if information we receive in our daily lives is to be assessed on its own merits, there is little need for an overconcern with the remote future or the remote past.[*] Most especially, a restraint is placed upon knowing the distant future since it cannot, by its very nature, be known.

The disciplined restraint upon the future is lifted if a person cannot or will not evaluate information on its own merits. Thus, in closed systems, the main cognitive basis is missing from the distinction between the immediate and remote future. Knowledge about the remote future is impossible to refute and, hence, one can be safely preoccupied with it. The more open the system, the more the immediate future should be in the service of confirming or not confirming predictions about the present. It is the other way around in closed systems. Things that happen in the present should be in the service of "confirming" the remote future. For this reason, a narrow, future-oriented time perspective, rather than a more balanced conception of past, present, and immediate future in relation to each other, is also seen to be a defining characteristic of closed systems.

Three Models of Man

Different schools of psychology have emphasized different models of man in building their systematic frames of reference. We would now like to comment briefly on how such differences in theoretical models are related to the main distinction we have drawn between open and closed systems. As we see it, Gestalt theory would be most appropriate if man were completely open in his belief system. This seems to be the position emphasized by such Gestalt psychologists as Wertheimer (1945), Köhler (1938), Katona (1940), Duncker (1945), and Asch (1952). For them, the model of man seems to be primarily a rational one. People act primarily in accord with the meaningful, structural, configurational requirements of the situation. Action on the basis of irrational motives or arbitrary external reinforcements is de-emphasized.

At the other extreme are those theoretical positions that have as their model a man closed in his belief system, evaluating and

---

[*] Unless the person happens to be vocationally or avocationally interested in science fiction or history.

acting only rarely in accord with situational requirements, but rather in accord with pressures irrelevant to the requirements of the situation. We are thinking here primarily of behaviorism and psychoanalysis, but for different reasons. Behaviorism emphasizes the importance of external reinforcements, or rewards and punishments, as determinants of behavior. If man were completely closed in his belief system, he could be completely controlled and directed by such arbitrary reinforcements. The mechanism by which reinforcements work, be it drive-reduction or contiguity (Hilgard, 1956), does not matter for the present. What does matter from our point of view is that they all seem to have as their model a man (also a rat or pigeon) completely closed in his belief system. The classical principles of learning that have been expounded should hold less and less as those doing the learning become more and more open in their belief systems.

Classical psychoanalysis also has as its model a person with a closed system, but here the emphasis is on irrelevant *internal* motivations rather than *external* reinforcements. For behaviorism, action is determined by arbitrary reinforcements and arbitrary associations; for classical psychoanalysis, action is determined by id and superego strivings. The ego tests reality only insofar as necessary to satisfy id and superego strivings, or to sublimate such strivings. Otherwise, the ego has little or no interest in reality-testing as such.* Thus, from the standpoint of classical psychoanalysis, we respond to a situation not so much in terms of its external requirements as in terms of our own inner requirements. The emphasis of psychoanalysis is on man's primary rather than secondary processes. As Witkin *et al.* have put it:

> Although psychoanalytic theory, in its conception of primary and secondary process, recognizes the relation between intellectual functioning and personality, it has not really been concerned with the nature of secondary processes. Furthermore, as many critics have validly pointed out, it has over-emphasized the affective foundations of intellectual life . . . there is still lacking in psychoanalytic theory any specific account of cognition or the nature of

---

* In all fairness, let us emphasize that we are here commenting on *classical* psychoanalysis. That the analytic movement itself has been unhappy with this one-sided view is seen in its more recent emphasis on ego psychology.

secondary process. Primary process involves learning by association—particularly by contiguity of affectively charged ideas. Secondary process is really not described, except in terms of its outcome—that it is reality oriented. By implication, it is suggested that the principle of learning by association is also involved here, although the associations are among rational ideas rather than the more primitive, undifferentiated ideas characteristic of the primary process. (1954, p. 481.)

The above considerations now lead us to the following view: Open and closed systems are but ideal types, convenient for purposes of analysis. However, the real people we all know have systems that are neither completely open nor completely closed. Furthermore, like the diaphragm on a camera, a system can expand and contract within limits, as conditions vary. Gestalt theory has contributed to psychological understanding, to the extent that man has open belief systems; psychoanalysis and behaviorism have likewise contributed, to the extent that man's belief systems are closed. But we will not behave as Gestalt psychology says we should, the more we are closed; or as psychoanalysis and behaviorism say we should, the more we are open. Like the blind man exploring different parts of the same elephant, not one of the three theories considered alone has adequately coped with man as he really and fully is. But considered all together, they each help—in differing degrees perhaps—to fill in the gaps left unexplored by the others.

A somewhat similar view, with respect to the function of an opinion, is expressed by Smith, Bruner, and White:

> . . . we have been impelled to treat the function of an opinion as a resultant or compromise between reality demands, social demands, and inner psychological demands. The three are inseparable. Emphasis upon the first alone leads one to the rationalism of the 19th-century writers on opinion who . . . would admit for study only those opinions based on "adequate knowledge." Emphasis on social factors alone leads to a passive conception of the individual, a mirror of culture or society. Emphasis on externalization alone [inner psychological demands] is the route to the kind of irrationalism that marked the earliest impact of the

psychoanalytic movement. Only by emphasis on the three together can one arrive at an adequate picture of the complex adjustments that go into the formation of a man's opinions. (1956, pp. 275–276.)

The Function of Belief-Disbelief Systems

As already implied in the preceding section, classical psychoanalysis has tried to account for man's behavior by seeing him as id-driven, egotistical, rationalizing, and sublimating. In recent years psychologists have become increasingly dissatisfied with this "negative" view. In addition to Asch, whom we have already cited, let us also draw attention here to the writings of Allport (1955), Fromm (1947), Maslow (1954), Rogers (1951), Tolman (1954), and White (1959). These writers prefer to place a greater emphasis on man's cognitive needs and his tendencies toward growth, productiveness, and self-actualization.

One danger of such a "protest movement" is that psychology will swing too far in the opposite direction to create a newer image of man as rational and self-actualizing. As already stated, we believe that there is validity in both positions. For we cannot think of a single person who is not driven by both rational and rationalizing forces. This assumption is at the core of our speculations regarding the functions served by belief-disbelief systems.

It is therefore assumed that all belief-disbelief systems serve two powerful and conflicting sets of motives at the same time: the need for a cognitive framework to know and to understand and the need to ward off threatening aspects of reality.* To the extent that the cognitive need to know is predominant and the need to ward off threat absent, open systems should result. In the service of the cognitive need to know, external pressures and irrational internal drives will often be pushed aside, so that information received from outside will be discriminated, assessed, and acted on according to the objective requirements of the situation. But as the need to ward off threat becomes stronger, the cognitive need to know should become weaker, resulting in more closed

* Sarnoff and Katz (1954), and Smith, Bruner, and White (1956) also recognize this duality of function in their analysis of the motivations served by attitudes and opinions.

belief systems. Under threat, information and source should become inseparable and should be evaluated arbitrarily in line with the rewards and punishments meted out by authority.

It is proposed, however, that for most persons in most situations, both sets of needs operate together to one degree or another. A person will be open to information *insofar as possible,* and will reject it, screen it out, or alter it *insofar as necessary.* In other words, no matter how much a person's system closes up to ward off threat and anxiety, it can still serve as a cognitive framework for satisfying the need to know. For the closed mind is *subjectively* experienced by the person who has it no differently from the way it is experienced by a person with an open mind. In this way the person's belief system may be thought of as a mechanism for having one's cake and eating it too. One can distort the world and narrow it down to whatever extent necessary, but at the same time preserve the illusion of understanding it. And if the closed or dogmatic mind is extremely resistant to change, it may be so not only because it allays anxiety but also because it satisfies the need to know.

If threat leads to dogmatism in individuals, by the same token it should also lead to dogma in institutions. Dogma serves the purpose of ensuring the continued existence of the institution and the belief-disbelief system for which it stands.

> In the early Church dogmatic formulation of an authoritative kind is minimal in extent and fundamentally negative in character. The Church only resorted to dogmatic formulation when it found itself confronted with some heresy which threatened to overthrow the very foundations of the characteristically Christian way of life and worship. The true purpose of the dogmatic formula is not to assert any particular solution of a theological problem, but rather to deny and decisively reject some proffered but inadequate solution. The essential virtue of the dogmatic formula is that the heretic against whose teachings it is aimed cannot sincerely repeat it.
>
> Dogma is not made for dogma's sake. Where there is no great heresy, there is not dogma. (Casserly, 1953, p. 57.)

Erasmus speaks of the self-preservative function of institutionalized dogma as the "Law of Degeneracy." As summarized by Salomon, this law refers to:

> . . . the thesis that all social institutions, including religious institutions, are driven by their desire to survive into programs of self-entrenchment and self-aggrandizement in the course of which their original faiths and ideals are perverted and abandoned. (1949, p. 599.)

At the individual level, threat may arise out of adverse experiences, temporary or enduring, which are shaped by and which, in turn, shape broader human conditions. To varying degrees, individuals may become disposed to accept or to form closed systems of thinking and believing in proportion to the degree to which they are made to feel alone, isolated, and helpless in the world in which they live (Fromm, 1947) and thus anxious of what the future holds in store for them. Such a state of affairs should lead to pervasive feelings of self-inadequacy and self-hate. Attempts may be made to overcome such feelings by becoming excessively concerned with needs for power and status. Along with such an overconcern follow compensatory attitudes of egotism on the one hand and misanthropy (Sullivan and Adelson, 1954) on the other. These, in turn, should lead to feelings of guilt and, by rationalization and projection, to a generally disaffected outlook on life.

Such then, in brief, is the constellation of conditions conceived to make the individual susceptible to cognitive confusion between information and source of information, and thus prone to closed systems of thinking and believing. By overidentification with absolute authority and a cause and by succumbing to the arbitrary reinforcements arising therefrom, an attempt is made to defend the self against feelings of aloneness and isolation, self-hate and misanthropy. At the same time something positive may be gained: closed belief-disbelief systems provide a systematic cognitive framework for rationalizing and justifying egocentric self-righteousness and the moral condemnation of others. Thus, the more closed the belief-disbelief system, the more do we conceive it to represent, in its totality, a tightly woven network of cognitive defenses against anxiety. Such psychoanalytic defense mechanisms as repression, rationalization, denial, projection, reaction formation, and overidentification may all be seen to have their representation in the belief-disbelief system in the form of some belief or in the form of some structural relation among beliefs. Indeed, we suggest that, in the extreme, the closed system is nothing more than the total network of psychoanalytic defense mechanisms organized together to form a cognitive system and designed to shield a vulnerable mind.

In this chapter we presented two definitions of what we mean by *open* and *closed*. Definition I is a working definition that describes various characteristics of the open and closed mind. Definition II is a more fundamental one that tries to tie together the various characteristics mentioned in Definition I. We then considered briefly how our formulation fits with those of the Gestalt theory, psychoanalysis, and behaviorism. Finally, we proposed the existence of two opposing sets of motives—the need to know and the need to defend against threat—which are conceived to jointly determine the extent to which a belief system is open or closed.

4

The Measurement of Open and Closed Systems

How can we tell whether the theory we have just outlined is a fruitful one? To find out is no simple matter. Like any other theory, it can only be tested step by step, by exploring its consequences. Like any other theory, it would be hard to prove or disprove. At best, research findings can only raise or lower the probability of its validity.

The rest of this book deals with these problems: evaluation of the theory, elaboration on it, and exploration of its applications. We first looked to the theory to tell us what sorts of measuring instruments to construct. This is what this chapter is mainly about.

The Dogmatism Scale

The primary purpose of this scale is to measure individual differences in openness or closedness of belief systems. Because of the way we have defined open and closed in Chapter 3, the scale should also serve to measure general authoritarianism and general intolerance. Our procedure in constructing the Dogmatism Scale was essentially deductive. We scrutinized the various defining characteristics of open and closed systems. We then tried to construct statements designed to tap these characteristics.

Our assumption was that if a person strongly agrees with such statements it would indicate that he possesses one extreme of the particular characteristic being tapped, and if he strongly disagrees, that he possesses the opposite extreme. Insofar as possible, we looked for statements that express ideas familiar to the average person in his everyday life. Some of the statements appearing in the Dogmatism Scale were inspired by spontaneous remarks we overheard being made by persons we thought intuitively to be closed-minded. Above all, each statement in the scale had to be designed to transcend specific ideological positions in order to penetrate to the formal and structural characteristics af all positions. Persons adhering dogmatically to such diverse viewpoints as capitalism and communism, Catholicism and anti-Catholicism, should all score together at one end of the continuum, and should all score in a direction opposite to others having equally diverse yet undogmatic viewpoints. Thus, it was our hope that the Dogmatism Scale could be employed as a research tool not only in the Western countries but also in the Soviet Union and in other Eastern countries.

The Dogmatism Scale is preceded by the following instructions, which are the same as those used with the F Scale:

> The following is a study of what the general public thinks and feels about a number of important social and personal questions. The best answer to each statement below is your *personal opinion*. We have tried to cover many different and opposing points of view; you may find yourself agreeing strongly with some of the statements, disagreeing just as strongly with others, and perhaps uncertain about others; whether you agree or disagree with any statement, you can be sure that many people feel the same as you do.
>
> Mark each statement in the left margin according to how much you agree or disagree with it. Please mark every one.

Write $+1$, $+2$, $+3$, or -1, -2, -3, depending on how you feel in each case.

+1: I AGREE A LITTLE	−1: I DISAGREE A LITTLE
+2: I AGREE ON THE WHOLE	−2: I DISAGREE ON THE WHOLE
+3: I AGREE VERY MUCH	−3: I DISAGREE VERY MUCH

The Dogmatism Scale went through five editions.[1] A total of 89 items were tried out in the initial scale and in four successive revisions. The aim of these revisions was to take advantage of continuing refinements in our theoretical formulations, and to increase reliability.*

For the sake of brevity we will discuss here only Forms D and E. Form D contains 66 items; the final Form E contains the best 40 items taken from Form D.[2] In the following discussion, the reader can identify a Form E item by the asterisk preceding it. For all statements, agreement is scored as closed, and disagreement as open.[3] The total score on the Dogmatism Scale is the sum of scores obtained on all items.

ITEMS INVOLVING THE BELIEF-DISBELIEF DIMENSION

Isolation within and between belief and disbelief systems. Isolation refers to the degree of segregation or lack of intercommunication between neighboring regions or subregions. It is assumed that the more closed the system the greater the isolation between and within the belief and the disbelief systems. Items reflecting various cognitive aspects of isolation are as follows:

(1) *Accentuation of differences between the belief and the disbelief systems*

   * 1. The United States and Russia have just about nothing in common.

* *Note to general readers:* A test is *reliable* if the person consistently responds to it in the same way on one or more occasions. A highly reliable test may or may not be *valid*. For example, consider a cloth tape measure that has shrunk badly after washing. It is still a reliable (consistent) measure, but it is hardly valid. Reliabilities are usually determined by noting the degree of consistency of a person's scores from one half the test to the other half, or by repeating the test on two separate occasions, or by taking two equivalent, but not identical, forms of the test. Consistency is typically expressed as a correlation ranging from 1.00 (perfect positive correlation), to zero (no correlation), to −1.00 (perfect negative correlation).

    2. Communism and Catholicism have nothing in common.

    3. The principles I have come to believe in are quite different from those believed in by most people.

(2) *The perception of irrelevance*

    4. In a heated discussion people have a way of bringing up irrelevant issues rather than sticking to the main issue.

(3) *The coexistence of contradictions within the belief system*

    *5. The highest form of government is a democracy and the highest form of democracy is a government run by those who are most intelligent.

    *6. Even though freedom of speech for all groups is a worthwhile goal, it is unfortunately necessary to restrict the freedom of certain political groups.

    7. While the use of force is wrong by and large, it is sometimes the only way possible to advance a noble ideal.

    8. Even though I have a lot of faith in the intelligence and wisdom of the common man I must say that the masses behave stupidly at times.

Relative degrees of differentiation of the belief and the disbelief systems. The belief system is assumed to be generally more differentiated than the disbelief system. It is further assumed that with an increase in closedness there will be less differentiation of disbelief subsystems with respect to each other; that is, different disbelief subsystems will be perceived as "the same."

(1) *Relative amount of knowledge possessed*

    *9. It is only natural that a person would have a much better acquaintance with ideas he believes in than with ideas he opposes.

(2) *Dedifferentiation within the disbelief system*

    10. There are certain "isms" which are really the same even though those who believe in these "isms" try to tell you they are different.

ITEMS INVOLVING THE CENTRAL-PERIPHERAL DIMENSION

Specific content of primitive beliefs. As noted in Chapter 2, the central region is composed of a constellation of "pre-ideological" primitive beliefs, for the most part unverbalized, that historically are prior to the rest of the beliefs in the system. These primitive beliefs are concerned with whether the world we live in is friendly or hostile, what the future has in store for us, the adequacy of the self, and what must be done to alleviate feelings of inadequacy. It is assumed that the more closed the system, the more will the content of such beliefs be to the effect that we live alone, isolated and helpless in a friendless world; that we live in a world wherein the future is uncertain; that the self is fundamentally unworthy and inadequate to cope alone with this friendless world; and that the way to overcome such feelings is by a self-aggrandizing and self-righteous identification with a cause, a concern with power and status, and by a compulsive self-proselytization about the justness of such a cause.

(1) *Beliefs regarding the aloneness, isolation, and helplessness of man*
     *11. Man on his own is a helpless and miserable creature.
     *12. Fundamentally, the world we live in is a pretty lonesome place.
     *13. Most people just don't give a "damn" for others.
     *14. I'd like it if I could find someone who would tell me how to solve my personal problems.
(2) *Beliefs regarding the uncertainty of the future*
     (a) *Fear of the future*
         *15. It is only natural for a person to be rather fearful of the future.
     (b) *A feeling of urgency* [4]
         *16. There is so much to be done and so little time to do it in.
     (c) *Compulsive repetition of ideas and arguments (self-proselytization)*
         *17. Once I get wound up in a heated discussion I just can't stop.
         *18. In a discussion I often find it necessary to re-

peat myself several times to make sure I am being understood.

*19. In a heated discussion I generally become so absorbed in what I am going to say that I forget to listen to what the others are saying.

20. In a discussion I sometimes interrupt others too much in my eagerness to put across my own point of view.

(3) *Beliefs about self-adequacy and inadequacy*

  (a) *Need for martyrdom*

  *21. It is better to be a dead hero than to be a live coward.[5]

  (b) *Conflict within the self*

  22. My hardest battles are with myself.

  (c) *Self-deprecation*

  23. At times I think I am no good at all.

  24. I am afraid of people who want to find out what I'm really like for fear they'll be disappointed in me.

(4) *Self-aggrandizement as a defense against self-inadequacy*

  (a) *Concern with power and status*

  *25. While I don't like to admit this even to myself, my secret ambition is to become a great man, like Einstein, or Beethoven, or Shakespeare.

  *26. The main thing in life is for a person to want to do something important.

  *27. If given the chance I would do something of great benefit to the world.

  28. If I had to choose between happiness and greatness, I'd choose greatness.

  (b) *Moral self-righteousness*

  29. It's all too true that people just won't practice what they preach.

(5) *Paranoid outlook on life*

  30. Most people are failures and it is the system which is responsible for this.

  31. I have often felt that strangers were looking at me critically.

  32. It is only natural for a person to have a guilty conscience.

33. People say insulting and vulgar things about me.
34. I am sure I am being talked about.

Formal content of the intermediate belief region. It will be recalled that in the intermediate region we have represented beliefs about the nature of positive and negative authority, ranging from rational at one extreme to arbitrary at the other, and beliefs about people, having to do with the extent to which people are accepted and rejected according to the positive and negative authorities they line up with. The more closed the belief-disbelief system, the more will authority be seen as absolute and the more will people be accepted and rejected because they agree or disagree with one's belief-disbelief system.

(1) *Authoritarianism*
    (a) *Beliefs in positive and negative authority*
        *35. In the history of mankind there have probably been just a handful of really great thinkers.
        *36. There are a number of people I have come to hate because of the things they stand for.
    (b) *Belief in the cause*
        *37. A man who does not believe in some great cause has not really lived.
        *38. It is only when a person devotes himself to an ideal or cause that life becomes meaningful.
        *39. Of all the different philosophies which exist in this world there is probably only one which is correct.
        *40. A person who gets enthusiastic about too many causes is likely to be a pretty "wishy-washy" sort of person.
        *41. To compromise with our political opponents is dangerous because it usually leads to the betrayal of our own side.
        *42. When it comes to differences of opinion in religion we must be careful not to compromise with those who believe differently from the way we do.
        *43. In times like these, a person must be pretty selfish if he considers primarily his own happiness.

44. To compromise with our political opponents is to be guilty of appeasement.

(2) *Intolerance*

(a) *Toward the renegade* [Persons adhering to disbelief subsystems most similar to one's own belief system—factional or renegade systems—are often likely to be perceived as especially threatening to the validity of the belief system. We assume that this will become increasingly the case the more closed the system.]

*45. The worst crime a person could commit is to attack publicly the people who believe in the same thing he does.

*46. In times like these it is often necessary to be more on guard against ideas put out by people or groups in one's own camp than by those in the opposing camp.

*47. A group which tolerates too much differences of opinion among its own members cannot exist for long.

(b) *Toward the disbeliever*

*48. There are two kinds of people in this world: those who are for the truth and those who are against the truth.

*49. My blood boils whenever a person stubbornly refuses to admit he's wrong.

*50. A person who thinks primarily of his own happiness is beneath contempt.

*51. Most of the ideas which get printed nowadays aren't worth the paper they are printed on.

52. I sometimes have a tendency to be too critical of the ideas of others.

Interrelations among primitive, intermediate, and peripheral beliefs. The more closed the system, the more will a change in a particular peripheral belief be determined by a prior change in the intermediate (authority) region. Further, the primitive and intermediate regions are assumed to control not only what will be represented in the peripheral region but also what will not be represented, that is, narrowed out.

(1) *Tendency to make a party-line change* [Referring to a change in peripheral beliefs following a change in intermediate beliefs.]

*53. In this complicated world of ours the only way we can know what's going on is to rely on leaders or experts who can be trusted.

*54. It is often desirable to reserve judgment about what's going on until one has had a chance to hear the opinions of those one respects.

(2) *Narrowing* [Referring to the selective avoidance of contact with facts, events, etc., incongruent with one's belief-disbelief system.]

*55. In the long run the best way to live is to pick friends and associates whose tastes and beliefs are the same as one's own.

56. There's no use wasting your money on newspapers which you know in advance are just plain propaganda.

57. Young people should not have too easy access to books which are likely to confuse them.

ITEMS INVOLVING THE TIME-PERSPECTIVE DIMENSION

It is assumed that the more closed the belief-disbelief system, the more will its organization be future- or past-oriented, and the more will the present be rejected as important in its own right. Expressions of such a time perspective are to be found in one's attitude toward the past, present, and future, in the extent to which one feels able to appraise accurately or to understand the future, and in one's attitude toward the use of force as a way of revising the present.

Attitude toward the past, present, and future

*58. The present is all too often full of unhappiness. It is only the future that counts.

59. It is by returning to our glorious and forgotten past that real social progress can be achieved.

60. To achieve the happiness of mankind in the future it is sometimes necessary to put up with injustices in the present.

Knowing the future

*61. If a man is to accomplish his mission in life it is sometimes necessary to gamble "all or nothing at all."

*62. Unfortunately, a good many people with whom I have discussed important social and moral problems don't really understand what's going on.

*63. Most people just don't know what's good for them.

64. There is nothing new under the sun.

65. To one who really takes the trouble to understand the world he lives in, it's an easy matter to predict future events.

Belief in force as a way to revise the present

66. It is sometimes necessary to resort to force to advance an ideal one strongly believes in.

This concludes our presentation of the Dogmatism Scale and of the theoretical considerations underlying it. The many statements in it cover a lot of territory—so much territory that one may well wonder whether it meaningfully measures anything at all. This is something that will concern us a good deal in the chapters that follow. But let us now describe our second instrument, the Opinionation Scale.

The Opinionation Scale

The purpose of the Opinionation Scale is to serve as a separate measure of general intolerance. Recall the assumption that the more closed our belief systems, the more we will reject others who disagree with us, and the more we will accept others *because* they agree with us. As already pointed out, opinionated language seems to be the best single indicator of such intolerance. In building the Opinionation Scale we have used two kinds of opinionated statements, as described below.

Opinionated rejection refers to a class of statements made by a speaker which imply that the speaker rejects a particular belief, and at the same time that he rejects people who accept it. Consider, for example, a person making the following statement: "Only a simple-minded fool would say that God exists." This statement gives us two kinds of information about the person making it: (1) It implies that the speaker rejects belief in God, and (2) he also rejects people who believe in God: they are "simple-minded fools." Half the items in the Opinionation Scale are of this type. The principle of construction is simply to link a variety of *opinionated rejection* phrases with a variety of beliefs: about God, socialized medicine, Franco, capitalism, communism, etc.

The remaining half of the items are *opinionated acceptance* statements. This refers to a class of statements that imply the speaker believes something and, along with this, accepts others who believe it too. Consider the example: "Any intelligent person will tell you God exists." This assertion also yields two kinds of information: (1) The person making it believes in God, and (2) he accepts those who agree with him as "intelligent." But notice the string attached to his accepting others. The statement carries the implication that you are no longer "intelligent" at the moment you have a change of heart.

We must now mention another important consideration we kept in mind in building the Opinionation Scale. Since this scale is meant to measure general intolerance it must, like the Dogmatism Scale, be kept free of specific ideological content. However, this is impossible because every opinionated phrase must end up with some sort of content. We solved this problem by building the scale with a *balanced* content. Half the items are worded in such a way that agreement with them indicates *left opinionation*, and half are worded in such a way that agreement with them indicates *right opinionation*. We defined "left" and "right" not in terms of extremist orientations but in terms of being either left of center or right of center.

This is easier to ascertain than it may seem at first glance. Consider again, for example, the following pair of opposites:

"Any intelligent person will tell you God exists."

"Any intelligent person will tell you God does not exist." Suppose we now ask which is "left" and which is "right"? The answer we typically get is that the first one is right and the second one is left. An opinionated statement is right of center if most judges generally see it as being to the right of an oppositely worded statement with which it is compared. Conversely, an opinionated statement is left of center if it is judged to be to the *left* of an oppositely worded statement with which it is compared. Thus, most judges will readily agree, regardless of their own views about God's existence, that a belief in God is to the right of a disbelief in God, and that a disbelief in God is to the left of a belief in God. To decide whether ideological statement A is left of center or right of center, proceed as follows: first conjure up statement $\bar{A}$, which is the ideological opposite of statement A. Then judge whether statement A is to the left or right of statement $\bar{A}$. Proceeding in this way, it is possible to decide easily and objectively, regardless of one's own ideological biases, whether a given ideological belief is politically to the left of center or to the right of center.[*]

As was the case with the Dogmatism Scale, the Opinionation Scale also went through several revisions. But all editions of the scale had the same design: half the items were *left-opinionation* items, and the other half, *right-opinionation* items. Each of the two halves was composed equally of *opinionated acceptance* and *opinionated rejection* items. This design makes it possible to measure the following variables for each person filling out the Opinionation Scale:

1. Total opinionation (left opinionation plus right opinionation);
2. Left opinionation;
3. Right opinionation;
4. Opinionated rejection; [†]
5. Opinionated acceptance;
6. Conservatism-liberalism (right opinionation minus left opinionation), low scores indicating liberalism, and high (positive) scores indicating conservatism.

[*] To obtain an independent check on whether the items so constructed were indeed left or right in direction, we asked two colleagues, Drs. Alfred Dietze and Donald M. Johnson, to judge whether each item is "left of center" or "right of center." These judges agreed perfectly with the writer.

[†] In the interest of brevity we will omit the correlational data on opinionated rejection and opinionated acceptance (scores 4 and 5). Each of these two subscales correlates in the .80's with total opinionation; each correlates about equally high with other variables. Thus, these two subscales appear to be equivalent halves of the total Opinionation Scale.

Table 4.1

The Opinionation Scale, American Version—Form C

Left opinionation	Right opinionation

OPINIONATED REJECTION

1. It's just plain stupid to say that it was Franklin Roosevelt who got us into the war.
2. A person must be pretty stupid if he still believes in differences between the races.
3. There are two kinds of people who fought Truman's Fair Deal program: the selfish and the stupid.
4. A person must be pretty shortsighted if he believes that college professors should be forced to take special loyalty oaths.
5. It's the people who believe everything they read in the papers who are convinced that Russia is pursuing a ruthless policy of imperialist aggression.
6. It's mainly those who believe the propaganda put out by the realestate interests who are against a federal slum clearance program.
7. A person must be pretty gullible if he really believes that the Communists have actually infiltrated into government and education.
8. It's mostly those who are itching for a fight who want a universal military training law.
9. It is very foolish to advocate government support of religion.
10. Only a simple-minded fool would think that Senator McCarthy is a defender of American democracy.

21. It's simply incredible that anyone should believe that socialized medicine will actually help solve our health problems.
22. A person must be pretty ignorant if he thinks that Eisenhower is going to let the "big boys" run this country.
23. It's the fellow travellers or Reds who keep yelling all the time about Civil Rights.
24. It's the radicals and labor racketeers who yell the loudest about labor's right to strike.
25. It is foolish to think that the Democratic Party is really the party of the common man.
26. You just can't help but feel sorry for the person who believes that the world could exist without a Creator.
27. It's usually the trouble-makers who talk about government ownership of public utilities.
28. Only a misguided idealist would believe that the United States is an imperialist warmonger.
29. It's mostly the noisy liberals who try to tell us that we will be better off under socialism.
30. It's the agitators and left-wingers who are trying to get Red China into the United Nations.

83

Left opinionation	*Right opinionation*

OPINIONATED ACCEPTANCE

11. It's perfectly clear that the decision to execute the Rosenbergs has done us more harm than good.
12. Any person with even a brain in his head knows that it would be dangerous to let our country be run by men like General MacArthur.
13. The truth of the matter is this! It is big business which wants to continue the cold war.
14. Make no mistake about it! The best way to achieve security is for the government to guarantee jobs for all.
15. It's perfectly clear to all decent Americans that Congressional Committees which investigate communism do more harm than good.
16. Thoughtful persons know that the American Legion is not really interested in democracy.
17. It's perfectly clear to all thinking persons that the way to solve our financial problem is by a soak-the-rich tax program.
18. It's all too true that the rich are getting richer and the poor are getting poorer.
19. History clearly shows that it is the private enterprise system which is at the root of depressions and wars.
20. Anyone who's old enough to remember the Hoover days will tell you that it's a lucky thing Hoover was never re-elected.

31. Any intelligent person can plainly see that the real reason America is rearming is to stop aggression.
32. Plain common sense tells you that prejudice can be removed by education, not legislation.
33. Anyone who is really for democracy knows very well that the only way for America to head off revolution and civil war in backward countries is to send military aid.
34. History will clearly show that Churchill's victory over the Labour Party in 1951 was a step forward for the British people.
35. The American rearmament program is clear and positive proof that we are willing to sacrifice to preserve our freedom.
36. This much is certain! The only way to defeat tyranny in China is to support Chiang Kai-Shek.
37. It's already crystal-clear that the United Nations is a failure.
38. A study of American history clearly shows that it is the American businessman who has contributed most to our society.
39. Even a person of average intelligence knows that to defend ourselves against aggression we should welcome all help—including Franco Spain.
40. Anyone who knows what's going on will tell you that Alger Hiss was a traitor who betrayed his country.

Table 4.2

The Opinionation Scale, British Version—Form C_E

Left opinionation	Right opinionation

OPINIONATED REJECTION

1. It is quite stupid to say that the Bevanites follow the Communist line.
2. A person must be pretty stupid if he still believes in differences between the races.
3. There are two kinds of people who opposed the Labour Government post-war programme: the selfish and the stupid.
4. A person must be pretty shortsighted if he thinks that the Conservatives represent the best interest of the British people.
5. It is the people who believe everything they read in the papers who are convinced that Russia is pursuing a ruthless policy of imperialist aggression.
6. It is mainly those who support the viewpoint put out by the landlord who believe that rents should be increased.
7. A person must be pretty gullible if he really believes that the Communists have actually infiltrated into the teaching profession.
8. It's mostly those who want a third World War who want to rearm Western Germany.
9. It is very foolish to advocate government support of religious education.
10. Only a simple-minded fool would think that the present Colonial Secretary is interested in Freedom.

21. It is simply incredible that anyone should believe that Dr. Jagan had the interest of the people of British Guiana at heart.
22. A person must be very ignorant if he thinks that Churchill is going to let big business run this country.
23. It's the Communists and fellow travellers who are always bringing up the issue of freedom for the Colonies.
24. It's the fellow travellers or Communists who are always on about the right to strike.
25. It is foolish to think that the Labour party is really the party of the common man.
26. You just can't help but feel sorry for the person who believes that the world could exist without a Creator.
27. It's usually the trouble-makers who talk about state ownership.
28. Only a misguided idealist would believe that the Soviet Union is for peace.
29. It's mostly the noisy radicals who try to tell us that we will be better off under socialism.
30. It's the agitators and left-wingers who wants to get Red China into the United Nations right away.

Left opinionation	*Right opinionation*

OPINIONATED ACCEPTANCE

11. It's perfectly clear to any thinking person that the execution of the Rosenbergs has done the United States more harm than good.
12. Any person with even a brain in his head knows that it would be danerous to let our country be run by men like Lord Beaverbrook.
13. The truth of the matter is this: It is big business which wants to continue the cold war.
14. Make no mistake about it! The best way to achieve security is for the government to guarantee full employment.
15. It's perfectly clear to all decent people that all this fuss about communism does more harm than good.
16. Thoughtful persons know that the Tories are not really interested in democracy.
17. It's perfectly clear to any thinking person that the way to solve our financial problems is by soak-the-rich taxation.
18. It's all too true that the rich are getting richer and the poor are getting poorer.
19. History clearly shows that it is the private enterprise system which is at the root of depressions and wars.
20. Anyone who truly understands America will tell you that the sooner we stop following in their footsteps the better off we will be.

31. Any intelligent person can plainly see that the real reason Britain is spending so much for defense is to stop aggression.
32. Plain common sense tells you that nationalization of industry has gone far enough.
33. Anyone who is really for democracy knows very well that the only way for Britain to avoid revolution and civil war is to support American foreign policy.
34. History will clearly show that Churchill's victory over the Labour Party in 1951 was a step forward for the British people.
35. The American re-armament program is clear and positive proof that they are willing to make sacrifices to preserve their freedom.
36. This much is certain: The only way to restore law and order in Kenya is to wipe out the Mau Mau terrorists.
37. It's already crystal-clear that the United Nations is a failure.
38. A study of British history clearly shows that it is the British merchant who has contributed most to our society.
39. Even a person of average intelligence knows that to defend ourselves against aggression we should welcome any kind of help—including Franco's.
40. Anyone who knows what's going on will tell you that the Foreign Office diplomats who disappeared in 1952 were traitors to their country.

Table 4.1 shows the final Form C of the Opinionation Scale. It is a 40-item test employed only in the United States. Note the fourfold classification of items in terms of left and right opiniona-tion, and opinionated acceptance and rejection. Note also the large variety of opinionated phrases employed, and the large vari-ety of political and religious issues sampled: Roosevelt, Truman, Hoover, McCarthy, MacArthur, Churchill, Eisenhower, Chiang Kai-Shek, the Rosenbergs, Alger Hiss, Russia, the United States, Spain, China, the United Nations, communism, socialism, capital-ism, God, religion, socialized medicine, the Democrats, civil rights, loyalty oaths, congressional committees, the American Legion, labor, race, housing, and military training.

Form C_E, the Opinionation Scale employed in England, is shown in Table 4.2. Forms C and C_E differ from the earlier Forms A and B in certain important respects. This can be discussed more profitably later, in connection with the discussion of their reliabil-ities.

In this and in the next section we will discuss the general pro-cedures followed in administering and scoring the Dogmatism and Opinionation Scales, the kinds of samples used to determine reliability, the mean scores obtained by the several samples, etc.*

General Procedure and Subjects

The Dogmatism and Opinionation Scales are typically admin-istered to persons meeting in groups. They take the tests without putting their names to them, in order to encourage frank and honest answers. Nevertheless, we often need to know the names of the subjects in order to obtain other data from the Registrar's office, or to identify extremely high and low scorers who are then invited to take part in various experiments. To identify subjects we ask them to write down their birth date, city and state of birth, sex, and religion. When this information is matched with class rosters and Registrar's records it enables us to identify each of the subjects by name.

The items of the Dogmatism and Opinionation Scales are typi-

* *Note to the general reader:* Those readers who may not be especially interested in the technical aspects of these issues may safely skip this material and still get the sense of it by reading the summary at the end of this chapter.

cally interspersed with each other and with items from other scales, in order better to disguise their purpose. The instructions are the same as those employed in the original research on the authoritarian personality. Also, the subjects indicate disagreement or agreement with each item on a scale ranging from —3 to +3, with the 0 point excluded in order to force responses toward disagreement or agreement. This scale is subsequently converted, for scoring purposes, to a 1-to-7 scale by adding a constant of 4 to each item score. The total score is the sum of scores obtained on all items in the test.

The questionnaires were administered to various groups, varying in size from 10 to 50 subjects, either in regular class periods or at other scheduled times. The questionnaires contained anywhere from 175 to 200 items and took from half an hour to an hour and a half to complete. Other information we usually obtained included sex, race, religion, political affiliation, and income.

The samples for whom reliability data were initially obtained came from three areas differing in social climate: the Midwest, New York, and England. In the Midwest, the subjects were college students at Michigan State University taking courses in beginning psychology. They were tested in the years 1952, 1953, 1955, and 1956. In New York, the subjects were beginning psychology students obtained from New York University and from Brooklyn College, and were tested in 1952. Other samples for whom we report reliabilities were from Purdue University (Ford, 1956), Ohio State University (Ehrlich, 1955), and a group of aged, destitute veterans living in a New York Veteran's Administration domiciliary (Alson, 1958). In England, college samples were obtained from University College in London and Birkbeck College; also obtained was a worker sample from a British automobile factory (Vauxhall Motors). All English samples were tested in 1954.

The English college sample was composed of first-year students recruited from psychology classes. We also obtained volunteers who were from the college at large. Among these were 13 members of the Communist Society, a student organization at University College.

Since English Communists are especially suspicious of American social scientists and of social science research in general, we

had to take special steps to find them and to secure their cooperation. This was done with the help of a graduate student in psychology who joined the Communist Society for the purpose of
getting to know each member individually. These members were
solicited and "fed into" larger groups one at a time so that it
would not be apparent that we were especially interested in Communists as such. The English worker group, on the other hand,
was obtained by yet other methods. It was composed of 15 of the
20 workers elected to the Management Advisory Committee (representing 14,000 workers). Forty-five additional workers were individually solicited by the members of this committee.

Reliability of the Dogmatism and Opinionation Scales

THE DOGMATISM SCALE

It has already been pointed out that the Dogmatism Scale went
through a number of revisions. These revisions were made in order to increase reliability and also to reflect the many modifications, elaborations, and refinements that took place in our thinking
over several years.

The reliabilities [6] for all forms of the Dogmatism Scale are
shown in Table 4.3. Also shown are the number of items in each
form, the groups to which they were administered, number of
cases, the means, and the standard deviations.

The initial Form A was composed of 57 items and its corrected
reliability was .70. Following an item analysis, we eliminated 14
items to get Form B. Its corrected reliability was .75. A second
item analysis led to Form C, which was essentially the same as
Form B except that the seven items with the poorest discriminatory power were further eliminated. Form C, however, yielded
reliabilities somewhat lower than expected, and in the next revi-
sion we added 30 new items. The corrected reliability of the 66-
item Form D was .91. Then, to shorten the scale, we eliminated
26 items on the basis of a third item analysis. This final 40-item
scale, Form E, was found to have a corrected reliability of .81 for
the English Colleges II sample and .78 for the English worker
sample. In other samples subsequently tested at Michigan State
University, Ohio State University, and at a VA domiciliary, the
reliabilities ranged from .68 to .93.

Table 4.3

Reliabilities, Means, and Standard Deviations of Successive Forms of the Dogmatism Scale

Form	Number of Items	Group	No. of Cases	Relia- bility	Mean	Standard Deviation
A	57	Mich. State U. I	202	.70	182.5	26.2
B	43	New York colleges	207	.75	141.4	27.2
C	36	Mich. State U. II	153	.73	126.9	20.1
		Mich. State U. III	186	.71	128.3	19.2
		Purdue U.	171	.76	—	—
D	66	English colleges I	137	.91	219.1	28.3
E	40	English colleges II	80	.81	152.8	26.2
		English workers	60	.78	175.8	26.0
		Ohio State U. I	22	.85	142.6	27.6
		Ohio State U. II	28	.74	143.8	22.1
		Ohio State U. III	21	.74	142.6	23.3
		Ohio State U. IV	29	.68	141.5	27.8
		Ohio State U. V[a]	58	.71	141.3	28.2
					143.2	27.9
		Mich. State U. IV	89	.78	—	—
		VA domiciliary	80	—	183.2	26.6
			24	.93	—	—
			17	.84	—	—

[a] The Ohio State U. V reliability was obtained by a test-retest, with five to six months between tests. The reliability of .84 for the VA group was obtained in the same way with at least a month between tests.

These reliabilities are considered to be quite satisfactory, especially when we remember that the Dogmatism Scale contains quite a strange collection of items that cover a lot of territory and appear on the surface to be unrelated to each other. The fact that subjects agree or disagree with these items in a consistent manner is borne out by item analyses. These analyses compare subjects scoring in the upper and lower quarters of the frequency distribution (which is leptokurtic) on each of the items. They typically show that high and low dogmatic subjects differ consistently and in a statistically significant manner on the great majority of items. These analyses are too complex to present here; the interested reader who wishes to consult them is referred to Rokeach (1956a).

Also shown in Table 4.3 are the means and standard deviations obtained. These normative data should be helpful to others who might want to use the Dogmatism Scale. The means obtained with the different forms are, of course, not comparable because the number of items differs from one form to the others. But it is possible to compare samples tested with the same form. Thus, Michigan State University II and III were both tested with Form C, and it is clear that their means and standard deviations are almost identical. More interesting, however, are the data obtained with Form E for the various British and American samples. Note first that the mean dogmatism score for the English workers is considerably larger than that for the English college students. This difference is highly significant. It is also larger than the comparable means obtained for the various American college groups, which are remarkably similar to each other. The only American group that scores about as high as the English workers is the aged, destitute veteran group. It is not possible to say whether this means that the English workers and the institutionalized veterans are really more closed in their belief systems than college students in both countries. The differences may be due to the fact that the workers and veterans, because of less education or senility or demoralization, generally agree more often with statements presented to them. The writer is more inclined toward the latter interpretation.

It will be noted also that the mean dogmatism score for the English college students is higher than the means obtained for any of the American college samples. The differences are rather small and not significant, and are possibly due to the fact that the English group contains a small number of Communists who, as we shall see later on, score higher in dogmatism than other political groups.

THE OPINIONATION SCALE

Let us now turn to the reliabilities obtained for the successive forms of the Opinionation Scale, and its various subscales. These are shown in Table 4.4. Also shown are the correlations obtained between left- and right-opinionation scores.

The initial 40-item Form A was composed of 20 pairs of statements, each pair consisting of a left-opinionated statement and an oppositely worded right-opinionated statement. Five pairs

Table 4.4

Reliabilities of the Total Opinionation Scale (T.O.), Left Opinionation (L.O.), Right Opinionation (R.O.), and Liberalism-Conservatism (R.O.−L.O.)

Form	Number of Items	Group	No. of Cases	T.O.	L.O.	R.O.	R.O. minus L.O.	Correlation between L.O. and R.O.
A	40	Mich. State U. I	202	.67	.64	.67	.66	−.22
		New York colleges	207	.75	.74	.77	.83	−.51
B	32	Mich. State U. II	153	.68	.39	.68	.50	.09
C	40	Mich. State U. III	186	.76	.68	.77	.70	.00
C$_E$	40	English colleges I	137	.75	.89	.88	.93	−.65
		English colleges II	80	.75	.90	.86	.93	−.61
		English workers	60	.75	.91	.91	.94	−.62

were presented together to the subject on a single page, and in all there were four such pages interspersed among other pages containing items measuring other variables. In responding to Form A, the subjects employed the usual +3 to —3 agree-disagree scale with the 0 point excluded. The reliabilities of this total scale are .67 and .75. Of special interest is that the two subscales—left opinionation and right opinionation—have reliabilities as high as the total scale, despite the fact that they are only half as long. The reliabilities of the conservatism-liberalism score (R.O. minus L.O.) are also as high or higher than those for the total scale.

Form B was composed of the best 16 pairs of items taken from Form A, as determined by item analysis. All 16 pairs were presented consecutively (without interspersing other items) and the subjects marked each item in terms of the following qualitative scale:

1. I disagree with the statement.
2. I agree with the statement in part.
3. I agree with the statement.

The purpose of this three-point *qualitative* scale was to give the subject the opportunity, if he so desired, to agree with the content of the statement but to disapprove of the opinionated manner in which it is put. We reasoned that a person agreeing with both the content of the statement *and* its opinionated style would respond with a "3"; however, another person agreeing with the content but *not* with its opinionated phraseology should give it a "2." Thus, only "3" responses can be assumed to indicate opinionation, and the total opinionation score is simply the number of statements to which the subject responds with a "3." (The "2"-type responses indicate nonopinionation, and "1"-type responses are indeterminate with respect to opinionation since the subject presumably disagrees with the content of the statement.[7])

It can be seen from Table 4.4 that this change in rating procedure in Form B did not raise the reliability of the total scale. It is about the same as in Form A. But it did lower substantially the reliability of the left opinionation ($r = .39$) and liberalism-conservatism scores ($r = .50$). For this reason, we dropped this type of rating in subsequent forms.

In a further attempt to increase reliability, we developed, finally, Forms C and C_E, used in America and in England, respectively. Form C_E is identical to Form C in design. The only exception is that the wording and content of Form C_E was altered as necessary to suit English conditions. Both forms contain 40 items, and once again the subject agrees or disagrees with each item on the -3 to $+3$ scale. In contrast to the preceding Forms A and B, the 20 left- and 20 right-opinionation items are not paired or matched in content, that is, they are highly diversified. Moreover, we interspersed these items with items from other tests. A major reason for abandoning the matched left and right pairs is that we suspected that many subjects, perceiving the pairs as opposites, felt that they had to agree with one of the items, and to disagree with its opposite.

This did not seem to affect the reliability of the total Opinionation Scale. It remains substantially the same for Forms A, C, and C_E ($r = .67$ to .76) despite revisions in wording and content, type of rating scale used, pairing and nonpairing of left and right items, and interspersing and not interspersing them among other scale items. But Forms C and C_E show consistently higher reliabilities than before for the left- and right-opinionation subscales and for the liberal-conservatism measure. This is especially evident for Form C_E.

At first glance these latter findings seem especially suspect because they violate the widely accepted notion that subscale reliabilities cannot be as high or higher than total scales reliabilities. These unusual findings are at least partly explained by the fact that scores on left and right opinionation generally correlate negligibly or negatively. This is shown in the last column of Table 4.4. It would seem that the total Opinionation Scale, by virtue of the logic of its design, is inherently more heterogeneous than either the left- or right-opinionation subscales, thereby accounting for the higher-than-expected reliabilities of the latter. These findings suggest also that further efforts to increase the reliability of the total scale would probably prove unrewarding, unless we increased its length.

Let us note one more extremely interesting finding on how the left- and right-opinionation subscales correlate with each other in the various groups. For the three Michigan State University groups, we observe that the correlations are —.22, .09, and .00; for the New York colleges group, the correlation is —.51; and for the three English groups, the correlations are —.65, —.61 and —.62. These findings strongly suggest that there are sharp discrepancies among the three sets of groups in the organization of attitudes, insofar as the left-right dimension is concerned. For the Michigan State University groups, the subjects are equally likely to adhere with varying degrees of opinionation to both left and right beliefs at the same time. That is, it is not possible to predict scores on left opinionation from scores on right opinionation. In contrast, the negative correlation of —.51 between left and right opinionation for the New York colleges group suggests a more consistent set of beliefs, insofar as the left-to-right dimension is concerned. This trend is even more apparent in the two English college groups, and in the English worker group.

These findings parallel the reliabilities found for the liberalism-conservatism measure. The highest reliabilities are obtained with the three English groups (.93, .93, and .94); the next highest is obtained with the New York group (.83); and the lowest are found for the three Michigan State University groups (.66, .50, and .70).

These regional differences, although incidental to our major purpose, are nevertheless extremely interesting. They are relevant to the study of regional or national character, and of modal personality (Inkeles and Levinson, 1954). They suggest that important differences exist in the organization of attitudes along a left-right dimension. It might prove rewarding to carry out further research on attitude organization in various regions of the United States and in foreign countries, and to study the implications of such differences for political conflicts in international relations.

Getting back to the main issue of reliability, we may conclude that the subjects all the way from the Midwest to England respond with respectable consistency to the Opinionation Scale and its subscales. Item analyses support this conclusion. Again we refer the interested reader who may want to see these analyses to Rokeach (1956a).

Table 4.5

Means and Standard Deviations on Left, Right, and Total Opinionation

Form	Number of Items	Group	No. of Cases	Left Opinionation		Right Opinionation		Total Opinionation	
				Mean	S.D.	Mean	S.D.	Mean	S.D.
A	40	Mich. State U. I	202	59.2	12.0	87.3	13.8	146.5	16.0
		New York colleges	207	66.7	17.3	79.6	18.4	146.3	17.7
B	32	Mich. State U. II	153	1.2	1.3	5.8	3.1	6.9	3.6
C	40	Mich. State U. III	186	61.2	11.9	80.8	14.6	142.0	18.9
C$_E$	40	English colleges I	137	77.8	21.8	67.2	21.3	145.0	17.8
		English colleges II	80	76.6	23.0	62.6	17.9	139.2	17.9
		English workers	60	75.4	25.5	80.9	25.7	156.3	19.4

Let us now look at the mean scores obtained by the various groups on the total Opinionation Scale and on its various subscales. Of special interest is that the right-opinionation means (Table 4.5) are significantly higher than the left-opinionation means in all American groups. The same is true for the English worker group (not significantly so). But the reverse is true for the two English college groups, whose mean left-opinionation scores are significantly higher than the mean right-opinionation scores. These findings are due to the fact that there is a small number of Communists and a more sizable number of Laborites among them (see Chapter 6).

Another point of interest is that the means on total opinionation are approximately the same for all the samples tested with
Forms A, C, and C_E (which all contain 40 items and are therefore
roughly comparable). The only exception is the English worker
group, which scores significantly higher than each of the remaining groups. This finding is consistent with those reported in Table
4.3 regarding the higher dogmatism of the English worker group.
Again, we cannot decide whether the higher total opinionation of
the workers means that this group is indeed more opinionated or,
more simply, is due to a greater tendency to endorse the statements put to them.

Synopsis

We have presented in this chapter the Dogmatism and Opinionation Scales, along with a discussion on how the theory of
belief systems guided their construction. The main purpose of the
Dogmatism Scale is to measure individual differences in open and
closed belief systems. By virtue of the way *open* and *closed* are
defined, this scale also purports to measure general authoritarianism and intolerance. In contrast, the Opinionation Scale is designed solely to measure general intolerance.

We then described how these scales are administered and
scored, and this was followed by a description of the particular
samples we tested in the Midwest, New York, and England. The
reliabilities of the final form of the Dogmatism Scale range from
.68 to .93. The reliabilities of the final form of the Opinionation
Scale are uniformly around .75. The left- and right-opinionation
reliabilities are higher than those obtained for the total scale. All
these results strongly indicate that subjects in the Midwest, New
York, and England respond consistently and predictably to the
highly diversified statements included in the two scales.

Two other incidental findings are of sufficient interest to warrant mentioning:

1. In midwestern college samples, a person's score on left
opinionation is unrelated to his score on right opinionation. This
is not true in New York or England, where a high score on one
typically goes with a low score on the other. These findings suggest that the left-to-right political spectrum does not exist psychologically in our midwestern samples. But it is more apparent

in the New York sample, and even more so in English samples.

2. Nevertheless, American college students are more right than left of center, politically speaking. This also seems to be true of the English worker sample, but not quite so sharply. In contrast, English college students are significantly more oriented to the political left than to the political right, due to the fact that there are sizable numbers of Communists and Laborites among them.

Notes

1. Most of the items in the Dogmatism Scale were constructed by the present writer. A few of the items were taken from the work of others, with or without modification. Item 21 was taken from Hoffer (1951); Items 14 and 24 from Berger (1952); Items 22, 23, 27, 31, 33, and 34 from the MMPI (Hathaway and McKinley, 1943).

2. As determined by item analysis. For details, see Rokeach (1956a).

3. This immediately raises the question of the extent to which "response set" or "acquiescence" is a determinant of scale scores. We will consider this issue in detail in Chapter 22.

4. We are indebted to Hoffer (1951) for this idea.

5. In the earlier forms we employed the item, obtained from Hoffer (1951), "It is better to be a dead lion than to be a live dog." This item turned out to be highly significant in earlier but not in later forms of the Dogmatism Scale.

6. Unless otherwise stated, the reliabilities reported are odd-even reliabilities, corrected by the Spearman-Brown formula.

7. It should be noted, furthermore, that the three possible responses represent a nominal, nonlinear scale because they are qualitatively different from each other (in contrast to the Likert-type scale employed in Form A, which is linear).

Part Two

The Nature of General Authoritarianism and General Intolerance

As we have already said, a theory has to be tested step by step. Thus far we have taken but one such step. Following the details of the theory's specifications, some reliable instruments have been forged. We now propose to use these instruments as levers to evaluate certain parts of the theory—those concerning the personality and cognitive characteristics of open and closed persons. Our strategy is to test indirectly the validity of those parts of the theory by testing the instruments' validity.* Other parts of the theory—those concerning the general nature of all belief systems—will be tested also, but in ways not involving the Dogmatism and Opinionation Scales.

In Part Two, our primary interest is to assess the validity of the formulations and tests insofar as they relate to general authoritarianism and intolerance. Later parts of the book deal with other aspects of the theory. Chapters 5 and 6 contain data concerning the extent to which the Dogmatism and Opinionation Scales validly measure general authoritarianism and intolerance.

* Cronbach and Meehl (1955) call this *construct* validity. Actually, we are also here concerned with what these authors call *predictive, concurrent,* and *content* validity. But in the present research the latter three kinds of validity are subordinated into the service of construct validity.

Chapter 7 deals further with the nature of general intolerance. We will try to find out to what extent all persons, regardless of how open or closed they are, discriminate against others according to their ethnic or their belief characteristics.

5

Two Validation Studies with High and Low Dogmatic Groups

Milton Rokeach, Leo Gladin, and Don A. Trumbo

One way to find out whether the Dogmatism and Opinionation Scales actually measure what they are supposed to is to try them out on people known on other grounds to be open or closed in their belief systems. This is the Method of Known Groups, and we used this method in two studies. In Study I, college professors selected from among their graduate students those they considered to have relatively open and relatively closed belief systems. In Study II, similar selections were made by graduate students in psychology from among their personal friends and acquaintances. Will the scales be able to distinguish between these two criterion groups?

Study I: The Professor as Judge

A letter was sent to members of the graduate faculty of the College of Science and Arts at Michigan State University explaining the nature of the study to be undertaken. They were invited to select from among the graduate students personally known to them those they regarded as *most* and *least* dogmatic. They were given a brief written description of the defining characteristics of persons with open and closed systems (closed mind, uncritical acceptance of authority, rejection of those who disagree, qualified acceptance of those who agree). Staff members wrote down their "nominations" on an enclosed form and returned them to us by mail. Through this procedure, we obtained the names of various graduate students in various departments, but not the Psychology Department. Letters were then sent to these students, inviting them to appear for testing. They were also told that those who did appear would be paid for their time. In this way we were able to collect data on 13 subjects judged by their professors to be high and 16 subjects judged to be low in dogmatism.

An analysis of the results showed no differences between the two criterion groups on the Dogmatism and Opinionation Scales. They were also given the F Scale and the Ethnocentrism Scale, and they did not differ on these either. On all four tests the two criterion groups obtained highly similar means and whatever differences were found among them were small and inconsistent in direction.

Study II: The Peer as Judge

The results in Study II were quite different. Psychology students in a graduate seminar conducted by the senior author selected high and low dogmatic persons from among their personal friends and acquaintances. In all cases the subjects were persons outside the field of psychology. Most of them were college students. A few were not in school. The criteria for selecting the subjects were similar to those of Study I. In this way, a total of 20 subjects was obtained, 10 judged to be extremely high and 10 extremely low in dogmatism. In the former group there were 6 men and 4 women; in the latter group, 4 men and 6 women. Each graduate student selected no more than one or two individuals at each extreme. The selected subjects were contacted and tested individually. Each was told that this was part of a larger "public opinion" study. The experiments stressed that anonymity would be respected and, to reinforce this point, the subject was specifically asked not to write his name on the questionnaire. Each subject then filled out the questionnaire, containing items from the Dogmatism, Opinionation, F, and Ethnocentrism Scales. Also, to find out whether the two extreme groups differed in intelligence, the subjects were given a brief IQ test devised by Wonderlic (1945).[1] When he finished, the subject inserted the completed questionnaire in a stamped envelope addressed to the senior writer. The experimenter sealed it and, wherever possible, mailed it in the subject's presence. Each envelope had a code letter on it that made it possible to identify whether the subject was judged high or low on dogmatism.

Let us now look at the results. It is obvious from Table 5.1 that the two selected groups differ sharply in mean dogmatism scores and in mean total opinionation scores. The high dogmatic group scores about 55 points higher on dogmatism than the low dogmatic group, and about 40 points higher on total opinionation. For both variables there is only about a 30 per cent overlap between the distributions of scores in the two groups. These differences are very significant from a statistical standpoint.*

* *Note to the general reader*: A difference in means will be reported as *not significant* if statistical tests show that the difference could reasonably have arisen by chance. A difference is conventionally regarded by research workers as *significant* if statistical tests show that it could have arisen by chance only five times (or less than five times) in a hundred. A difference is judged to be *very significant* if statistical tests show that it could have arisen by chance only once (or less than once) in a hundred. Throughout this book we will use the following abbreviations or terms:

| Not significant: | N. S. | Significant: | $p = .05$ or less |
| Nearly significant: | $p = .10$ or less | Very significant: | $p = .01$ or less |

A further nontechnical explanation is in order about the meaning of *standard deviation*, abbreviated to S.D. in Table 5.1 and in subsequent tables. The standard deviation is, broadly speaking, a measure of the amount of spread or variability of scores around a mean. The greater the standard deviation, the greater the spread. It might also be helpful to say that the main reason we present the standard deviations is because they are needed to calculate the degree of statistical significance of a difference between two means. Therefore, in the great majority of instances the general reader will probably be less interested in looking at the standard deviations and more interested in (1) the means shown, (2) the differences between means of groups being compared, and (3) whether or not the differences in means are statistically significant.

Table 5.1

Comparison Between High and Low Dogmatic Groups on Dogmatism and Opinionation

	High Dogmatic		Low Dogmatic		
	Mean	S.D.	Mean	S.D.	Difference [a]
Dogmatism	157.2	27.9	101.1	33.8	56.1 [b]
Total opinionation	142.3	20.3	102.9	36.2	39.4 [b]
Left opinionation	52.2	11.0	48.0	17.2	4.2
Right opinionation	90.1	21.0	54.9	22.9	35.2 [b]

[a] The p values are determined by t tests. Since the direction of the difference is predicted in advance, one-tailed tests of significance are employed.
[b] Very significant, $p = .01$. The difference of 4.2 is not significant.

It is clear, then, that the Dogmatism and Opinionation Scales differentiate between the two groups selected by our judges. However, it is strongly suggested by the data on left and right opinionation that both groups are more right than left of center in their political orientation. The high dogmatic group seems to be a "right authoritarian" group, and the low dogmatic group, a "right anti-authoritarian" group.

This interpretation can be independently checked by comparing the two groups in their performance on the California F Scale and the Ethnocentrism Scale.[2] It will be recalled that we advanced reasons earlier for believing that these scales measure, respectively, right authoritarianism and right intolerance. It

Table 5.2

Comparison Between High and Low Dogmatic Groups on the F and Ethnocentrism Scales

	High Dogmatic		Low Dogmatic		
	Mean	S.D.	Mean	S.D.	Difference [a]
F Scale	116.1	23.4	68.7	26.1	47.4 [b]
E Scale	54.6	27.6	34.9	13.5	19.7 [c]

[a] As determined by one-tailed t tests. The F test for homogeneity of variance for the two groups approaches significance on the Ethnocentrism Scale. The Cochran-Cox approximation was therefore employed (see Edwards, 1954, p. 167). The level of significance remains unchanged.
[b] Very significant, $p = .01$.
[c] Significant, $p = .05$.

should therefore be expected that the high dogmatic group should score higher than the low dogmatic group on these scales also. This expectation is fully borne out, as can be seen in Table 5.2. There are quite sizable and significant differences between the two groups in mean F score and in mean Ethnocentrism score.

Before going on to interpret the findings, let us now see whether the differences reported between the two extreme groups on dogmatism, opinionation, F, and ethnocentrism can be attributed or explained away on other grounds. Perhaps the subjects were unwittingly selected by judges on some other basis, such as age, education, or intelligence. The results shown in Table 5.3 show that this is not so. Although there are differences between high and low dogmatic groups in age, education, and intelligence, they are quite small and statistically not significant; they could easily have arisen by chance. It is therefore safe to conclude that the significant differences shown in Tables 5.1 and 5.2 cannot be attributed to selections made by the judges on these extraneous considerations.

Table 5.3

Mean Age, Years of Education, and Intelligence Test Scores of Persons Judged High and Low in Dogmatism

Group	Age	Education	Intelligence
High dogmatic	25.6	14.9	32.8
Low dogmatic	27.1	15.6	36.1

Interpretation of Studies I and II

The results of Study II seem to suggest two things: first, judges can meaningfully pick out people in everyday life on the basis of their being open and closed in their belief systems; second, our scales can identify persons so judged with considerable validity. However, it should not be overlooked that the judges in Study II are the peers of those they judge. By contrast, and to our surprise, we find no differences in scale scores when professors are the judges. How can we account for the positive findings of Study II, and the negative findings of Study I?

One possibility that occurs to us is that the professors (none of them were psychology professors) were simply poor judges of character or, at least, poor judges of the particular variables they were asked to judge. The graduate students in Study II might have been better judges, perhaps because they majored in psychology or because they had a richer understanding of the variables they were judging.

A second possibility, which we think is more likely, is that the professor-student relationship introduces a "masking" effect on the professor's judgment that is not present in the peer's judgment. We assume that the dogmatic, authoritarian person is typically very sensitive to the presence of authority in his social environment. In such a situation he is likely to adopt a respectful, acquiescent, and at the same time enlightened and objective façade. As best he can, he will inhibit or cloak expressions of a closed belief system. The classroom is one place where such a role may be systematically developed and, indeed, sometimes encouraged. Such a person might be expected to behave in a typically different manner when interacting with a professor than when interacting with fellow students. There is little room for arrogance, bigotry, or cocksureness in dealings with professorial authority. As a result, the professor may typically see only one of the several faces of his students. If his students behave differently in their dormitories in the presence of peers and subordinates, the professor is typically in no position to become aware of it. In most cases, all he knows about his students is based on the inferences he makes from student behavior he himself observes.

In the past few years we have had occasion once or twice to get informal reports from roommates about the behavior of relatively dogmatic students in their dormitories. In contrast to their observed respectful docility in professor-student relationships, they were reported to betray many of the characteristics of the closed mind discussed earlier. Among peers, such persons are apparently less inhibited in their expressions.

The fact that the professor sees his students solely, or primarily, in a teacher-student context may serve unwittingly to bias his judgment of at least some students. Add to this now another possible complication: The person characteristically more open in his belief system may play his student role somewhat differently.

106

His behavior within halls of learning may be premised on a more equalitarian appreciation of his academic environment. It may lead him to a greater willingness to venture sincere opinions which sometimes challenge or amend those made by his professors. It is thus conceivable that the professor may to one degree or another see such nondogmatic students as dogmatic, and at the same time see as open-minded the conforming student who flatteringly agrees with him while seeking his favor. This might become increasingly true the more the professor himself is closed in his belief system. In other words, in addition to the possible differences in role behavior of students with closed and open systems, the personality and cognitive structure of the professor himself may influence his reactions to real and fancied infringements of his authority position. It may, consequently, influence the accuracy of his judgments in a context such as that provided in Study I.

Although we tentatively favor the second interpretation of our findings, we unfortunately have no data to help us decide which one is the more tenable. Such data would not be hard to obtain, and would provide interesting information about the daily interactions existing among open and closed minds.

In any event, we have one study in which rather striking results have been obtained. The Dogmatism and Opinionation Scales clearly differentiate the two groups in Study II. But how do these results pertain to the hypothesis that these scales, by virtue of the way they were built, represent measures of general authoritarianism and general intolerance? It is fairly clear from the data that (1) the groups selected are relatively right-oriented and (2) the Berkeley measures of authoritarianism and intolerance (the F and Ethnocentrism Scales) also distinguish between the two groups. All we can say, then, is that we have demonstrated thus far that our scales perform essentially the same diagnostic function as those performed by the comparable Berkeley scales. It is therefore premature to conclude from the data that the Dogmatism and Opinionation Scales are *general* measures. Nevertheless, the results of Study II encourage us to feel that we are on the right track. We are referring particularly to those results showing sizeable differences between high and low dogmatic groups on right opinionation, but not on left opiniona-

107

tion. What we need to find is a group high on left opinionation but low on right opinionation.

We will try to come to closer grips with this issue in the next chapter.

Synopsis

Our main purpose here was to try to validate the Dogmatism and Opinionation Scales by the Method of Known Groups. In Study I, college professors selected high and low dogmatic subjects from among graduate students working with them. No differences in dogmatism or opinionation were found between these two groups. In Study II, graduate students in psychology selected high and low dogmatic subjects from among their personal friends or acquaintances. The high dogmatic subjects scored considerably and significantly higher than the low dogmatic subjects on both the Dogmatism and total Opinionation Scales. The difference on total opinionation was traceable to a difference between the two groups on right opinionation, and not on left opinionation. These findings as well as others suggest that the total sample selected was primarily oriented to the right of center, politically speaking. This was borne out by additional findings which showed that the high dogmatic subjects also scored higher on the Berkeley F and Ethnocentrism Scales.

We then tried to account for the positive findings in Study II and the negative findings in Study I by analyzing the differences in field conditions under which the two sets of subjects were selected. Finally, we concluded that it is as yet premature to say to what extent our measures are *general* measures of authoritarianism and intolerance.

Notes

1. Wonderlic's Personnel Test, Form A, is reported to correlate between .81 and .87 with the Otis Self-Administering Test of Mental Ability.

2. A 19-item E Scale was used, as shown on p. 142 of *The Authoritarian Personality* (1950). The "zootsuiter" item, C1, was omitted.

6

Dogmatism and Opinionation in Religion and Politics

To pursue further the line of inquiry begun in the last chapter, we will next compare various religious and political groups tested in the Midwest, New York, and England. In the course of doing so we hope to find out more about the general nature of the Dogmatism and Opinionation Scales, and at the same time about differences in authoritarianism and intolerance characterizing certain religious and political groups. In the midwestern and New York universities the comparison will be among religious groups; in the English university the comparisons will be among political groups ranging from Conservative to Communist. The kinds of data to be considered here are essentially the same as those presented in the last chapter.

But let us first see if there are not grounds for anticipating what will be found. If our theoretical formulations are reasonable,

Table 6.1

Comparisons Among Various Religious Groups in the Michigan State University 1 Sample on the Opinionation, Dogmatism, F, and Ethnocentrism Scales

Group	Number	Left Opinionation Mean	S.D.	Right Opinionation Mean	S.D.	Total Opinionation Mean	S.D.	Dogmatism Mean	S.D.	F Scale Mean	S.D.	Ethnocentrism Scale Mean	S.D.
1. Catholics	42	58.4	11.8	94.7	12.9	153.1	12.2	191.1	27.1	109.8	20.8	34.3	11.1
2. Protestants	145	58.5	12.0	86.4	12.8	144.9	17.0	180.1	25.4	99.2	21.8	30.0	11.0
3. Nonbelievers	15	67.7	9.3	76.7	11.8	144.4	15.3	174.6	21.1	91.6	21.4	24.3	7.5

DIFFERENCES BETWEEN MEANS [a]

		Left Opinionation		Right Opinionation		Total Opinionation		Dogmatism		F Scale		Ethnocentrism Scale	
1 vs. 2		−.1		8.3 [b]		8.2 [b]		11.0 [b]		10.6 [b]		4.3 [c]	
1 vs. 3		−9.3 [b]		18.0 [b]		8.7 [c]		16.5 [b]		18.2 [b]		10.0 [b]	
2 vs. 3		−9.2 [b]		9.7 [b]		.5		5.5		7.6		5.7 [b]	

[a] All significance tests are determined by one-tailed t tests. This is also the case for Tables 6.2 and 6.3.
[b] Very significant, p = .01.
[c] Significant, p = .05.

then we should expect to find that authoritarian left-of-center groups and authoritarian right-of-center groups should both score relatively high on the Dogmatism and Opinionation Scales. However, if the California F and Ethnocentrism Scales indeed measure only right authoritarianism and intolerance, then only authoritarian right-of-center groups should score high on these scales.

Table 6.1 shows the results obtained for Catholics, Protestants,[1] and those professing no religion. The subjects are from the Michigan State University I sample described in Chapter 4. (Jews and Negroes were excluded from this study because they were only a small handful.)[2] To find out where the three groups stand politically, let us first compare their mean scores on left and right opinionation. By subtracting the left from the right scores we see that the Catholics are the most conservative, the Protestants are next, and the nonbelievers are the least conservative. At the same time we learn that all three groups are more to the right of center than to the left of center: the mean right-opinionation scores are all higher than the mean left-opinionation scores.

Having identified the political leanings of the Catholics, Protestants, and nonbelievers, we next compare them on the main variables under consideration. On all four variables—opinionation, dogmatism, F, and ethnocentrism—the means for the Catholics are significantly or very significantly higher than those obtained by the Protestants and nonbelievers. The nonbelievers score lowest on all variables and the Protestants score in between. These differences cannot be attributed to differences in the social status of the groups because they are about equal in this respect, as determined by parents' income. Also, independent checks show that the four variables under consideration are unrelated to social status and to sex.

Of further interest are the differences in mean scores on left and on right opinionation. The nonbelievers are significantly more left-opinionated than the Catholics and Protestants, who do not differ from each other in this respect. On right opinionation, it is the Catholics who score highest, the Protestants next highest, and the nonbelievers lowest. Each of these means is significantly different from each of the others.

Despite the differences on left and right opinionation between Protestants and nonbelievers, their total opinionation means are

Table 6.2

Comparisons Among Various Religious Groups in the New York Colleges Sample on Opinionation, Dogmatism, F, and Ethnocentrism Scales

Group	Number	Left Opinionation		Right Opinionation		Total Opinionation		Dogmatism		F Scale		Ethnocentrism Scale	
		Mean	S.D.	Mean	S.D.	Mean	S.D.	Mean	S.D.	Mean	S.D.	Mean	S.D.
1. Catholics	46	58.3	14.2	86.4	19.9	144.6	15.9	147.4	30.0	105.2	27.8	26.5	10.0
2. Protestants	24	56.7	16.0	88.8	19.0	145.6	22.4	138.3	32.2	95.8	23.2	25.0	8.2
3. Jews	131	70.2	15.8	76.4	16.0	146.6	18.0	139.5	24.5	94.7	22.2	20.3	7.5
4. Nonbelievers	6	94.4	16.8	61.0	18.5	155.4	14.9	147.2	30.6	93.7	20.2	18.7	5.7
DIFFERENCES BETWEEN MEANS													
1 vs. 2		1.6		−2.4		−1.0		9.1		9.4		1.5	
1 vs. 3		−11.9 c		10.0 c		−2.0		7.9 a		10.5 b		6.2 c	
1 vs. 4		−36.1 c		25.4 c		−10.8		.2		11.5		7.8 b	
2 vs. 3		−13.5 c		12.4 c		−1.0		−1.2		1.1		4.7 c	
2 vs. 4		−37.7 c		27.8 c		−9.8		−8.9		2.1		6.3 b	
3 vs. 4		−24.2 c		15.4 b		−8.8		−7.7		1.0		1.6	

[a] Nearly significant, $p = .10$.
[b] Significant, $p = .05$.
[c] Very significant, $p = .01$.

almost identical, and both of these means are significantly lower than the Catholic mean on total opinionation.

It is evident that the results shown in Table 6.1 are very similar to those presented in Chapter 5, wherein we compared high and low dogmatic groups. In both cases the highly dogmatic groups are to the right of center. In both cases, the pattern of scores obtained by such groups shows high scores on right opinionation, total opinionation, dogmatism, F, and ethnocentrism, and they go with a low score on left opinionation.

So much for the Michigan data. We turn next to the New York data, shown in Table 6.2, which compare in the same way Catholics, Protestants, Jews, and nonbelievers.[3]

The Catholics, Protestants, and Jews are again seen to lean more to the right than to the left of center. But the New York nonbelievers, small in number as they are, are clearly to the left of center. This is the first time we encounter such a group. By subtracting the left-opinionation from the right-opinionation scores we get 28, 32, 6, and —33, respectively for the four groups. The Catholic and Protestant groups are clearly right-oriented, and the Jewish is slightly more to the right than to the left of center. All the differences on left and right opinionation are significant except those between the Catholics and Protestants.

However, the four groups do not differ significantly from each other on total opinionation. But note that the mean total opinionation score for the nonbelievers is higher than the rest.

The Catholics and nonbelievers score equally high on dogmatism, and both these groups score higher on this variable than do the Protestants and Jews. However, the only difference that approaches statistical significance ($p = .10$) is that between the Catholic and Jewish groups.

As was the case with the Michigan Catholics, here too the Catholics score highest on the F and Ethnocentrism Scales. They are followed in order by the Protestants, Jews, and nonbelievers.

Finally, quite aside from the question of statistical significance, the over-all trend of results shown in Table 6.2 is that the right-oriented Catholic group scores relatively high on right opinionation, dogmatism, F, and ethnocentrism. The left-oriented nonbelievers score relatively high on left opinionation, total opin-

Table 6.3

Comparisons Among Various Political Groups Among English University Students on Opinionation, Dogmatism, F, and Ethnocentrism Scales

Group	Number	Left Opinionation Mean	Left Opinionation S.D.	Right Opinionation Mean	Right Opinionation S.D.	Total Opinionation Mean	Total Opinionation S.D.	Dogmatism Mean	Dogmatism S.D.	F Scale Mean	F Scale S.D.	Ethnocentrism Scale Mean	Ethnocentrism Scale S.D.
1. Conservatives	54	56.2	13.4	83.0	18.8	139.2	17.6	258.8	49.7	115.5	25.0	29.9	9.0
2. Liberals	22	68.7	11.5	68.2	13.9	136.9	13.4	242.9	29.2	98.4	14.0	24.8	7.9
3. Attleeites	27	76.8	12.6	59.2	11.8	135.9	18.5	252.7	36.6	101.8	21.4	22.7	9.3
4. Bevanites	19	96.5	19.4	44.5	10.0	141.1	17.3	255.2	37.9	90.4	24.3	23.5	9.4
5. Communists	13	107.9	18.1	46.6	7.3	154.5	18.4	261.6	32.6	82.9	20.3	16.5	4.2

DIFFERENCES BETWEEN MEANS

		Left Opinionation		Right Opinionation		Total Opinionation		Dogmatism		F Scale		Ethnocentrism Scale	
5 vs. 1		51.7[c]		−36.4[c]		15.3[c]		2.8		−32.6[c]		−13.4[c]	
5 vs. 2		39.2[c]		−21.6[c]		17.6[c]		18.7[a]		−15.5[b]		−8.3[c]	
5 vs. 3		31.1[c]		−12.6[c]		18.6[c]		8.9		−18.9[c]		−6.2[b]	
5 vs. 4		11.4		2.1		13.4[b]		6.4		−7.5		−7.0[b]	

[a] Nearly significant, $p = .06$.
[b] Significant, $p = .05$.
[c] Very significant, $p = .01$.

ionation, and dogmatism, but they score relatively low on the California F Scale and Ethnocentrism Scale.

Before discussing further the differences found among religious groups, let us study the data obtained in England for various political groups. Table 6.3 [4] shows the mean scores obtained by English college students who identified themselves as Conservative, Liberal, Attleeite Laborite, Bevanite Laborite, and Communist.* From a study of these data we abstract the following points for discussion:

As before, we first look to their political orientations from right to left. The five groups score exactly as one would expect. The mean conservatism-liberalism scores (right minus left opinionation) for the five groups go in order: 27, 0, —18, —52, and —61. These findings independently show that the Conservatives are a right-of-center party, the Liberals almost a dead-center political party, the Atleeites are to the left of center, and the Bevanites are almost, but not quite, as extremely left as the Communists.

The pattern of Communist means on the several variables seems to be very much like that of the New York nonbelievers, only more so. They score the highest of all groups on left opinionation, total opinionation, and dogmatism; they score the lowest of all groups on the F Scale and the Ethnocentrism Scale. The Communists are significantly higher on total opinionation than each of the other groups. On dogmatism, the Communists are again higher than all other groups, but the only difference that is close to statistical significance (6 per cent level) is the difference between Communists and Liberals. On F and ethnocentrism the Communists are clearly lower than each of the remaining political groups.

The Communists are highest on left opinionation and lowest on right opinionation. All differences are significant except those between the Bevanites and Communists. Conversely, the Conservatives show exactly the opposite trend. They are lowest on left opinionation and highest on right opinionation. The five political groups, arranged in order from right to left, follow in clear-cut ascending order on left opinionation and in clear-cut descending order on right opinionation.

* These data were collected in the early part of 1954.

Despite these findings for left and right opinionation, it is interesting to note that on total opinionation the five groups do not follow any particular ascending or descending order in relation to the right-left continuum. When left and right opinionation are combined to yield a total opinionation score the Communists are seen to be the most opinionated, followed in order by the Bevanites, Conservatives, Liberals, and Attleeites.

The mean dogmatism scores also do not follow any particular order in relation to leftness-rightness. The Communists are the most dogmatic and they are followed in order by the Conservatives, Attleeites, Bevanites, and Liberals.

In contrast to the above two points, a fairly clear-cut relationship is seen between leftness-rightness and scores on the F Scale and the Ethnocentrism Scale. The Conservatives score highest on F and ethnocentrism and these means generally decrease as we proceed from the political right to the political left.

Finally, attention is drawn to the fact that although the Communists are highest on dogmatism, their mean score (261.6) is only slightly higher than that for the Conservatives (258.8). Also, the difference in means between the Conservatives and Liberals is significant ($p = .05$), the Conservatives being more dogmatic than the Liberals.

Interpretation of Findings

What do these results tell us about the religious and political groups tested, and what do they tell us about the theoretical nature of the scales purporting to measure general authoritarianism and intolerance? To help us answer this question let us focus primary attention on the pattern of results obtained for the groups who are clearly the most right-oriented, and the most left-oriented. These are the Michigan and New York Catholics on the one hand, and the New York nonbelievers and the English Communists on the other. To aid us in our discussion we will first summarize in Table 6.4 the scoring patterns obtained by these groups.

It is clear that the right-oriented Catholics diverge sharply from the left-oriented nonbelievers and Communists in their performance on the California F and Ethnocentrism Scales. The former groups score higher than the other religious groups on both variables; the nonbelievers and Communists score the lowest.*

Table 6.4

*Summary of Score Patterns Obtained by the Most
Right-of-center and Left-of-center Groups*

	Left Opinion-ation	Right Opinion-ation	Total Opinion-ation	Dogma-tism	F Scale	Ethno-centrism Scale
Right of center						
Michigan Catholics	Low	High	High	High	High	High
New York Catholics	Low	High	Average	High	High	High
Left of center						
New York nonbelievers	High	Low	High	High	Low	Low
English Communists	High	Low	High	High	Low	Low

If we had only the F and ethnocentrism means to go on, we would be tempted to conclude that the Catholic groups are relatively high in authoritarianism and prejudice, while the nonbelievers and Communists are relatively low. We would also be tempted to conclude (from Table 6.3) that the Conservatives in England are politically the most authoritarian and intolerant, and the Communists the least.

The findings on dogmatism and opinionation clearly contradict the preceding. Even though the rightist and leftist groups score at opposite poles on F and ethnocentrism, they both generally score high on dogmatism and opinionation. And although the English Conservatives and Communists are also at opposite poles on F and ethnocentrism, no relation is apparent between radicalism-conservatism on the one hand and dogmatism and opinionation on the other.

These findings provide the strongest evidence we have been able to obtain thus far indicating that the Dogmatism and Opinionation Scales are measuring *something* relatively independent of ideological content. We infer this "something" to be general

* We hesitate to make formal, direct comparisons between Communist and Catholic groups because the former group was obtained in England, the latter in America. Nevertheless, it is worth pointing out that a direct comparison of the mean F and ethnocentrism scores for Catholic and Communist groups, shown in Tables 6.1, 6.2, and 6.3, reveal marked differences between them.

authoritarianism and general intolerance on the basis of three considerations:

First, this is what the Dogmatism and Opinionation Scales were meant to measure by the theory that generated them.

Second, the groups that score high on these scales may be reasonably expected to do so. It is well known that there exist certain institutionalized, hierarchically organized groups—among them the Catholic Church and the Communist party—which require of their members strict adherence to doctrine. Whether a person becomes a member of such a group by birth or by joining it later, once he is a member he is subject to its social pressures of reward and punishment. These pressures are meant to coerce him to commit himself in advance to the group's ideology and to reject in advance alternative ideologies. Such social pressures should, over time, leave their mark on the adherent's belief system—that is, his belief system should increasingly betray the defining characteristics of the closed mind. The results found with the Dogmatism and Opinionation Scales fit in well with this interpretation. What also fits in with expectations is the fact that the Catholics score at opposite poles from the Communists and nonbelievers on the California F and Ethnocentrism Scales. These findings indicate that they do indeed measure right authoritarianism and intolerance.

Third, additional evidence suggesting that the Dogmatism and Opinionation Scales measure general authoritarianism and intolerance comes from an analysis of the way the scores a person obtains on these scales are related to scores he obtains on the F and Ethnocentrism Scales. But before we turn to this evidence, it is first necessary to temper somewhat the conclusions arrived at on the basis of the particular group data already presented.

FURTHER REMARKS CONCERNING THE CATHOLIC GROUPS

Although the New York Catholic group does not differ from the remaining religious groups on opinionation, it is clearly the highest on the F and Ethnocentrism Scales, and it is also highest on the Dogmatism Scale. The latter finding, however, only borders on statistical significance ($p = .10$). The trend of results for the New York Catholics is not completely in the same direction as that for the Michigan Catholics. Why these results are somewhat less conclusive is something about which we can only speculate. One possible explanation is that students attending New York colleges are less representative of college students in general. They are generally believed to be more liberal than students found elsewhere. This is supported by the data presented in Tables 6.1 and 6.2. They show that the New York Catholics have lower means than the Michigan State University I Catholics on right opinionation, total opinionation, F, and ethnocentrism.[5]

It is important to mention also that although the means for Catholics are on the whole higher than those for the other religious groups on the major variables under consideration, the ranges of individual differences for both the Michigan and New York Catholics are about as great as they are for the other religious groups. This is seen from the size of the standard deviations shown in Tables 6.1 and 6.2. Thus, other unanalyzed variables in addition to group pressures toward commitment are undoubtedly operating to produce the results.

FURTHER REMARKS CONCERNING THE COMMUNIST GROUP

The English Communists score lower than do the Socialists, Liberals, and Conservatives on the right opinionation, F Scale, and Ethnocentrism Scale.[6] These findings are exactly as predicted. It is especially interesting to note that the Communists have a much narrower spread of scores (see standard deviations) on ethnocentrism and right opinionation than any of the other groups. These are consistent with what is known about the content of Communist ideology. Communists can be counted on to score low on ethnocentrism because they cannot ideologically endorse hostile statements about Jews, Negroes, and other minority groups.

However, although they are clearly the most tolerant toward ethnic and racial groups, they are the most intolerant toward those who disagree with their views. Thus, if we relied solely on the Ethnocentrism Scale to measure their level of prejudice we would have to conclude that the Communists are the most tolerant of all the groups tested. But with the information gained from the Opinionation Scale a clearer, more complete, and different picture emerges.

We have already had occasion to mention that on all variables the range of individual differences for the Michigan and New York Catholics is generally as great as it is for the other religious groups. A similar point must now be made for the English Communists. Except for the Ethnocentrism Scale and the right opinionation subscale, the spread of Communist scores is about as great as those found for the other political groups. Thus, it is necessary to emphasize that the differences we have reported are group differences. There are, no doubt, other personality factors at work that account for the differences in scores obtained by individual Communists.

CONCERNING THE NONBELIEVERS

In our analysis we have showered more attention on the New York than on the Michigan nonbelievers. Our reason for doing so is that the latter are politically to the left of center. And the behavior of leftists is more crucial than that of rightists for the purpose of evaluating the adequacy of our conceptualizations and measuring instruments. We conclude that the New York nonbelievers are relatively authoritarian and prejudiced despite their low scores on the California F Scale and Ethnocentrism Scale because they score relatively high on dogmatism and opinionation.

The findings for this group are from a statistical standpoint not generally significant; they are based on only six cases. They are interesting nevertheless because their pattern of scores clearly differs from the Michigan nonbelievers (who are apparently right-oriented anti-authoritarians), and because their pattern of scores is remarkably similar to that found for the English Communists. This does not mean that the New York nonbelievers are also Communist. All we can safely say about them as a group is that they are apparently authoritarian with a left-of-center political orientation.

Extending the Chain of Evidence

Despite the evidence already considered, it is logically not sufficiently airtight to justify the conclusion that our formulations and scales are really about general authoritarianism and intolerance. Perhaps the scales merely measure political extremism rather than all varieties of authoritarianism and intolerance. How can we tell whether the scales measure what they are supposed to at *all* positions of the political spectrum?

One way to find out is to examine some additional correlational evidence that was obtained in America and in England.

THE DOGMATISM SCALE AS A MEASURE OF
GENERAL AUTHORITARIANISM

First of all, we have computed correlations between the scores on the Dogmatism Scale and on the F Scale. If our hypothesis is correct that one scale measures a general form of the phenomenon and the other a particular form, then we should expect to get sizable positive correlations for persons who take both tests.

This is exactly what we find. For the seven groups (described in Chapter 4) who were tested at Michigan State University, New York, and England the correlations range from .54 to .77.[7] People who score relatively high on one test tend to score relatively high on the other. This is even true for the English Communists. Even though their mean dogmatism score is high and their mean F score is low, we still get a positive correlation between their dogmatism and F scores.[8]

How do these dogmatism and F scores correlate with scores measuring attitudes toward liberalism-conservatism? We have already had occasion to mention one way in which liberalism-conservatism was measured: the right-opinionation score minus the left-opinionation score. The more positive the score the more the conservatism; the more negative the score the more the liberalism. A second measure we employed was the 5-item Political-Economic Conservatism Scale, which was originally used in the Berkeley investigations (Adorno *et al.*, 1950). It contains statements testing attitudes toward such things as government control of industry, labor, capitalism, etc. Here, too, the higher the score the more the conservatism.

Table 6.5 shows the results obtained with both these measures. It will be noticed that the dogmatism scores are related to a negligible extent with scores obtained on the two liberalism-conservatism tests. In other words, these low correlations support the conclusion that the Dogmatism Scale is actually measuring general authoritarianism, since it is found with approximately equal frequency along all positions of the political spectrum. The Dogmatism Scale is thus also seen to be relatively free of political content. However, this does not seem to be the case for the F Scale. In every group without exception, the F Scale correlates more highly than does the Dogmatism Scale with the two liberalism-conservatism measures, the high F scorers being the more conservative. This finding once more supports the suspicion that the F Scale is measuring right authoritarianism.[9]

Table 6.5

The Dogmatism and California F Scales in Relation to Liberalism-Conservatism

| | | Correlations Between: | | | |
| | | Dogmatism and | | F Scale and | |
Group	Number	R.O.— L.O.[a]	Polit.- Econ. Conserv. Scale [b]	R.O.— L.O.	Polit.- Econ. Conserv. Scale
Mich. State U. I	202	.13	.13	.28	.22
New York colleges	207	.04	.11	.37	.43
Mich. State U. II	153	.13	.20	.21	.29
Mich. State U. III	186	.17	.28	.35	.40
English colleges I	137	.12	—	.36	—
English colleges II	80	—.03	—	.31	—
English workers	60	.11	—	.15	—

[a] Right-opinionation score minus left-opinionation score. Positive differences indicate a rightist orientation; negative differences indicate a leftist orientation.
[b] The P.E.C. Scale was not employed in the English research.

There is one additional finding shown in Table 6.5 that must not be overlooked. Even though the correlations between dogmatism and conservatism are quite negligible, they are consistently positive. The chances are somewhat better than even that a closed-minded person will be conservative rather than liberal in his politics. Several interpretations are possible to account for this finding and will be considered after we present additional evidence bearing on the general nature of the Opinionation Scale.

THE OPINIONATION SCALE AS A MEASURE OF
GENERAL INTOLERANCE

We examine next the way in which scores on left, right, and total opinionation correlate with scores obtained on other variables. These are shown in Table 6.6. Recall first that the total Opinionation Scale contains 40 items, 20 of which are left- and 20 right-opinionation items. Recall also that among Michigan State University students scores on left opinionation are not related to scores on right opinionation, while in the New York and in the English samples left- and right-opinionation scores are negatively related to each other.

From a study of Table 6.6, we select the following points to discuss: In accord with theoretical expectation we find that people who score high on dogmatism also tend to score high on total opinionation. Also in accord with theoretical expectations is the fact that in every sample dogmatism scores are positively related to left *and* to right opinionation. The latter finding is all the more interesting when we keep in mind the fact that left and right opinionation are negatively correlated with each other in the New York and English samples. These findings all suggest that a person's scores on left and right opinionation may be *meaningfully* added together to yield a measure of general opinionation or intolerance, as predicted by our theory.

But let us not overlook here a fact that is similar to one already noted in the preceding section. It will be recalled that the Dogmatism Scale correlates slightly but in a consistently positive manner with political conservatism. We now see that dogmatism also correlates more positively with right than with left opinionation.

This point is noted once again when we examine the correlations between the Political-Economic Conservatism Scale and total opinionation. The correlations are again seen to be quite small but consistently positive. They are due to the fact that the positive correlations with right opinionation outweigh the negative correlations with left opinionation. Thus, although the total Opinionation Scale seems to be measuring left-of-center bigotry as well as right-of-center bigotry, the findings show that bigotry has a somewhat greater affinity with right-of-center ideologies.

Table 6.6

Left, Right, and Total Opinionation: Correlations with Other Variables

Correlation between:

Group	Number[a]	Dogmatism and			P.E.C. Scale[b] and			F Scale and			Ethnocentrism and		
		Left Opin.	Right Opin.	Total Opin.	Left Opin.	Right Opin.	Total Opin.	Left Opin.	Right Opin.	Total Opin.	Left Opin.	Right Opin.	Total Opin.
Mich. State U. I	202	.22	.40	.51	−.20	.41	.19	.11	.53	.54	−.08	.50	.37
New York colleges	207	.20	.23	.43	−.39	.60	.25	−.08	.56	.50	−.22	.62	.43
Mich. State U. II	153	.20	.31	.34	−.10	.26	.21	.12	.46	.45	.02	.44	.41
Mich. State U. III	186	.24	.42	.47	−.18	.48	.26	.12	.55	.49	.01	.50	.39
English colleges I	137	.17	.38	.61	—	—	—	−.27	.64	.40	−.21	.58	.38
English colleges II	80	.25	.25	.55	—	—	—	−.06	.56	.46	−.22	.49	.20
English workers	60	.22	.43	.63	—	—	—	.18	.47	.63	−.18	.59	.50

[a] The N's for the English colleges I and II and the English workers samples are 116, 69, and 59, respectively for the ethnocentrism correlations since Jewish subjects were omitted.
[b] The Political-Economic Conservatism Scale was not given in England.

Turning next to the correlations concerning the F Scale and Ethnocentrism Scale, we note that the correlations clearly show, in line with theoretical expectations, that these scales are sensitive primarily as measures of rightist forms of intolerance and insensitive to leftist forms. Both the F and ethnocentrism scores correlate relatively highly with right-opinionation scores, but negligibly and sometimes even negatively with left-opinionation scores. Because of the "suppressing" effect of left opinionation, the F and ethnocentrism scores generally correlate *less* with total opinionation than with right opinionation.

A final comment concerns the correlations between ethnocentrism and opinionation. It is evident that the two forms of discrimination (one racial or ethnic, the other based on belief) tend to go together. The correlations range from .20 to .50. However, these relationships are a long way from perfect. A person may score high on one and low on the other. Recall that this is exactly what was found with the English Communists; they scored high on opinionation but low on ethnocentrism. By the same token it is not inconceivable that we might find people—perhaps in the South—who would score high on ethnocentrism but low on opinionation. Such persons may well have negative stereotypes and even believe ideologically in separation of races, but not necessarily harbor hostile feelings toward other races. We cannot, for example, assume that every southerner who believes in segregation in education has necessarily an underlying need to be hostile toward Negroes. No doubt some do, but others may believe in segregation for no other reason than that it is the social norm. There thus emerges the need to isolate and to study further tolerant and intolerant persons who believe in racial segregation and, by the same token, tolerant and intolerant persons who do not. And the Opinionation Scale is seen to be an instrument which, when used alongside the usual scales of prejudice, can help us to identify such persons.

Ideological Content versus Ideological Structure

When we view all the findings presented in this chapter, they indicate that we have on the whole succeeded in our aims to formulate and to measure general authoritarianism and intolerance. Nevertheless, the data also stubbornly suggest that people to the right of center are somewhat more prone to authoritarianism and intolerance than people to the left of center. The dogmatism scores show slight but consistent positive correlations with conservatism. So do the opinionation scores. Also, the dogmatism scores correlate more highly with right than with left opinionation. How can we account for these findings?

One possible explanation is the following: The results found may be simply due to the fact that the samples tested in the United States and in England are predominantly right- rather than left-oriented in their politics. As a result, there is a greater spread or *heterogeneity* in the degree to which the subjects accept right-oriented ideologies, and a smaller spread or homogeneity in the degree to which they reject left-oriented ideology. If true, this could account for the findings. But the available evidence seems to rule out this possibility. All four American samples and the English worker sample do indeed show higher mean scores and greater variability (standard deviations) on right opinionation than on left opinionation (see Table 4.5). However, this is clearly not so for the two groups of English university students who are more left- than right-oriented. Furthermore, the latter two groups are more variable on left opinionation than on right opinionation. Despite such differences, however, all the data show the consistently small but positive correlations already referred to.

A second possibility is that despite our best efforts to build ideologically contentless scales, the Dogmatism and Opinionation Scales still contain some ideological content, and what there is of it is somewhat more weighted to the right than to the left. We cannot definitely rule out this possibility without further research. Nor can we accept it as highly likely in view of the procedures we followed in designing the tests. This brings us to a third and perhaps the most fascinating explanation of the findings.

Let us consider the most extreme forms that political conservatism and liberalism have taken—fascism and communism. Viewed from the standpoint of ideological *structure* both ideologies may be said to be authoritarian. Both exert powerful pressures to maintain discipline among their members; both advocate repressive measures to stifle opposition; both believe in leadership by an elite; and so on. But the case is different when we look at the ideological *content* of communism and fascism. Communism, considered purely as an ideology, is humanitarian and antiauthoritarian. Its ideological aim is to establish a classless society, to wither away the state, and to take care of the individual according to the doctrine: "From each according to his abilities, to each according to his needs." However, in the case of fascism, particularly naziism, the ideological content is frankly antihumanitarian. It advances as its ideological aim the establishment of the Aryan race as master race, to rule and subjugate forever the rest of mankind.

We thus see in the case of fascism that ideological content and structure support each other. There is no incompatibility between them and thus psychological conflict is not engendered or guilt feelings aroused. For this reason, authoritarian ideological structures may be psychologically more reconcilable—more easily "attachable"—to ideologies that are antidemocratic than to those that are democratic in content. If a person's underlying motivations are served by forming a closed belief system, then it is more than likely that his motivations can also be served by embracing an ideology that is blatantly anti-equalitarian. If this is so, it would account for the somewhat greater affinity we have observed between authoritarian belief structure and conservatism than between the same belief structure and liberalism.

But in the case of a person who embraces communism there is a sharp discrepancy between content and structure. Such a person may have seen a lot of social injustice around him and may want to do something about it. He may read the literature of Marxism and discover that it proposes humanitarian, equalitarian solutions. He may join the Communist party in the hope of alleviating or eliminating such injustices. But somewhere along the line he may become aware, at one level or another, that the methods advocated, the discipline, and the hierarchical structure of the party are somehow at odds with the humanitarian aims advocated. He may sense, perhaps without being quite able to make it explicit, that there is an inherent conflict between the content of communist ideology and its structure.

These interpretations are in line with those of Lindner's (1953). According to Lindner, there is a neurotic component to communism, but a psychopathic component to fascism. Neurosis is characterized by conflict, guilt, and anxiety. These are absent in psychopathic personalities because here the superego or conscience is weak and poorly developed. A person is in a neurotic conflict situation if he is committed to a humanitarian ideology but at the same time strives to achieve its goals by inhuman means. But it takes a psychopath, a person without a conscience or the capacity to experience guilt, to commit himself to an antihumanitarian ideology and to an antihumanitarian program to achieve its aims.

The analysis of conflict or harmony between ideological content and structure seems to suggest that there is a compelling theoretical reason for our finding a somewhat greater affinity of authoritarian belief structure with political conservatism. That is, they are somewhat more compatible with each other. We say "somewhat more compatible" rather than "compatible" because the conservatism we have dealt with in our American and English samples is a far cry from the extreme, fascistic conservatism of Nazi Germany.

The analysis also seems to have application to the better understanding of certain recent political events. Ernst and Loth (1952) report an extremely high turnover rate among American Communist party members. There were wholesale defections from the Communist party as a result of the Nazi-Soviet Friendship Pact in 1939 and as a result of the Soviet Army's putting down the Hungarian rebellion of 1956. We have ourselves noticed and wondered why the state of *disillusionment* is experienced far more often by adherents to causes of the left than the right. All these events seem to become more understandable if we think of disillusionment as a psychological state in which the person experiencing it becomes aware of a discrepancy between ideological content and structure, between what he believes and how he believes. This discrepancy is so painful that only the inner core of party members (Almond, 1954), by virtue of heavy investments, can withstand it for long. The rest seem to defect at opportune moments, sooner or later.

Along the same lines let us offer for whatever they may be worth some additional observations about the character of the Soviet state itself. We detect, in contrast to the unyielding, fanatical stance of the Nazi regime under Hitler, an oscillating pattern in the history of the Soviet state. Within the period of one year, for example, we all witnessed Khrushchev's repudiation of Stalin's totalitarianism and the quelling of the Hungarian rebellion. The freedom of Soviet artists, writers, and scientists are expanded and contracted according to the times. Genuine self-criticism within the Communist party is sometimes officially encouraged and sometimes unofficially discouraged. "Enemies of the people" are at different times in Soviet history punished with different degrees of harshness. Soviet relations with Tito were at first friendly, then hostile, friendly again, and are now hostile again. Russia's attitude toward the United States, foreign tourists, and cultural and scientific interchange blows cold and warm with the times. These facts suggest that those who see no difference between the Soviet regime and the Nazi regime under Hitler may be seriously mistaken when they assume that because they are both equally totalitarian, they are therefore "the same." What they fail to take into account, according to our view, is that the fluctuations in Communist Russia's policies over the years may be theoretically fated and therefore predictable from the inherent conflicts between Marxist ideological content and its structure.

Synopsis

We have tried in this chapter to test the validity of our conceptualizations and tests measuring general authoritarianism and intolerance. The results on the whole show that authoritarian left-of-center groups (Communists and religious nonbelievers) and authoritarian right-of-center groups (Catholics) score relatively high on the Dogmatism and Opinionation Scales. However, only the authoritarian groups to the right of center score high on the California F and Ethnocentrism Scales.

These results support theoretical expectations about the general nature of the Dogmatism and Opinionation Scales. Other evidence of a correlational nature extends these findings. But these results notwithstanding, the data nevertheless show that there is a somewhat greater tendency for persons to the right of center to be more authoritarian than persons to the left of center.

Several explanations are offered to account for the results. The one considered most seriously is that there is a theoretically necessary reason for authoritarianism to have a somewhat greater affinity with right than with left ideologies. This explanation involves the distinction between the content and the structure of an ideology and whether such content and structure are compatible or not compatible with each other.

Notes

1. Of the total group of 145 Protestants, 75 wrote in "Protestant" on the face sheet in response to the question on religion. The remainder wrote in "Episcopalian" or "Presbyterian" (N = 22), "Methodist" (N = 16), "Congregational" (N = 6), "Baptist" (N = 9), "Lutheran" (N = 10), or some other denomination (N = 7). Means and sigmas for dogmatism, opinionation, F, and ethnocentrism were computed separately for the Protestant denominations. None of the differences were statistically significant. The mean dogmatism, opinionation, F, and ethnocentrism scores for the Catholic group were found to be higher than for any one of these denominations considered separately.

2. In view of the fact that the California Ethnocentrism Scale (we employed the 10-item E Scale, reported in Adorno et al., p. 128) contains items about Jews and Negroes, questionnaires obtained from Jews and Negroes were eliminated from consideration in the Michigan State University groups. In the New York study, where many Jewish subjects participated in the research, we employed a revised 10-item E Scale, taken from a longer scale employed in the California research, in which none of the items referred to Jews. By virtue of the fact that Negro items were included, we eliminated Negro subjects in analyzing these results. In England yet other revisions were necessary. Three E items (Adorno et al., Items 5, 10, and 15 on p. 128) were not relevant and other items were substituted. Also, the word "Britain" was substituted for the word "America" in the last E item. Jewish subjects were retained, but all data involving the E Scale were analyzed with the Jews omitted from consideration.

3. The 10-item Ethnocentrism Scale employed in New York did not contain any items about Jews. It is interesting to note that the variances decrease as the means decrease, the Catholics having the highest variance, and the nonbelievers the lowest. The difference between these two groups is significant. Accordingly, in testing these means for significance we used the Cochran-Cox approximation for significance of differences in means when the variances differ significantly (see Edwards, 1954, p. 167).

4. The N's on which the mean E scores are based are 51, 16, 23, 14, and 10 for groups 1, 2, 3, 4, and 5, respectively. Jewish subjects were excluded from these computations.

The N for the English colleges I is 137. Seven of these gave "other" political affiliations (e.g., Anarchist, Trotskyite, ex-Communist, Celtic Alliance). Five of the 13 Communists were from the English colleges II sample, and the full 66-item Dogmatism Scale (Form D) was scored for these five subjects for purposes of the present analysis.

As was found in the New York sample, here too the variances for ethnocentrism decrease as the means decrease. This is also the case for right opinionation. For both of these variables, therefore, we again used the Cochran-Cox approximation (see Note 3). Likewise for left opinionation, comparison 5 vs. 2.

5. Six of the ten Ethnocentrism Scale items employed in the two studies were identical (non-Jewish items); four were not. Thus, the mean ethnocentrism scores

are only roughly comparable. The Dogmatism Scale employed in the two groups was different in length and wording and thus direct comparisons are not justified.

6. Eysenck (1954) reports that the mean F scores for the Communists in England are higher than for other groups. We are dubious of this as well as other findings of Eysenck. For a justification of this position, see Rokeach and Hanley (1956e), and Christie (1956a). The interested reader will also wish to consult Eysenck's rejoinders (1956a, 1956b), and reactions to the rejoinders by Hanley and Rokeach (1956) and by Christie (1956b).

7. Pettigrew (1958) reports a correlation of .82 between dogmatism and the F Scale on a sample of North Carolina students.

8. Such opposing trends are quite possible even though all the correlations are positive. The product-moment correlations between dogmatism and opinionation (N = 13), dogmatism and F (N = 13), dogmatism and ethnocentrism (N = 10), opinionation and F (N = 13), opinionation and ethnocentrism (N = 10), and F and ethnocentrism (N = 10) are .66, .56, .54, .33, .25, and .46, respectively. They are all positive, even though the Communist means for dogmatism and opinionation are relatively high, while the means for F and ethnocentrism are relatively low.

9. We are omitting here for the sake of brevity additional and more detailed correlational evidence that further supports the above conclusions regarding the nature of the Dogmatism and F Scales. The interested reader is referred to Rokeach (1956a) for this evidence. Attention is also drawn to the results of two factor analyses by Rokeach and Fruchter (1956d), and by Fruchter, Rokeach, and Novak (1958). The rotated factors found in these two studies strongly support the interpretations offered in this text regarding the differential properties of the Dogmatism and F Scales as measures of authoritarianism.

7

Two Kinds of Prejudice or One?

Milton Rokeach, Patricia W. Smith, and Richard I. Evans

There is a logical point raised in the preceding chapter that continues to bother us. It is obvious, from a purely logical standpoint, that the relation between the two kinds of authoritarianism measured by the F and Dogmatism Scales is a relation between a specific form and a general form of authoritarianism. This being the case, the Dogmatism Scale is more inclusive than the F Scale. But shall we say that a similar relation exists between the two kinds of intolerances measured by the Ethnocentrism and Opinionation Scales? Is the latter logically more inclusive than the former? One kind implies an ethnic or racial basis for prejudice; the other implies belief as a basis.

The data presented in the last chapter suggest that ethnic or racial prejudice is largely a phenomenon of the political right, while "belief prejudice" is the more general phenomenon. However, this does not seem to make good theoretical sense because the two forms of prejudice appear to be qualitatively quite different from each other. As we have said, one involves an ethnic criterion; the other a belief criterion. We do not see how one of these can logically be subsumed under the other—even though the empirical findings seem to suggest that they are—unless further research can demonstrate that race prejudice is further analyzable or reducible to belief prejudice.

The question we then ask is this: Are there really two kinds of prejudice, or is there some conceptual way of seeing ethnic or race prejudice as a special case of belief prejudice? Let us make the issue more concrete by considering a hypothetical person who is a member of the Ku Klux Klan. We note that he not only expresses prejudice toward Negroes but that he also makes a cognitive distinction between "good Negroes" and "bad Negroes." If we may presume to speak for him, a "good Negro" is one who agrees with the Ku Klux Klanners on how Negroes ought to behave, and a "bad Negro" is one who does not. The cognitive distinction is apparently based on belief.

Consider next the parallel cognitive distinction between "good" and "bad" whites. Again, the definition seems to be defined in terms of agreement or disagreement with the Ku Klux Klanner's belief about how Negroes ought to behave. But this time the object of prejudice is a white person, not a Negro.

In this way we emerge with four cognitive distinctions which appear to be relevant parts of the Ku Klux Klanner's anti-Negro prejudice. These are shown below in tabular form:

RACE

		White	Negro
BELIEF	Agree	A. "Good white"	B. "Good nigger"
	Disagree	C. "Nigger lover"	D. "Uppity nigger"

Without belaboring the point, it could be argued from this analysis that the Ku Klux Klanner's actual, day-to-day bigotries seem to be analyzable on the basis of belief rather than race.

133

The example chosen is probably not a unique one. We may observe similar cognitive distinctions between "good" and "bad" Jews, gentiles, Catholics, Russians, etc. Such distinctions are apparently made by minority-group members as well as majority-group members (Adelson, 1953). However, in almost all studies of attitudes toward minority groups this distinction is usually glossed over, and it is generally assumed that a person's attitude toward minority-group members is homogeneous, the same toward one minority member and another. Furthermore, in studying attitudes toward minorities we rarely go to the trouble to contrast such attitudes with those held toward majority-group members. It is hard to see how we can assess a person's attitude toward a minority group without at the same time also assessing, for the sake of having a base line or control, his attitude toward the majority group. Yet, this is what we typically do not do. Furthermore, we typically have nothing to say about the possibly different attitudes a person may hold toward different members of the majority group. In other words, instead of addressing ourselves in our thinking and research to all four categories shown in the above chart, categories B and D are usually collapsed into one, and categories A and C are ignored altogether.

It seems to us that an adequate theory about the nature of prejudice should be capable of bringing under scrutiny the total phenomenon of prejudice, not merely a part of it. In line with our analysis, it should be able to take into account at least the following differential attitudes: (1) toward different members of the minority group, (2) toward different members of the majority group, (3) toward those who agree regardless of ethnic character, and (4) toward those who disagree. It should also try to take into account (5) qualified, conditional acceptance as well as frank rejection as expressions of intolerance.

In our opinion, current conceptions of the psychological nature of intolerance, stereotyping, and categorizing do not seem to embrace all these facets. The full richness of the phenomenon is collapsed into a lone concern with the rejection of an undifferentiated ethnic outgroup. It seems to us that our theory about the nature of belief systems provides us with an opportunity to help restore this richness. In line with this theory, let us conjecture that the basic principle governing the way in which we organize the world of people is not in terms of abstract ethnic or racial categories as such, but in terms of how congruent or incongruent others' belief systems are to our own. The more significance we attach to another's agreement or disagreement with us as grounds for reacting to him, the more the intolerance. In other words, we are here taking the view that we organize our social world not once and for all in terms of, say, Negro-white distinctions, but in terms of Negroes and whites who agree with us and Negroes and whites who disagree with us on specific issues we care about. Thus, we would say of the current conflict in the South that it is not a conflict between Negroes and whites, but a conflict between two sides, each composed of Negroes and whites, one for desegregation in education and the other for segregation. Furthermore, this view relieves us of the necessity of seeing such conflicts as fixed or rigidly drawn. The particular alignment is unique to the specific issue of desegregation in education. As the specific social context changes, the issues over which there is conflict will also change and, along with this, realignments will take place in the make-up of opposing groups, each side composed of Negroes and whites.

In short, then, we hypothesize that *insofar as psychological processes are involved,* belief is more important than ethnic or racial membership as a determinant of social discrimination. Our theory leads us to propose that what appears at first glance to be discriminations among men on the basis of race or ethnic group may turn out upon closer analysis to be discriminations on the basis of belief congruence over specific issues.*

How can we find out if this hypothesis is tenable? One way to test it experimentally is systematically to pit the belief characteristics of people against their ethnic or racial characteristics. Would subjects confronted with both kinds of social cues discriminate between people on the basis of one kind of cue or the other, or both?

Two kinds of studies will be discussed: (1) *The North-South Study* is concerned with the Negro-white distinction. Results were obtained for a northern and a southern sample. The north-

---

* Note that our hypothesis is about *psychological* processes associated with prejudice. We will comment at the end of the chapter on the *institutionalization* of ethnic or racial prejudice.

ern sample was composed of 65 white students in introductory psychology at Michigan State University. The southern sample consisted of a similar group of 136 white students in introductory psychology at the University of Houston in Texas. Of these, 95 were born in Texas, 10 in other parts of the South, 8 in the border states, 8 in the East, 9 in the Midwest, 5 in the West, and 1 in Panama. (2) *The Jewish Study*, concerned with the Jew-gentile distinction, was conducted with Jewish children of two age groups.*

The North-South Study

THE EXPERIMENTAL DESIGN

Subjects are presented with pairs of social stimuli and asked to rate each of them on a 9-point scale: "1" means "I *can't* see myself being friends with such a person." "9" means "I can *very easily* see myself being friends with such a person." Consider first the following two pairs:

Type R: Race varied, belief held constant
    a. A white person who believes in God 1 2 3 4 5 6 7 8 9
    b. A Negro who believes in God   1 2 3 4 5 6 7 8 9

    c. A white person who is an atheist   1 2 3 4 5 6 7 8 9
    d. A Negro who is an atheist   1 2 3 4 5 6 7 8 9

We will say that a person is discriminating if he rates one member of the pair differently from the other member of the pair. In Type R pairs, all discriminations must be attributed to race, since belief is constant in both members of the pair. We present next Type B pairs:

Type B: Belief varied, race held constant
    a. A white person who believes in God 1 2 3 4 5 6 7 8 9
    b. A white person who is an atheist   1 2 3 4 5 6 7 8 9

    c. A Negro who believes in God   1 2 3 4 5 6 7 8 9
    d. A Negro who is an atheist   1 2 3 4 5 6 7 8 9

* We gratefully acknowledge our indebtedness to Mr. Pat Harkins, who helped collect and analyze the southern data; and to Mr. Jacob Frankel, who collected the Jewish data.

Here any discriminatory response is clearly on the basis of belief, since race is held constant. Consider finally Type RB pairs:

Type RB: Race varied, belief varied
  a. A white person who believes in God 1 2 3 4 5 6 7 8 9
  b. A Negro who is an atheist   1 2 3 4 5 6 7 8 9

  c. A white person who is an atheist   1 2 3 4 5 6 7 8 9
  d. A Negro who believes in God   1 2 3 4 5 6 7 8 9

Suppose a subject gives a discriminatory response to a Type RB pair. Such a response may be due solely to race, or solely to belief, or to both. Our major purpose is to ascertain which of these possibilities forms the main basis for discrimination. If our theoretical analysis is correct the responses to Type RB pairs should be primarily on the basis of belief. One way to find out whether this is so is to inspect the data to see if the subjects consistently prefer persons holding to their own belief regardless of whether the person is white or Negro. There are also other methods for testing the hypothesis and these will be discussed shortly.

Note that there are 2 Type R pairs, 2 Type B, and 2 Type RB pairs for the God-atheism issue described above—a total of 6 pairs. Actually this issue is only one of eight issues included in the experiment: four concern Negro-white relations and the remaining four issues are more general in nature, having nothing to do with race. Type R, Type B, and Type RB pairs were constructed for each of these eight issues in exactly the same way as described above.

The four *general beliefs* are:

  1. a. A ——— who is for socialized medicine
     b. A ——— who is against socialized medicine
  2. a. A ——— who believes in God
     b. A ——— who is an atheist
  3. a. A ——— who is a Communist
     b. A ——— who is anti-Communist
  4. a. A ——— who is pro-labor unions
     b. A ——— who is anti-labor unions

The four *Negro-white beliefs* are:

5. a. A ——— who is for immediate desegregation
   b. A ——— who is for gradual desegregation
6. a. A ——— who believes that fraternities and sororities should be interracial
   b. A ——— who believes that each race should have its own fraternities and sororities
7. a. A ——— who believes that, fundamentally, all races are equal
   b. A ——— who believes that there are fundamental differences between races
8. a. A ——— who believes that Negroes should be allowed to own homes anywhere they want to
   b. A ——— who believes that Negroes should be allowed to own homes only in certain areas

We thus end up with 48 pairs of statements, a third of which are Type R, a third Type B, and a third Type RB pairs. The pairs are thoroughly mixed together and presented to the subject on a mimeographed sheet.

Each subject must, of course, be first given the opportunity to state where he stands on each of the eight issues. At the beginning of the experiment we therefore ask him to check whether he is for or against each of the eight issues shown above. He is then given the following instructions:

> The following is a study of what the general public thinks and feels about a number of important social and personal questions. In the questionnaire below are a number of paired statements. Your task is to express the degree to which you can or cannot see yourself being friends with each of the two persons described in each pair. Make your judgments on a scale from 1 to 9 by circling the number which best expresses your degree of preference. Use the following scale as your guide.

I *can't* see myself being friends with such a person						I can *very easily* see myself being friends with such a person

1	2	3	4	5	6	7	8	9

Let us take an example: Circle the number which best expresses your degree of preference for 1a and 1b.

1a. A person who likes classical music   1 2 3 4 5 6 7 8 9
1b. A person who likes popular music   1 2 3 4 5 6 7 8 9

Your task is simply to circle the number which best expresses how much you can see yourself being friends with the person described. Remember, encircle one number after "a" and one number after "b" for each pair in the questionnaire. Please assume that the two persons described in each pair are alike *in all other respects.*

SCORING PROCEDURE

For each subject, separate scores are obtained for the four Negro-white beliefs considered together, and for the four general beliefs considered together. The scores are of two types: a *difference score* is the value obtained by subtracting from each other the ratings given to the two members of a pair. The larger the difference, the larger the discrimination; an *absolute score* is simply the rating from 1 to 9 circled by the subject. More specifically, the following scores were computed for the four general issues, and for the four Negro-white issues:

1. *R difference score*: A race score representing the total differences in ratings given to whites as compared to Negroes, when belief is held constant (Type R pairs). The larger the score, the greater the preference for whites over Negroes.

2. *B difference score*: A belief score representing the total differences in ratings given to those who agree as compared to those who disagree with the subject, when race is held constant (Type B pairs). The larger the score, the greater the preference for those who agree.

3. *RB difference score*: [1] A race-belief score representing the total differences in ratings given to pairs (Type RB) in which both race and belief are varied.

4. *N*: The total absolute score given Negroes holding the *same* belief preferences as the subject. The larger the score, the greater the preference.

5. *n*: The total absolute score given Negroes holding beliefs *contrary* to those professed by the subject.

6. W: The total absolute score given whites holding the *same* belief preferences as the subject.

7. w: The total absolute score given whites holding beliefs *contrary* to those professed by the subject.

In every case, the decision that the subject was "for" or "against" a belief is made by noting where he stands on each issue, as determined by responses at the beginning of the experiment.

RESULTS

A first requirement is to determine how reliable or consistent are the discrimination ratings thus obtained. We find that the reliabilities are uniformly quite high.[2] They range from .73 to .89 for the race and the belief difference scores. The reliabilities of the various absolute scores are even higher, ranging from .85 to .95. In addition, the reliabilities are about equally high for the northern and southern groups.

Having determined the reliability of the data, let us now look to them for an answer to the major question: To what extent is discrimination based upon race, or belief, or both? Several kinds of analyses are relevant to this issue:

1. Suppose that a white subject is in the process of responding to a Type RB pair (both race and belief vary). How will he rate Negroes who agree with him as compared to whites who disagree? If race is more important than belief, then whites who disagree should be preferred to Negroes who agree. If on the other hand belief is the more important determinant, then Negroes who agree should be preferred to whites who disagree. Table 7.1 shows the results found for all issues, for northern and southern groups.

It is seen that for all eight issues the great majority of the subjects prefer Negroes who agree with them to whites who disagree with them. This is so for issues involving Negro-white relations as well as for nonracial issues, and the results hold for southerners as well as for northerners. In all instances without exception the preference is made primarily in terms of belief.

However, the relative frequency of preference for Negroes who agree over whites who disagree varies from one issue to the next. It is almost unanimous for communism, and next most clear-cut

Table 7.1

*Number of Subjects Who Prefer Negroes Who Agree More than,
Equal to, and Less than Whites Who Disagree*

| Beliefs | | Negro Is Rated: | | | |
		Higher Than White	Equal to White	Lower Than White	Total
General beliefs					
1. Socialized	North	39	20	6	65
medicine	South	84	26	26	136
2. Belief in God	North	55	9	1	65
vs. atheism	South	110	16	10	136
3. Communism	North	63	1	1	65
	South	123	8	5	136
4. Labor unions	North	42	17	6	65
	South	71	39	26	136
Negro-white beliefs					
5. Immed. vs. gradual	North	42	18	5	65
desegregation	South	92	30	14	136
6. Interracial	North	47	12	6	65
fraternities	South	85	30	21	136
7. Races differ	North	47	8	10	65
fundamentally	South	85	26	25	136
8. Segregation in	North	41	13	11	65
housing	South	100	23	13	136

on belief in God. The frequency of "equal" ratings also varies from issue to issue. These fluctuations are probably due to the saliency of the issue combined with a desire, genuine or not, to appear tolerant by showing no preference. Note also that the unanimity of preference on the basis of belief is somewhat less on Negro-white issues than on general issues. But this tendency is not impressively great and does not minimize the subjects' strikingly greater preference for Negroes who agree over whites who disagree.

2. The results presented thus far do not tell us the *degree* to which race and belief are determining the discrimination response. Perhaps the discrimination response is the result of a sum-

mative or interactive effect between race and belief. Table 7.2 helps us answer this question.

Table 7.2

Correlations Between Discrimination Responses When Both Race and Belief Are Varied (Type RB) with Race Discrimination (Type R) and Belief Discrimination (Type B) Responses

Correlation [a] Between Race-belief Difference Score and:		Negro-White Beliefs	General Beliefs
Race difference score	North	.15	−.07
	South	.28	−.20
Belief difference score	North	.86	.91
	South	.74	.83

[a] The five highest correlations are significant beyond the .01 level. The $r = -.20$ is significant at the .05 level. The remaining two correlations are not significant. As we have pointed out in the text, the correlations with the race difference scores are negligible. However, we cannot overlook the fact that these correlations are significant for the South. Furthermore, we wonder whether the two negative correlations are psychologically meaningful. These findings, although difficult to interpret, do not detract from the main findings discussed in the text. $N = 65$ in northern group; $N = 136$ in southern group.

If the discrimination responses to Type RB pairs (race and belief varied) are due *solely* to race, then such responses should be highly related to the race discrimination responses (Type R), but not to the belief discrimination responses (Type B). On the other hand, if Type RB responses arise *solely* from belief, then they should correlate highly with belief but not with race discrimination responses. If Type RB discrimination responses are determined by both race and belief, then they should correlate substantially with both race and belief discrimination responses.

The results in Table 7.2 clearly show that the Type RB discrimination responses are negligibly correlated with race discrimination responses, and highly correlated with belief discrimination responses. Again, the results are highly similar for northerners and southerners for beliefs involving Negro-white relations as well as nonracial beliefs. Again the results show that the discriminations made by the subjects are almost exclusively on the basis of belief, with race playing a negligible role.

3. If the discriminatory response is indeed made in terms of belief rather than race, then those who agree with us, Negro and white, should be far more preferred in absolute terms than those who disagree with us, Negro and white. At the same time, we should expect to find relatively more equal preferences for Negroes and whites when each race is composed equally of those who agree and disagree. The results are shown in Table 7.3.

Table 7.3

Mean Acceptance of Negroes and Whites When Belief Is Held Constant, and Mean Acceptance of Those Who Agree And Disagree When Race Is Held Constant

Group		Negro-White Beliefs			General Beliefs		
		Mean	S.D.	Diff.[a]	Mean	S.D.	Diff.
North	White (*Ww*)	54.0	10.2	2.5	50.1	9.1	2.4
	Negro (*Nn*)	51.5	11.5		47.7	9.5	
South	White (*Ww*)	48.1	9.8	9.5	45.8	7.4	8.3
	Negro (*Nn*)	38.6	12.2		37.5	9.7	
North	Agree (*WN*)	61.8	9.2	20.0	62.9	8.2	29.5
	Disagree (*wn*)	41.8	14.7		33.4	13.3	
South	Agree (*WN*)	56.7	8.9	28.7	59.0	8.8	36.2
	Disagree (*wn*)	28.0	14.4		22.8	11.0	

[a] The significance levels are determined by *t* tests for correlated measures. Also the sum of the means for *Negro* and *white* is only approximately equal to the sum of the means for *agree* and *disagree* because the former are computed from Type R pairs, while the latter are computed from Type B pairs.
All differences shown are very significant, $p = .01$.

The results show without exception that whites are accepted more than Negroes, and that those who agree are accepted more than those who disagree. For the first time we see in these data a suggestion that the subjects discriminate on the basis of race as well as belief, although much more strongly on the basis of belief. All differences, North and South, are statistically very significant. But the most striking finding is that the differences between mean acceptances of whites and Negroes are relatively small compared to the impressively large differences between mean acceptances of those who agree and those who disagree.

The reader should be reminded that the mean acceptance scores for whites vs. Negroes are with belief held constant, and the agree vs. disagree comparisons are with race held constant.

But there are also some interesting differences between northerners and southerners which should be noted: (a) The southerners reject *both* whites and Negroes significantly more than do northerners. (b) For the southerners the gap between their acceptance of whites and Negroes is greater than the gap for northerners. (c) This is also true for those who agree vs. disagree. The gap is again larger for southerners than for northerners. (d) Furthermore, the southerners reject both those who agree and disagree with their views more than do the northerners. (e) Considering the results as a whole, it would seem that the southerners generally reject everybody—whites and Negroes, those who agree and those who disagree with them—more than northerners do.

4. Racial discrimination implies that the outgroup (Negro in this case) is discriminated against, but that the ingroup is favored. If we keep in mind that the concept of ethnocentrism (Levinson, 1949) refers to vilification of the outgroup and overglorification of the ingroup, we should expect to find a negative relation between rejection of the Negro and rejection of the white—the more the Negro is rejected, the more should the white be accepted. Should this turn out to be the case, it would be quite meaningful to speak of racial discrimination against the Negro. But what if we should find a positive relation instead? The results are shown in Table 7.4. Also shown are the correlations between preference for those who agree and disagree.

Table 7.4

Correlations Between Acceptance of Negroes and Whites, and Between Acceptance of Those Who Agree and Disagree

Correlation Between Acceptance of:		Negro-White Beliefs	General Beliefs
Negro (*Nn*) and white (*Ww*)	North	.81 [a]	.79 [a]
	South	.51 [a]	.35 [a]
Those who agree (*NW*)	North	.60 [a]	.43 [a]
and disagree (*nw*)	South	.20 [b]	−.14

[a] $p = .01$.
[b] $p = .05$.

The results clearly show that the greater the rejection of Negroes, the greater also the rejection of whites. The correlations are .81 and .79 for the northerners and .51 and .35 for the southerners. The fact that all these correlations are positive reminds us of a *New Yorker* cartoon of a few years back, showing a man sitting at a bar with drink in hand. He is saying: "I hate everybody, regardless of race, creed, or color." It seems that we are finding here evidence for *misanthropy* rather than discrimination, with the rejection of the Negro as but a special case of a wider rejection of all people, "regardless of race, creed, or color." It is thus difficult to talk *psychologically* of racial discrimination if those who reject Negroes also reject whites.

At the same time we cannot help but note that the positive correlations for southerners are smaller than those for northerners. These smaller correlations probably point to important differences between North and South. They indicate that the attitude toward the Negro does not altogether vary directly with the attitude toward the white. Perhaps this is due to the greater institutionalization of prejudice toward the Negro in the South. Perhaps there is some discrimination based on race as such. At the moment we do not know which is more likely. It would be worth investigating this problem further.

Consider now the following question: Is there any relation between our liking of those who agree with us and of those who disagree with us? The correlations are .60 and .43 for the northerners and .20 and —.14 for the southerners. In the North, the more we like those who agree with us the more we like those who disagree with us; in the South, there seems to be little or no relation between the two. Again, the findings seem to point to basic differences between North and South, and again we are by no means clear on what interpretation to give these findings. But we will come back to them when we consider the comparable findings for Jewish children.

5. We have already presented theoretical considerations and data suggesting that the Opinionation Scale is not only a measure of individual differences in belief prejudice, but also a broader measure under which ethnic prejudice may be subsumed. Let us therefore see how the discriminatory responses made to Type R, Type B, and Type RB pairs are related to the Opinionation Scale

on the one hand, and to a conventional measure of anti-Negro prejudice. On theoretical grounds, we should expect scores on an anti-Negro scale,[3] obtained from subjects' responses to attitude statements about the Negro, to be positively related only to Type R discriminations, but not to Type B or to Type RB discriminations. In contrast, we should expect the Opinionation Scale to be related not only to Type B but *also* to Type RB discriminations, since Type RB discriminations (wherein race and belief are both varied) have been shown to be primarily based on belief.

Data to test these expectations were available and analyzed only for the northern sample, and results are shown in Table 7.5.

Table 7.5

Correlations Between Anti-Negro and Opinionation Scales
with Race, Belief, and Race-Belief Difference Scores

Scales	Race Difference Score		Belief Difference Score		Race-Belief Difference Score	
	Negro-White Beliefs	General Beliefs	Negro-White Beliefs	General Beliefs	Negro-White Beliefs	General Beliefs
Anti-Negro scale	.41[a]	.41[a]	.03	—.03	.15	.04
Opinionation scale	—.03	—.02	.13	.26[b]	.12	.33[a]

$N = 65$.
[a] $p = .01$.
[b] $p = .05$.

It is seen that although all the correlations are relatively low, the anti-Negro scale scores correlate significantly with race discrimination responses, but not with belief or with race-belief discrimination scores. The Opinionation Scale, on the other hand, does not correlate with race discrimination responses, but does show a significant correlation with belief and, more importantly, with race-belief discrimination scores. These results all line up with theoretical expectations regarding the limited nature of the traditional types of prejudice tests, and they also suggest that belief prejudice, as measured by the Opinionation Scale, is a more powerful indicator of prejudice since it correlates significantly with Type RB (as well as with Type B) discriminations.

But again the conclusions must be tempered by certain unexpected aspects of the data shown in Table 7.5. Why are not the significant correlations higher than they are? And why are the significant correlations with opinionation found only with "general beliefs" but not with "Negro-white beliefs"? We could engage in lengthy speculations about these, but we prefer to let it go by simply saying we do not know. All we can reasonably do now is to draw attention to these puzzling findings in the hope that they will be clarified with further analysis and research.

The Jewish Study

METHOD

We will now describe a second study with 50 middle-class Jewish children, students attending a Hebrew school in Grand Rapids, Michigan. Instead of Negro-white distinctions, this study deals with Jew-gentile distinctions. Below are the six issues employed: three deal with anti-Semitism; the other three deal with other issues. As before, three types of pairs were constructed for each of the issues: Type E (ethnic group varied), Type B (belief varied), and Type EB (both ethnic group and belief varied).

General beliefs

1. a. A ——— who is for democracy
   b. A ——— who is against democracy
2. a. A ——— who is for Communists
   b. A ——— who is against Communists
3. a. A ——— who believes in God
   b. A ——— who does not believe in God

Beliefs about Jews

4. a. A ——— who believes Jews are mostly interested in money
   b. A ——— who believes Jews are not mostly interested in money
5. a. A ——— who believes Jews are loud and noisy
   b. A ——— who believes Jews are not loud and noisy
6. a. A ——— who is for Israel
   b. A ——— who is against Israel

The general design of this study is otherwise identical with the preceding one in every respect, and the same scores were obtained. In the hope of getting some insights into the development of ethnic and belief discriminations in children, the children were divided into two age groups of 25 each: a younger group between 7 years, 7 months and 11 years, 1 month of age; and an older group between 11 years, 4 months and 16 years, 3 months of age. Eleven other children had to be eliminated from the study because it was obvious from the material they filled out that they did not understand what was expected of them.

RESULTS

The results are presented in Tables 7.6 to 7.9. These four tables are exactly parallel to Tables 7.1 to 7.4, for the North-South study.*

Before considering the main results let us again discuss first how reliable the scores obtained are.[4] We find that the reliabilities of the ethnic difference scores are close to zero for the younger, 7–11-age group. They are fairly high (.66 and .87) for the older, 11–16-age group. Apparently children between the ages of 7 and 11 have not yet learned to discriminate reliably between the terms, Jew and gentile. It is our guess that the main source of the unreliability is that the term "gentile" is simply unfamiliar to Jewish children of this age.†

As for the belief differences scores, these are found to be about equally reliable for both age groups. The reliabilities are .71 and .75 for the younger group, .73 and .78 for the older group. These findings, along with those on the reliability of the ethnic differences scores, suggest that at least within the context of the present study (1) children between the ages of 7 and 11 discriminate with relatively high consistency on the basis of belief, but not on the basis of the particular ethnic categories used; (2) children between 11 and 16 discriminate reliably on both the ethnic and belief criteria.

* *Note to the general reader:* On the whole, the findings reported here for the Jewish children are in agreement with the findings of the North-South study. Those readers who might wish to skip this section can still get the gist of it by turning to the next section on "Interpretations, Implications, and Applications."

† We have confirmed this point informally by questioning Jewish children on the meaning of this term.

Table 7.6

Number of Subjects Who Prefer Gentiles Who Disagree More than, Equal to, and Less than Jews Who Disagree

| | Gentile is Rated: | | | |
| | Higher Than Jew | Equal to Jew | Lower Than Jew | |
Beliefs				Total
General beliefs				
1. Democracy	42	4	4	50
2. Communism	42	4	4	50
3. God	45	4	1	50
Beliefs about Jews				
4. Interested in money	39	9	2	50
5. Loud and noisy	33	12	5	50
6. Israel	49	0	1	50

N = 50.

The reliabilities of the absolute scores generally range from moderate to high, the younger group scoring somewhat less reliably. The reliabilities for the 11–16 group range from .43 to .94, while those for the younger group range from .46 to .72, with one exception. The only reliability figure that is clearly out of line is the correlation of .20 for the 7–11 group on absolute scores measuring amount of acceptance of gentiles. This low reliability fits in with the comment just made about the Jewish children being unfamiliar with the term "gentile."

Table 7.6 is comparable to Table 7.1 for the North-South study. It shows how frequently the children prefer gentiles who agree with them to Jews who disagree with them. The data have been combined into a single group because the results are very similar for the two age groups. These data show, as in the North-South study, that in the great majority of instances the preference is for gentiles who agree over Jews who disagree. Again, there are differences in results from one issue to another. Unanimity is lowest on beliefs 4 and 5, highest on belief 6. But the over-all trend of results is unmistakable. The Jewish children seem to be responding primarily to belief.

Table 7.7 shows the correlations between discriminatory responses given to Type EB pairs (both ethnic group and belief varied) with ethnic discrimination (Type E) and belief discrimination (Type B). The results show that the discriminatory responses made to Type EB pairs are not significantly related to ethnic discrimination, but are significantly related to belief discrimination. These results are highly consistent with those found for northerners and southerners (Table 7.2) dealing with the Negro-white distinction and suggest that when discriminations are made to stimuli that have both belief and ethnic characteristics the discriminations are made primary on belief characteristics.

Table 7.7

Correlations Between Discrimination Responses When Both Ethnic Group and Belief Are Varied (Type EB) with Ethnic Discrimination (Type E) and Belief Discrimination (Type B) Responses

Correlation Between Ethnic-Belief Difference Score and:	Group	Beliefs About Jews	General Beliefs
Ethnic difference score	7–11	−.31	−.36
	11–16	−.04	−.11
Belief difference score	7–11	.47 [a]	.80 [b]
	11–16	.66 [b]	.70 [b]

N = 25 in each age group.
[a] $p = .05$.
[b] $p = .01$.

An additional finding is noted which is also extremely interesting. It will be recalled that although the younger Jewish children do not discriminate reliably between Jew and gentile, the older Jewish children do. We now see from Table 7.7 that whether they do or do not makes no difference. Both younger and older Jewish children discriminate on the basis of belief rather than ethnic group when given a choice between the two. These findings suggest that belief discriminations develop relatively early in life, and clearly earlier than the time they learn the distinction between Jew and gentile.[*]

Next shown, in Table 7.8, is the degree to which the Jewish children accept Jews and gentiles and the degree to which they

[*] These results cannot be generalized to include Negro-white and other ethnic distinctions. Further research with children of various ages on various ethnic and racial distinctions would be highly illuminating.

Table 7.8

*Mean Acceptance of Jews and Gentiles When Belief Is Held Constant,
and Mean Acceptance of Those Who Agree and Disagree When
Ethnic Group Is Held Constant*

Group	Beliefs About Jews			General Beliefs		
	Mean [a]	S.D.	Diff.	Mean	S.D.	Diff.
7–11						
Jew (*Jj*)	30.5	6.0	1.2	30.1	4.3	.5
Gentile (*Gg*)	29.3	6.7		29.6	3.9	
11–16						
Jew (*Jj*)	32.0	7.5	1.4	31.9	6.1	1.5
Gentile (*Gg*)	30.6	5.6		30.4	4.8	
7–11						
Agree (*JG*)	46.1	7.1	31.1[b]	47.8	8.1	35.4[b]
Disagree (*jg*)	15.0	8.2		12.4	6.5	
11–16						
Agree (*JG*)	46.6	7.0	27.6[b]	48.8	5.5	34.9[b]
Disagree (*jg*)	19.0	11.7		13.9	9.4	

[a] The sum of the means for Jew and gentile is only approximately equal to the sum
of the means for agree and disagree because the former are computed from Type
E pairs, the latter from Type B pairs.
[b] Very significant, $p = .01$.

Table 7.9

*Correlations Between Acceptance of Jews and Gentiles, and Between
Acceptance of Those Who Agree and Disagree*

Correlation Between Acceptance of:	Group	Beliefs About Jews	General Beliefs
Jew (*Jj*) and Gentile (*Gg*)	7–11	.52[a]	.59[a]
	11–16	.20	.21
Those who agree (*JG*) and disagree (*jg*)	7–11	−.17	−.79[a]
	11–16	−.53[a]	−.44[b]

[a] $p = .01$.
[b] $p = .05$.

accept those who agree and disagree with them. Very little difference is found in either age group in the extent to which they
accept Jews and gentiles, when they both hold to the same beliefs;
but tremendous differences are found for both age groups in the

extent to which they accept those who agree and disagree with them, when those who agree and disagree are all Jews, or all gentiles.

Finally, Table 7.9 shows the correlations between amount of acceptance of Jews and of gentiles, and between amount of acceptance of those who agree and those who disagree. Again we see that the correlations between acceptance of Jews and gentiles are positive, although the correlations are lower for the older group. Why this is so is unclear. Our guess is that it is probably due to sampling fluctuations. We will have to reserve judgment on this pending further study with larger samples and more age groups. More surprising, though, are the negative correlations between amount of acceptance of those who agree and those who disagree with the subjects. When these correlations are compared with those found in the North-South study (Table 7.4), we are confronted with an apparent contradiction. With Jewish children the amount of acceptance of those who agree is negatively related to the amount of acceptance of those who disagree; in the North-South study, the correlations between acceptance of those who agree and disagree are positive in the North and fluctuate around zero in the South. We can only speculate about why these results come out as they do. Is it possible that the correlations between liking for those who agree and disagree with us change from negative to positive as a result of increasing maturity?

We gain the impression from an inspection of the raw data that the Jewish children tend to rate at the extreme of the 9-point scale; that is, if they rate those who agree with them absolutely high (9), then they rate those who disagree with them, absolutely low (1), thus accounting for the negative correlations. But the northern college students generally seem to be more subtle in the way they rate others. They typically do not use the total scale from 1 to 9 in making their ratings. Instead they restrict themselves to only a part of the scale, and express their likes and dislikes in a relative rather than absolute way. A particular subject, for example, rates everybody relatively high—from 6 to 9. At the same time he consistently rates those who agree with him higher than those who disagree with him. In this way he can maintain for himself a self-image of tolerance and at the same time still have a free hand within these limits to discriminate among people according to whether they agree or disagree with him. This may possibly account for the positive correlations found among northern college students on ratings of those who agree and disagree with them.

As for the southern college students, their behavior seems to fall somewhere between the Jewish children and the northern college students. Some of them polarize and others rate the social stimuli in a more relative manner, thereby possibly leading to close-to-zero correlations.

But let us stress that these interpretations are tentative. Further analysis and research with larger samples seem called for before anything more definitive can be said.

Interpretations, Implications, and Applications

Despite the many interesting side questions raised, let us not lose sight of the main threads running through all the findings. Pulling them all together we see that northern and southern whites and Jewish children generally react in strikingly similar ways to the following:

1. Most of the time they discriminate on the basis of belief and not on the basis of racial or ethnic group when they are given the opportunity to react to social stimuli differing simultaneously on both characteristics.

2. Discriminations made between social stimuli that differ on both characteristics are negligibly correlated with independently obtained racial or ethnic discriminations, but they are highly correlated with independently obtained belief discriminations.

3. The subjects generally prefer as friends those who agree with them far more than those who disagree with them, regardless of race or ethnic group. But when beliefs are held constant, the subjects prefer other ethnic and racial groups almost but not quite as much as their own.

4. The more the subjects reject the ethnic or racial outgroup, the more they also reject their own group.

Recall that four of the eight issues in the North-South study concern Negro-white relations while the other four are issues having nothing to do with race. Similarly, three of the six issues in the Jewish study concern anti-Semitism, and the remaining three deal with other topics. It is remarkable how similar the findings are in all studies regardless of the kind of issues on which they are based. But, it may be asked, are these issues a fair sample of the total population of issues? They are obviously not. We deliberately selected issues we believed to be relevantly salient in everyday life. Thus, whatever conclusions are to be drawn regarding the relative potency of belief vs. racial or ethnic cues have to be qualified by this consideration. We doubt if any or *all* beliefs would serve equally as primary determinants. The more trivial the belief the more would we expect discriminations to be made on the basis of race or ethnic group. For example, do we prefer Negroes who believe that red bow ties are pretty to Negroes who believe blue bow ties are pretty? The issue is trivial, and had we pitted such an issue against race, we would probably have got a trivial effect. In real life, issues involving intergroup conflict are far from being this trivial, so perhaps it is more accurate to say that the particular issues we selected for study are more representative as a sample of salient everyday issues rather than all issues.

Not to be overlooked either is the question as to whether the subject samples used are representative. Had we obtained data only for northern college students, generalizations to southern students would have been less warranted because northerners are typically more tolerant than southerners, or at least may desire to appear so in testing situations such as this. But then again, northern and southern college students are hardly representative of the total population either. This we have partly corrected for by including the Jewish children. This broadens the base from which generalizations can be made. There are yet additional data (Smith, 1957), which we omit here for lack of space, that enable us to generalize our findings yet further. The two college groups filled out an anti-Negro attitude scale, and the Jewish children filled out an anti-Semitism scale. On the basis of these scores, the subjects were divided equally into high and low prejudice groups. A major portion of the results presented in this chapter for the various groups was also analyzed separately for these high and low prejudice subgroups. The results for these subgroups were remarkably identical and are essentially the same as those reported here for the total groups. They thus enable us to say that

154

whether a person is high or low in prejudice against Jews and Negroes, he responds to belief rather than to racial or ethnic cues when given the opportunity to do so.

The over-all results obtained for the Jewish children are interesting for several reasons. They enable us to broaden the scope of our generalizations not only from the point of view of broader sampling, but also from the point of view of including the Jew-gentile distinction as well as the Negro-white distinction. And, perhaps most important, the Jewish data provide us with at least a few insights into what is happening developmentally with respect to ethnic vs. belief discrimination. Apparently, 7–11-year-olds already have firmly established belief discriminations even though they cannot yet fully understand the Jew-gentile distinction. This does not necessarily mean that children of this age range do not make ethnic distinctions. Perhaps we would have got different results had we used instead of Jew-gentile the terms Jew-Christian or Jew-*goy*. In any event, both groups of Jewish children, the 7–11-year-olds who cannot yet make the Jew-gentile discrimination and the 11–16-year-olds who can, respond primarily on the basis of belief.

Before going on to explore further the broader implications of the findings, we are obliged to examine several methodological issues that may possibly raise doubts about the meaningfulness of the findings. One such issue is that the data are obtained from *verbal* reports of discrimination. What can we then conclude about discrimination in everyday life? This issue, of course, arises in all attitude research where questionnaires or verbal reports are obtained. This is not the place to enter into a systematic consideration of the relative validity of verbal vs. nonverbal expressions of prejudice. Suffice it to say here that it would certainly be desirable to replicate the present studies in real life situations wherein an opportunity is given to discriminate against people on the basis of both sets of cues. For example, we are now in the process of setting up a group study in which a naive subject (that is, a subject who is ignorant of the set-up of the experiment) discusses his stand on a particular issue with four other people. The latter are confederates, two whites and two Negroes. One white and one Negro take the same stand as the naive subject, and the other two take the opposing stand. In such a way the stage can be set to see whether behavioral discriminations will be made on the basis of belief or race. Suppose that only three persons at a time are permitted to go out for a coffee break. Whom will the naive subject pick to go with him? *

There is yet another objection that may be raised about the present research. Perhaps our subjects responded on the basis of belief rather than ethnic group or race because they "saw through" the purpose of the study, and wished to appear tolerant. This is of course possible but we can think of four reasons why it is unlikely. First, our subjects responded under conditions of anonymity. Second, they could have disguised their discriminatory tendencies by giving the *identical* rating to each member of the pair. This in the main they did not do, as can be seen from Tables 7.1 and 7.6. On the whole, they responded differently to the two members of the pair, and these differences are generally quite reliable. Third, our subjects also filled out an anti-Semitism or an anti-Negro attitude scale. Marked individual differences in responses were apparent. So it is hardly likely that the group as a whole was trying to appear tolerant on ethnic or racial issues. Fourth, the criticism might at best apply to our college students who might conceivably be sufficiently sophisticated to "see through" the purpose of the study. But surely this would not be likely to apply to the Jewish children.

Another possible methodological objection concerns the specific nature of the rating scale used. The subjects responded to each social stimulus on a 9-point rating scale in which 1 means, "I *can't* see myself being friends with such a person," and 9 means, "I can

---

* As we prepare to go to press at the end of 1959, a preliminary answer to this question becomes available. In collaboration with Robert I. Mendelsohn and Milan J. Reban, data have been obtained for nine white subjects who vary widely in their scores on an anti-Negro attitude scale. In all nine cases without exception the subjects selected on the basis of belief rather than race. Four subjects picked the Negro and white confederates who agreed with their views on democracy, fraternities, and religion. One subject picked the two confederates, one Negro and one white, who disagreed with his views because, he told us afterwards, he wanted to argue with them further over coffee. The remaining four subjects picked one confederate who agreed and a second confederate who disagreed with their views, in all cases cutting across race lines.

It must be emphasized, however, that these are merely preliminary results. A definitive answer to the question as to whether the principle of belief congruence governs discrimination in everyday life as well as verbal discrimination will have to be delayed until additional results are forthcoming from experiments such as the one just described.

very easily see myself being friends with such a person." We have no way of knowing at this point whether the results would have been different had we, instead, asked for ratings of acceptance-rejection on some other basis, for example, in terms of working on the same job, living in the same apartment house, eating together, etc. It will be interesting to see what results will be obtained with such variations. For research workers who may contemplate using such variations, it should be pointed out that each variation may bring to the fore a different set of beliefs. For example, a rating scale on "living in the same apartment house" invokes or arouses the subject's beliefs about the consequences of living close together. Such beliefs should be brought under experimental control in further attempts to evaluate the race vs. belief issue.

Pending further research, then, the present findings must be interpreted cautiously. To return to the original question posed at the beginning of this chapter: Are there two qualitatively different kinds of prejudice, or can racial and ethnic prejudice be subsumed under belief prejudice? The data, such as they are, seem to yield up a primarily "no" answer to the first part, and a primarily "yes" answer to the second part of the question. If we can accept the results at face value, anti-Negro prejudice seems to reduce psychologically to how we feel differently toward Negroes who agree and disagree with us, and toward whites who agree and disagree with us. Likewise with anti-Jewish prejudice, and presumably with other ethnic and racial prejudices not directly investigated here.

But not *all* of the subjects react primarily to belief. From Tables 7.1 and 7.6 we observe that on various issues 2 to 20 per cent of the subjects respond primarily to race or ethnic group. It would be extremely interesting to know why these subjects react so differently from the majority. It should prove worthwhile to isolate out such persons for more intensive future study.

Getting back to the majority findings, we must anticipate some scepticism over the interpretation offered to account for them because it goes against social-science conceptions and common-sense conceptions about social prejudice, and in this area many people are expert because they have felt deeply and thought deeply about it. Let us therefore carefully explore their implications, possible applications, and the way they might be fitted in with current conceptions.

Allport, in his comprehensive work, *The Nature of Prejudice* (1954), describes three stages in the child's learning of ethnic prejudice. The first he calls *pregeneralized* or prelogical learning. It refers to the learning of linguistic categories that arouse emotion prior to the learning of the referent. Allport gives a number of interesting examples of children who know such words as "nigger," "Polack," "wop," "kike," and "goy" but have no conception of the groups to which they refer. "The child seems to live his mental life in specific contexts. What exists here and now makes up the only reality" (p. 308). The second stage is the period of *total rejection*. This occurs when the child has learned to distinguish ethnic and racial groups from each other. The third stage is *differentiation*.

> Escape clauses are written into the attitude in order to make it more rational and more acceptable to the individual. One says, "Some of my best friends are Jews." Or, "I am not prejudiced against Negroes—I always loved my black Mammy." The child who is first learning adult categories of rejection is not able to make such gracious exceptions. It takes him the first six to eight years of his life to learn total rejection, and another six years or so to modify it (p. 309).

The question may be raised whether Allport's description of the three stages of learning is a description of the development of racial and ethnic prejudice or of belief prejudice. In defense of the latter viewpoint it could be said that in the process of indoctrinating the child, the white parent usually offers him some specific *reason* (of course, accompanied by rewards and punishments) to make him understand why he cannot play with Negro children—for example, they are dirty or lazy. Indoctrination about race takes place within a yet broader learning context aimed at inculcating beliefs about the virtues of cleanliness, hard work, monogamous sexual behavior, middle-class values, and so on. In such a broader context the child also builds up beliefs about racial, ethnic, social, religious, political, and occupational groups. Such-and-such behavioral characteristics, the child is taught to believe, are or are not desirable. Such-and-such groups, the child is further taught to believe, are acceptable or unacceptable because they exemplify such-and-such characteristics. If children learn violent epithets such as "kike," "nigger," and "dago" before they learn which groups they refer to, they also learn nonethnic epithets as well, such as "stinker," "dummy," and "stupid," the meanings of which are also vague, except that they are all appelations to be hurled without regard for "race, creed, or color" at those who express behavior and beliefs at odds with the child's. Thus, to isolate out for study only ethnic or racial cleavages is, possibly, to delimit artificially the full story of what is happening developmentally. We also stand in danger of projecting into the child's psyche adult, sociological conceptions that may or may not exist in the phenomenal world of the child. In other words, we are trying to say that prejudice may develop in children along a far broader front than an ethnic or racial one. It cannot be said on the basis of the limited data considered here how the learning of belief prejudice proceeds in the child, or precisely how ethnic discriminations fit into such a total picture. But with these limited data as a point of departure, perhaps we can go back with a fresh eye to take another look at the origins of prejudice in children.

In the meantime, let us point to a few examples taken from everyday behavior which seem to become more understandable in the light of the present formulations and findings. In August, 1956, two hangings in effigy were reported in Montgomery, Ala., in connection with the Negro boycott of the bus lines. One was a Negro; the other was a white. On the white was a placard: "He talked integration." Another example involves the Little Rock situation following Governor Faubus' calling out the militia to prevent integration at Central High School in September, 1957. One of his most vocal opponents in Little Rock was Harry Ashmore, the white executive editor of the *Arkansas Gazette*. Some other forces arrayed against Faubus were President Eisenhower, the federalized National Guard, and many white ministers. It would be hard to conclude from these examples that the conflict was drawn on racial lines. A third example is given by Gunther (1955) in connection with his report on the Mau Mau oath. Gunther writes:

Mau Mau is beyond doubt an anti-white, anti-European movement, but one striking thing about it is . . . that the terrorists have killed extremely few white men. . . . By far the greatest number of those butchered by the Mau Mau are, then, Africans. Why are these slain? Mostly because they were Kikuyus who . . . refused to take the Mau Mau oath, in spite of formidable pressures to make them do so, or because they became informers. The Mau Mau wanted above all . . . to enforce conformity (pp. 358–359).

A fourth example is the case of a 7-year-old Jewish girl who, one day in late December, was wondering aloud about which neighbors were "like us" and "not like us." The criteria she used to decide this issue were three: were they Democrats? did they believe in Chanukah? did they believe in God? All these examples point to the possibility that in everyday life it is congruencies in belief that seem to orient us to the social world. They all suggest, too, that this principle may hold for "nonverbal" as well as "verbal" behavior.

The present conceptualizations and findings should in no way be construed as denying the facts of anti-Semitism, Jim Crow, and similar bigotries. They merely reformulate our way of thinking about these phenomena. For many, such concepts as Negro, Jew, Mexican, Catholic, and Communist symbolize learned, often institutionalized, *complexes* that bring to mind all at once groups of persons thought to adhere to certain belief systems at variance with their own. Such complexes bring to mind a cluster of stereotypes, where each stereotype is a "picture in our head" about a specific belief or characteristic we attribute to other groups. When a non-Jew says of the Jew that he is *exclusive,* he apparently attributes to the Jew the belief: "Jews should stick together to prevent gentiles from entering into competition with them." What he may also be saying is that he, a non-Jew, believes that Jews should not stick together for such a purpose. When he says that Jews are *intrusive,* what he apparently believes is that Jews believe, and act on the belief, that they should be permitted social entrance to places that exclude Jews. What he may also be saying is that he, as a non-Jew, believes the opposite. When a non-Jew says "Some of my best friends are Jews" he may be trying to say that he knows and likes some Jews because they hold to the same beliefs he does. It may also mean that his homogeneous complex image, the Jew, has broken down upon contact with certain Jews who believe as he does.

Nor can the present conceptualizations and findings be interpreted to mean that everybody is equally prejudiced on the criterion of belief congruence. As we have seen, the *amount* of discrimination on this basis varies from one subject to another, even though cleavages along belief lines seem generally to be the guiding principle of organization. The subjects differ in *relative* preference for those who agree and disagree with them, and they also differ in their *absolute* preferences.

Nor are we prepared to say that associations among people with compatible belief systems are necessarily an indication of hostility toward those with incompatible belief systems. There seems to be a natural tendency for people to associate with, socialize with, and be more comfortable with others having similar belief systems. We observe, for example, that in a large academic community such as ours, social intercourse is relatively infrequent between faculty members of, say, the College of Science and Arts and the College of Agriculture; between college people on the one hand and businessmen, Oldsmobile workers, and construction workers on the other; between college people and Negroes and Mexicans living in Lansing. It would be psychologically unparsimonious to say that these associations are sometimes due to ethnic similarities, sometimes to class, occupation, values, and so forth. Conceptually they may be more simply attributed to compatibilities in belief systems. To varying degrees in various people, to be sure, such associations are rooted in a desire to exclude others because of hostility or prejudice, but not necessarily so.

The reformulation we have proposed here is to our mind more "field-theoretical" in its orientation than the traditional view. It gives proper due to the *social situation* as well as to *personality* as determinants of social bigotry. The *specificity* of prejudice can be more readily understood and defended * if we think of prejudice as psychologically based on belief rather than ethnic or racial group. It emphasizes the fact that men take sides over specific

* See Cook (1957), for example.

issues in the context of specific social situations. As the social situation changes, a given person's behavior and alignments will also change.* Alignments among men are not necessarily the same on the issue of FEPC, interracial housing, desegregation in education, and desegregation in public transportation. A southern realtor, teenager's parent, personnel manager, construction worker, and high-school senior cannot all be expected to feel the same way about such issues because they have different kinds and degrees of stakes in them. But at the same time no one can deny there is also the *generality* of prejudice to be reckoned with. The generality of prejudice can also be more readily understood and defended † if we think of the structure rather than the content of bigotry—if we think of the bigot as one who, due to his over-all motivational structure, finds it necessary to reject others on the simple criterion that they agree or disagree with him, regardless of the content of what he happens to believe. Thus, in our view both specificity and generality of prejudice are real—specificity of prejudice when the focus is on content of beliefs, generality of prejudice when the focus is on structure of beliefs.

Lectures on group relations and other propaganda for brotherhood often fail to produce the desired effect. At best, they seem to change the specific beliefs to which the propaganda is directed and not the global attitudes toward ethnic or racial groups.‡ Perhaps the reason such efforts to change global attitudes are generally unsuccessful is that propaganda for brotherhood is based on the assumption that cognitive organization proceeds along ethnic rather than belief lines. One of the most widely cited studies that do show a change in attitude is the one by Smith (1943). He found that prejudice was reduced in a group of white college students as a result of contact with Negroes having a social status equal to their own. The reason this approach may have been successful is that the college students were really given an opportu-

---

* Robin Williams writes: "the explanation of conflict requires taking into account the actual content of beliefs and values; it is not enough to note that Protestants, Jews and Catholics are culturally defined as 'different' and that real social groupings develop on the basis of that definition" (1956, p. 17). Williams' view is, of course, similar to our own. But we would add ethnic and racial groups as well as religious groups.

† See Allport and MacKinnon (1944), for example.

‡ For example, Krech and Crutchfield (1948) cite an empirical study by Rosenthal which supports this view.

nity, through contact with persons of equal status, to discover that there exist Negroes who have belief systems congruent with their own. A similar interpretation may be made of Deutsch and Collins' (1951) findings on the effects of interracial housing on changing attitudes. Perhaps it is not equal status as such that is the crucial variable. Rather, persons of equal status generally form congruent belief systems and, psychologically speaking, it is this perceived congruence that produces the effects noted.* What would have happened in Smith's study or in the interracial housing study if the contacts were deliberately arranged with equal-status persons holding to belief systems incongruent with the subjects'? In such a case, our theory would lead us to predict opposite effects.

What we are leading up to is the proposal that we should be able to change race-prejudiced attitudes and behavior by bringing together people of varying racial or ethnic groups who have congruent belief systems. There are some psychologists who would contend that you cannot really expect to eliminate social discrimination unless you first change the underlying personality structure or deep-lying motivations served by such attitudes and behavior. According to the present view, this is not at all necessary. As we interpret Deutsch and Collins' (1951) data, a prejudiced white housewife moving into an interracial housing project may change her attitudes and actions with respect to her Negro neighbors without necessarily changing her underlying psychodynamic structure. She may do so because there has been a change in social norms. Or, to put it more in our terms, when she discovers that there is belief congruence with respect to sanitation, child rearing, sexual behavior, etc., where before she expected none, and when it further dawns on her that socializing with her new-found neighbors will not result in a *loss* of belief congruence with respect to her white neighbors, she will become increasingly more friendly toward her Negro neighbors.

Thus, our theory about the organization of belief systems is relatively optimistic regarding the possibilities of social change with respect to intergroup relations because it is not predicated

---

* Consistent with the above, Westie (1952) has shown that extent of preference for whites and Negroes varies with the occupations held by whites and Negroes.

163

on the doctrine that deep changes in personality and motivation are essential.

It is now necessary to add an important qualification. At the point where ethnic discrimination becomes institutionalized or sanctioned by law, as is most clearly the case in the South and in South Africa, social discrimination obviously will become coerced along ethnic and racial rather than belief lines. For economic and political reasons too complex to go into here, man often finds it desirable to set up social castes and classes which are, insofar as possible, visibly distinguishable from each other—and ethnic and racial cues are more visible than belief cues. It is perhaps for this reason that the institutionalization of social discrimination proceeds more readily along such lines. In Germany under Hitler, for example, visibility was artificially increased by wearing arm bands and other insignia that helped identify who was Jew and who was not. Another method is to segregate the minority group into the ghetto. The more institutionalized such discrimination becomes, the more is the illusion created that there is a deep-rooted instinctual or psychological basis for it. But as the data in the present research suggest, this is not so. The *psychological* basis for discriminating one person from another and one group from another seems to be belief. From an individual standpoint, prejudice is conceived to arise from a conditioned avoidance of belief systems incongruent with one's own, and not from a general conditioning to hate outgroups as a class, this being a secondary development that arises as prejudice becomes institutionalized. Allport describes the psychological arbitrariness of ethnic cleavage under institutionalization in the following passage:

> The nearest to the all-duty scapegoat then is a religious, ethnic, or race group. Having permanence and stability, they can be given a definite status and stereotyped as a group. The *arbitrariness of the categorization we have already commented upon—many people being included or excluded by a kind of social fiat* [italics ours]. A given Negro may have more white ancestry than colored—but what is wanted is a "socially supposed" race, and so he is arbitrarily included. Occasionally the process is reversed. A Vienna mayor during Nazi days wished to accord some privilege to a prominent Jew. He met the objection that

his beneficiary came from a Jewish family by saying, "It is up to me to decide whether he is a Jew or not." The fact that Nazis made certain favored Jews into "honorary Aryans" shows the importance of maintaining the persecuted minority intact (1954, p. 246).

To Allport's comment about the "honorary Aryan" we might add that the existence of this category (and also the "yellow Aryan") is interesting from a psychological standpoint because it points further to the importance of belief as a determinant of discrimination. The "favored Jew" is a Jew who by his actions or verbalizations has indicated that he agrees with, condones, or is useful to the Nazi belief system. This is formalized by making him an "honorary Aryan" which distinguishes him from other Jews who, by fiat, are all assumed to disagree with the Nazi belief system.

Racial or ethnic prejudice is therefore a sociological fact. This does not necessarily also make it a *psychological* fact. The psychological representation of a phenomenon need not be bound slavishly to sociological representations because psychology has to try to understand man's noninstitutionalized as well as his institutionalized behavior and prejudices. This we have tried to do by focusing on man's belief systems, which to some extent reflect institutionalization and to some extent do not.

There is always the danger of overstating a new theoretical position for the sake of emphasizing it. To avoid this danger we have tried to be cautious in our interpretation of the findings. In the same spirit let us now cite some counterexamples that are perhaps not so easy to reformulate in terms of belief prejudice. First, it has been observed that boys' gangs in large cities are sometimes formed spontaneously on the basis of ethnic groupings —Italian gangs, Puerto Rican gangs, Negro gangs, Jewish gangs. A second point we get from Allport: "A minor offense, overlooked in a member of our group, seems intolerable when committed by a member of the outgroup" (1954, p. 139). A third counterexample is that the southern white bigot would not want his daughter to marry the "good" Negro any more than the "bad" one. The reader will, no doubt, think of other examples.

As we have said, we mention these counterexamples in order

to point up the fact that we ourselves are wary of the sweeping contention that ethnic and racial prejudice can be generally subsumed under belief prejudice. To each of the above counterexamples it is perhaps possible to save our position. For example, in the case of the Ku Klux Klanner who would not want a "good" Negro, any more than the "bad" Negro, to marry his daughter, it can be counter-counterargued that in the act of wanting to marry his daughter, the "good" Negro automatically forfeits his claim as "good" and automatically becomes "bad." It is to be admitted, however, that not all will find this way of looking at the problem convincing. In any event, rightly or wrongly, our theoretical analysis of the nature of belief-disbelief systems has led us to push to the limits this line of inquiry, in order to see how far we can get with it. Perhaps it will provide us with a fresh approach to an age-old problem. Perhaps not. Whether it does or does not, we have more or less deliberately played the role of devil's advocate in the hope that it will goad others to join us in pursuing this issue further.

Synopsis

To delve further into the psychological nature of general intolerance we have investigated whether ethnic and racial discrimination on the one hand and discrimination on the basis of belief congruence on the other, are qualitatively different forms of prejudice, or whether the former is reducible to the latter. Studies were conducted with northerners and southerners and with two groups of Jewish children of different ages. The subjects were asked to rate their preferences for whites and Negroes, or for Jews and gentiles holding to various beliefs similar to or opposed to their own. The major finding in all samples was that discriminatory preferences are made primarily on the basis of belief congruence rather than on the basis of ethnic or racial congruence.

Notes

1. An important methodological point should be noted here. The score here is the difference between the two members of the pair, regardless of direction. There are no negative scores. The rule is: Subtract the smaller number from the larger, regardless of race or belief.

2. It is possible to obtain the various race and belief scores indirectly as well as directly—that is, from pairs not specifically set up for this purpose—for all members

of Type R pairs are repeated again in Type B and again in Type RB pairs, but in different permutations and combinations. Thus, a race difference score can be obtained directly from a given Type R pair and indirectly from the identical two members found in Type B or Type RB material. For example, if the reader will turn back to the Type R pairs shown on page 136 he will note that the race difference score is (a-b) plus (c-d). A second race difference score can be obtained indirectly from the Type B pairs; that is, (a-c) plus (b-d). And a third race difference score, obtained from Type RB pairs, is (a-d) plus (c-b). These three scores are really all race difference scores obtained from the same basic material because each single member of a pair is repeated three times in the three types, except that they are paired off differently.

In exactly the same way, the belief difference score can also be obtained directly from Type B pairs, or indirectly from Type R or Type RB pairs. And similarly for the various absolute scores, N (preference for Negroes who agree), n (disagree), W, and w. So if we want to find out, for example, how reliable the race difference score is, all we have to do is to compute two race difference scores for each person and then see how closely they correspond with each other. The results are shown in Table 7.10.

The fact that these reliabilities are relatively high suggests to us that in general we have essentially three sets of duplicative data from Type R, B, and RB pair-

Table 7.10

Reliability Coefficients for Difference Scores and Absolute Scores on Negro-White and General Beliefs

Correlating:	Group	Negro-White Beliefs	General Beliefs
A. DIFFERENCE SCORES			
$R_r{}^a$ and R_b	North	.81	.73
	South	.83	.81
B_b and B_r	North	.89	.86
	South	.87	.83
B. ABSOLUTE SCORES			
Nn_r and Nn_{rb}	North	.93	.93
	South	.93	.92
Ww_r and Ww_{rb}	North	.95	.91
	South	.88	.86
NW_b and NW_{rb}	North	.89	.92
	South	.85	.91
nw_b and nw_{rb}	North	.92	.94
	South	.94	.93

$N = 65$ in northern group; $N = 136$ in southern group.

[a] The subscript r means that the score was obtained from Type R pairs (race varied, belief constant); the subscript b means that the score was obtained from Type B pairs (belief varied, race constant); the subscript rb means that the score was obtained from Type RB pairs (race and belief varied).

ings. It suggests too that, in future research along similar lines, it will be possible to get essentially the same data obtained herein with only one-third of the material, and without presenting the members in pairs. Thus, had we known the outcome of the results on reliability in advance, we could have used only 16 instead of 48 pairs (32 instead of 96 members) to obtain all the data needed to test our major hypotheses.

3. To measure anti-Negro prejudice, we used the six Negro items shown on p. 142 of Adorno *et al.* (1950).

4. The full details on reliability are shown below in Table 7.11.

Table 7.11

Reliability Coefficients for Difference Scores and Absolute Scores on Jew-Gentile and General Beliefs

Correlating:	Group	Beliefs About Jews	General Beliefs
A. DIFFERENCE SCORES			
$E_e{}^a$ and E_b	7–11	.03	.21
	11–16	.66	.87
B_b and B_e	7–11	.71	.75
	11–16	.73	.78
B. ABSOLUTE SCORES			
Gg_e and Gg_{eb}	7–11	.65	.20
	11–16	.68	.75
Jj_e and Jj_{eb}	7–11	.46	.61
	11–16	.77	.88
JG_b and jg_{eb}	7–11	.51	.68
	11–16	.43	.51
jg_b and jg_{eb}	7–11	.67	.72
	11–16	.94	.83

N = 25 in each age group.

a Exactly the same notational system is used here as before with the exception that E (ethnic group) has been substituted for R (race). E_e is the ethnic difference score obtained from Type E pairs, wherein ethnic group is varied, belief held constant. E_b is the ethnic difference score obtained from Type B pairs wherein belief is varied, ethnic group held constant. B_b and B_e refer to belief difference scores, the former obtained from Type B, the latter from Type E pairs; G and J refer to absolute scores given to gentiles and Jews who agree with the subject, g and j to gentiles and Jews who disagree with the subject. The subscript *eb* refers to a score obtained from Type EB pairs, wherein both ethnic group and belief are varied.

Part Three

*Experimental Cosmology: Explorations
into the Relation Between Belief
and the Cognitive Processes*

In Part Two, we were primarily concerned with what
the theory of belief-disbelief systems has to say about
the nature of general authoritarianism and general intolerance. We now turn away from these issues to investigate the more purely cognitive workings of the
open and closed mind. To aid us in this undertaking,
we will have frequent occasion to compare extreme
high and extreme low scorers on the Dogmatism Scale
on various cognitive tasks put to them. Up to now, we
have restricted our use of the Dogmatism Scale to serve
solely as a measure of authoritarianism. From now on
we intend to use it more fully and literally for the purpose it was originally intended—as a measure of the extent to which a person's total belief system is open or
closed. For this reason, persons making extreme scores
on the Dogmatism Scale will henceforth be called
"closed" and "open" persons, rather than "high dogmatic" and "low dogmatic" persons. This should help us
to keep more clearly in mind what the Dogmatism
Scale is purporting to tap, and to evaluate whether it
can be meaningfully used to measure a variable as tre-
mendously complex as the open and closed mind. But,
far more important, we are not so much interested in

testing the validity of the Dogmatism Scale as in using it as a lever to help test the validity, and as a probative device to help extend the scope, of the theory of belief-disbelief systems.

8

The Doodlebug Problem
A Miniature Cosmology

Imagine a fictitious world wherein the rules of the game are in contradiction to those of our everyday world. Let these rules be organized into a system of beliefs which are highly interrelated with each other. Let the total number of such beliefs be relatively small so that we can keep track of them, and so that we will be able to introduce changes in them to suit our theoretical and experimental purposes. Our aim is to invent a miniature cosmology, a miniature belief system, that will be at odds with the one we employ in everyday life. Then let us set up various problems within the framework of such a miniature cosmology and give these problems to subjects under laboratory conditions, and let the solution of these problems hinge upon the subject's willingness or capacity to adopt such a new system as temporarily "true"; to pretend playfully, at least for the moment, that it is part of his everyday belief system.

The more closed a person's everyday system, the more difficulty he should encounter in solving problems within a new system. Or, to put it the other way around, the more difficulty a person has in switching over to a new system, the more closed must be the organization of his present system.

In a variety of experiments to be considered shortly, subjects are confronted with just such a hypothetical world. The hero is a little creature named Joe Doodlebug. Joe, the subjects are told, is a strange sort of bug. He can jump in only four directions: north, south, east, or west—not diagonally. Once he starts in any direction, he must jump four times in that direction before he can switch directions. He cannot crawl, fly, or walk—he can only jump; he can jump very large distances and very small distances. And he cannot turn around.

Joe's master, the subject is further told, places some food, larger in diameter than Joe, three feet directly west of him. Joe stops dead in his tracks, facing north. After surveying the situation, Joe concludes that he will have to jump four times to get to the food. We impress upon the subject that Joe is dead right in his conclusion. He must take four jumps, no more, no less. We then ask the subject to describe the circumstances Joe must have been in which led him to reach this conclusion. He is given anywhere from 30 to 45 minutes, in different experiments, to tell us why Joe reaches the conclusion he does. Like the detective in a murder story, the subject is confronted with the end result and is asked to reconstruct the circumstances that led up to it.*

Let us see if we can analyze the structural texture of this problem and what we hope to find out about the subjects as they struggle to solve it. There are three beliefs the subject must first overcome one by one, and three new beliefs which must replace the ones overcome. Then he must somehow integrate these new beliefs into the problem solution.

1. *The facing belief.* In everyday life we have to face the food we are about eat. But Joe does not have to face the food in order to eat it. He can land on top of it.

2. *The direction belief.* In everyday life we can change direction at will. But Joe is not able to do so because he is forever

* At this point, the reader may wish to pause long enough to see if he can solve the problem for himself.

trapped facing north. Thus, the only way Joe can change direction is by jumping sideways and backwards.

3. *The movement belief.* When we wish to change direction in everyday life there is nothing to stop us from doing so immediately. But Joe's freedom of movement is restricted by the fact that once he moves in a particular direction—north, south, east or west —he has to continue four times in this direction before he can change it. Thus, when Joe stops to survey the situation at the moment his master places the food down three feet west of him, he may or may not necessarily be a free agent. He may have stopped in the middle of a sequence of jumps rather than at the end of a sequence. Many subjects have difficulty because they assume that Joe is at the end rather than possibly in the middle of a sequence.

This problem is known as the Denny Doodlebug Problem, after M. Ray Denny who devised it in 1945. In its original form it was a mazelike sort of problem designed to test certain aspects of learning theory. It was modified from this form to its present "cosmological" form by Rokeach and Denny to permit the testing of a variety of hypotheses designed to throw light on the nature of open and closed cognitive functioning.

The Doodlebug Problem is quite difficult to solve. The solution is as follows: At the moment Joe's master placed the food down, Joe had already jumped once to the east. He therefore has to jump sideways three times more to the east, and once sideways back to the west, landing on top of the food. He can now eat. Simple as it may appear in retrospect, most subjects need help if they are to solve it within a 30- to 45-minute time limit. The reason it is so difficult to solve is that the subject must first overcome not one but three currently held beliefs, and replace them with three new ones. This is the *analytic* phase of the problem. But this is not all. Even if the subject overcomes and replaces all three beliefs with new ones, he still has work to do. He must then organize them together, or integrate them, into a new system. This is the *synthesizing* phase of the problem.* The two processes are depicted graphically in Figure 8.1.

---

* In typical research on thinking (Duncker, 1945; Luchins, 1942; Johnson, 1955; Maier, 1930), the obstacle to the problem solution is usually a single belief or set, the overcoming of which is equivalent to the solution. But real-life problems

PHASE 1: ANALYSIS   PHASE 2: SYNTHESIS

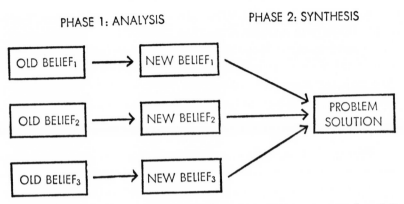

FIGURE 8.1. Graphic representation of two phases of mental activity in problem-solving. In the analysis phase the thinker's activity is directed toward the overcoming of old beliefs or sets and their replacement with new ones. Then in the synthesis phase the new beliefs must somehow be organized together by some process of integration into a new system. The end result is the solution of the problem.

A person may have difficulty in solving the problem because he is poor in analytic ability, in synthesizing ability, or in both. How can we tell objectively? To keep track, these thought processes must somehow be slowed down so that we will be in a more leisurely position to observe them. For this reason the Doodlebug Problem is deliberately made difficult, the subject is encouraged to think out loud, and his spontaneous remarks are recorded either by the experimenter or by tape recorder. For if the problem were too easy, the subject would solve it too soon and we would not be any the wiser as to how he arrived at the solution.

There is yet another important procedure that we typically employ in order to find out what goes on by way of mental activity. If the subject shows no analytic sign of having overcome any of the beliefs by himself at the end of a specified time (10 or 15 minutes in different experiments) he is given, in the form of a hint, the new *facing* belief; then five minutes later, the *direction* belief, and five minutes later yet the *movement* belief. This paves

---

are generally more complicated than this, typically involving the overcoming of multiple rather than single. beliefs, and involving further their integration into a new system. In other words, real-life problems typically involve both analysis and synthesis.

the way to isolate and to measure separately the two discrete stages of analysis and synthesis in problem-solving, as follows:

1. *Analysis.* How long does it take the thinker to overcome each of the individual beliefs? From his comments and questions during the course of the experiment it is relatively easy to tell. For example, a subject might say: "He can jump sideways, can't he?" or, "Does he have to face the food in order to eat it?" The first remark indicates that the subject has overcome by himself the *direction* belief, and the second remark, the *facing* belief. The examiner records the time during the experiment when such remarks are made, and this time represents a quantitative measure of how long it took him to overcome each of the individual beliefs by himself. Following this procedure we can obtain five separate measures of the thinker's ability to analyze:

    a. Time taken to overcome one belief.

    b. Time taken to overcome two beliefs.

    c. Time taken to overcome all three beliefs.

    d. Number of beliefs overcome without outside help by the time the first belief is given as a hint (5 or 10 minutes in different experiments).

    e. Number of beliefs overcome by the time the second belief is given as a hint (10 or 15 minutes in different experiments).

2. *Synthesis.* This refers to how fast the thinker can integrate new beliefs into a new belief system. It is reasonable to assume that when the thinker finally states correctly the solution to the problem, it is merely the end result of a prior process of synthesizing activity. Who is to say when this process begins? Clearly it does not begin at the moment the problem is first presented, but sometime afterwards. For there must first be *something* to synthesize—there must first be some "bricks" to start with—before the activity we call synthesizing can occur. Our problem then is to try to dissect out and to measure this process independently of the process of analysis. We have not been able to pinpoint precisely where in the problem-solving activity analysis ends and synthesis begins. Indeed, we regard it as likely that the two overlap each other. We will now describe, with the aid of Figure 8.2, how we went about isolating and measuring the synthesis phase independently of the analysis phase. If we know at what point in the experiment the subject has overcome the various beliefs (by him-

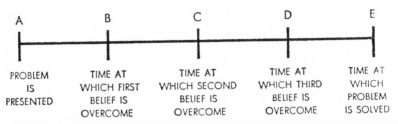

FIGURE 8.2. Graphic representation of how the analysis and synthesis phases of problem-solving are measured. Time *AB*, *AC*, and *AD* represent, respectively, time taken to overcome one belief, two beliefs, and all three beliefs. These measure the analysis phase. Time *BE*, *CE*, and *DE* represent, respectively, the time taken to solve the problem after the first belief is overcome, after the second belief is overcome, and after all three beliefs are overcome. These latter measure the synthesis phase of problem-solving.

self or with the experimenter's hints), and if we know the total time he takes to solve the problem, it is possible by simple subtraction to obtain the following three measures of synthesis:

a. Time taken to solve the problem after the first belief is overcome.

b. Time taken to solve the problem after the second belief is overcome.

c. Time taken to solve the problem after all three beliefs are overcome.

As we have said, it is difficult to say which of these measures of synthesis is the best one. So to play it safe we will use them all.

There are undoubtedly other things that go on during problem-solving in addition to the processes we have already discussed. One is memory. The integration of new beliefs into a new system can proceed smoothly only if the thinker can keep in mind simultaneously all the new beliefs to be synthesized. If there is any malfunctioning of memory, for whatever reason, it should slow down the synthesizing process. It would therefore be helpful to know what goes on in the person's memory processes during the experiment. But this would be hard to investigate directly, because it would require interrupting the subject while he is working. So the next best thing is to ask the subject to recall the new beliefs immediately after the experiment is over, or later. How many of the new beliefs can he remember? How much time does he take to recall each one? We will assume that the number of beliefs recalled and the latency of recall right after the experiment are at least rough measures of memory functioning during the experiment. Such recall measures, along with the analysis and synthesis measures already discussed, should prove very helpful in studying the relation between memory and thought in problem-solving, and how they determine the final outcome of problem-solving.

Thought and memory processes, however, are not the only determinants of problem-solving. There is also the basic emotional and motivational attitude of the thinker to be reckoned with. It is reasonable to suppose that a person who dislikes playing around with new ideas, a person who resists entertaining new modes of thought which shake his everyday modes, would typically approach new problems with resistance and defensiveness. This he may reflect by rejecting the problem, or the experimenter, or the experimental situation, which should show up in the spontaneous comments he makes as he continues to work on the problem. Another way to find out if this is indeed the case is to interrogate the subject at the end of the experiment. Did he enjoy working on the problem? Would he like to come back again to work on similar problems? and so on. We can then relate such emotional indices of acceptance-rejection to indices of memory functioning, analysis and synthesis, and to our personality measure of openness and closedness of belief systems. Considered all together, they should tell us a good deal about the general processes and dynamics of problem-solving, and more particularly whether these processes run their course differently in persons with open and closed belief systems.

Let us then probe more deeply into these processes by introducing our subjects to a number of variations in the world of Joe Doodlebug. Suppose we want to find out whether a person who has learned the rules governing Joe Doodlebug's behavior is able to transfer what he has learned in order to solve another similar problem. The subject is therefore asked, in one variation, to imagine that there is a canopy over the food. Now Joe cannot eat when he lands on top of it. He has to find some other way to get at the food. Joe has to jump off the canopy and, somehow, face the food in order to eat. What we have actually done in building the canopy is to manipulate the new facing belief so that it no longer applies. Now there are only two new beliefs to learn instead of three, and everything else remains the same. Joe again decides (correctly, the subject is told) that it will take him four jumps to reach the food. What must have been his circumstances at the time his master placed the food down that led him to make this decision? We will refer to this problem as the Canopy Problem, to distinguish it from the original problem, the No Canopy Problem. This time the solution is that Joe had already jumped once to the *west*. He must therefore take three more jumps to the west, landing on top of the canopy. He then jumps once backward off the canopy and is now in a position to eat.

Another variation will be known as the Impossible Problem. Its purpose is to help us study psychologically the process of defection from a system. Once again there is a canopy over the food. Once again Joe decides (correctly, the subject is told) that he must jump four times to get to the food. But he is also told that Joe had been jumping *east* when his master placed the food down. This introduces a basic contradiction into Joe's world. The problem is exactly like the Canopy Problem the subject had solved prior to the Impossible Problem. He remembers—and if he forgets, we remind him—that the correct solution to the Canopy Problem is that Joe had jumped once to the *west*. How, then, could Joe have been jumping east? To get to the food, Joe would have to change directions *twice*—from east to west, and from west to south. This will take at least five jumps, not four. The problem is then impossible to solve, and we credit the subject with a correct solution if he discovers that it is impossible to solve and can tell us why.

But despite our best attempts to design this problem so that it is impossible to solve, it turns out that there *is* a solution. A very few of our subjects creatively inform us that Joe's world is really round. This makes it possible for Joe to jump three more times to the east, thereby landing on top of the canopy. He then jumps once backwards to the south off the canopy. He is now in a position to eat. But the psychological significance of this ingenious solution will be discussed in Chapter 13.

Let us mention a final variation to be used, which will be called the Chessboard Problem. This is identical with the No Canopy Problem, except that it has been reformulated as a game to be played between two opposing players on a chessboard. Joe Doodlebug's stand-in is now a piece of wood painted red on one side, black on top, and black on the three remaining sides. It moves according to certain rules, which are of course identical with Joe's rules. Its job is to capture the opponent's piece. Our purpose in introducing this variation is to make the Doodlebug system psychologically more familiar to some—those who play chess—and psychologically new to others—those who do not play chess—without in any way affecting the internal structure of the problem. Exactly the same thought processes are involved, but now we can study the effects of past experience and basic attitude toward *newness* on the ability to synthesize new beliefs into new systems.

For yet other theoretical purposes, to be discussed in more detail at the appropriate time, we will introduce yet other variations in the experimental conditions under which the beliefs are presented. In one experiment, the new beliefs are presented on cards which, when kept in the visual field of the subject, eliminate his reliance on memory. When the cards are removed, the subject is thereby forced to rely on his memory. What difference will it make to the subject's ability to form new systems? In another experiment, the individual beliefs are sometimes presented all together at the beginning of the experiment and sometimes doled out one at a time in a temporally spaced fashion. What difference will *this* make? And what can it tell us about open and closed cognitive functioning in real life?

Let us take inventory now. We have described four variations of the Doodlebug Problem: the No Canopy Problem (Denny Doodlebug Problem), the Canopy Problem, the Impossible Problem, and the Chessboard Problem. We have described the various quanitative ways in which we propose to measure analysis and synthesis in thinking, memory, and basic emotional attitude toward these problems. And we have described several experimental conditions under which these problems will be presented to persons with relatively open and closed belief systems. With all these methods we hope to find out more about what goes on in open and closed minds.

Current psychological thought about the nature of cognition, which includes perception, thinking, and memory, is that it is essentially a very private affair. Its locus is inside the individual. With this view we would agree. But it is also our view that most of man's cognitive activity is also highly social in nature, dependent upon some external check against the cognitions or beliefs of others. Thinking inside the head often takes place within a social system that can affect processes inside the head.

One of the things that has impressed us greatly in the research with the Doodlebug Problems is the way in which the problem-solver stands in a position of dependence on the person who gives him the problem. As the subject thinks out loud, and at every step along the way, he is constantly looking to the experimenter for confirmation or disconfirmation of his hypotheses or beliefs. Throughout the course of the experiment, the subject is saying to the experimenter, sometimes explicitly but most of the time implicitly: "Am I right or wrong in assuming thus-and-so?" "Am I on the right track or not?" "Is this the correct solution?" The experimenter thus stands in a position of authority over the subject exploring the new cosmology. At every turn, the fate of his mental explorations is dependent upon what the experimenter chooses to confirm or disconfirm. If, after the subject states the correct solution, the experimenter were to say "That's right," activity ceases; if, on the other hand, the experimenter were to say maliciously "That's wrong" or "How stupid of you to give such a solution," activity continues. For there is no way for the subject to know for sure that he has arrived at the correct solution except to check with the "gatekeeper" to the new cosmology.

Generalizing somewhat from these observations, we suspect that most problem-solving activities of human beings are probably not solely intrapsychic in nature. We must also look to the social context, the social system within which intrapsychic activity takes place. We will have occasion again in the chapters that follow to point to the social character of problem-solving.

To summarize: we have set forth here a miniature cosmology, its content, its structural properties, its variations, and a series of measures that we propose to employ in studying quantitatively the problem-solving processes of persons scoring extremely low and extremely high on the Dogmatism Scale; that is, persons who may be characterized as having relatively open and relatively closed minds. Our general hypothesis is that the more closed a person's belief system, as measured by the Dogmatism Scale, the more resistance he will put up to forming new belief systems. The specific hypotheses, the further elaboration of theoretical notions, the modifications introduced into the world of Joe Doodlebug, and the details regarding subjects, procedure, and instructions will be considered more fully in the chapters that follow.

9

Dogmatic Thinking Versus Rigid Thinking

An Experimental Distinction

Milton Rokeach, Warren C. McGovney, and
M. Ray Denny

We first used the Doodlebug Problem to help us clarify a possible distinction used in everyday language between two kinds of thinking: dogmatic thinking and rigid thinking. At first glance they appear to refer to synonymous thought processes. At least, the two terms are often used interchangeably in everyday discourse. If so, the term dogmatic thinking is superfluous, and in the interest of economy, ought not to be introduced into psychological thinking, since the concept of rigidity has had a considerably longer history.[1] If, on the other

182

hand, dogmatic and rigid thinking are discriminably different psychological processes, then the burden of proof is squarely on us to demonstrate that this is indeed the case.

We have said that at first glance rigid and dogmatic thinking appear to be synonymous: they both refer to resistance to change. On second thought, however, we see a possibly legitimate distinction between them: the first refers to the resistance to change of *single* beliefs (or sets or habits), and the second refers to the resistance to change of *systems* of beliefs. For example, we ordinarily say that a person is performing a task rigidly, not dogmatically. The research literature contains references to studies showing that rats are under certain conditions rigid (also fixated), but hardly dogmatic, or closed in their belief system. Similarly, there are studies that show that the feeble-minded and the brain-injured are rigid (also compulsive, pedantic, perseverative, and inflexible) but, again, not dogmatic or closed. Conversely, in everyday life we speak of a dogmatic rather than a rigid theorist, or Marxist, or Freudian.

Thus, the referent of dogmatic thinking seems to be a total cognitive configuration of ideas and beliefs organized into a relatively closed system; rigidity, on the other hand, points to difficulties in overcoming single sets or beliefs encountered in attacking, solving, or learning specific tasks or problems. But how can we be sure that the distinction is a real one? In order to find out, let us first try to relate it to what was said in the last chapter on the ability to analyze and to synthesize. It seems to us that to the extent a person is said to be characteristically rigid, his analytic thinking should suffer. The source of his cognitive troubles should be traceable to the fact that he cannot break down or overcome beliefs when they are no longer appropriate, in order to replace them with more appropriate ones. Thus, rigid thinking should be expected to lead to difficulties in thinking analytically.

On the other hand, to the extent a person is said to be characteristically dogmatic or closed in his thinking, the preservation of his total system will be at stake rather than the preservation of a particular belief in his system. This should not lead to difficulties in analytic thinking; analysis by itself, if not followed up by synthesis, cannot topple a person's total belief system. Nor should synthesis in thinking topple it, so long as new beliefs can be readily integrated into the belief system. But what if a person in the course of solving a problem were to push his synthesizing or integrative thinking to the point where he begins to see the outlines of another system that threatens his present belief system? As he approaches this point, we should expect the synthesizing processes of thinking to slow down or be disrupted, to the extent that his belief system is dogmatic or closed.

We have already shown in Chapters 5 and 6 that the Dogmatism Scale can be thought of as a device to measure authoritarianism. Because the F Scale is also such a device, we have gone to considerable trouble to delineate the way in which the two are distinguishable from each other. We are now confronted with a similar problem. Is the Dogmatism Scale measuring the same kind of a cognitive variable as is being measured by scales purporting to measure rigidity? Our speculations suggest they are not. But how can we test this empirically? This is where the Doodlebug Problem comes in. Recall that with it we are able to measure the ability to analyze separately from the ability to synthesize. If the distinction we have drawn between rigid and dogmatic thinking is a valid one, then high rigidity should lead to difficulties in the analytic phase of thinking, and high dogmatism (or, what amounts to the same thing, closed systems) should lead to difficulties in the synthesizing phase of thinking.

To test these deductions experimentally we will need a measure of rigidity as well as of openness-closedness. Let us therefore examine a rigidity scale that has been widely used—one constructed by Gough and Sanford (1952)*—to see if the items in it actually reflect rigidity as we have described it. We select for inspection the following more or less typical items from this scale, to each of which the subject can respond by agreeing or disagreeing:

> "I always put on and take off my clothes in the same order."
> "I never miss going to church."
> "I usually check more than once to be sure that I have locked a door, put out a light, or something of the sort."
> "I often find myself thinking of the same tunes or phrases for days at a time."

* The full scale is reproduced in Appendix C.

184

"I prefer to stop and think before I act even on trifling matters."

The impression we get from looking at these statements is that they are in line with our analysis of the nature of rigid thinking. The referents seem to be specific tasks or habits rather than total belief systems.

These considerations set the stage for the experiment to be reported here. Let us now set forth quite explicitly the hypotheses to be tested.

A. Concerning analysis:
  1. Persons high in rigidity should have greater difficulty in the analytic phase of problem-solving than persons low in rigidity,
  2. but persons open and closed in their belief systems, as measured by the Dogmatism Scale, should not differ from each other in this respect.

B. Concerning synthesis:
  1. Persons with closed systems should have a greater difficulty in the synthesizing phase of problem-solving than persons with open systems,
  2. but persons high and low in rigidity should not differ from each other in this respect.

Subjects and Procedure

One hundred and nine students enrolled in introductory psychology at Michigan State University were given a battery of Likert-type personality tests among which were included Form C of the Dogmatism Scale and the 22-item Gough-Sanford Rigidity Scale. Three degrees of agreement and three degrees of disagreement were employed in responding to the individual items.

From among these 109 subjects, 60 were selected for individual experimentation with the Denny Doodlebug Problem.[2] These 60 subjects were selected from the larger group in such a way that 15 scored relatively high on both the Rigidity and Dogmatism Scales, and 15 scored relatively low on both scales; another 15 subjects scored high on the Rigidity Scale and low on the Dogmatism Scale, and the remaining 15 scored the other way around. Thus, the sample consisted of a total of 30 subjects high and 30 low in rigidity who were equated for openness-closedness, and at the same time it consisted of a total of 30 open subjects and 30 closed subjects, equated for rigidity. The setup can perhaps be more immediately grasped with the help of the following:

	Open Group	Closed Group	Total
Rigid group	15	15	30
Nonrigid group	15	15	30
TOTALS	30	30	60

The interview took approximately 45 minutes. To prevent bias, the experimenter did not look at the subjects' scores on the personality tests until afterwards.

The examiner begins the experiment with the following comments: "Today you are going to be given a newly devised test of general intelligence. The problem is not a simple one but the solution can be reached by good logical analysis. Here is the problem. Read it over carefully." (Hands subject a mimeographed sheet).

The Conditions

Joe Doodlebug is a strange sort of imaginary bug. He can and cannot do the following things:
1. He can jump in only four different directions, north, south, east, and west. He cannot jump diagonally (e.g., southeast, northwest, etc.).
2. Once he starts in any direction, that is, north, south, east, or west, he must jump four times in that same direction before he can switch to another direction.
3. He can only jump, not crawl, fly, or walk.
4. He can jump very large distances or very small distances, but not less than one inch per jump.
5. Joe cannot turn around.

The Situation

Joe has been jumping all over the place getting some exercise when his master places a pile of food three feet directly west of him. Joe notices that the pile of food is a little larger than he. As soon as Joe sees all this food he stops dead in his tracks facing north. After all his exercise Joe is very hungry and wants to get the food as quickly as he possibly can. Joe examines the situation and then says, "Darn it, I'll have to jump four times to get the food."

The Problem

Joe Doodlebug was a smart bug and he was dead right in his conclusion. Why do you suppose Joe Doodlebug had to take four jumps, no more and no less, to reach the food?

After the subject has read the problem, the examiner continues: "I'd like to ask you to think out loud as you work the problem so I can let you know whether you are correct or not. You may ask questions as you go along and you may refer to the problem at any time. You may use the scratch paper in any way you wish. Now let's read the problem over together."

The total time allowed is 30 minutes. For the first 15 minutes the subject works continuously regardless of whether he overcomes any of the three beliefs by himself. If he overcomes any belief by himself, the time taken to do so is recorded. At the end of 15 minutes the experimenter asks: "Have you figured it out yet?"

If the problem is not yet solved, the examiner gives hints at the end of 15, 20, and 25 minutes designed to overcome each of the three beliefs. Which hint is given depends upon which belief the subject had previously overcome by himself. But in general the *facing* belief is given first, the *direction* belief second, and the *movement* belief third. Whether or not a solution is reached, the session is terminated 30 minutes after the problem is given to the subject.

In the event that the subject overcomes one belief on his own within the first 15 minutes, he is given the second hint at the end of 15 minutes and the third hint at the end of 20 minutes. In the case where the subject overcomes two beliefs within the first 15 minutes by himself, he is given the third hint at the end of 15 minutes. This procedure is followed for all the subjects without exception.

The hints are give as needed and as follows:

1. *The facing belief.* "I'm going to give you a hint: Joe does not have to face the food in order to eat it. [Repeat hint.] OK, I'll give you five minutes more."

2. *The direction belief.* "I'll give you another hint: Joe can jump sideways and backwards as well as forwards. [Repeat hint.] I'll give you five minutes more."

3. *The movement belief.* "Let's read the problem again. [The experimenter and subject reread the problem.] Now here is the last hint: Joe was moving east when the food was presented. [Repeat hint.] You have five more minutes."

At the end of the formal session the subject is given an opportunity to comment freely on his reactions to the experiment. At this time too the subject is told the correct solution if he does not already know it, is disabused of the idea that the problem is a test of intelligence, and is asked not to discuss the experiment with others.

Results

Let us first consider the data with respect to analysis or ease of overcoming the individual beliefs. In Table 9.1 is shown the mean time, in minutes, taken by the rigid and nonrigid groups, and by the closed and open groups to overcome the first belief, the first two beliefs, and all three beliefs. It is seen that the closed and open groups do not differ from each other in analytic thinking. They overcome the individual beliefs at about the same time. But the rigid group usually takes longer to analyze than the nonrigid group. This is particularly evident on the mean time taken to overcome the first belief. Unfortunately, however, it is ex-

Table 9.1

Ability to Analyze: Comparison Between Rigid and Nonrigid Groups and Between Closed and Open Groups on Mean Number of Minutes Taken to Overcome the First Belief, the First Two Beliefs, and All Three Beliefs

Group	First Belief	First Two Beliefs	All Three Beliefs
Rigid	8.6	15.9	19.8
Nonrigid	5.9	14.4	18.4
Closed	7.4	14.9	19.2
Open	7.0	15.3	19.0

N = 30 in each group.

tremely difficult to evaluate the statistical significance of these results because certain statistical assumptions that are prerequisite to such tests are not met; the distributions of scores are extremely skewed and there are a large number of tied scores because many subjects did not overcome the beliefs by themselves. For this reason we used another set of measures to circumvent these statistical difficulties: The number of beliefs overcome by the subject within the first 10 minutes of the experiment, and the number of beliefs overcome by him within the first 15 minutes. These results are shown in Table 9.2.

Table 9.2

Ability to Analyze: Number of Beliefs Overcome Within the First 10 Minutes and Within the First 15 Minutes by Rigid and Nonrigid Groups and by Closed and Open Groups

	Beliefs Overcome				
	0	1	2	3	p
I. NUMBER OF BELIEFS OVERCOME WITHIN FIRST 10 MINUTES					
Rigid	13	17	0	0	
Nonrigid	5	20	3	2	.05
Closed	10	17	3	0	
Open	8	20	0	2	N.S.
II. NUMBER OF BELIEFS OVERCOME WITHIN FIRST 15 MINUTES					
Rigid	10	17	2	1	
Nonrigid	5	16	4	5	.05
Closed	7	17	4	2	
Open	8	16	2	4	N.S.

N = 30 in each group.

Looking first at the results for the rigid and nonrigid groups, the table may be read as follows: 13 out of 30 in the rigid group, as compared with only 5 out of 30 in the nonrigid group, did not overcome any beliefs by themselves at the end of 10 minutes. And not a single one of the rigid subjects, as compared with 5 of the nonrigid subjects, overcame 2 or 3 beliefs by themselves in the first 10 minutes of the experiment. These two groups differ significantly [3] in speed of analysis, as measured at the end of 10 minutes, and they also differ significantly at the end of 15 minutes.* But looking at the closed and open groups, we see that they do not differ from each other on these analysis measures.

These results, then, are as theoretically predicted. High and low scorers on rigidity differ significantly from each other in analytic thinking, but high and low scorers on the Dogmatism Scale do not.

Consider now the data on synthesis in thinking. Recall that there are three measures available in this connection—time taken to solve the problem after the first, second, and third beliefs are overcome. We should expect to find that the closed group will take longer to synthesize the new beliefs than the open group (Hypothesis B1), but that the rigid and nonrigid groups will not differ in this respect (Hypothesis B2).

As can be seen in Table 9.3, the mean time taken to solve the problem after the first belief was overcome is not significantly different[4] for either set of groups. But the closed group takes about a minute longer to synthesize than the open group. The comparable differences between rigid and nonrigid groups is in the wrong direction.

However, on the second measure the closed group takes significantly longer than the open group. This is not so for rigid and nonrigid groups, whose mean scores are about the same. On the third measure (time taken to solve after the third belief was overcome) there are again no significant differences. But there is over a minute difference between closed and open groups, while there is a difference of about half a minute between rigid and nonrigid groups.

Before going on any further in the interpretation of these findings it would help to know to what extent they can be accounted for by differences in intelligence between the groups. A rough measure of intelligence was available for most of the subjects— the American Council on Education Test. Correlations found between intelligence and scores on the Dogmatism Scale are —.02, and the correlations are generally small between intelligence and rigidity, and between intelligence and ability to solve the

---

* It will be recalled that the first hint was given at the end of 15 minutes. The two measures being discussed, then, represent the number of beliefs overcome by the subject himself before any hint was given by the experimenter.

Table 9.3

Ability to Synthesize: Time Taken to Solve the Doodlebug Problem after the First, Second, and Third Beliefs Were Overcome by Rigid and Nonrigid Groups and by Closed and Open Groups

Group	Mean	S.D.	p
I. NUMBER OF MINUTES TAKEN TO SOLVE PROBLEM AFTER FIRST BELIEF OVERCOME			
Rigid	14.5	5.5	
Nonrigid	15.1	5.6	N.S.
Closed	15.2	5.7	
Open	14.4	5.4	N.S.
II. NUMBER OF MINUTES TAKEN TO SOLVE PROBLEM AFTER SECOND BELIEF OVERCOME			
Rigid	7.2	4.1	
Nonrigid	6.6	4.0	N.S.
Closed	7.7	4.4	
Open	6.1	3.6	.05
III. NUMBER OF MINUTES TAKEN TO SOLVE PROBLEM AFTER THIRD BELIEF OVERCOME			
Rigid	3.2	3.6	
Nonrigid	2.6	2.8	N.S.
Closed	3.4	3.4	
Open	2.4	2.9	N.S.

N = 30 in each group.

Doodlebug Problem.[5] On the whole, then, it can be safely concluded that the findings in the present experiment cannot be accounted for by differences in intelligence.

Additional Findings and Interpretations

Looking at the results as a whole we get the impression that they come out partially, but not wholly, as expected. With respect to analytic thinking, the rigid group performs significantly more poorly than the nonrigid group, but the closed and open subjects do not differ from each other. With respect to synthesizing, it is the other way around, as expected, but only on one of the three synthesis measures. Thus, these data are not conclusive. We do not know why the second measure of synthesis (time taken to solve after the first two beliefs had been overcome) significantly differentiates closed from open subjects, while the other two measures do not. In the chapters that follow we will see that in general all three measures of synthesis consistently and significantly differentiate between closed and open groups. Our guess is that the present results do not turn out to be consistently significant because the extreme Dogmatism Scale groups are not extreme enough (60 extreme subjects picked from a pool of 109) to bring out the cognitive differences between them.

But the significant differences that are found fall neatly in line with the theoretical distinction drawn between rigid and dogmatic thinking. These are bolstered by certain additional qualitative findings. As has already been indicated, the Dogmatism Scale purports to measure not only closed systems of thinking and believing but also the rejection of ideas and people perceived to threaten such closed systems. The following are some examples of spontaneous comments made by the subjects during the course of the experiment which are indicative of such dogmatic rejections:

"Stupid bug! He could get there in one jump."
"Let him starve to death!"
"There is probably a catch here."
"What if you don't agree with it?"
"That's crazy!"
"That's irrelevant."

From the hundreds of comments made by the subjects we were able to cull a total of 50 statements, such as those cited above, which we judged to be indicative of rejection. These statements were selected "blindly" by two judges, that is, without knowing the identification of the subject. The question we then asked was whether these comments were made equally often by the four groups under consideration.

Apparently not. Thirty-three of the 50 dogmatic statements were found to come from the closed group, as compared with only 17 which came from the open group. This difference is significant.[6] In contrast, the rigid and nonrigid groups do not differ

192

significantly in this respect. Twenty-six of the statements were found to come from the former and 24 from the latter group.

The theoretical import of these results considered together with the main results of the study are seen to be as follows:

1. Dogmatic or closed thinking, and its operational measurement by means of the Dogmatism Scale, can now with some empirical backing be said to refer to the resistance to change of *total belief systems*. This is evidenced by the greater difficulty shown by the closed subjects in synthesizing or integrating beliefs into a new system which contradicts their everyday system. It is also evidenced by the finding that closed and open subjects do not differ from each other with respect to analysis, or the breaking down of individual beliefs.

2. The findings lend empirical support to the theoretical distinction drawn between dogmatic and rigid thinking. As has been shown, high and low scorers on rigidity differ on measures of analysis but not of synthesis.

3. Finally, the findings suggest that information about personality organization can reliably predict the outcome of different phases of thinking in problem-solving. This is indicated by the fact that differential responses to the Denny Doodlebug Problem can be systematically related to differential responses to the two personality scales employed in this study.

All the conclusions above imply that dogmatic and rigid thinking are *discriminable* processes, but this does not mean that they are necessarily *independent* processes. In fact, in the various groups we have studied the correlations found between the Dogmatism and Rigidity Scales range from .37 to .55; and the correlation in this study between analysis and synthesis of thinking is around .45, suggesting that rigidity and dogmatism in the personality, and the ability to analyze and the ability to synthesize, tend to go together. Nevertheless, the present data point to the fact that they are discriminably different psychological processes. This conclusion is further supported by the results of two factor analyses,* one by Rokeach and Fruchter (1956d), the other by

---

* *Note to the general reader:* Factor analysis is a statistical method for ascertaining the least number of independent psychological dimensions or variables needed to describe or to account for all the correlations of each test with every other in a given battery of tests.

Fruchter, Rokeach, and Novak (1958). Both studies indicate that the Dogmatism and Rigidity Scales are measuring essentially independent psychological dimensions.

But we are not content to let the matter rest here. As we have already stated, the differences between open and closed persons in their ability to form new systems are clearly suggestive but not conclusive. We therefore propose to look again at the issue in the next chapter, and at the same time try to probe more deeply into the heart of the synthesizing process, which seems to be so essential to the formation of new belief systems. This will lead us to study the memory processes and the ability to entertain new beliefs as well as the processes of analysis and synthesis in thinking.

Synopsis

We have here tried to distinguish experimentally between two kinds of thinking, dogmatic and rigid, and also to study the relation between personality and problem-solving.

One hundred and nine subjects were given the Dogmatism Scale and the Gough-Sanford Rigidity Scale. From this pool we selected 60 subjects so that 30 were closed and 30 were open, as measured by the Dogmatism Scale; in addition, 30 were high in rigidity and 30 were low. These subjects were then tested with the Denny Doodlebug Problem. If the distinction made between rigid and dogmatic thinking is valid, then high and low rigid individuals should differ primarily in their ability to think *analytically,* and closed and open individuals should differ primarily in their ability to think *synthetically.*

Those differences that turned out to be statistically significant clearly support the distinction drawn between dogmatic and rigid thinking. But the results on differences in synthesis between closed and open subjects were not consistently conclusive. We will therefore pursue this matter further in the next chapter and at the same time try to gain a deeper understanding of the nature of integrative thinking as a prerequisite to the formation of new belief systems.

Notes

1. See, for example, the discussions on rigidity by Cattell (1949), Kounin (1948), Levitt (1956), Luchins (1949), and Werner (1946).

2. Of these, 58 showed up. Two additional subjects were selected from the larger pool to complete the sample of 60.

3. All tests in this research are one-tailed since direction of differences are predicted in advance. Significance of difference in Table 9.2 was determined by chi-square. To eliminate theoretical frequencies smaller than 5 the data for one, two, and three beliefs have been combined on measure I (Yates' correction applied). The chi-square for the high vs. low rigid groups is 3.89 with one degree of freedom. For the same reason, the data for two and three beliefs have been combined on measure II. The significant chi-square is 4.70, with two degrees of freedom. The significance levels reported may err slightly on the conservative side in view of the continuous nature of the measures employed.

4. The first measure (number of minutes taken to solve the problem after the first is overcome) is normally distributed, but the remaining two are clearly positively skewed Pearson Type III distributions. Accordingly, in the latter two cases Festinger's F Test (1943) was used to test for statistical significance.

5. The ACE scores are standard scores. They were available for 61 out of the original 109 subjects and for 46 of the 60 subjects tested individually with the Doodlebug Problem. The product-moment correlations that were found are shown in Table 9.4.

Table 9.4

Correlations Between ACE and Other Variables

Variable	N	r
Dogmatism Scale	61	—.02
Rigidity Scale	61	—.31[a]
Number of beliefs overcome in first 15 minutes	46	+.19
Time taken to solve problem after 2nd belief was overcome	46	—.25
Total time taken to solve the problem	46	—.36[a]

[a] Significant at .05 level.

6. The chi-square is 4.50, which is significant at the .05 level. Since the judges did not know where the statements came from or whether two or more of these statements came (or did not come) from a particular subject, the judgments are independent. The sample is not from a universe of subjects but from a universe of statements. Hence, the assumption of independence of observations is met and the chi-square test, which assumes such independence, is considered to be appropriate.

10

The Formation of New Belief Systems

The Roles of Memory and the Capacity to Entertain

Milton Rokeach and Robert N. Vidulich

We have seen in the preceding chapter that closed persons betray more difficulty than open persons in synthesizing or integrating new beliefs into a new system. This suggests that different things are happening psychologically in the thought processes of the two groups. Our purpose now is to try to dig deeper into the nature of these processes in order to gain more insight into the workings of the open and closed mind.

We have also seen in the last chapter that closed persons reject the experimental situation more than do open persons. The former do not like to become involved in situations that necessitate new systems of thought. Their rejecting comments, considered alongside their poorer performances in synthesizing, suggest that even though they can overcome one or more of the individual beliefs by themselves, they have no intention of "going all the way" to organize such beliefs into a new belief system. Moreover, we have observed that some of our closed subjects want to change the Doodlebug Problem, as if to solve it on their own terms rather than on the experimenter's. For example, one subject said: "I don't believe Joe has to take four jumps. I think he can do it in one!"

Wanting to change a problem or rejecting it hardly seems conducive to the formation of a new belief system. If new beliefs are not really accepted, then they will not be remembered, and if they are not remembered there is nothing to synthesize or integrate. If your source of supply (the memory apparatus) is not able to deliver the bricks (beliefs), your mortar (your ability to synthesize) will do you no good and the new building (the new belief system) will not get built. Is this a reasonable model of what happens frequently in the cognitive processes of those with closed systems? If so, we should expect to find that those with relatively closed systems as compared to those with relatively open systems should: reject the problem situation more completely ⟶ display a poorer memory for the new beliefs ⟶ take longer to synthesize ⟶ take longer to solve the Doodlebug Problem. Furthermore, if the synthesizing thought process is indeed dependent upon memory, then making the new beliefs available in the person's visual field so that memory is by-passed, should clearly facilitate the synthesis of new beliefs into a new system. If the person is forced to pay attention to new beliefs, whether he wants to or not, and if he does not have to rely on his memory, there will at least exist some beliefs to start with and this should increase the chances that his synthesizing powers will be brought into play to the end of forming new systems.

Above is our conception of what may be happening, at least in part, in the course of problem-solving by closed and open persons. We will now describe how these deductions were tested. As before, the task is the Denny Doodlebug Problem. The three new beliefs (the facing, direction, and movement beliefs) are typed on separate cards. As the subject discovers one or more of these by himself the appropriate card is placed before him. If the subject fails to discover the new beliefs for himself, the cards containing the beliefs are placed before him at specified time intervals in the form of hints. The experimental group, composed equally of closed and open subgroups, is allowed to keep the belief cards in front of them throughout the experiment. We will call this the "visual field" condition. The control group, also composed equally of closed and open subgroups, is also shown the belief cards in the same way. But each card is taken away immediately after its contents are read. We will call this the "memory field" condition. The psychological difference between the two conditions is that in the latter case the subject is required to rely on memory and in the former case reliance on memory is less necessary because the beliefs are present in the visual field. As before, the subject is encouraged to think out loud, his spontaneous comments are recorded, hints are given at specified time intervals, and the time taken to complete the two problem-solving phases is recorded. Shortly after the end of the experiment and also one week later, the subject is asked to recall the three new beliefs and the recall time is measured. The subject is also asked to answer several questions designed to find out to what extent he "accepted" the new world of Joe Doodlebug.

In this way the effects of both personality and situational variables are studied within the confines of a single experiment. Both sets of variables (closed vs. open, visual field vs. memory field condition) address themselves fundamentally to the same issue; namely, what are some of the conditions that may facilitate and hinder the synthesizing process and, with this, the formation of new belief systems?

In order for the reader to keep more clearly in his "visual field" all the theoretical considerations discussed above, let us set them forth below in the form of specific hypotheses:

A. Concerning the total time taken to solve the problem, which involves both analysis and synthesis in thinking:

    1. The open group should solve the problem faster than the closed group,

2. and the visual group should solve the problem faster than the memory group.

B. Concerning analysis:
  1. Open and closed groups should not differ in this respect,
  2. nor should visual and memory groups differ in this respect because analytic thinking precedes the establishment of the "keep card" and "remove card" conditions.

C. Concerning synthesis:
  1. The open group should be faster than the closed group,
  2. and the visual group should be faster than the memory group.

D. Concerning the incidental recall of new beliefs at the end of the experiment:
  1. The open group should be superior to the closed group,
  2. and the visual group should be superior to the memory group.

E. Concerning the acceptance-rejection of the experimental situation:
  1. The open group should accept the experimental situation more than the closed group,
  2. and the visual group should accept the experimental situation more than the memory group.

Subjects and Procedure

From a group of 249 Sophomores, we selected for individual testing the 30 subjects scoring highest and the 30 subjects scoring lowest on the Dogmatism Scale, Form E.[1] Fifteen closed and 15 open subjects were randomly assigned to the visual field condition; the other 15 closed and 15 open subjects were assigned to the memory field condition. These assignments were made by someone other than the experimenter so that the latter did not know the dogmatism score of the subject while conducting the examination.

The subjects were told that they had been selected randomly and were asked to appear for individual experimentation. The instructions employed in the individual sessions were identical with those employed in the previous study, as described in Chapter 9. But certain modifications were made in procedure. Instead of a 30-minute time limit, the total time to solve the problem was extended to 40 minutes. Instead of the first, second, and third hints being given at the end of 15, 20, and 25 minutes, respectively, the hints were given at the end of 10, 15, and 20 minutes.

The hints were presented to the subject typed on 3″ × 5″ cards. Under the visual field condition, the subject was allowed to keep the cards before him throughout the experiment. Under the memory field condition, the subject was allowed to read the hints for about ten seconds, and they were then removed.

The hints were given as needed and as follows:

1. *The facing belief:* "I'm going to give you a hint. It's on this card." [On card: "Joe does not have to face the food in order to eat it."] "OK, I'll give you five minutes more."

2. *The direction belief:* "I'm going to give you another hint." [On card: "Joe can jump sideways and backwards as well as forwards."] "I'll give you five minutes more."

3. *The movement belief:* "Here is one more hint." [On card: "Joe was moving east when the food was presented."] "You have five more minutes."

After the subject had solved the problem, or at the end of 40 minutes, the subject was told the solution to the problem if he had not solved it and was asked to read magazines "for a few minutes while I work on something." After 10 minutes, the experimenter said:

Now I would like you to tell me what the three hints were that I gave you, or that you figured out by yourself, while you were trying to solve the problem. You have three minutes. Go ahead.

As soon as the subject had recalled the beliefs, or at the end of three minutes if he had not recalled all of them, the experimenter asked the subject to fill out a short five-item questionnaire designed to test the subject's acceptance or rejection of the problem situation. This questionnaire, with instructions, is given here:

Below are five questions which we would like you to answer. Indicate how you feel by circling the number which best reflects your true feelings. 1 means that you disagree very strongly; 2 means you disagree somewhat; 3 means you have no feelings one way or the other; 4 means you agree somewhat; 5 means you agree very strongly.

[The five questions to which responses were requested are:]
1. Do you think the hints helped you to solve the problem?
2. Do you feel that you understood the hints?
3. Did you enjoy the problem?
4. Did you get angry with me or with the problem during the experiment?
5. Did you think that this experiment was worth your time and effort?

The questionnaire was scored by giving the same number of points for each question as to the number circled ($1 = 1$ point, $2 = 2$ points, etc.), with the exception of question number 4, for which the scoring was reversed. Thus, the lowest possible score on the questionnaire was 5 (extreme rejection), while the highest possible score was 25 (extreme acceptance).

Following the questionnaire, the subject was asked to return for "a very few minutes" in seven days for "another part of the experiment." He was also requested not to discuss the problem with others. When the subject returned in seven days, he was again asked to recall the three hints within a three-minute time limit.

Results

Table 10.1 shows the results [2] on total time taken to solve the Doodlebug Problem. It is seen that the closed group takes significantly longer to solve the problem than the open group. The former takes a mean time of about 24 minutes while the latter takes about 17 minutes. Similar significant differences are also found separately between the closed and open subgroups solving the problem under the memory condition, and under the visual condition.

As for the differences between the memory and the visual conditions, it is seen that the memory group takes longer to solve the problem than the visual group. Likewise, the differences between

Table 10.1

Total Time Taken to Solve the Denny Doodlebug Problem

Group	Number	Mean Time	p
Closed	30	24.0	
Open	30	17.2	.01
Closed-memory	15	25.7	
Open-memory	15	18.1	.02
Closed-visual	15	22.4	
Open-visual	15	16.2	.03
Memory field	30	21.9	
Visual field	30	19.3	.15
Memory-closed	15	25.7	
Visual-closed	15	22.4	.22
Memory-open	15	18.1	
Visual-open	15	16.2	.22

Table 10.2

Analysis: Mean Time Taken to Overcome the First Belief,
the First Two Beliefs, and All Three Beliefs

Group	Number	First Belief	First Two Beliefs	All Three Beliefs
Closed	30	4.9	9.8	14.6
Open	30	4.3	8.8	13.6
Closed-memory	15	3.8	9.7	14.3
Open-memory	15	3.9	9.1	14.0
Closed-visual	15	6.0	9.9	14.9
Open-visual	15	4.7	8.4	13.3
Memory field	30	3.9	9.4	14.2
Visual field	30	5.4	9.2	14.1
Memory-closed	15	3.8	9.7	14.3
Visual-closed	15	6.0	9.9	14.9
Memory-open	15	3.9	9.1	14.0
Visual-open	15	4.7	8.4	13.3

memory and visual conditions show up in a consistent fashion for the two open subgroups considered separately. However, although all these differences are in the expected direction they do not reach the usual standard of significance (5 per cent).

What about the thought processes preceding these end results? How do the various groups do on analysis and synthesis? Concerning analysis, recall that we do not expect any differences between open and closed groups (Hypothesis B1), or between the two experimental conditions (Hypothesis B2). If there are any differences between these groups it should turn up in the synthesis rather than in the analysis measures. In Table 10.2 is shown the mean time taken by the several groups and subgroups to overcome one belief, two beliefs, and all three beliefs. The results are all seen to be very similar for the two personality groups and for the two experimental conditions under consideration. However, as was the case with the Doodlebug study reported in the last chapter, it was not possible to ascertain the significance level of these results, primarily because of the large number of ties in scores resulting from failure to overcome the individual beliefs in the specified time. We therefore present in Table 10.3, as we did before in Chapter 9, another measure of analysis which can be tested for statistical significance: the number of beliefs overcome within the first five minutes, and the number of beliefs overcome within the first 10 minutes.[3]

It is clear from Table 10.3 as well as from Table 10.2 that the closed and open groups on the one hand, and the memory and visual groups on the other, do not differ from each other in analytic thinking. Not one of the differences is found to be significant. These results substantiate fully those reported in the last chapter, which also show no differences in analysis between closed and open groups.

This being the case, let us now consider how the several groups behave with respect to synthesis or integration of the new beliefs into a new system. These data are given in Table 10.4. Here we see that on all measures—times taken to solve the problem after one, two, and after three beliefs had been overcome—the closed group takes longer than the open group. The same is true for the closed and open subgroups under memory and under visual conditions, considered separately. All differences without exception

Table 10.3

Analysis: Number of Beliefs Overcome Within the First Five Minutes and Within the First Ten Minutes

Group	Beliefs Overcome				p
	0	1	2	3	
I. NUMBER OF BELIEFS OVERCOME WITHIN FIRST 5 MINUTES					
Closed	12	15	3	0	N.S.
Open	12	12	5	1	
Memory field	9	18	3	0	N.S.
Visual field	15	9	5	1	
II. NUMBER OF BELIEFS OVERCOME WITHIN FIRST 10 MINUTES					
Closed	7	16	6	1	N.S.
Open	4	17	8	1	
Memory field	3	19	8	0	N.S.
Visual field	8	14	6	2	

Table 10.4

Synthesis: Mean Time Taken to Solve the Doodlebug Problem After the First, Second, and Third Beliefs Had Been Overcome

Group	Number	After First Belief		After Second Belief		After Third Belief	
		Mean Time	p	Mean Time	p	Mean Time	p
Closed	30	19.1	.01	14.3	.01	9.4	.01
Open	30	12.9		8.4		3.6	
Closed-memory	15	21.9	.01	16.0	.03	11.3	.01
Open-memory	15	14.2		9.0		4.2	
Closed-visual	15	16.4	.04	12.5	.01	7.5	.03
Open-visual	15	11.5		7.8		2.9	
Memory field	30	18.0	.03	12.5	.26	7.8	.09
Visual field	30	14.0		10.2		5.2	
Memory-closed	15	21.9	.05	16.0	.25	11.3	.15
Visual-closed	15	16.4		12.5		7.5	
Memory-open	15	14.2	.07	9.0	.29	4.2	.15
Visual-open	15	11.5		7.8		2.9	

are statistically significant. These results are thus considerably more clear-cut than the comparable results presented in the preceding chapter, because the subjects in the present study are more extremely open and closed, since they are selected from a larger pool of subjects (60 extreme scorers selected from a pool of 249 subjects). Both sets of results support the hypothesis that persons with relatively closed systems, as measured by the Dogmatism Scale, differ from those with relatively open systems with respect to their capacity to integrate new beliefs into new systems.

What effect does the experimental variable have on the synthesis of new systems? Two points are noted in Table 10.4: (1) The visual group requires less time than the memory group to integrate the new beliefs into a new system. This is true for the total groups and it is also true for subgroups composed only of closed subjects and subgroups composed only of open subjects. Without exception, the time to synthesize or integrate is less for those allowed to keep the belief cards in view than for those not allowed to do so. The differences are statistically significant, or nearly so, for the first measure (time taken to solve the problem after the first belief is overcome) but do not reach significance for the remaining two measures. (2) The differences found between the experimental groups are, however, consistently of a lesser order of magnitude than those found for the personality variable under consideration.

The data considered thus far have to do with the thought processes involved in the solution of the Doodlebug Problem. These results are in close accord with the theoretical expectations regarding total time to solve (Hypotheses A1 and A2), analysis (Hypotheses B1 and B2), and synthesis (Hypotheses C1 and C2). These results tell us that the faster solutions of the total problem by the open as compared with the closed group, and by the visual as compared with the memory group, are definitely not a function of analysis or speed of overcoming the individual beliefs. They are clearly seen to be a function of a superior facility to integrate by the open group as compared with the closed group, and by the visual group as compared with the memory group.

Why do the differences in synthesis emerge as they do? Hypothesis D1 is concerned with this question. It states that persons with relatively open systems can form new systems more easily than persons with relatively closed system because they are somehow better able to remember the separate elements that are to be integrated into the new system; Hypothesis D2 states that subjects under the experimental condition in which they are allowed to keep the beliefs in view will form new systems more easily than subjects not allowed to do so because in the former group there is less dependence on memory.

Ten minutes after the end of the experiment and also a week afterwards the subjects were tested for incidental recall of the three beliefs. If Hypotheses D1 and D2 are correct we should expect the open group to be superior in recall to the closed group, and the visual group to be superior to the memory group. Let us first consider the immediate recall results, shown in Table 10.5. The closed group takes an average of about 46 seconds and the open group takes only half this time—an average of 23 seconds—

Table 10.5

Mean Time (in Seconds) Taken to Recall Each Belief Ten Minutes After and One Week After End of Experiment

| | | After 10 Min. | | After 1 Week | |
Group	Number	Mean Time	p	Mean Time	p
Closed	30	45.9	.02	25.0	.05
Open	30	22.7		22.4	
Closed-memory	15	70.9	.02	29.7	.34
Open-memory	15	29.1		34.6	
Closed-visual	15	21.0	.22	20.3	.02
Open-visual	15	16.3		10.2	
Memory field	30	50.0	.01	32.1	.15
Visual field	30	18.6		15.2	
Memory-closed	15	70.9	.01	29.7	.43
Visual-closed	15	21.0		20.3	
Memory-open	15	29.1	.16	34.6	.11
Visual-open	15	16.3		10.2	

to recall each of the three new beliefs. The closed-memory subgroup takes 71 seconds to recall each belief while the open-memory subgroup takes under 30 seconds. The closed-visual subgroup takes 21 seconds while the open-visual subgroup takes about 16 seconds. Two of these three differences are statistically significant. Similar results in the expected direction are obtained for the two experimental groups. The visual group takes considerably less time than the memory group to recall the new beliefs. These results are also found for the subgroups, and two of the three differences are statistically significant.

Consider now the recall results obtained one week later, which are also shown in Table 10.5. Again, superiority of recall generally favors the open group over the closed group (two of the three differences are significant), and the visual condition over the memory condition (but none of the differences are significant). But on the whole, the differences are smaller on delayed recall (one week later) than on immediate recall (10 minutes later).

The fact that the differences between groups are smaller on delayed recall than on immediate recall merits further scrutiny. If we inspect the differences in recall on the two occasions it immediately becomes evident that recall a week later is generally no worse than recall ten minutes after the end of the experiment. In fact there is a tremendous improvement of recall in the closed group working under the memory condition wherein the beliefs were not in the visual field: the average recall drops from 70 seconds to 30 seconds. The only way we can account for this unexpected finding is to suggest that the closed subjects under this condition, perhaps because they are insecure or anxious about their poor performance, reminisce more than the open subjects about the experiment during the intervening week. As a result they improve in their recall of the beliefs on the later occasion. But for the present this must remain a tentative interpretation, pending future confirmation.

The results presented thus far can be reasonably interpreted to suggest the following sequence in problem-solving: A relatively efficient solution of the Doodlebug Problem is not so much a function of efficiency in analytic thinking as in integrative thinking. Speed of integration is, in turn, a function of the ability to remember the beliefs to be integrated. Pushing this analysis back one step more leads us to inquire about the possible determinants of the ability to remember the beliefs.

Hypothesis E1 states that those with relatively closed systems, as compared to those with relatively open systems, will more frequently reject situations requiring new modes of thought. Similarly, Hypothesis E2 is to the effect that those in the memory condition, as compared with those in the visual condition, will also more frequently reject the experimental situation. It will be recalled that immediately after the experiment the subjects filled out a brief questionnaire of five items pertaining to their accep-

Table 10.6

Mean Rejection of Problem Situation

Group	Number	Mean	p
Closed	30	20.8	.04
Open	30	22.1	
Closed-memory	15	20.0	.16
Open-memory	15	21.3	
Closed-visual	15	21.6	.06
Open-visual	15	22.9	
Memory field	30	20.7	.02
Visual field	30	22.2	
Memory-closed	15	20.0	.13
Visual-closed	15	21.6	
Memory-open	15	21.3	.04
Visual-open	15	22.9	

tance-rejection of the experimental situation. The data are shown in Table 10.6. The mean score for the closed group is 20.8, as compared with a mean of 22.1 for the open group. In other words, the closed subjects reject the problem more than the open subjects. This difference is actually larger than it looks because the scores are bunched together close to the maximum score of 25. In fact, the open and closed groups differ significantly from each other at the .05 level. The results for the two sets of closed and open subgroups, one under the memory, and the other under the visual condition, are consistent with those found for the larger group. These differences, however, do not quite reach statistical significance.

As for the memory vs. visual conditions, the group permitted to keep the belief cards in view accept the problem situation significantly more than do those not permitted to do so. Again, the results are highly consistent for the two sets of subgroups.

The greater rejection of the problem by the closed group is further evident from the spontaneous comments made by the subjects during the test situation. A record was kept of all comments made during the experiment and these were analyzed in a manner similar to that discussed in the preceding chapter. Three judges selected all comments which they thought were indicative of dogmatic rejection of the experimental situation. The comments were typed on separate cards, without identification of the subject, and were thus "blind" judgments.

Typical comments judged to indicate rejection are the following:

> "Are you sure he wants to eat the food?"
> "That's illogical!"
> "He could have died of hunger when he stopped dead."
> "If he's so smart, why doesn't he do it in one jump?"
> "Maybe he really doesn't want the food."
> "He can starve for all I care."
> "Jeez, what a screwball of an outfit."
> "This is impossible."
> "I know there's a tricky answer to this."
> "There's no solution. How in hell can he change directions if he can't turn around?"

From the total pool of comments made by the subjects, 41 were selected by two of the three judges as indicating rejection of the problem. By pure chance we should expect half of these to come from the closed and the other half from the open group. Instead we find that 30 of the 41 comments were made by individuals in the closed group, while 11 were made by individuals in the open group. This difference is significant.

So much for the main findings of the study. It is now once more proper to ask whether the differences found could be due to differences in intelligence rather than to openness-closedness or to the experimental variable. As before, American Council on Education scores, assumed to provide a rough measure of intelligence, were available for 59 out of the 60 subjects. The results, shown in Table 10.7, do not support the hypothesis that there are differences in intelligence, either between open and closed subjects or between memory and visual subjects. Furthermore, correlation

Table 10.7

Mean ACE Scores for High and Low Dogmatic Groups and for Memory Card and Visual Card Groups

Group	Mean	S.D.	p
Closed	5.6	1.7	N.S.
Open	6.0	1.7	
Memory field	5.6	1.5	N.S.
Visual field	6.0	1.9	

coefficients were computed between these intelligence scores and the total time required to solve the problem, the time taken to overcome the first belief, and the time taken to solve the problem after the second belief was overcome. These correlations are —.08, —.16, and —.22, respectively, and are not statistically significant. Whatever differences are found in problem-solving between the closed and open groups, or between the experimental conditions, cannot be attributed to differences in intelligence. The results also suggest that intelligence, as measured, has very little to do with the way our subjects solve the Denny Doodlebug Problem, at least in the particular sample tested. These results confirm the findings reported in Chapter 9 regarding negligible correlations between intelligence and problem-solving, and a correlation of .02 between dogmatism scores and American Council on Education scores. To all of this let us add a finding by Ehrlich (1955) with Ohio State University students. He reports a —.01 correlation between dogmatism and intelligence where the latter was measured by the Ohio State Psychological Examination.

Interpretations

It may be safely said that all theoretical expectations are strongly supported by the findings. Those having relatively open systems take less time to solve the Doodlebug Problem (Hypothesis A), not because they overcome beliefs faster (Hypothesis B) but because they can more readily integrate new beliefs, once the older ones have been overcome, into a new system (Hypothesis C). Their greater capacity to integrate is seen to be related to and possibly a function of a greater capacity to remember the elements to be integrated (Hypothesis D). This capacity, in turn, is related to and possibly a function of a greater capacity to entertain novel problem-solving situations (Hypothesis E).

The findings with respect to Hypotheses B and C and E confirm those found in the first Doodlebug study but, in general, are more clear cut. Hypothesis D, with respect to memory functioning, and Hypothesis E, with respect to acceptance-rejection, throw additional light on some other psychological factors that seem to affect problem-solving. Concerning Hypothesis E, it should be pointed out that acceptance-rejection was ascertained in two ways: quantitatively, from the questionnaire given at the end of the experiment, and qualitatively, from the spontaneous comments made by the subjects during the experiment. Both measures yield similar results.

To understand better the differences in cognitive and emotional functioning between open and closed subjects, let us anticipate certain evidence to be considered later in Chapters 19 and 20. The gist of this evidence is that closed persons have considerably more anxiety than open persons and have different childhood experiences which can reasonably account for such differences in anxiety. In line with such findings it may be assumed that persons with closed systems find the strange world of Joe Doodlebug more threatening than do persons with open systems. It is this threat, rather than intellectual ability as such, that seems to be the basis of their cognitive malfunctioning. It is reasonable to say that the greater rejection of Joe's world by closed-minded subjects is an attempt to defend themselves against the threat inherent in new belief systems contradicting old ones. The closed person may perhaps "go along" with the experimenter's invitation to solve the Doodlebug Problem, but only on the surface. He is not really prepared psychologically to entertain it seriously. As one of our closed subjects puts it: "The hints just seemed to go in one ear and out the other." This spontaneous remark elegantly sums up why the findings in this experiment may have emerged as they do. It is small wonder that closed persons are poorer in recalling the new beliefs, are slower to synthesize them, and are thus delayed in solving the problem as a whole. For as we have said earlier, if nothing is remembered, there is nothing to integrate.

These results are important not only because they show the role of personality in problem-solving behavior but also because they tell us something of the interplay of underlying processes of thought, of memory, and of basic emotional attitudes which may facilitate or retard problem solution.

What does it take to get the unreceptive mind into a more receptive mood? How can we help a person to "empty out" old beliefs and really to replace them with new ones? Considering that one major obstacle to synthesizing is often to be found in a reluctance to remember, one way to help is to "short-circuit" the person's reliance on memory. This is exactly what our experimental manipulation tries to accomplish. The difference between the visual field condition and the memory field condition is exactly this. We reasoned that with the beliefs in view the subject's resistance to the problem should decrease because his dependence on memory is reduced. Consequently, when all the new beliefs together are "pumped" into the phenomenal field by artificial means, the synthesis of these beliefs into a new system should be significantly facilitated. The data clearly support this view. More important, they serve also to increase confidence in our speculations regarding the nature of the interplay among cognitive and emotional processes, which are necessary prerequisites to the formation of new belief systems.

The findings on intelligence indicate once more that the differences in cognitive synthesis or integration between open-minded and closed-minded persons are not attributable to differences in intelligence as such. Instead we find it necessary to account for the differences in synthesis, as well as the lack of differences in analysis, in more psychodynamic terms, in terms of the closed person finding the Doodlebug Problem *as a system* more threatening to his own belief system. But what is it precisely about the Doodlebug Problem that is so threatening? We have suggested that it is the newness of a system which in its totality contradicts already cherished systems. If only we could, by somehow sugarcoating it, get rid of the sheer newness of the Doodlebug system and leave everything else the same, then the threat would be removed and, consequently, the cognitive functioning of the closed mind, particularly its synthesizing functions, should reveal itself as *fully intact* as that of the open mind. We will see in the next chapter if this is so.

Synopsis

The purpose of this study was to investigate some of the variables thought to aid or hinder the formation of new belief systems. The results show that subjects with relatively closed systems, as measured by the Dogmatism Scale, take longer to solve the Doodlebug Problem than do subjects with relatively open systems. This is clearly due to differences in the ability to synthesize, and not in the ability to analyze. These findings become more understandable in the light of additional findings which suggest that relatively closed persons have greater difficulty in remembering the beliefs to be integrated. Greater difficulty in recall, in turn, seems to be related to an unwillingness to play along, or to entertain new belief systems.

The results show also that permitting the subjects to keep the beliefs before them in their perceptual field, as compared with not permitting them to do so, produces the following effects: it increases acceptance of the experimental situation, it facilitates memory for the beliefs, it facilitates the synthesis of the new beliefs into a new system, and it decreases the total amount of time needed to solve the Doodlebug Problem. The experimental condition of keeping the beliefs in the visual field seems to serve the function of by-passing the subject's reliance on his memory processes and consequently serves to facilitate the formation of new belief systems.

The results found cannot be attributed to differences in intelligence between closed and open subjects, or between subjects under the two experimental conditions. We favor the view that the differences can better be understood as arising from the greater threat to closed persons of the new Doodlebug system. In the next chapter we will consider what happens in the cognitive functioning of open and closed persons when the *newness* of the Doodlebug system is no longer at issue.

Notes

1. All references to the Dogmatism Scale from now on will be to Form E.

2. Because of the skewness of many of the measures employed in the Doodlebug research it was necessary to find a distribution-free statistic to test for significance of difference. Festinger's *F* test, used in Chapter 9, is not ideal because it applies only to Pearson Type III distributions. This means that in each case we would have to first determine whether each and every one of our distributions conform to Type III distributions. A simpler distribution-free statistic was recently made available by White (1952) and is given in Siegel's book on nonparametric statistics (1956). This test will be used routinely from now on, in this chapter and in all the remaining chapters in Part III, *unless otherwise stated.* The mean times presented in the various tables which follow are for comparison purposes only. They do not enter into the computation of White's rank-order statistic used to test for significance. Also, *unless otherwise stated,* all tests are one-tailed tests, since we usually predict the direction of differences in advance.

3. The data were tested for significance by the chi-square method. To eliminate small theoretical frequencies, the data for two and three beliefs have been combined for measure I and also for measure II. Since Hypotheses B1 and B2 predict no differences, two-tailed tests of significance were employed.

11

The Role of Past Experience

A Comparison Between Chess Players and Non-Chess Players

Milton Rokeach, Theodore S. Swanson, and
M. Ray Denny

W e will now describe an experiment in which the Doodlebug Problem is converted into a game played by two opponents on a chessboard. The structure of the Chessboard Problem, as it will be called, is identical in all respects with the Doodlebug Problem discussed in the last two chapters. Our reason for constructing the Chessboard Problem is to find out what happens in the problem-solving process when cognitive synthesis proceeds in a setting more familiar to the person than the strange world of Joe Doodlebug. We may reasonably suppose that a person who has had past experience with such a game—for example, a person who plays chess and is thus familiar with the rules governing the movements of the chessmen—should encounter less difficulty in integrating new beliefs into a problem solution than one who has not had this experience. In such a case, the "new" system within which he is to do his thinking and synthesizing is not, psychologically speaking, new for him. He has experienced something like it before, and thus the problem of reconciling a new system with an old one simply does not arise. Instead, he can readily integrate the "new" beliefs with similar beliefs he has previously encountered. For example, Joe Doodlebug's movements in sequences of four jumps in one direction (the movement belief) are not too different from the movements of the knight in chess; many of the chessmen "face" in the direction of the opponent, but can nevertheless move backwards and sideways (the direction belief); and the chessmen capture their opponent's pieces by landing on top of them (the facing belief). It may thus be expected that those who play chess should do better on the Chessboard Problem than those who do not because the rules of the system to be integrated are not new.

But our theoretical concern is not primarily with the synthesizing capacities of those who do and do not play chess. Rather, we seek to understand more fully the nature of the thought processes of persons characteristically open and closed in their belief systems. We have already seen in the last two chapters that closed persons, as compared with open persons, are typically more resistant to the integration of new beliefs into new systems. This is not attributable to lesser intelligence on their part but to their greater reluctance to change their everyday belief systems. These considerations suggest that if a problem were placed in a more familiar context, so that the system within which they have to work is not seen as new, then closed persons should do about as well as open persons. Hence our interest in chess players. We should expect little or no differences between open-minded chess players and closed-minded chess players when they are both solving problems well within the scope of their everyday belief systems.

Now what about those who have had no experience with chess? For them the Chessboard Problem is relatively unfamiliar—as unfamiliar as the orginal Doodlebug Problem. Both problems involve a psychologically new system. We therefore conjecture once again that relatively closed persons who do not play chess should take longer than relatively open persons who do not play chess to synthesize the new beliefs.

In short, then, we expect the following three things to happen: (1) Those who play chess should synthesize faster than those who do not. (2) Open and closed chess players should not differ from each other on synthesis because, for them, the Chessboard Problem is not a psychologically new system. (3) Open persons who do not play chess should synthesize faster than closed persons who do not play chess because closed persons will characteristically resist more the formation of new systems.

Let us now see to what extent the empirical findings conform to theoretical expectations. But first the Chessboard Problem:

The Conditions:

A new kind of game has just come on the market. It is played on a board like a checkerboard 15 squares wide and 15 squares long. As in checkers, two people play the game. Each player has two kinds of pieces, a flat red piece to be captured, and a capturing piece. Your capturing piece is a thick block which is painted red on one side, black on top, and black on the three remaining sides. The piece to be captured is the size of the checkerboard square and the capturing piece is smaller. The object of the game is to capture all of your opponent's flat red pieces before he can capture all of yours. The rules for moving the pieces are as follows:

1. The flat red pieces cannot be moved once they have been placed on the board.
2. You can move the capturing piece in only four different directions, north, south, east, and west. It cannot be moved diagonally.
3. Once the piece is started in any one direction, that is, north, south, east, or west, it must be moved four times in that direction before you can change its direction.
4. The piece can be moved any number of squares at one time, from one to fifteen squares.
5. The capturing piece cannot be turned around or rotated.

6. To capture the opponent's pieces, the flat red side of the capturing piece must form a right angle with the flat red surface of the piece to be captured.

The Situation:

The game has been in progress for some time and there is now only one more piece for you to capture in order to win. A penalty has just been exacted against your opponent, and you now have four moves to make before your opponent can move. The piece you want to capture is ten squares directly west of your capturing piece, and the red side of your capturing piece faces north. After some deliberation, you decide that you cannot capture the piece in one, two, or three moves, but that you *can* capture it in four moves and win the game.

The Problem:

You are dead right in your conclusion. Why do you suppose that it takes four moves, *no more and no less*, in order to capture the remaining piece?

As in the original Doodlebug Problem, there are three sets of new beliefs that the subject must learn: (1) *the facing belief:* the capturing piece does not have to face the piece it is capturing, but can land on top of it; (2) *the direction belief:* the capturing piece can move sideways and backwards as well as forwards; and (3) *the movement belief:* the capturing piece could have been in the middle of a sequence of moves as well as at the beginning of a sequence when the penalty was invoked. The solution is exactly the same as in the original problem: the capturing piece had already been moved once to the east. It must therefore be moved three more times to the east to complete its sequence of four moves, and then once back to the west to land on top of the piece to be captured.

As before, the three new beliefs—the facing, direction, and movement beliefs—are typed on 3″ × 5″ cards. As the subject overcomes one or more beliefs by himself, the appropriate card is placed before him, and then taken away immediately after the contents are read. In the event the subject does not overcome the individual beliefs on his own, the card bearing the specific belief is placed before him as a hint, and then removed after it is read.

Six hundred and fourteen subjects, primarily Sophomores, enrolled in introductory psychology in the spring of 1956, were given the Dogmatism Scale. From these, 48 were selected for individual testing with the Chessboard Problem, half scoring extremely high and half extremely low on the Dogmatism Scale. The experimenter did not, of course, know the dogmatism score of the subjects. For all but two subjects, information was obtained on whether or not they played chess. The total time allowed to solve the problem was 40 minutes. The three hints were given at the end of 10, 15, and 20 minutes, respectively.

The hints were as follows:

1. *The facing set:* "I'm going to give you a hint. It's on this card." [On card: "The two pieces do not have to occupy separate squares to form a right angle."]
2. *The direction set:* "I'm going to give you another hint." [On card: "The capturing piece can be moved sideways and backwards as well as forward."]
3. *The movement set:* "I have one more hint for you." [On card: "The capturing piece was moved east when you last moved it."]

Results and Interpretations

The Chessboard Problem turned out to be generally more difficult than the original Doodlebug Problem (No Canopy Problem). The mean solution time for the latter is about 22 minutes (see Chapter 10, memory condition), but the mean solution time for the Chessboard Problem is about 28 minutes. The greater solution time of the Chessboard Problem is clearly due to the fact that both processes—analysis and synthesis—take longer. Thirty-three of the 48 subjects, for example, could not overcome any of the three beliefs by themselves, and thus had to be given a hint at the end of 10 minutes. Only three persons out of 48 were able to overcome two or three beliefs by themselves. The greater difficulty of the Chessboard Problem is also shown by the fact that 19 out of the 48 subjects were not able to solve the problem at all at the end of 40 minutes.* This is in contrast to

---

* For a more detailed consideration of these data, see Swanson (1958).

the Doodlebug Problem, which is failed by about 10 per cent of the subjects.

In view of the fact that so very few of the subjects overcame the individual beliefs by themselves and thus had to be given the hints, there are virtually no individual differences in analytic thinking. Therefore, for the sake of brevity we will depart from our usual procedure and assume that individual differences in total time to solve the Chessboard Problem are essentially a measure of individual differences in time to synthesize. Table 11.1 shows the mean total time taken to solve by the closed and open groups.

It is obvious that the open group solves the problem in less time—about six minutes less—than the closed group. The difference is significant. It might also be pointed out that 13 of the 24 closed subjects failed to solve the problem in 40 minutes, but only 6 of the open subjects failed to do so.

Table 11.1

Total Time to Solve the Chessboard Problem by Closed and Open Groups

Group	Number	Mean Time	p
Closed	24	31.4	.02
Open	24	25.2	

We come now to the question of past experience with chesslike problems. Information was obtained for 46 out of the 48 subjects on whether or not they played chess. It happened that 9 out of 23 closed subjects, and also 9 out of 23 open subjects stated that they did. Thus, we had 18 subjects who played chess and 28 subjects who did not, half of each group scoring extremely high and half extremely low on the Dogmatism Scale. The mean time to solve for the chess players and the non-chess players is shown in Table 11.2. It was about 22 minutes for the chess players and about 32 minutes for the non-chess players—a difference of about 10 minutes. The difference in performance between the two groups is very significant and confirms theoretical expectations. Furthermore, although only 4 of the 18 chess players failed to solve the problem, 15 out of 28 of the non-chess players failed to

Table 11.2

Total Time to Solve the Chessboard Problem by
Chess and Non-chess Players

Group	Number	Mean Time	p
Chess players	18	22.4	
Non-chess players	28	31.9	.01

solve it. This difference is also significant. Apparently, then, past experience with chess increases familiarity with the Chessboard Problem and this results in faster synthesis (and solution time) for the chess players because they are dealing with a system that is not new to them.

Let us now compare open with closed chess players and open with closed non-chess players on total time to solve. The results are shown in Table 11.3.

Table 11.3

Total Time to Solve the Chessboard Problem by Open and Closed
Chess Players and Non-chess Players

Group	Number	Mean Time	p
Closed chess players	9	23.0	
Open chess players	9	21.7	N.S.
Closed non-chess players	14	36.5	
Open non-chess players	14	27.2	.01

A glance at Table 11.3 shows a marked difference in results for the two sets of chess players and non-chess players. There is a small and insignificant difference of about a minute and a half between open and closed chess players.[1] But there is a difference of about nine minutes between open and closed non-chess players. It should also be pointed out that of the 14 closed persons who did not play chess, 10 failed to solve the problem altogether in the allotted 40 minutes. The comparable figure for the 14 open subjects was 5 failures. The difference between the two groups of non-chess players is very significant from a statistical standpoint.

These findings fit in quite well with theoretical expectations. They demonstrate the psychological importance of newness of system as a determinant of problem-solving behavior. For the non-chess players, the Chessboard Problem is psychologically new in the same way that the original Doodlebug Problem is psychologically new. To integrate the new beliefs into a new system requires an openness to experience, a capacity to entertain new systems that are in one way or another in opposition to everyday systems. It is essentially in this respect that those with open systems are seen to differ from those with closed systems. This seems to account for the relatively large and significant difference found between open-minded and closed-minded persons who do not play chess.

That the difference between closed and open subjects who do not play chess is considerably larger than the comparable difference between the closed and open subjects who do, suggests once more that factors other than intelligence are probably responsible for the difference. The synthesizing capacities of the closed chess players are about as good as those of the open chess players. There is no evidence here of inferior cognitive functioning on the part of closed persons. Nor do we expect any, so long as they are in "familiar territory." Lest there be any doubt about this point we once again obtained the subjects' scores on the American Council on Education test. As in the previous studies, closed and open groups did not differ from each other on intelligence thus measured. The mean ACE score for the closed group was 5.4 and for the open group, 5.6. Nor did the chess players and the non-chess players differ from each other on intelligence. The means for the two groups were 5.9 and 5.3, a difference that is not significant. It is thus necessary to conceive of other dynamic forces at work, rather than intelligence, to account for the differences found. The one that seems to fit the data best is the extent to which the subject resists the formation of new systems.

Before we take leave of our chess players and non-chess players, let us speculate about what would be expected of them if they were to work on the Doodlebug Problem instead of the Chessboard Problem. Since they differ in synthesizing on the

Chessboard Problem, should they not likewise differ on the Doodlebug Problem? If our theoretical analysis is correct we should expect little if any difference between chess players and non-chess players on the Doodlebug Problem because it should be psychologically new, relatively speaking, for both. In a recent study concerned primarily with other issues (Rokeach, Oram, and Marr, 1959) we had the opportunity to compare chess players with non-chess players on the Doodlebug Problem. We find small differences between them on synthesis which are in the expected direction, but these differences are not significant. Chess players and non-chess players do not particularly differ from each other on the Doodlebug Problem even though they differ substantially on the Chessboard Problem, which is essentially the same—except in one big respect.

Synopsis

To study the effects of past experience in determining when a system is psychologically new or not new, the Doodlebug Problem was converted into a chesslike game. We assumed that for chess players the Chessboard Problem would not be psychologically new and, hence, that they would more readily synthesize the materials into the problem solution than would non-chess players, for whom the Chessboard Problem is psychologically new. The findings clearly confirm this expectation. It was further conjectured, for the same reason, that open-minded and closed-minded chess players would not differ from each other in their solution to the Chessboard Problem, but that open and closed persons who do not play chess would differ. The results are again in accord with these expectations. Further, no significant differences were found in intelligence between open and closed persons, or between chess players and non-chess players. The over-all findings, then, suggest that differences in synthesizing are often attributable to (1) past experience which determines whether a system is psychologically new or not, and (2) the basic attitude a person has toward new systems as such.

Notes

1. Since no differences are predicted between open and closed chess players a two-tailed test (White's t) was used, and $p = .27$. A one-tailed test was used to test the significance of the difference between open and closed non-chess players, since direction of difference was theoretically predicted in advance.

12

On Party-Line Thinking

An Experimental Analogy

*Milton Rokeach, Alfred Oram, John J. Laffey, and
M. Ray Denny*

A party-line thinker is a person who not only resists change but can also change only too easily. What he does depends on what his authorities do, and his changes and refusals to change conform with authority. What happens at the cognitive level when one is said to have engaged in party-line thinking? In this chapter our purpose is to try to probe into the underlying cognitive structure of party-line thinking.

It is first necessary to elaborate on certain theoretical aspects discussed in Chapters 2 and 3. Recall first our notion of peripheral beliefs, which are the beliefs a person perceives to emanate from authority. We assume that all persons have peripheral beliefs, regardless of how open or closed their belief systems.

But peripheral beliefs may hang together in different ways in different persons. In open systems, the peripheral beliefs are intrinsically related to each other as well as to beliefs about authority. In closed systems, however, peripheral beliefs are conceived to be isolated or segregated from each other, but are interconnected via the authority region; that is, they are arbitrarily seen to be interrelated because they are all seen to emanate together from the same authority. Party-line thinking can now be described as a thought process wherein each peripheral belief is isolated from every other, but is still in communication with the others through the intermediate region. It is this common origin in authority rather than intrinsic logical connections that gives the party-liner's closed system the *appearance* of a systematic, integrated system. He may appear to the outsider to have a systematic position even though the component beliefs are isolated from each other. But the closed system is a fortuitous one—it is the authority's system rather than the adherent's. Let us try to clarify this further with the aid of Figure 12.1.

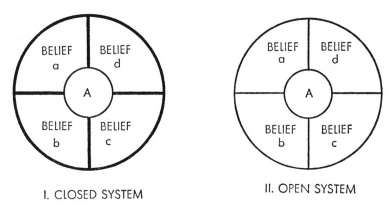

I. CLOSED SYSTEM   II. OPEN SYSTEM

Figure 12.1. A diagrammatic representation of party-line and non-party-line thinking.

In I, which represents a closed belief system, beliefs *a*, *b*, *c*, and *d* are isolated from each other so that logical connections are not seen. But they are still in indirect communication with each other because they each communicate with the authority region (*A*).°

° We are omitting here a consideration of the most central region, having to do with primitive beliefs.

They all belong together as part of a system because they are all seen to have a common origin. A change in belief a will occur only if it is seen to originate with one's authority. But this change will have no effect on, and will not be integrated with, beliefs b, c, or d, nor will it have any effect on beliefs regarding the credence of one's authority. To go back to an example we have used before, some Communists were observed to change their beliefs about Communist collaboration with the Nazis immediately following the announcement of the Hitler-Stalin pact in 1939. When asked for their reason for doing so, such persons were typically evasive until they could learn the reason for themselves from the next morning's *Daily Worker* or through some other party channel. However, other beliefs relevant to communism did not change. The change was an isolated one, a party-line change restricted to one belief, without altering the total belief system.

In II, which represents an open system, beliefs a, b, c, and d are in high communication with each other as well as with the authority region. A change anywhere will spread in all directions and will be seen to have implications for changing the remaining beliefs, including beliefs about the credence of authority. Thus, some Communists, when confronted with the demand that they change their beliefs about Communist collaboration with the Nazis, saw implications for changing other beliefs about the theory and practice of communism. Sometimes it led to disillusionment and defection, and sometimes to a qualitatively different view of the nature of communism so that it was still acceptable. Instead of a single belief giving way within a belief system which must at all costs be preserved intact, the whole system is modified in order to assimilate the change, or in order to give way to an altogether new system.

How do these considerations apply to the problem-solving activities of open and closed persons? In the Doodlebug experiments, the subject is left to his own devices. There is no authority to look to or to give out the answers. He has to do his own synthesizing of peripheral beliefs without benefit of external authority. Recall that the world of Joe Doodlebug involves three new beliefs—the facing belief, the direction belief, and the movement belief. These beliefs are in contradiction to those we ordinarily have about how to get to food. Let us call the three everyday beliefs *a, b,* and *c,* and the three new, opposing beliefs *ā, b̄,* and *c̄.* In Figure 12.2, let each one of the circles represent a belief system, each one composed of three beliefs. No authority region is represented in Systems II and III because the thinker cannot look to the experimenter-authority for the answer. He is strictly on his own. Let belief *a* represent the everyday belief that to eat food we must first face it; belief *b,* that when we want to change direction we simply turn to the left, or right, or around; belief *c,* that when we wish to change direction we can do so immediately without having to finish a sequence of steps in the old direction.

In solving the Doodlebug Problem considered thus far (to be called henceforth the No Canopy Problem), the subject is required to give up thinking in terms of System I and instead to think within the framework of System II. But, as we have seen, closed persons find it more difficult than open persons to do so, and this is attributed to the fact that they adhere to System I in a more closed manner. Our theory suggests that to the extent that a person's System I is closed it is characterized by a pervasive

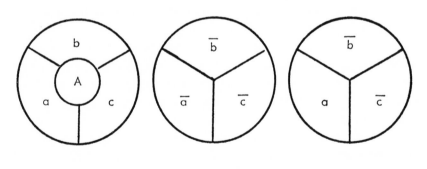

I. EVERYDAY BELIEFS   II. NO CANOPY PROBLEM   III. CANOPY PROBLEM

FIGURE 12.2. A diagrammatic representation of three belief systems.

state of isolation existing between each belief and every other belief; there is isolation between beliefs *a* and *b, a* and *c,* and *b* and *c.* In our conceptualizations, this *pervasive* state of isolation in System I structurally retards the synthesizing process and prevents System I from breaking down as a system,* and it therefore hinders the formation of new systems.

Let us try to observe the disruptive effects of isolation on the synthesizing process under the simplest possible condition. Analogous to instances of party-line thinking in real life, let us experimentally introduce a single change into the rules governing Joe Doodlebug's behavior. Without authority to lean on, how will open and closed persons integrate such a lone change into their belief systems? To this end imagine yet another system, System III, which is to be identical with System II except for one belief. The subject is, first, to solve and learn System II, then work on System III. The only difference between them (see Figure 12.2) is that belief $\bar{a}$ in System II is to be replaced by belief a in System III. Otherwise, the two systems are to be identical.

We thus need to redesign the Doodlebug Problem (System II) so that it will conform with the requirements of System III, that is, so that it will contain beliefs $\bar{b}$, $\bar{c}$, and a. After some trial and error we succeeded in satisfying these requirements by "building" (in our imagination, of course) a canopy over the food. Now Joe can not eat when he lands on top. He will have to jump off the canopy and face the food in order to eat it, just as we do in everyday life. In other words, we have changed the new facing belief, $\bar{a}$, back to the old facing belief, a. But we have not changed anything else because the problem is exactly as before: Joe decides (correctly of course) that it will take four jumps to get to the food. Where was Joe when his master placed the food down under the canopy three feet west of him?

How will open and closed persons do on the Canopy Problem? And, more important, suppose they were to work first on the No Canopy Problem (System II) and then on the Canopy Problem (System III). Should not the synthesis phase of thinking on the second problem take relatively less time, since two of the three beliefs in it are identical with the first problem? This is what we may reasonably expect in open persons, but in closed persons, if their beliefs are indeed as isolated from each other as we have conjectured, no such facilitation or saving in time should be expected. For without authority to guide them, they may take

---

* Without necessarily interfering with the *analytic*, temporally spaced breaking down of individual beliefs, which are worked through by the person one at a time.

note of the single change that has taken place but they will not know how to cope with it or how to integrate it with the rest of their system.

Thus, party-line thinking is reformulated as a problem in the positive transfer of learning from one situation to similar situations. If our analysis is essentially correct, closed persons should generally show less positive transfer than open persons do because the parts within their belief systems are more isolated from each other.*

The Canopy Problem

The Conditions:

Joe Doodlebug is a strange sort of imaginary bug. He can and cannot do the following things:

1. He can jump in only four different directions: north, south, east, and west. He cannot jump diagonally (southeast, northwest, etc.).
2. Once he starts in any direction, that is, north, south, east, or west, he must jump four times in that same direction before he can switch to another direction.
3. He can only jump, not crawl, fly, or walk.
4. He can jump very large distances or very small distances, but not less than one inch per jump.
5. Joe cannot turn around.

The Situation:

Joe has been jumping all over the place getting some exercise when his master places a pile of food three feet directly west of him. Joe notices that the pile of food is a little larger than he. As soon as Joe sees all this food he stops dead in his tracks, facing north. After all his exercise, Joe is very hungry and wants to get to the food as quickly as he possibly can. Joe examines the situation, noticing that there is a low canopy over the food, then says, "Darn it, I'll have to jump four times to get the food."

---

* For a study of transfer effects within a similar, Lewinian framework, see Kounin's research on rigidity in the feeble-minded (1941). But there is an important difference between Kounin's and the present work, which points up once more the distinction made between rigid and dogmatic thinking. Kounin defines rigidity in terms of isolation between two regions or activities, a and b. In the present work we are talking about pervasive isolation within a whole system, the isolation of belief a from b, belief a from c, and belief b from c.

The Problem:

Joe Doodlebug was a smart bug and he was dead right in his conclusion. Why do you suppose Joe Doodlebug had to take four jumps, no more and no less, to reach the food?

Inspection of the Canopy Problem readily illustrates how it differs from the No Canopy Problem; the two problems are identical except for the single phrase, "Joe examines the situation, noticing that there is a low canopy over the food." Thus, Joe can no longer eat the food by landing on top of it. The correct solution is that Joe had already taken one jump to the *west*, and therefore has to take three more jumps to the west, his third jump landing him on top of the canopy. He now takes a fourth jump backward off the canopy, landing to the south of the food and, thus facing the food, he is now in a position to eat.

EXPERIMENT I: PRESENTING THE NEW BELIEFS ALL AT ONCE

Experiment I was conducted with 20 extremely open and 20 extremely closed subjects. They were selected from a pool of over 600 introductory psychology students who filled out the Dogmatism Scale in January, 1956. The general procedure and instructions are the same as those described in Chaper 10. The No Canopy and Canopy Problems are presented in a counterbalanced order, half the subjects in the closed and open groups solving them in the order AB (No Canopy → Canopy), the other half in the order BA (Canopy → No Canopy). The total time allowed to solve each problem is 45 minutes.

Since we were not particularly interested in the analytic phase of problem-solving, the beliefs were presented to the subjects on $3'' \times 5''$ cards *all at once* at the beginning of the experiment and left in view. The hints on the cards read as follows:

1a. *Facing belief (No Canopy Problem):* "Joe does not have to face the food in order to eat it."

1b. *Facing belief (Canopy Problem):* "Joe must face the food in order to eat it."

2. *Direction belief (No Canopy and Canopy Problems):* "Joe can jump sideways and backwards as well as forwards."

3. *Movement belief (No Canopy and Canopy Problems):* "Joe is not necessarily at the beginning or end of a series of jumps. He may have been somewhere in a series of jumps."

It is important to emphasize the fact that when the subject is presented his second Doodlebug Problem, the hints and instructions of his first problem lie before him on the table and are available for consultation. Thus, when solving the second problem, the subject has immediate access to all three beliefs, two of which are still applicable.

Since the subjects are given all the new beliefs immediately at the beginning of the experiment, we assume that the analytic phase of thinking is more or less nonexistent and therefore that the total time to solve the problem is essentially a measure of the synthesis phase of thinking. The results on total time are shown in Table 12.1. In order to show the results as clearly as possible the total time means are presented separately for the No Canopy and Canopy Problems when each is solved first, and solved second.

Table 12.1

Total Time to Solve Canopy and No Canopy Problems by Open and Closed Groups

Doodlebug Problem	Group	Mean Total Time	p
A. Presented First			
No Canopy	Closed	18.7	N.S.
	Open	20.1	
Canopy	Closed	24.8	N.S.
	Open	25.4	
B. Presented Second			
No Canopy	Closed	4.1	N.S.
	Open	5.3	
Canopy	Closed	15.8	N.S.
	Open	21.2	

$N = 10$ in each subgroup.

Much to our surprise, we find no differences between closed and open groups. This is in marked contrast to the findings reported in Chapters 9, 10, and 11, which show consistently that closed subjects take longer to synthesize than open subjects. Even more remarkable is the fact that for the first time we see the open group taking *longer* than the closed group to synthesize. Although this longer time is not significant, we hesitate to dismiss it because it is found consistently on both Canopy and No Canopy Problems, when solved first and when solved second.[1]

Now what about transfer effects? Is the problem that is presented second solved faster than the same problem when presented first? The results are shown in Table 12.2.

Table 12.2

Comparison Between Problems When Solved First and When Solved Second

Transfer Effect for:	Order of Presentation	Group	Mean Total Time	p
No Canopy problem	First	Closed	18.7	.01
	Second	Closed	4.1	
	First	Open	20.1	.01
	Second	Open	5.3	
Canopy problem	First	Closed	24.8	.02
	Second	Closed	15.8	
	First	Open	25.4	.15
	Second	Open	21.2	

N = 10 in each subgroup.

Again to our surprise, we find marked and generally significant improvements in *both* groups, the closed group as well as the open group. Solving one variation of the Doodlebug Problem facilitates greatly the solution of the second. The results for the open group are as expected, but those for the closed group are opposite to those expected.

These results provide no support whatever for the theoretical formulations put forward about the nature of party-line thinking. Closed persons show as much positive transfer of learning as open persons. There is no evidence here for the view that there is greater isolation in closed-minded persons. Moreover, the findings do not even substantiate the earlier findings on differences in synthesis between open and closed persons. Both groups show equal facility in forming new systems.

Whenever a research study produces unexpected findings the investigator is obligated to weigh carefully two alternatives which might possibly account for such findings. First, the theory or hypothesis may be wrong. Second, the method for testing the hypothesis may not be appropriate. The method used may be unreliable or, even though it may be reliable, it may introduce other variables that produce unknown systematic effects complicating the expected outcome.

Is it possible that we unknowingly introduced such a complication by presenting all the beliefs immediately at the beginning of the experiment? The metaphor that comes to mind here is a silver platter. Could it be that presenting all the beliefs on a silver platter radically alters the cognitive activities leading to the formation of new belief systems. Perhaps our closed subjects no longer resist the formation of new systems when the new beliefs are presented on a silver platter.

Let us therefore do the experiment over again, exactly as before, but this time let us present the new beliefs gradually as we did in Chapters 9, 10, and 11.

EXPERIMENT II: PRESENTING THE NEW BELIEFS GRADUALLY

Experiment II is exactly like Experiment I, except that the new beliefs are presented one at a time, one each at the end of 5 minutes, 10 minutes, and 15 minutes. It was conducted in the spring of 1956 with 20 extremely open and 20 extremely closed subjects, as determined by the Dogmatism Scale, selected from a pool of over 600 students in introductory psychology. The major theoretical question we are concerned with is whether closed persons can adequately cope with a single change introduced into their belief system. But first let us see whether the differences in synthesizing previously found between open and closed persons (see Chapters 9, 10, and 11) are substantiated.

A glance at Table 12.3 shows that they are. The substantiation is very satisfying. Once again there are no significant differences between closed and open subjects in analytic thinking. This is true for the Canopy and the No Canopy Problems, solved in the first position and solved in the second position.[2]

But the usual differences emerge between closed and open subjects on synthesis. These differences are quite consistent from

Table 12.3

Mean Times to Analyze and Synthesize, and Total Time to Solve Canopy and No Canopy Problems by Open and Closed Groups

Doodlebug Problem	Group	Time to Analyze		Time to Synthesize		Total Time	
		Mean [a]	p	Mean	p	Mean	p
		A. PRESENTED FIRST					
No Canopy	Closed	10.9	N.S.	20.1	.03	31.1	.02
	Open	9.4		9.0		18.4	
Canopy	Closed	13.9	N.S.	21.0	.08	34.8	.07
	Open	12.2		15.3		27.6	
		B. PRESENTED SECOND					
No Canopy	Closed	1.3	N.S.	17.2	.05	18.5	.06
	Open	1.7		6.5		8.1	
Canopy	Closed	2.6	N.S.	17.6	.09	20.2	.08
	Open	3.7		12.0		15.6	

N = 10 in each subgroup.

[a] Mean time to analyze refers to total time taken to overcome all three beliefs, and mean time to synthesize refers to total time taken to solve the problem after all three beliefs were overcome.

one problem to the other, and from one position to the other. They are statistically significant or nearly so. And, of course, these differences between open and closed persons are also reflected in the total time they take to solve the problems.

Another finding to which attention is drawn is the sharp improvement in "mean time to analyze" a problem when it is presented second as compared with first. There is really nothing surprising about this. Remember that the three new beliefs of the first problem are clearly in the subject's view on the 3″ × 5″ cards placed before him.

There findings not only strongly support the earlier findings but also extend them in two ways. We now have evidence that the findings on analysis and synthesis hold for the Canopy Problem as well as the No Canopy Problem, and they hold for two problems solved in a row as well as for one problem solved alone. But striking as these results are, they do not yet answer the major question posed at the beginning of this chapter. What about improvements in synthesis—positive transfer effects—from the first to the second position? Naturally, we expect everybody to improve in total time because less time is needed for analysis on the problem that is presented second. This is an artifact of the experiment. Improvements in analysis have to come out as they do because of the way the experiment is conducted. The crucial question is whether open and closed persons improve in the *synthesis* phase of problem-solving. The results are shown in Table 12.4.

Table 12.4

Comparisons Between Problems When Solved First and When Solved Second

Transfer Effect for:	Order of Presentation	Group	Mean Time to Synthesize	p [a]
No Canopy problem	First	Closed	20.1	.50
	Second	Closed	17.2	
	First	Open	9.0	.05
	Second	Open	6.5	
Canopy problem	First	Closed	21.0	.26
	Second	Closed	17.6	
	First	Open	15.3	.08
	Second	Open	12.0	

N = 10 in each subgroup.

[a] In the closed group comparisons two-tail tests are employed since no positive transfer is predicted. In the open group comparisons, one-tail tests are employed since differences are predicted in advance.

Table 12.4 is of course a regrouping of data shown in Table 12.3. It may be read in the following manner: When the closed group solves the No Canopy Problem presented in the first position, its mean time to synthesize is 20.1 minutes; when the No Canopy Problem is presented second, its mean time to synthesize is reduced to 17.2 minutes. This difference is not statistically significant, suggesting an absence of significant improvement or positive transfer. In other words, it takes the closed group almost as long to synthesize the solution to the No Canopy Problem when it is solved after as when it is solved before the Canopy Problem. Likewise, no significant improvement in synthesis is evident for the closed group on the Canopy Problem. In both sets of comparisons, the improvement in synthesizing is roughly 15 per cent, but it is not significant.

In contrast, the open subjects are generally not only more efficient in synthesizing than the closed subjects, but in addition improve significantly or nearly significantly on the second problems they work on. The improvement is roughly 25 per cent. These findings are, then, in contrast to those of Experiment I and in accord with expectations derived from the analysis of party-line thinking presented at the beginning of this chapter. The open group shows significant or nearly significant transfer effects in synthesizing activity; the closed group does not.

COMPARISON BETWEEN THE SILVER-PLATTER AND
WORKING-THROUGH CONDITIONS

Having supported our party-line hypothesis in Condition II but not in Condition I, the question arises: why the difference in results between the two experimental conditions? We have already suggested that in Condition I the beliefs are presented all at once, on a silver platter as it were. In Condition II, the new beliefs are presented gradually, and the subject is given the chance to work them through in his cognitive processes. In both conditions two variations of the Doodlebug Problem are employed. The two variations are identical in all respects but one: one of the three beliefs of the original No Canopy Problem is no longer applicable in the Canopy Problem. Our reason for doing this was to find out how readily subjects readjust their thinking to take this single alteration into realistic account. According to our theory, the greater the isolation of beliefs the less the positive transfer to be expected in moving from one variation of the problem to the other. This is what we find in Condition II, now to be called the Working-Through Condition. Having only themselves to depend on and being unable to rely on external authority for the solution, the closed group takes about as long to integrate the new Doodlebug beliefs when they are presented in the second position as when they are presented in the first position. This absence of significant transfer occurs despite the fact that two of the three beliefs had been already encountered earlier in the first problem. This failure of transfer has been attributed to the relatively greater isolation of beliefs characteristic of those with closed belief systems. It is in these terms that we have attempted to describe what happens in the thought processes of persons said to engage in party-line thinking. The results found with the closed-minded subjects in Condition II are in line with this analysis. Left to their own devices they cannot transfer what they have learned in one problem-solving situation to another one like it. It is almost as if the second problem is a brand new one, not encountered before. In contrast, the open-minded subjects show significantly positive transfer effects, suggesting a state of lesser isolation among beliefs in their belief systems.

Consider now the way in which the results of Condition I differ from those of Condition II. In Condition I, which we will now call the Silver-Platter Condition, we find that the closed group performs as well as the open group in all respects. In fact, the positive transfer effects in the closed group are even somewhat greater than in the open group. These results are quite puzzling until we look more closely at the way in which Condition I differs psychologically from Condition II. In the Silver-Platter Condition, the new beliefs are handed over to the subject all at once. He does not have to "struggle" to grasp them. This being the case, the closed subject encounters no resistance and does not have to reconcile them with his older, everyday beliefs. The problem-solving process can thus proceed more smoothly, more quickly than before, perhaps because the main psychological obstacle has been removed. In this way we may account for the fact that all differences in problem-solving behavior between closed and open subjects are erased in Condition I, and also for the fact that there are sizable transfer effects in both groups. The fact that the closed and open subjects do about as well in the Silver-Platter Condition also shows once more that basically closed-minded persons do not differ from open-minded persons in sheer intellectual ability to synthesize, but rather in dynamic resistances stemming from investments and commitments to everyday belief systems.

We are now content to leave this issue of party-line thinking. The interpretation given above seems to account reasonably well for the absence of party-line thinking in Condition I and for its presence in Condition II. Both sets of results now seem to be reconciled and compatible with the theoretical views stated at the beginning of this chapter. But we are not content to say that our job is altogether finished. Advances in knowledge often come about by capitalizing on unforeseen accidents which require experiments to be done over again. Let us therefore focus more directly on the psychological effects on the thinker when the materials of thought are presented or not presented on "silver platters."

It is highly reasonable to expect that it should take less time to solve the problems when the new beliefs are presented all at once at the outset than when they are presented gradually, because in the former case the thinker does not have to invest any time in analyzing or breaking down old beliefs. It is already done for him. Let us see if total time to solve is indeed less under the Silver-Platter Condition. The results for the closed subjects, which are shown in Table 12.5,* are exactly in accord with this expectation. Their total time to solve is significantly less, at least 10 minutes less, under the Silver-Platter Condition than under the Working-Through Condition. The time saved seems to be clearly due to the fact that analysis is unnecessary. They therefore can proceed forthwith to the synthesis phase of problem-solving.

But not so for the open group. Their total time to solve, surprisingly, is just as long under the Silver-Platter as under the

---

* The results shown in Table 12.5 are for the problems presented in the first position. The comparable data for the second position are not relevant because they are complicated by differential transfer effects for closed and open groups.

Table 12.5

Comparisons Between Silver-Platter and Working-Through Conditions
For Closed and Open Groups for No Canopy and Canopy Problems
Presented in First Position

Group	Experimental Condition	Prob-lem	Mean Time to Analyze	Time to Synthesize		Total Time	
				Mean	p	Mean	p [a]
Closed	Working-through	No	10.9	20.1	N.S.	31.1	.03
	Silver-platter	Canopy	—	18.7		18.7	
	Working-through	Canopy	13.9	21.0	N.S.	34.8	.03
	Silver-platter		—	24.8		24.8	
Open	Working-through	No	9.4	9.0	.01	18.4	N.S.
	Silver-platter	Canopy	—	20.1		20.1	
	Working-through	Canopy	12.2	15.3	.04	27.6	N.S.
	Silver-platter		—	25.4		25.4	

N = 10 in each subgroup.

[a] One-tail tests were used in testing for the significance of differences in mean total time. Two-tail tests were used in testing for the significance of differences in mean time to synthesize, since we were testing the null hypothesis.

Working-Through Condition. How is it that the open-minded subjects fail to "improve" under the Silver-Platter Condition? An inspection of their results on synthesis throws considerable light on the reason. The open-minded subjects take considerably and significantly *longer* to synthesize under the Silver-Platter than under the Working-Through Condition. Why should they take longer? The only sensible way we have thought of to account for these results is to assume that the open-minded subjects are not using all this "extra" time to synthesize, but to analyze, because they reject "silver-platter handouts." It is as if they refuse to have the new beliefs of a system "rammed down their throats" without first trying to relate them to their everyday beliefs. One of our open-minded subjects put this very nicely when he said, at the end of the experiment: "I didn't pay attention to the hints you gave me until I understood the problem."

We thus begin to see why the open group takes as long to arrive at the solution under the two experimental conditions. The greater time they allegedly take to synthesize may not be all spent on this cognitive activity. Part of it seems to be "stolen" for analytic activity in order to compare and to reconcile the new with the old, even if they do not have to, and even if it delays solution. This process seems to be the very thing that the Silver-Platter Condition renders superfluous for the closed group.

But note that the open group can well afford to spend more time to "synthesize" in the Silver-Platter Condition. In the end they are no worse off than the closed group: their total time to solve under the Silver-Platter Condition is no more than the closed group's total time to solve under the Silver-Platter Condition. Also, it is no worse than the open group's total time to solve under the Working-Through Condition. These findings suggest that the open subjects *work through* under the Silver-Platter as well as the Working-Through Condition.

Synopsis

To clarify the process of party-line thinking we have studied here the role of isolation in problem-solving. Would closed and open persons do equally well in solving a second Doodlebug Problem wherein a single change is introduced into the belief system?

Two experiments were conducted. In Experiment I, the Silver-Platter experiment, the new beliefs are given all at once at the beginning. Closed persons solve the two Doodlebug Problems as efficiently as open subjects. Both groups improve to an equal extent in solving the second problem after having solved the first one. These results appear to contradict the hypothesis that closed persons, by virtue of their greater isolation of peripheral beliefs, should function less efficiently than open persons. In Experiment II, the Working-Through experiment, the new beliefs are presented gradually rather than all at once. The usual differences in synthesis emerge between closed and open persons. Moreover, open persons show significant or nearly significant transfer effects from one problem to the next, but the closed persons do not.

We then compared directly the results found in the two experiments in order to learn more about conditions that facilitate the formation of new systems. The closed group, as expected, solves the problems faster in the Silver-Platter than in the Working-Through Condition. But, surprisingly, the open group takes just as long under the two conditions. Furthermore, open subjects take longer to synthesize in the Silver-Platter than in the Working-Through Condition. From these results we tentatively conclude that closed persons work more efficiently with "silver-platter handouts" because the new beliefs need not be reconciled with old beliefs, thereby removing a major obstacle to synthesis leading to the formation of new systems. Open persons, however, resist having new beliefs "rammed down their throats" without first working them through cognitively for themselves. This may account for the fact that open persons take longer than necessary over the problems in the Silver-Platter Condition. In the end this pays off, because it leads to creative problem-solving which in no case, under any experimental condition, is inferior to the problem-solving behavior of persons with closed belief systems.

Notes

1. An interesting incidental finding is that the Canopy Problem is obviously much more difficult than the No Canopy Problem. This may appear puzzling in view of the fact that the Canopy Problem contains two new beliefs while the No Canopy Problem contains three new beliefs. The reason the Canopy Problem is harder is that even though it contains fewer new beliefs the thinker has to take Joe Doodlebug through *more steps* to get him to the food. This takes more time.

2. At this point, the reader may raise the following question. In view of the fact that open and closed groups are not equated for rigidity, and in view of the fact that there is a positive correlation around .45 between dogmatism and rigidity, why do not open and closed groups differ in analysis as well as in synthesis? We must confess that we are not completely clear on the answer to this question. It seems reasonable to expect that open and closed groups should also differ in analysis. Looking back at all the analysis data presented in Chapters 9, 10, and 11, we note that the closed groups are consistently poorer in analysis but that the differences are slight and never reach statistical significance. The consistent trends are in line with theoretical expectations. That these trends are not statistically significant is not in line with theoretical expectations.

13

On Loyalty to and Defection from a Belief System

An Experimental Analogy

Milton Rokeach, John J. Laffey, Alfred Oram, and M. Ray Denny

We speak of defection from the conservative camp, from communism, Catholicism, from a particular theoretical position in psychology. We also speak of defection from a group, but this implies that the group embraces a particular belief system. By defection we mean the relinquishing of a belief system. The belief system is held to be unworkable, false, or impossible; it fails to answer questions or to solve problems to which it addresses itself. The emphasis is not on the giving up of single beliefs, but on the giving up of a whole system of beliefs. Thus, it is not quite appropriate to speak of defecting from, say, a single belief about segregation, or God, or socialized medicine. Defection is a more global phenomenon.

The opposite of defection is loyalty, allegiance, or commitment to a belief system in the face of challenge to its validity. Again, the referent is the total belief system rather than a single belief. One example is the continued adherence to the free enterprise system maintained by many Americans in North Korean prison camps despite pressures to adopt an opposing one. Another is the refusal of many southerners in the United States to submit to what they see to be federal encroachments on the southern way of life.

In the preceding chapter, we have seen how certain theoretical considerations regarding the cognitive structure underlying party-line thinking led us to build a canopy over Joe's food, thereby changing the structural character of the problem, and thus permitting us to test certain hypotheses regarding the role of isolation in party-line thinking and in the formation of new belief systems. In this chapter, we will describe yet another variation of the Doodlebug Problem, designed to explore the processes of loyalty to and defection from a belief system. All the subjects participating in the present research also took part in the research with the No Canopy and Canopy Problems, reported in the preceding chapter. Thus it will be possible not only to compare differences between persons with open and closed belief systems with respect to the processes of loyalty and defection, but also to relate such performances to their earlier problem-solving behavior on the No Canopy and Canopy Problems.

With these remarks, let us now return to the miniature world of Joe Doodlebug. By the time the subject has solved the No Canopy and Canopy Problems he has learned a new set of beliefs and, with or without the experimenter's help, has learned to feel more or less at home within the new system.* We will now introduce the subject to yet a third variation, which has the structure shown in Figure 13.1.

In Figure 13.1, beliefs a, $\bar{b}$ and $\bar{c}$ represent the three beliefs employed in the Canopy Problem. The symbols stand, respec-

---

* The vast majority of subjects solve the problems within the prescribed time limits. If at the end of this time limit the subject has not solved the problem, the solution is presented and explained by the experimenter.

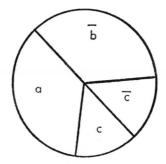

FIGURE 13.1. The impossible world of Joe Doodlebug.

tively, for the old facing belief and for the new direction and new movement beliefs. But this time, we also propose to add belief c in opposition to belief $\bar{c}$. In other words, contradictory information regarding one of the beliefs (the movement belief) will be presented so that the Doodlebug world is an impossible one for Joe to live in. What is to be required of the thinker is the discovery that the problem is impossible to solve and the discovery of the contradiction that makes it so. When he has done so, we will say he has defected from the new belief system, thus providing us with an operational definition of defection. On the other hand, we will say that the subject remains loyal to the new system if he continues to insist over a specified period of time that there *is* a solution, even though he cannot see it.

What can we expect of persons with open and closed belief systems when confronted with this impossible world of Joe Doodlebug? Our views on what should happen at the cognitive level are very similar to those put forward to account for party-line thinking: The structural differences underlying defection on the one hand and loyalty on the other may again be thought of in terms of differences in degree of isolation of beliefs. The greater the isolation, the less the ability to see logical contradictions between beliefs. Consequently, the integration or synthesizing process will be more slowed down when the problem solution hinges upon the discovery of such contradictions. We are thus led to expect that those with relatively closed belief systems will, by virtue of relatively greater isolation within their belief systems, be unable to see logical contradictions between beliefs. The greater isolation arises from the fact that they have "faith" in the experimenter-authority, refuse to believe that they would be given a problem that has no solution, and thus remain dogmatically loyal to an impossible belief system. On the other hand, we expect persons with relatively open systems, by virtue of the greater intercommunication among their beliefs, to be less dependent upon authority, to see through the internal contradiction, and thus to defect from the impossible system.

The Impossible World of Joe Doodlebug

The situation that enables us to test the loyalty-defection hypothesis will be called the Impossible Problem, which is presented to the subject in typewritten form as follows:

The Conditions

Joe Doodlebug is a strange sort of imaginary bug. He can and cannot do the following things:
1. He can jump in only four different directions: north, south, east, and west. He cannot jump diagonally (southeast, northwest, etc.).
2. Once he starts in any direction, that is, north, south, east, or west, he must jump four times in that same direction before he can switch to another direction.
3. He can only jump, not crawl, fly, or walk.
4. He can jump very large distances or very small distances, but not less than one inch per jump.
5. Joe cannot turn around.

The Situation

Joe has been jumping all over the place getting some exercise when his master places a pile of food three feet directly west of him. Joe notices that the pile of food is a little larger than he. As soon as Joe sees all this food he stops dead in his tracks, facing north. After all his exercise, Joe is very tired and wants to get to the food as quickly as he possibly can. Joe examines the situation, noticing that there is a low canopy over the food, then says, *"Darn it, since I have already made one jump to the east, I'll have to jump four times to get to the food."* *

* This sentence was, of course, not italicized in the instructions given to the subjects. It is the added condition that Joe had been traveling east which makes the problem impossible to solve.

The Problem

Joe Doodlebug was a smart bug and he was dead right in his conclusion. Why do you suppose Joe Doodlebug had to take four jumps, no more and no less, to reach the food?

Hints

1. Joe must face the food in order to eat it.
2. Joe can jump sideways and backwards as well as forwards.
3. Joe is not necessarily at the beginning or end of a series of jumps. He may have been somewhere in a series of jumps.

Recall that the solution to the Canopy Problem is that Joe had jumped once to the *west*. The only way in which the Impossible Problem differs from the Canopy Problem is the addition of the instruction that Joe had been traveling *east* at the time the food was placed down. Were it not for this addition, the problem and the solution would be identical with that of the Canopy Problem. The subject, confronted with the Impossible Problem, is fully aware of the solutions to the Canopy Problem and to the No Canopy Problem because he had solved them a week before, and because these problems, the hints, and the solutions are now all before him in written form by way of reminder. Thus, the additional notion that Joe was traveling east does not make sense. It contradicts the subject's belief that Joe had been traveling to the *west*. How can Joe possibly get there now in four jumps? The fact is that under the conditions stated Joe can no longer get to the food in four jumps. He must take more than four jumps since he now has to change his direction of movement *twice*—from east to west and from west to south. Actually he must take eight jumps: three more to the east, four to the west, landing on top of the canopy, and one to the south.

METHOD: WHEREIN THE SUBJECT BECOMES THE EXPERIMENTER AND THE EXPERIMENTER BECOMES THE SUBJECT

The procedure we employed is unusual from a methodological standpoint if for no other reason than that it involves a reversal of the experimenter and subject roles: the subject is paid to be the

experimenter and the experimenter pretends he is the subject.*
Our reason for adopting this procedure is that in a preliminary
study we found it very difficult to get subjects to defect. Even
after generous amounts of time, the subjects continued to assume
that there was a solution to the problem and interpreted their
failure to solve it as a reflection on their own intellectual abilities. In two cases the experiment was continued over a period of
several days. With repeated failure to find a solution we observed
a withdrawal. The two subjects, close acquaintances of the senior
author, went out of their way to avoid him. When pressed for a
solution, they replied that they "got tired" of seeking a solution
or were "too busy." Accordingly, the reversal of experimenter and
subject roles was adopted with the hope that it would prevent
the subjects' withdrawal and encourage defection.

Let us for the record describe the procedure in its exact details.
Upon returning to work on the Impossible Problem—about a
week after having worked on the No Canopy and Canopy Problems—the subject is met by one of the two experimenters † and
told the following:

> You did pretty well on those problems last time. They are
> so difficult many people never solve them at all. Do you do
> much work with problems like that?
>
> You don't say. Say, we have a project going on here that
> ought to interest you. You know, whenever we give prob-
> lems to people to solve, there's always the chance we get
> biased results through the experimenter giving unconscious
> clues to the subject. In other words, the experimenter un-
> consciously tips off the subject when he gets close to the
> solution. It's probably something like ESP, you know, ex-
> trasensory perception.
>
> We are trying something that's never been done before
> in psychology. We are testing subjects who, of course,
> don't know the answer to the problem but the unusual
> thing is that we are also using experimenters who don't
> know the answer either.
>
> The trouble is, that for each subject we need a new ex-
> perimenter, and there just aren't that many people in the

* We gratefully acknowledge the help of Dr. Charles Hanley, who gave us the
idea and helped us design the experimental procedure.
† J. L. and A. O.

Psychology Department to do the job. So we've had our eye out for intelligent undergraduates who seem to know their way around these problems, to act as an experimenter for us just once.

For work like this you really ought to be paid pretty well, but our research budget is limited, and we can afford to pay you only one dollar. Your job is simply to give the third problem to another person to solve, and we'll pay you a dollar for doing so. We have it worked out so that there is very little for you to do. Since you haven't been trained in taking notes, everything will be recorded automatically on this tape recorder, which I'll put on, so you won't have to worry about this at all.

You just read the instructions to the subject, and put the problem and hints on the table for him to look at, and then start the stop watch. He's already had the first two problems, so he shouldn't have any questions.

The rest is very simple. If the subject gives an answer, and you agree with it, just tell him so. On the other hand, if he gives an answer which you think is wrong, tell him so also. In other words, act natural.

Let the subject work for 30 minutes, or until he solves the problem, whichever comes first. If you should notice anything interesting that the subject says or does, you might tell me about it when you finish.

Are there any questions?

We have a subject scheduled to come in about now. You could be the experimenter for him."

Proceeding in this way, it was possible to enlist the cooperation of each subject who appeared for the third problem.

At this point the experimenter introduces the subject to a third person, the alleged subject, who is really a confederate of the experimenter. This confederate is dressed in typical campus apparel and appears friendly and cooperative, but naive. Thus, the two roles are reversed: the subject acts the role of experimenter; the confederate acts the role of subject.

When the experimenter leaves the room, the recorder is on. The subject reads the Impossible Problem aloud to the confederate and in this way they both become familiar with it. The subject finds all this quite natural since he had experienced this procedure a week before as a subject in the No Canopy and Canopy experiments.

At the end of five minutes, the confederate states: "Are you sure there's a solution to this problem?"

At five-minute intervals thereafter, the confederate states. "This problem is impossible. Could that be the answer, that Joe can't make it in four jumps?"

At no time does the confederate give reasons for his statements, but each time merely tries to elicit a response of agreement or disagreement from the subject regarding the impossibility of the problem.

At the end of 30 minutes or sooner, if defection has occurred, (i.e., the subject agrees with the confederate and correctly says why he agrees) the watch is stopped, and the subject contacts the original experimenter. The latter thanks the confederate for his cooperation, pledges him to secrecy, and dismisses him. The subject is then asked for his impressions of the experiment, and if defection has occurred, he is asked why he thinks the problem is impossible to solve. If defection has not yet occurred, the subject is asked what he thinks the answer is and why. The subject is then thanked, pledged to secrecy, and paid.

Results

The subjects were 26 of the 40 individuals who had participated in Experiment II (Working-Through Condition) which we reported in the preceding chapter. Twelve scored extremely high on the Dogmatism Scale, 14 low. It is unfortunate that the number of cases is small, since differences between closed and open subjects must be quite substantial to reach statistical significance. Nevertheless, the results are fairly clear, as shown in Table 13.1.

There were three kinds of responses to the Impossible Problem, rather than the two originally anticipated: (1) Six out of the 12 closed subjects (50 per cent) as against 3 out of the 14 open subjects (21 per cent) remained loyal to the end of the experiment; they continued to believe that a solution was possible—in spite of repeated suggestions at five-minute intervals by the confederate that there was no solution. (2) Exactly half of the closed group and half of the open group defected, said that the problem was

Table 13.1

Frequency of Loyalty, Defection, and Round-the-world
Solutions in Closed and Open Groups

| | Number of Persons Who: | | | |
Group	Remained Loyal	Defected	Emerged with New Solution	Total
Closed	6 (50%)	6 (50%)	0 (0%)	12
Open	3 (21%)	7 (50%)	4 (29%)	14

impossible to solve, and were able to state why it was impossible to solve. (3) An unexpected finding was that 4 subjects, all open-minded, emerged with a new creative solution which was correct even though unanticipated by us when we had designed the problem: Joe could get to the food by jumping three times to the east, *around the world,* thereby landing with the third jump on top of the canopy. Joe then jumps once backward off the canopy to the south and is in a position to eat. This solution occurs quite rarely. In other research with the Doodlebug Problem we have encountered it less than 5 times in a 100. In the present experiment, it occurred 4 times among the 14 open-minded subjects and not once in the 12 closed-minded subjects.

Are the over-all results found for closed and open subjects statistically significant, or could they have arisen by chance? Statistical analysis shows that the differences between the two groups are significant.[1] The psychological significance of these results will be discussed shortly.

We will now consider whether nonintegrative (isolated) vs. integrative performance in solving the Impossible Problem is related to nonintegrative vs. integrative performance in solving the No Canopy and Canopy Problems, described in the preceding chapter. It will be recalled that we regarded the absence of improvement or positive transfer from one problem to the second to be an index of nonintegrative, party-line thinking, that is, isolated thinking. Subjects were given the two problems in either of two orders: the No Canopy Problem followed by the Canopy Problem, or vice versa. We first determined for each subject whether there was a savings effect (improvement) in proceeding from one problem to the next. This was done in the following way: let the mean time to solve by the closed and open groups who had the No Canopy Problem first provide us with two base lines of how long it normally takes to solve this problem; let the groups solving the Canopy Problem first provide us with similar base lines. Then, if a subject solves a given problem when it is in the second position in less than the normal time for his group we may say that there has been a savings effect. Such a savings effect is indicative of a relatively nonisolated, integrative belief system. On the other hand, if a subject's solution time in the second position is equal to or greater than the mean solution time required by his group when it is given in the first position, there is no saving, and we may assume this as indicative of a relatively more isolated belief system. In this way we can classify our subjects into two groups, regardless of their being closed or open, on the basis of whether they do or do not show a positive transfer effect. We can then compare these two groups on their problem-solving behavior on the Impossible Problem in order to see whether behavior on the Canopy and No Canopy Problems is related to behavior on the Impossible Problem. The results of this comparison are shown in Table 13.2.

Table 13.2

Relation Between Transfer Effect on the No Canopy and Canopy Problems and Behavior on the Impossible Problem

	Number of Subjects Showing:		
	Positive Transfer	No Positive Transfer	Total
Remained loyal	3 (33%)	6 (67%)	9
Defected or found new solution	13 (76%)	4 (24%)	17

The results come out as expected in 19 of the 26 cases. Of the 17 subjects who defected or found the "round-the-world" solution, 13 showed positive transfer effects; of the 9 who remained loyal, only 3 showed positive transfer effects. The differences are very significant.[2]

Interpretations and Implications

In discussing these findings we may say, in the language of politics and religion, that the subject is first indoctrinated with a new cause. The work he does on the No Canopy and Canopy Problems, the hints given, the review of these problems and solutions immediately prior to the presentation of the Impossible Problem, all serve to indoctrinate the subject to think comfortably in terms of Joe Doodlebug's cosmological framework. As the subject works on the Impossible Problem he is put to the test by an infidel who heckles him with insinuations that his cause is an impossible one. The infidel is, of course, the confederate disguised as subject. The true believer is the subject appointed (we are also tempted to say, anointed) by the experimenter. His loyalty comes naturally and perhaps, just a little bit, is bought by the experimenter.

Despite the small number of cases, two fairly clear findings emerge:

1. Although closed and open groups do not differ from each other in frequency of defection, the closed-minded subjects persist twice as often as open-minded subjects in their belief that there is a solution, despite repeated suggestions by the confederate that the problem has no solution. Furthermore, four creative solutions are obtained, all from open-minded subjects, saving the theory underlying the new cause from logical annihilation, and thereby obviating the need to defect from it.

What is the theoretical significance of this novel, round-the-world solution? It has already been stated that continued loyalty to an inherently contradictory belief system is regarded as an indication of relative isolation, and defection an indication of relative intercommunication among beliefs. The round-the-world solution likewise points to high intercommunication among beliefs, a fuller appreciation of the requirement that a system has to be internally consistent. The round-the-world solution neatly and correctly staves off the annihilation of the system. Thus, the results suggest that more of the closed subjects remain dogmatically loyal, once more indicating greater isolation among their beliefs; in contrast, more of the open subjects find creative solutions that save the new cosmology, suggesting greater intercommunication among their beliefs.

2. The great majority of the subjects who either defect or find creative solutions to the Impossible Problem also show positive transfer effects in proceeding from the No Canopy to the Canopy Problem, or from the Canopy to the No Canopy Problem; in contrast, most of the subjects who remain loyal in the Impossible Problem show no positive transfer.

Both sets of results fit in well with our conception of the differential role of isolation in open and closed belief systems. Because of the greater isolation of boundaries with closed belief systems, persons thus characterized have greater difficulty in integrating or synthesizing the new rules governing Joe's behavior. Their grasp of the system is precarious and when a contradiction arises within it, they are less prepared to entertain it. In this way people in everyday life may become trapped within impossible systems without knowing it, and strive for solutions that may never come. In this way, the absence of isolation may account for the fact that those who defect or find creative solutions also show positive transfer effects.

There is one further point to which we now wish to draw attention. What is the social-psychological situation for the subject as he proceeds to solve the Impossible Problem? Scrutiny of our method reveals that our subjects are confronted with the task of mastering a new miniature belief system. But note also that all efforts to this end take place within the framework of a social system composed of three persons who each play prescribed roles. First, there is the original experimenter who is in an authority position. He sets the stage, structures the situation, poses the task. In sociological terms, he is the subject's "significant other." Then there is the subject to whom authority is relegated to serve as an experimenter, who is responsible to authority, and who reports back to the authority at the end of the experiment. The subject agrees to join this social system partly because he is required to participate in a psychological experiment to satisfy a course requirement, partly because he is motivated by curiosity, and partly because he is getting paid for it. Finally, there is the third person, the confederate who plays the role of subject.

It is within such a miniature social system that the problem-solving behavior of the subject takes place. True, the social system we have just described is not a typical one. But the point is that *every* research on human cognitive activity includes an experimenter and a subject who bear explicit and implicit relations to each other. Thus, every experimental situation represents some sort of social system and, in the final analysis, cognitive behavior is a joint function of mental activity and the social system in which it takes place. In the series of Doodlebug experiments reported herein we have admittedly concentrated primarily on the analysis of individual rather than social variables as determinants of the fate of cognitive activity. But what we learned from the present series of experiments, especially the one now under discussion, is that in everyday life there is an inherent social character to most of our problem-solving activity which is often overlooked. At every step we observe the thinker to be dependent upon the experimenter as authority figure. He looks to the experimenter for confirmation of each step he takes toward the solution. Moreover, contrary to present-day psychological theory, the activity of the subject does *not* seem to cease with the problem solution. It goes on until the subject is able to check the end result of his mental activity against external authority. Imagine what would happen if, after the solution were achieved, there is no experimenter to tell it to? *

Most research on cognitive activity has ignored the miniature social system within which it necessarily takes place, as if to say that thinking is purely a private affair, a purely intrapsychic process. The experimenter is seen to be merely an observer rather than one who because he knows the answer is an authority figure in the eyes of the subject. It is hoped that by pointing to the social structures within which thinking takes place we will become more sensitized to them so that future research on the cognitive processes will give them greater due.

---

* An experiment is now in progress, in collaboration with R. Hoppe and J. Marr, that is designed to study how the thought processes are affected when there is no opportunity for confirmation with external authority.

Synopsis

The research reported herein compares the problem-solving behavior of persons with relatively open and closed systems when they are confronted with a new system that has contradictions built into it. Defection is a process wherein it is discovered that such a belief system is unworkable and why it is so. Conversely, loyalty is a process wherein the thinker continues to have faith that there is a solution. The results show no differences between closed and open subjects in frequency of defection. But closed subjects more frequently remain loyal, that is, continue to believe that there is a solution. Conversely, open subjects more frequently find an ingenious, creative solution that saves the system so that it is unnecessary to defect from it.

It was also found that those who defect or find the ingenious solution to the Impossible Problem more frequently show positive transfer in solving the No Canopy and Canopy Problems. Conversely, those who remain loyal exhibit positive transfer less frequently.

All results are interpreted in terms of the property of isolation of belief systems, which is assumed to be greater in those with relatively closed systems as compared to those with relatively open systems.

Notes

1. To test for significance a modification of Fisher's exact test was used. We are grateful to Drs. Ingram Olkin and Charles Kraft of the Statistics Department at Michigan State University for working out this test. According to their analysis, the model under consideration is that of two independent trinomial distributions with parameters (p_1, p_2, p_3) and (q_1, q_2, q_3), and the hypothesis to be tested is $p_1 = q_1$, $p_2 = q_2$. A particular choice of alternative will dictate a most powerful similar test against the alternative. The problem does not specify a single alternative, but instead indicates a set of alternatives to be considered; namely, p_1 larger than q_1 and p_2 larger than q_2. Since there is no uniformly most powerful similar test for this set of alternatives, the test employed is a compromise among several of the most powerful similar tests. Within this context, the null hypothesis was rejected at the .03 level.

2. As determined by chi-square. The value is 6.58, which with a one-tail test is significant beyond the .01 level.

14

The Formation of New
Perceptual Systems

Jacques M. Levy and Milton Rokeach

$\mathbf{W}$e think of Joe Doodlebug's world as a conceptual system. It involves a set of rules that are to be manipulated in one's head for the purpose of solving problems. All the Doodlebug investigations concern the formation of new conceptual systems, and concern various psychological factors that speed it up and slow it down in open and closed persons. We will now try, in this chapter[*] and in the one that follows, to broaden the scope of our investigations to include perceptual and esthetic systems as well as conceptual ones. Our structural approach commits us to expect consistencies in open and

[*] We wish to express our gratitude to Miss Joann S. Maryo for her help in carrying out this research.

closed persons with respect to all kinds of systems and to search them out in widely separated areas of behavior. For, if a person's *total* belief system can indeed be meaningfully placed along a spectrum from open to closed, then this total state of mind should be reflected in any area of human functioning that requires that new systems be entertained and formed.

In this chapter we will ask whether open and closed persons differ in their ease of synthesizing perceptual systems in the same way they differ in ease of synthesizing conceptual systems. Most directly relevant as a point of departure is the work of Witkin and his associates, who have long concerned themselves with the relation between personality and perceptual functioning. Using many and varied testing procedures, they emerge with a body of findings which they systematically relate to a personality continuum ranging from "field-dependent" to "field-independent."

> Field-dependent persons tend to be characterized by passivity in dealing with the environment; by unfamiliarity with and fear of their own impulses, together with poor control over them; by lack of self-esteem; and by the perception of a relatively primitive, undifferentiated body image. Independent or analytical perceptual performers, in contrast, tend to be characterized by activity and independence in relation to the environment; by closer communication with, and better control of, their own impulses; and by relatively high self-esteem and a more differentiated, mature body image (1954, p. 469).

It is in terms of this basic characteristic of field-dependence vs. field-independence that Witkin and his associates account for many of the empirical relations they find between various personality measures and their battery of perceptual tests. And they describe the basic purpose of these perceptual tasks as being the measurement of individual differences in the ability to separate "item from field." (p. 116.)

The ability to separate item from field is the ability to break down the field, that is, to perceive *analytically*. This ability to analyze is what their battery of perceptual tasks appears to be tapping, and differences in this ability to analyze constitute the essence of the differences in perception between field-independent and field-dependent persons.

The present research will deal not only with the ability to perceive in an analytic manner—the concern of Witkin and his associates—but also with the ability to perceive in a synthesizing manner. Recall that in the Doodlebug experiments we have had a lot to say about the phases of analysis and synthesis in thinking. The conceptual breaking down of beliefs embedded in a belief system seems to be closely analogous to the perceptual "separation of item from field." The synthesizing of new beliefs into a new system seems likewise analogous to the building up of "items into a new field."

Recall also our distinction between rigid and dogmatic thinking. Persons differing in rigidity differ primarily in analytic ability; persons differing in dogmatism differ primarily in synthesizing ability. It would thus seem reasonable to interpret tentatively the findings by Witkin and his associates as being concerned with the problem of rigidity, but not of dogmatism. By the same token we also see the field-dependent person as a rigid person because he is relatively unable to break down analytically perceptual sets.[1]

These considerations set the stage for the research to be reported here. More specifically, our experiment is designed to pit the two modes of perceptual functioning—analysis and synthesis—against each other. People with relatively closed systems should not differ from those with relatively open systems on tasks requiring perceptual analysis, but they should differ from each other on tasks requiring perceptual synthesis. In Witkin's term, closed individuals should adequately handle tasks requiring separation of item from field, but should differ on tasks requiring synthesis or integration of perceptual items into a new field.

The Perceptual Tasks

The perceptual task used to tap analytic functioning is the Gottschaldt embedded-figures test developed by Witkin (1950).* The full test is made up of 24 complex designs, and the subject is instructed to locate simple figures contained within each complex design. A sample is shown in Figure 14.1. In this study, we used a short form of this test, as suggested by Jackson (1956). It con-

* We are grateful to Dr. H. A. Witkin for making this test available to us.

sists of 12 instead of the original 24 complex figures, with a three-minute time limit given to locate each simple figure contained within the complex figure. Jackson reports that this abbreviated test correlates from .96 to .99 with the longer test.

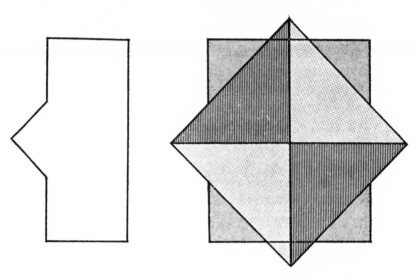

FIGURE 14.1. Sample of simple and complex figures used in embedded-figures test.

The perceptual task used to study perceptual synthesis is adapted from the well-known block-design test. Such designs were originally constructed by Kohs (1923), and the ones we will use here are those taken from the Wechsler Adult Intelligence Scale (1955) and from the Goldstein-Scheerer Cube Test (1941). In the usual administration of this test the subject is presented with a series of printed red-and-white designs of varying complexity. He is also given from 4 to 16 cubes or blocks. Each block has some of its sides painted white, some painted red, and some painted half red and half white (diagonally). The subject's task is to reproduce the printed design with these blocks. A sample is shown in Figure 14.2.

In the adaptation used here, which we call the perceptual synthesis task, the subject is first shown a red-and-white design and is asked to reproduce it with four blocks. He is then asked to reproduce it once again, but this time the design is (1) to be enlarged (built with 9 or 16 blocks) *and at the same time* (2) rotated 90 degrees to the left or right (it must not be built first and then rotated) *and at the same time* (3) the colors must be interchanged—red replaces white and white replaces red. All of this takes place with the printed colored design placed in front of the subject in its original position.

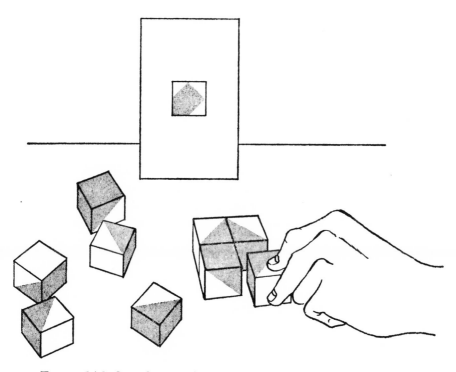

FIGURE 14.2. Sample item from the block-design test.

As in the Doodlebug experiments, there are three beliefs or sets which the subject has to overcome and then reintegrate—a size set, a position set, and a color set. The main task confronting the subject is to replace the sets he builds up while working with four blocks with three new sets in order to reconstruct the same design in accord with instructions. By the very nature of this task he cannot deal with the three new sets one at a time. He must deal with them all at once in an integrative fashion. In contrast to the Gottschaldt embedded-figures task, which requires the analytic separation of item from field, the perceptual synthesis task requires the simultaneous integration of three new items into a new field.

The perceptual synthesis test is composed of 6 designs, with a 5-minute time limit given for each one. In 4 of them (Type A), the subject is required to expand the 4-block design to a 16-block design; in 2 (Type B), the design is rebuilt with 9 blocks.*

Subjects and Procedure

A total of 41 subjects scoring extremely high and low on the Dogmatism Scale were tested individually with both tests. They were selected from a pool of about 400 students. For the first time in our research program we discovered that open subjects scored significantly higher than closed subjects on intelligence, again as measured by the American Council on Education Test. To equate the two groups on intelligence, it was necessary to eliminate 8 subjects who scored at the extremes. This procedure left us with 33 subjects, 17 scoring extremely high and 16 scoring extremely low on the Dogmatism Scale. These groups now no longer differed significantly in intelligence although the open group still scored somewhat higher on the average. Seven of the closed group and 6 of the open group were women.

Each subject is tested individually, the session lasting from one to one-and-a-half hours. The embedded-figures test is given first, followed by the block-designs test. This order of presentation of the figures and designs tests is the same for all subjects.

The directions for the embedded-figures test are as follows:

> "I am going to show you a series of colored designs. Each time I show you one of these designs, I want you to describe the over-all pattern that you see in it. After you have examined each design, I will show you a simpler figure which is contained in that larger design. You will be given that larger design again, and your job will be to locate the smaller figure in it. Let's go through one to show you how it's done."

Show subject the larger design (sample) for 15 seconds.

---

* A seventh design was also used. It was to be built with 9 blocks but it is actually impossible to do so. The solution is to discover that the problem is impossible. Only 10 of the 33 subjects (6 open and 4 closed subjects) discovered this fact.

Then have him turn it over and show him the smaller figure for 10 seconds. After that, say: "I will now show you the original figure again and you are to find the smaller figure in it." Remove the smaller figure. After subject finds the figure, say: "Would you now trace the figure with this [a pencil] without touching the paper."

Then: "This is how we will proceed on all trials. I would like to add that in every case the smaller figure will be present in the larger design. It will always be in the upright position. Work as quickly as possible since I will be timing you, but be sure that the figure you find is exactly the same as the original figure, both in size and in proportions. As soon as you have found the figure, tell me at once. If you ever forget what the small figure looks like, you may ask to see it again. Are there any questions?"

If the subject asks to see the smaller figure again, the watch is stopped, and the smaller figure is shown for 10 seconds with the larger figure hidden from view. Then the larger figure is again placed in view, the smaller figure removed, and the watch is started again. If an incorrect solution is offered, the subject is told it is incorrect and urged to continue.

Next comes the perceptual synthesis tasks. The first one is a sample, and if the subject encounters difficulty he is given sparing help. After the sample has been explained, he is told that the tasks to follow are all of the same general kind. The subject is shown a colored block design on a card and asked to reproduce it with 4 blocks. After the design is built with 4 blocks, it is broken up and 9 (or 16) blocks are now placed on the table before him. His task is to reproduce the design again, but this time with the 9 (or 16) blocks, with the colors interchanged and the design rotated 90 degrees. The subject is not permitted to turn his head to the side in order to see the card at a 90-degree angle. Throughout, the card remains in the original position. If the design is rebuilt without rotating it and the subject offers it as a finished product, he is informed that this is not correct and is told that it must be rebuilt. In the case where reproduction is required with 9 blocks, it is stressed that the reproduction will be symmetrical, but not exactly proportional to the design on the card.

Finally, the subject is told he is being timed and asked to report when he is finished with each design. When he does so, the time is recorded and the next design is placed before him.

Table 14.1

Mean Solution Time to Each of the 12 Embedded-Figures Tasks by Closed and Open Groups

	Means		
Embedded-Figures Tasks	Closed Group (N = 17)	Open Group (N = 16)	Difference [a]
1-C1	1:00	1:09	—:09
2-D1	1:09	1:05	:04
3-E1	:50	1:05	—:15
4-A2	2:16	2:45	—:29
5-C2	:53	:32	:21
6-G1	:25	:14	:11
7-A3	:29	:32	—:03
8-H1	1:51	1:24	:27
9-E3	1:30	1:28	:02
10-C3	1:08	:52	:16
11-D2	:17	:07	:10
12-E5	:52	:39	:13

[a] Not one of these differences is significant.

Results

Table 14.1 shows the average time taken by open and closed subjects in the 12 embedded figures. They are presented in the order in which they were given to the subject, the code number in each case corresponding to Witkin's (1950). Open and closed persons, then, do not seem to differ on the ability to perceive analytically.

As for perceptual synthesis, the results are shown in Table 14.2. They are again arranged in the order in which they were given to the subjects. If our hypothesis is correct, we would expect to find that the closed group takes longer than the open group to synthesize. We see that this expectation is fairly well borne out. On all 6 designs the closed group takes longer than the open group. The differences on the fourth, fifth, and sixth designs are nearly significant.[2]

Note also the appearance of a definite order effect. The differ-

Table 14.2

Mean Solution Time to Each of the 6 Perceptual Synthesis Tasks for Closed and Open Groups

Perceptual Synthesis Tasks	Means		Difference	p
	Closed Group (N = 17)	Open Group (N = 16)		
1-A1	3:57	3:49	:08	.39
2-A2	3:15	3:06	:09	.47
3-B1	3:27	2:47	:40	.19
4-A3	3:22	2:11	1:11	.06
5-A4	3:59	3:03	:56	.06
6-B2	3:34	2:47	:47	.09

ences between the closed and open groups tend to get larger as we proceed from the first to the last block design. A possible reason for this order effect will be considered shortly.

The results shown in Table 14.2 may be fruitfully supplemented with a further analysis of the number of open and closed

Table 14.3

Number of Closed and Open Subjects Who Pass and Fail Each of the 6 Perceptual Synthesis Tasks

Group	Perceptual Synthesis Tasks											
	A1		A2		B1		A3		A4		B2	
	Pass	Fail	Pass	Fail	Pass	Fail	Pass	Fail	Pass	Fail	Pass	Fail
Closed	12	5	12	5	10	7	10	7	8	9	11	6
Open	11	5	10	6	14	2	14	2	13	3	13	3

subjects who reconstruct or fail to reconstruct each block design within the 5-minute time limit given them. The results are shown in Table 14.3. Open and closed persons apparently do not differ from each other on the first two designs. But on the last four there are more failures in the closed group than in the open group. The differences are significant for designs B1, A3, and A4.[3]

Interpretations

There is little doubt, as Witkin and his associates have shown, that the process of perceptual analysis plays an important role in the personality functioning of the individual. These investigators have presented a substantial body of evidence which suggests that this ability penetrates to the very core of personality. The "field-dependent" person—the person who cannot function adequately in terms of perceptual analysis—is regarded by them as passive, not able to struggle actively and independently with his world, and not able to manipulate his external environment to any degree.

Our own theoretical pursuits require us to investigate the nature of perceptual synthesis as well as perceptual analysis. It is fairly clear from the data presented that there is empirical support for the distinction we have made between analysis and synthesis in perceptual functioning. And, as was the case with conceptual functioning, we find here also that relatively open-minded and closed-minded subjects do not differ with respect to the ability to analyze. They both seem equally adequate in this respect. But we do find the expected differences on perceptual synthesis. Open-minded individuals are consistently better able than closed-minded individuals to reconstruct the block designs into a new field.

Let us reflect for a moment on exactly what the subject is required to do in the perceptual synthesis task. He is first asked to reproduce tridimensionally with four blocks a complex colored design printed bidimensionally on a card. Then he is asked to reproduce it—enlarged, rotated, and with colors reversed—all at once. Most of our subjects balk and some of them audibly groan at this request when it is first made because it requires a real effort. They have to imagine how the reconstructed design will look before it is reconstructed. However, as the experimental situation progresses, we observe some of our subjects to be more willing to "go along," to put up less resistance to the perceptual tasks. As they continue to work, some of them find that the tasks are not so hard after all, and that they can successfully complete them if they put their minds to it.

Herein lies what we think is the significance of the order effect to which we have already drawn attention. At the very outset, the closed and open groups are fairly equal in their ability to reconstruct the designs perceptually. As the series progresses, however, the gap between them seems to grow larger. The open-minded subjects appear to resist less, or in Rogers' (1951) terms, to be "more open to experience." Thus, they generally seem to take less time than the closed-minded subjects to synthesize as they proceed from problem to problem. Of the 16 open-minded subjects, 5 or 6 fail to reconstruct the first two tasks and this is reduced to 2 or 3 out of 16 who fail to do so on the last four tasks. But the closed-minded group appears to resist more as the test progresses. Although 5 out of 17 fail to reconstruct the first two tasks, this is increased to anywhere from 6 to 9 out of 17 who fail to do so on the last four tasks.

These improvements or lack of improvements are of course reminiscent of similar findings noted in the subjects who solved both the Canopy and No Canopy Problems in the party-line experiment. In Chapter 12 we attributed the degree of positive transfer effects to the degree of isolation in the belief system. The order effects noted here on perceptual synthesis can be theoretically accounted for in the same way.

We will soon see similar order effects in the next chapter, which deals with open and closed reactions to continued exposure to new musical systems. Closed subjects do not appear to like new kinds of music, and like it even less after repeated exposure. Open subjects also do not like new music at first, but they get to like it with repeated exposure.

The fact that open and closed persons differ on perceptual synthesis but not on perceptual analysis does not mean that the two processes are mutually exclusive. They are probably no more so than the processes of conceptual analysis and synthesis. In the present study, as in the Doodlebug studies, we have deliberately set up procedures for separating them in order to expose them better to view. But in everyday life the two processes of analysis and synthesis undoubtedly go on at once, interwoven.

As in our previous studies, it is necessary to consider again the role of intelligence as possibly accounting for the differences found between open and closed groups. It has already been pointed out that the closed group initially selected was significantly lower in intelligence than the open group, as measured by the American Council on Education Test. To match these groups more closely on intelligence we had to eliminate some of the cases. But even after matching, the closed group was still slightly lower than the open group on this variable, although not significantly. Is it possible that this slight difference in intelligence between the two groups can account for the differences found on perceptual synthesis? Our opinion, once more, is that this is not likely.

Recall that the two groups do not differ in perceptual analysis, as measured by the embedded-figures test. Jackson (1957) reports a correlation of —.53 between intelligence and scores obtained on the embedded-figures test. Thus, since the closed and open groups differ slightly in intelligence, we should expect that they would also differ on the embedded-figures test. But this is not the case. They differ only on the perceptual synthesis test. We therefore conclude that the two sets of findings—the absence of differences in perceptual analysis, and the presence of differences in perceptual synthesis—cannot be accounted for by the small differences in intelligence between closed and open groups.

Synopsis

In this chapter we have tried to extend our hypothesis and research findings in the area of conceptual functioning to that of perceptual functioning. In an experiment analogous to our investigation of the processes of conceptual analysis and synthesis, we have here distinguished between perceptual analysis and synthesis. On the basis of previous theory and research it was anticipated that closed and open persons should not differ from each other on perceptual analysis, but should differ from each other on perceptual synthesis.

Witkin's embedded-figures test was used to measure individual differences in the ability to perceive analytically. A second test was specially devised to measure perceptual synthesis. The subjects were first required to reproduce a colored Kohs design with 4 blocks, then to reconstruct it again with 9 or 16 blocks, with colors reversed and rotated 90 degrees—all at once. Closed and open subjects do not differ in speed of perceptual analysis, as measured by Witkin's embedded-figures test, but they do differ in speed of perceptual synthesis, as measured by the block-design tasks.

The findings suggest further that Witkin's distinction between "field-dependence" and "field-independence" is, basically, a distinction between the ability and inability to analyze perceptually. Thus conceived, it does not concern itself with the additional ability to synthesize perceptually. It might thus be fruitful to try to reconsider and reformulate the nature of "field-dependence" and "field-independence" so that it will include synthesis as well as analysis. For it is reasonable to suppose that a person who is really "field-independent" is a person who is not only able to "separate item from field" but to "reorganize old fields into new ones."

Notes

1. In a personal communication, Witkin provides empirical support for this view. He writes:

"Beverly Goodman of our laboratory gave the embedded-figures test to a group of college students who also went through the waterjug Einstellung situation. Two measures of performance for the Einstellung situation were used, one reflecting susceptibility to set, the other reflecting capacity to overcome set. Whereas the first type of measure was not related to perceptual scores, there was a significant correlation of .653 between measures of the second kind and perceptual scores. In other words, subjects with a more field-dependent (less analytical) mode of perceiving found it more difficult to overcome set."

2. Since the distributions of scores on the embedded-figures and block-design tests were not normal, White's rank test was used. For the embedded figures we used two-tailed tests of significance since we predicted no differences between open and closed groups. For the block designs we used one-tailed tests of significance since the direction of differences was predicted beforehand.

3. As determined by chi-square. One-tailed tests were used.

15

The Enjoyment of New
Musical Systems *

Bernard Mikol

We propose here to extend fur-
ther the scope and generality of the notions already developed
about the organization of open and closed cognitive systems to
the realm of esthetic functioning. That esthetic experience is not
purely an affective experience, but is cognitive as well, is suggested by Aiken, who writes:

> When we ascribe "coherence" or "unity" to a work of
> art . . . we are merely giving evidence of the artist's power
> to evoke and sustain an integrated system of beliefs. The
> sensory and imaginal content of a work of art does not

* Abridged from a Ph.D. dissertation submitted to the School for Advanced
Graduate Studies at Michigan State University (1958).

establish its own unity as an aesthetic whole; nor do its parts "fit" together simply because they coexist. What is required if the elements are to be composed into an aesthetic whole is the presence of an ordering system of beliefs and attitudes which make them mutually relevant to one another; and, conversely, the materials handled in a work of art and the emotions which they express, may vary indefinitely without endangering the integrity of the whole so long as they are held together by a controlling system of expectations. Beliefs thus have the effect of creating and sustaining an aesthetic "world" in which an indefinite variety of elements may be held together without strain or confusion (1951, pp. 305–6).

In a similar vein, Meyer (1956) remarks that the listener brings to music not only specific musical experiences, associations, and dispositions, but also important beliefs as to the nature and significance of esthetic experience in general and the expected musical experience in particular. According to Meyer, much of the information supplied in the program notes for a symphony concert has the effect of creating a willing attitude and of aiding appreciation by strengthening the beliefs about the seriousness, purposefulness, and "logic" of the creative artist and the work he produces. This is supported empirically by Williams (1943), who found that, given sufficient training, the listener is aided significantly by program notes in the enjoyment of a musical program. And Riemann asserts that "practice and good will are required for the understanding of a great and complicated work of art" (1956, pp. 61–2).

These observations by musicians suggest that feeling and thinking about music are not completely different experiences, but are separate yet interrelated facets of the same esthetic experience. The "ordering system of beliefs and attitudes which make them [the elements in the esthetic whole] mutually relevant to one another" does not seem to be substantially different from the process of synthesis or integration required in forming new conceptual or perceptual systems. Likewise, the "willing attitude" and "good will" noted by Meyer and Riemann seem essential to the entertaining of the Doodlebug Problems no less than to the enhancement of esthetic appreciation.

When a person is exposed to music he brings with him to the listening situation a set of beliefs concerning the nature of music, expectations about how music should sound, a set of preconceptions about what constitutes good and bad music, and even beliefs about what is and what is not music. Nowadays, for example, Stravinsky's "Rite of Spring" is highly regarded as a musical composition. Half a century ago it caused a riot when first performed, so strongly polarized were beliefs and feelings about whether it should even be called music. All of this leads us to ask if there is a basis for predicting which persons are likely to be receptive or unreceptive to new musical experience.

The musical medium affords us an opportunity to expose persons who differ in the degree to which their belief systems are open or closed to a world of sound whose organization is governed by laws radically different from those of the everyday world of music. In the same way that the Doodlebug cosmology may be said to represent a psychologically new conceptual system that is at variance with one's everyday belief system, so can we find ready-made, psychologically new musical systems that violate everyday belief systems about what constitutes pleasing music. To Western ears, for example, the music of Beethoven or Brahms is relatively pleasing, even if never heard before, because it belongs to a class of music that is familiar. It is familiar because the rules governing its construction are somehow internalized over time into one's everyday belief system. But to many Western ears, Japanese, Chinese, Hindu, and Persian music probably sound strange and unpleasant when first heard because the system of rules governing their construction are at odds with those of Western types of music.

It is thus expected that while open and closed persons may not differ in their receptivity to music written in the conventional, familiar style, they should differ in their receptivity to music constructed in accord with new systems of rules.

For present research purposes, the music of Arnold Schönberg's later creative period seems particularly well suited as an example of "new system" music. It is written in the twelve-tone technique which involves, among other things, the use of the twelve tones of the chromatic scale in a predetermined order called a row. In contrast, conventional music does not depend upon such rows.

Schönberg's music is atonal; that is, it is written without a key center,* while conventional music, as exemplified by most of the music of the nineteenth century, has a definite key center and is therefore tonal. In Schönberg's music, the melodies are based upon the twelve-tone row constructed according to certain rules,† while conventional melodies are based on major and minor scales. Schönberg's harmonies are often based on the tone row; i.e., the tones of the row are used not only in succession but simultaneously as well. In conventional music, harmonies are based on the triad; i.e., chords are built by superimposing thirds.

The music of Bartók, though less rigorously systematized than that of Schönberg, also differs from conventional music in certain respects. Contrasted with the single key center of conventional music, it is often polytonal; that is, it makes simultaneous use of more than one key center. Conventional melodies are relatively linear (movement by step), but Bartók's melodies are often extremely angular (movement by leap). And although conventional music is relatively consonant and not outstandingly complex rhythmically, Bartók's music is characterized by the frequent use of dissonance and of a high degree of rhythmic complexity.

Our basic plan, then, is to study the reactions of open and closed persons to conventional music on the one hand and to unconventional music on the other. Conventional music is written within the framework of a musical system with which we are familiar, which is part of our everyday belief system. Accordingly we should expect closed persons to enjoy conventional music to about the same extent as open persons. But we should expect closed persons to reject more frequently music written within musical frameworks that are incongruent with the ones they build up in everyday life.

* "Key center" refers to that tone which serves as a focus for the organization of a piece or section. In twelve-tone music, there are assumed to be twelve such foci of equal importance rather than just a single one.

† An example of such a rule would be that the composer decides in advance in which order he will use the twelve tones. Should he, for example, decide, for his own esthetic reasons, that the order will be C, E flat, E, G♯, B, D, C♯, F♯, F, G, A, B flat, this sequence of tones, called a tone row, is either maintained in its original form or is varied according to still other rules (e.g., played backward or inverted).

Experiment I

We compared the musical responses of 40 subjects, 20 scoring extremely high and 20 extremely low on the Dogmatism Scale. These subjects represented the top and bottom 15 per cent of the total distribution of Dogmatism Scale scores for 133 subjects. The subjects responded under group conditions to two selections played by tape recorder—Brahms' C Minor String Quartet and Schönberg's Fourth String Quartet. The choice of these particular chamber works was dictated by three considerations: (1) The two works should be more or less equated for instrumentation. (2) The two works should be equally unfamiliar to all subjects. (3) If differences in reaction to the "new system" music are to be attributed to differences in openness-closedness of belief systems, it is necessary to show also that no such differences in reaction will occur to conventional music. For these reasons Brahms' Quartet, considered to represent conventional music, was paired with Schönberg's Quartet, considered to represent "new system" music.

The instructions were as follows:

> This is a musical interest survey. We are sampling the musical likes and dislikes of college students and we would like to get your reactions to the music you are about to hear. It has been said that in matters of taste, there is no dispute. This is certainly the rule here. We would like you to be perfectly free in expressing how you feel about the music.
>
> A word about procedure. You are about to hear two excerpts of music. After each excerpt, write the name of the composition and the composer. If you don't know, write "don't know." If you have heard either of these compositions before, please indicate by circling the appropriate number. Any questions?

The two excerpts were each two-and-a-half minutes long. Each was taken from the opening section of the quartet. The subjects were first asked to identify the selections and the composers. Then:

> You will now hear the same compositions again. This time, I would like your reaction to the compositions; that

is, the way you feel about them as music, whether you like or dislike them. Please be as frank as you can. Remember, it is your personal opinion we want. Will you please check the adjectives which you feel apply to the first composition? Do not place a check if in your opinion the adjective doesn't apply.

Immediately following the replaying of the Brahms piece and of the Schönberg piece, the subjects were given the opportunity to react to the musical excerpt. They did so by selecting from lists of adjectives those which described their feelings. One list was designed to elicit reactions to the music, and a second list, to the composer. Each list consisted of 20 adjectives, half positive and half negative. For the music, the adjectives were listed as follows: beautiful, ugly, melodious, noisy, refined, vulgar, graceful, clumsy, creative, gibberish, interesting, dull, imaginative, simple-minded, profound, senseless, attractive, superficial, stimulating, repulsive.

For the composers: genius, crack-pot, brilliant, dull, sensitive, inspired, disorganized, alert, apathetic, profound, shallow, playful, muddle-headed, democratic, autocratic, tolerant, intolerant, witty, fearful.

The score obtained for each subject is the difference between the number of positive and negative adjectives checked, with a constant of 10 added to each person's score to eliminate negative scores. Thus, the range of possible scores is between 0 and 20, the higher scores indicating greater acceptance of the music or composer.

Following the marking of these check lists, other information was obtained about the subject's formal music background and general knowledge of classical music.

The main results of the experiment are summarized in Table 15.1. Considering first the differences in reaction to the conventional and unconventional music, it is obvious that the conventional excerpt and composer are liked much more than the unconventional ones. This is to be expected. Schönberg's music does not arouse much positive feeling in our subjects. But far more important to the issue at hand is whether open and closed subjects react similarly or differently to the unconventional music. Consider first the reactions to the conventional music. The two groups of subjects do not differ from each other in their reactions

275

Table 15.1

Mean Acceptance of Conventional and Unconventional Music and Composers by Closed and Open Groups

	Group	Mean	S.D.	Diff.[a]
Conventional music				
Quartet (Brahms)	Closed	14.9	3.4	−.5
	Open	14.4	3.2	
Composer (Brahms)	Closed	12.7	2.2	.1
	Open	12.8	2.1	
Unconventional music				
Quartet (Schönberg)	Closed	5.8	3.5	2.5[b]
	Open	8.3	4.0	
Composer (Schönberg)	Closed	7.5	2.6	2.3[c]
	Open	9.8	2.5	

N = 20 in each group.

[a] As determined by *t* tests. Where differences are predicted in advance, one-tailed tests are used.
[b] Significant, $p = .05$.
[c] Very significant, $p = .01$.

to the music of Brahms or to the composer himself. However, we do find significant differences between open-minded and closed-minded subjects in their reactions to the new music of Schönberg and to Schönberg himself.

These reactions occur without a single one of the subjects knowing the name of the composers or the compositions listened to. When asked to identify the piece or composer not one of the subjects could do so correctly. Further analysis reveals few if any differences in the musical backgrounds of the two groups of subjects. The closed and open groups do not differ in years of study of classical music, or in frequency of attending concerts, or in the number of courses taken in classical music. Nor do they differ in preference for classical, semiclassical, and jazz music. In a test of musical knowledge, in which the subjects are asked to match correctly a series of composers with compositions, the differences are again not significant, although the open subjects score somewhat higher in knowledge.

There is, however, a nearly significant difference between the two groups in their reports on how many hours a week they spend listening to music, the closed group reporting more hours spent in listening. This difference is probably not a stable one, for it does not appear again in Experiment II, to be described shortly. Moreover, even if the closed group does spend more time listening to classical music, it seems to have no observable effect on its liking for the conventional music, not to speak of the unconventional music.

Additional data show that the two groups are also fairly well matched on age and intelligence. The mean ages of the closed and open groups are 21.7 and 22.3 years respectively. Mean American Council on Education scores for the two groups are 5.37 and 5.89, respectively. Neither set of differences is statistically significant.

Summarizing, closed and open groups differ in their reactions to the "new system" music of Schönberg and to Schönberg himself, but do not differ in their reactions to the conventional music of Brahms or to Brahms, the composer. These findings cannot be accounted for by differences in familiarity with the particular pieces played, or general musical background, or training, or knowledge of music, or age, or intelligence.

Experiment II

In Experiment II an attempt was made to enlarge the scope of the previous study in two ways: by increasing the number of musical samples and by determining whether there are changes in receptivity to new music as the subject continues to listen to it. The procedure followed was essentially the same as in Experiment I, with certain modifications in the number and length of excerpts. Added to the Brahms sample of conventional music was Saint-Saëns' Violin and Piano Sonata in D Minor. Added to the Schönberg sample of unconventional music was Bartók's First Violin and Piano Sonata. In Experiment I, a single excerpt was played twice. In Experiment II, two successive excerpts, each two minutes long, were played from the opening of each composition. The excerpts were played in the following sequence: Brahms, Schönberg, Saint-Saëns, and Bartók. After each excerpt the subject reacted to the music and composer as before, using the same adjective check list.

Thus we are in a position to test again the same hypotheses tested in Experiment I. But in addition, we should be able also to determine whether open persons, more than closed persons, increase in their receptivity to "new system" music and to its composers as they listen to successive excerpts.

There are 44 subjects in Experiment II, 22 scoring extremely high and 22 scoring extremely low on the Dogmatism Scale. They represent the top and bottom 15 per cent of the total distribution of scores obtained by 147 subjects.

Table 15.2

Mean Acceptance of Conventional and Unconventional Music and Composers by Closed and Open Groups

		Excerpt 1			Excerpt 2		
	Group	Mean	S.D.	Diff.	Mean	S.D.	Diff.
Conventional music							
Sonata (Saint-Saëns)	Closed	15.0	2.5	.0	15.0	2.8	−.2
	Open	15.0	2.9		14.8	2.4	
Composer (Saint-Saëns)	Closed	12.9	1.5	−.2	12.8	1.4	−.1
	Open	12.7	2.1		12.7	1.8	
Quartet (Brahms)	Closed	12.9	3.4	.2	12.7	2.8	.3
	Open	13.1	2.5		13.0	3.1	
Composer (Brahms)	Closed	11.4	2.1	.6	11.7	1.9	.1
	Open	12.0	1.7		11.8	2.0	
Unconventional music							
Sonata (Bartók)	Closed	9.0	3.5	.8	10.1	3.5	.8
	Open	9.8	3.3		10.9	3.8	
Composer (Bartók)	Closed	9.0	2.3	.8	9.8	2.6	.4
	Open	9.8	2.3		10.2	2.7	
Quartet (Schönberg)	Closed	8.4	2.7	−.1	8.0	3.2	1.1[a]
	Open	8.3	3.1		9.1	3.6	
Composer (Schönberg)	Closed	9.1	2.0	.2	8.7	2.5	1.2[b]
	Open	9.3	2.2		9.9	2.2	

N = 22 in each group.

[a] p = .15.
[b] p = .08.

Table 15.2 shows responses by open and closed groups to conventional and unconventional music and composers. The results are shown separately for excerpts 1 and 2. In general, the results are consistent with, but not nearly as clear-cut as those found in Experiment I. The mean acceptance of conventional music and their composers (Saint-Saëns or Brahms) for closed and open groups are as expected—the two groups do not differ from each other. Nor do we observe here any consistent trends in one direction or the other.

Less conclusive, however, are the differences between closed and open groups on unconventional music and composers. Not one of the differences reaches an acceptable level of significance for either Bartók or Schönberg.

At the same time, we should not overlook the fact that the largest differences are obtained between closed and open groups in their responses to the second Schönberg excerpt and to Schönberg as composer. These are in the expected direction and approach statistical significance. The former is significant at the .15 level, and the latter at the .08 level. When these differences are considered in relation to the comparable differences in Experiment I, the results of the two experiments, insofar as reactions to Schönberg are concerned, are in close agreement. If the results of the two experiments are pooled, the differences between the closed and open groups in their reaction to the Schönberg Quartet is significant ($p = .03$), as are also the differences in reaction to Schönberg as composer ($p = .01$). As for the differences in reactions to Bartók, the results are again in the expected direction, but do not even approach statistical significance. Insofar as reactions to Bartók are concerned, the hypothesis cannot be said to be supported.

Let us now look at the changes that take place in the listeners' reaction to music and composer as they proceed from the first to the second excerpt. The mean increases and decreases in acceptance are shown in Table 15.3. At a glance, it is seen that there are practically no changes in reactions to the conventional music for either of the two groups. With respect to Bartók and his music, it is apparent that both open and closed groups increase in their acceptance from the first to the second excerpt.

It is only with respect to Schönberg and his music that the two

279

groups show a parting of ways. The closed group likes Schönberg and his music less on the second excerpt; but the open group likes music and composer more. These changes from first to second excerpt are significant for both music and composer.

Table 15.3

Relative Changes in Acceptance of Conventional and Unconventional Music in Closed and Open Groups

	Group	Mean Gain	S.D.	Diff.
Conventional music				
Sonata (Saint-Saëns)	Closed	.0	2.0	−.2
	Open	−.2	1.9	
Composer (Saint-Saëns)	Closed	−.1	1.7	.1
	Open	.0	1.9	
Quartet (Brahms)	Closed	−.2	2.1	.1
	Open	−.1	1.9	
Composer (Brahms)	Closed	+.3	0.3	−.5
	Open	−.2	1.2	
Unconventional music				
Sonata (Bartók)	Closed	+1.1	2.3	.0
	Open	+1.1	2.0	
Composer (Bartók)	Closed	+.8	2.5	−.4
	Open	+.4	1.7	
Quartet (Schönberg)	Closed	−.4	1.9	1.2[a]
	Open	+.8	2.3	
Composer (Schönberg)	Closed	−.4	1.7	1.0[a]
	Open	+.6	1.4	

N = 22 in each group.

[a] Significant, $p = .05$.

Again it may be asked whether the results of Experiment II can be accounted for on grounds other than differences in openness or closedness of belief systems. As in Experiment I, the two groups are found to be equally unfamiliar with the selections played. Not one of the subjects correctly identified either the music or the composers. The two groups do not differ significantly in age or intelligence, or years of study in music, hours per week spent listening to music, number of concerts attended, number of music courses taken, or relative preference for classical, semi-classical, or jazz music. However, the open group does score significantly higher on knowledge of classical music, doing better on a test in which a set of compositions is to be matched with a set of composers. A similar comparison between the closed and open groups in Experiment I, although not significant, is in the same direction. This raises the question as to whether greater general knowledge of classical music, as determined by the matching test, can account for the results found in Experiments I and II. To this question we shall return shortly.

Interpretations

Let us begin our discussion by saying that the reactions to music considered here are regarded to be *structurally* similar to the reactions of the subjects in the problem-solving and perceptual experiments, however different such reactions may appear to be in content. Both music experiments seem to lend support to the hypothesis that persons with closed systems are less receptive to "new system" music and their composers, insofar as exemplified by Schönberg—but not insofar as exemplified by Bartók. Thus, some restraints are necessary in generalizing from these findings. At the same time, we cannot help but speculate about possible reasons why the results do not come out as expected with the Bartók music.

From Table 15.2, it can be seen that both open and closed groups react more favorably to the Bartók than to the Schönberg music. An examination of the musical score of the Bartók First Violin and Piano Sonata suggests some possible reasons. Although the Bartók and Schönberg compositions are equally unfamiliar to all the subjects, it is possible that there may have been some familiar stylistic elements in the Bartók composition that were not present in the Schönberg composition. Bartók uses tonal combinations reminiscent in some ways of the conventional nineteenth-century music. Examination of the score reveals that these occur at a time when they would be likely to exert a strong influence on the subject's response to the music; that is, just prior to the end of the second excerpt. Bartók uses simultaneous major and minor thirds to introduce a new section in the music in measures 103–114 of the score. It might be pointed out that the third is one of the sounds most characteristic of the nineteenth century and hence reasonably conventional music. Although most nineteenth-century composers do not generally juxtapose major and minor thirds simultaneously, this use of thirds by Bartók may well have functioned as an element of familiarity and therefore increased the general acceptance of the composition.

Further analysis of the Bartók score reveals another aspect that may have been responsible for its greater acceptance—the fact that the mood of the music changes from one of stormy agitation to a quiet lyricism. The point at which the music stops may well have been experienced as tension-reducing and hence pleasant. Thus, we are inclined to say in retrospect that the selection of Bartók's music as an example of "new system" music was not as judicious a choice as that of Schönberg's.

Regarding the differences between relatively open and closed persons in their responses to Schönberg, it should be noted that in Experiment II the differences between the two groups emerge fairly clearly after the second excerpt but not after the first excerpt. But in Experiment I the two groups differ significantly at the end of excerpt 1. This discrepancy in results is more apparent than real. It can readily be explained by differences in methodology between the two experiments. Recall that in Experiment I the subjects listened to the same excerpt (two and a half minutes long) *twice* and then gave their reaction to it only after it was played the second time. In Experiment II, the subjects listened to two successive excerpts, each two minutes long, and responded to each excerpt. Thus, in both experiments, the results for the closed and open groups are really quite similar; the differences between the two groups emerge in both cases after the second exposure.

Rigg (1948) found that repetition increases liking for music. Our results on enjoyment of successive excerpts support Rigg's findings, but only to a limited degree. Both groups clearly increase in their enjoyment of Bartók's Sonata, but there is no gain or loss to speak of in the enjoyment of Saint-Saëns or Brahms. Even more interesting is the fact that repetition of the new music of Schönberg increases enjoyment for the open-minded subjects, but decreases it for the closed-minded subjects, thus leading to a widening of the differences between the two groups after the second excerpt. In this connection, the results seem to be similar to those considered on the formation of perceptual systems, discussed in the last chapter. There, too, an order effect was noted. The differences between closed and open groups are nonexistent at first but appear and get generally larger as the experiment progresses.

Another finding worth commenting on is that the reactions are approximately the same for music and for composers. There is apparently a close connection between the two. It seems to make little difference whether you ask a person: "What do you think of the music?" or "What do you think of the composer who wrote it?" Either way the question is put leads to essentially the same psychological information about the person answering it. That it should make such little difference is to our minds theoretically significant, for it supports the view expressed earlier in this work that there is often a close connection between the way we accept and reject ideas—in this context, a composition represents the composer's musical ideas—and the way we accept and reject persons holding to such ideas.

Let us now return to the finding that those with open systems have a generally greater knowledge of music than those with closed systems. It is, of course, conceivable that the results found in Experiments I and II could be explained on this basis. But there are reasons to doubt this. First, despite the difference in *general* knowledge of classical music, not one of the subjects in either experiment recognized the specific compositions or their composers. Second, it is clear that the difference in general knowledge of music between the two groups does not lead to differences in enjoyment of Brahms, or of Saint-Saëns, or of Bartók. How, then, can it account for the differences found in the enjoyment of Schönberg? If general knowledge of classical music were a relevant consideration, it would more likely lead to a greater enjoyment of all kinds of classical music, rather than to a selectively greater enjoyment of only Schönberg's music.

Finally, if one thinks of esthetic values as signifying an interest in the novel ways in which artists and writers order their unique experiences and as signifying an openness to new experience, then it is not at all surprising to find that open persons are more attracted to things esthetic than closed persons. Along with this greater appreciation, it should not be surprising if they also know a bit more about music.

Synopsis

Two experiments have been described here on the reactions of open and closed persons to conventional music and "new system" music. In Experiment I it was hypothesized that persons with closed belief systems would be less accepting of new music and its composers than persons with open belief systems. Subjects were exposed to two unfamiliar samples of music, a conventional piece by Brahms and an unconventional one by Schönberg. No significant differences were found between open and closed groups with respect to their acceptance of the conventional Brahms music; but open persons are more accepting than closed persons of the unconventional Schönberg music. These results cannot be attributed to differences between the two groups in age, intelligence, or musical background.

In Experiment II, the number of musical samples was increased and the subjects' reactions were obtained to successive excerpts from the same musical composition. Thus it was possible to study changes in receptivity to new music as a function of repeated exposure to it, in addition to testing again the hypotheses of Experiment I. Brahms and Saint-Saëns were used as examples of conventional music, and Schönberg and Bartók as examples of new music. The results support the hypotheses of Experiment I insofar as they relate to Schönberg and his music, but not insofar as they relate to Bartók and his music. The absence of differences on the Bartók music was interpreted as being due to the fact that Bartók's music was less extreme than Schönberg's as an example of "new system" music. More important is the significant finding that closed persons like Schönberg's music less with repeated exposure to it, but open persons like it more. All these results are consistent with earlier findings, which suggest that closed persons have greater difficulty than open persons in forming new conceptual and perceptual systems.

Recapitulation of Part Three

Before going on to Part Four, we feel obliged to pull together the many ideas and findings contained within the eight chapters of Part Three. This should serve to fix them more firmly in mind and to integrate them more explicitly with our theoretical formulations about the nature of belief systems. Central to the work reported in Part Three is the Dogmatism Scale. As we have already said in the Introduction to Part Three, we are concerned with the validity of the Dogmatism Scale not as an end in itself but as a means to an end. First and foremost, we prefer to think of it as an instrument designed to help us test that part of our conceptualizations which deal with the open or closed character of belief systems. If the Dogmatism Scale behaves as it is meant to, it increases our confidence in its validity; but more important, it increases our confidence in the validity of our ideas and encourages us to extend them yet further.

In the various investigations reported in Part Three, the typical procedure has been to compare high and low scorers on the

Dogmatism Scale on a variety of laboratory tests. Our reasons for doing so are several: to gain a better understanding of the cognitive and emotional functioning of open-minded and closed-minded persons; to relate such functioning to personality; to study by analogy certain ideological phenomena such as party-line thinking and loyalty to and defection from an ideological system; to gain a better understanding of variables that facilitate and retard the formation of new systems. The laboratory tasks put to our subjects are deliberately chosen to represent different areas of psychological functioning—conceptual, perceptual, and esthetic. But all these tasks are seen to have something structural in common. They all involve a new belief system that is at odds with a previously held belief system. To deal with such tasks in terms of their intrinsic requirements entails a willingness to relinquish old systems, a capacity to entertain and enjoy new systems, and actively to synthesize new materials into an integrated whole. In isolating and in measuring this aspect of thought, perception, and feeling we are dealing with the most complicated, perhaps the most creative aspect of cognitive and emotional activity.

High scorers on the Dogmatism Scale are repeatedly found to differ from low scorers in the ability to synthesize new beliefs into a new system, but not in the ability to analyze or to break down single beliefs. These findings, as well as the converse of these for rigid vs. nonrigid persons, provide empirical support for a distinction that has been previously sloughed off—the distinction between dogmatism and rigidity in thought and personality. Dogmatism is a *system* variable, a characteristic of the total system; rigidity is a characteristic of the elements within a system. Thus, in using the Dogmatism Scale to measure a total state of mind we are necessarily committed to study people's behavior vis-à-vis systems. The various laboratory tasks presented to open and closed persons are designed to bring out, to throw into relief, differences in their behavior with respect to the formation of new systems. Let us now summarize what we have learned about some of the variables that aid and hinder the formation of new systems.

One variable that seems to account for the differences in the formation of new systems between open and closed persons is the ability to remember, or to keep in mind all the new parts to be integrated. When memory is by-passed by seeing to it that the parts are all in the visual field, and thus all in mind, synthesis is facilitated.

A second variable is the extent to which one is willing to "play along," or to entertain new systems. Again, those with relatively open systems have been shown to be better off in this respect than those with relatively closed systems. It is reasonable to suppose that the capacity to entertain new systems leads to better memory for the parts of the new system. Consequently, the probability is increased that synthesis will take place.

A third variable is past experience, which defines whether a particular system is, psychologically speaking, new or not new. A particular task may be equally unfamiliar to two persons, but may be new to one and not new to the other. A system is not new, psychologically speaking, if it can be shown to be rooted in specific past experience, and in beliefs formed as a result of such experience. Notions of non-Euclidian space, for example, are psychologically new to most people because they violate built-in Euclidian-type systems of beliefs learned through everyday experience. But such notions would probably be less new to the student of mathematics, by virtue of his past experience with various kinds of real and unreal systems. In the same way, a given style of architecture, or music, or painting may or may not be new, depending on unique past experience or cultural background. The less new a system, the more will synthesis be facilitated; conversely, the newer a system, the more will synthesis be blocked. Also, the newer a system, the more important is the role of individual differences in the capacity to entertain new systems.

A fourth variable is whether the beliefs of a new system (political, religious, scientific, etc.) are exposed, imposed, taught, or promulgated all at once or gradually. In those with relatively closed systems, problem-solving is clearly facilitated when the parts of the new system are presented all at once "on a silver platter." The dish is very tempting, and therefore swallowed whole. There is no need to predigest it because little or no resistance to synthesis is offered by the everyday belief system. Consequently, problem-solving proceeds more smoothly in closed persons when new beliefs are presented all at once than when presented gradually. However, it makes no difference to those with relatively open systems whether the beliefs are presented gradually or all at once. The total solution of problems takes just as long in either case, suggesting that open persons genuinely feel the need to work through, to reconcile the new with the old, even if they do not have to.

A fifth variable that has been shown to facilitate or hinder the formation of new systems is the degree of isolation of beliefs within the system. The greater the isolation within a system, the less the positive transfer from one system to a similar one, and the more difficult it is to discover inherent contradictions within the system. Here, again, relatively closed persons are found to differ consistently from relatively open persons. In the language of politics, isolation within a belief system may be thought of as the structural basis for party-line thinking, and also of the inability to defect from an inherently contradictory system.

Let us point to some theoretical implications of the findings just considered. First, the findings suggest that important aspects of mental functioning are attributable to personality rather than to intellectual ability as such.* Second, the findings suggest that a person's belief system has pervasive effects on different spheres of activity—ideological, conceptual, perceptual, and esthetic. What these different spheres of activity seem to have in common is something structural. On the surface, they are indeed different kinds of behavior; but beneath the surface (genotypically) they are seen to have something in common. This accounts for the generality of man's behavior in spheres of activity that are apparently different. Seen in this way we can perhaps better grasp why it is that a person's score on a personality test enables us to predict such diverse things as how he will behave on a perceptual task, whether he will enjoy a problem put to him, whether he will solve it, and remember it, whether he will enjoy a musical composition, and so on.

Third, our research demonstrates that the psychological processes involved in ideological functioning can be studied in labo-

---

* In this respect our findings add to the increasingly widespread recognition of the importance of nonintellectual determinants of cognition. See Fishman (1957), for example.

ratory situations by analogy. Fourth, our findings point to the fact that we have succeeded reasonably well in distinguishing and measuring two interrelated aspects of personality and of cognitive functioning. There are many ways of talking about these two aspects: the resistance to change of beliefs and the resistance to change of systems of beliefs; rigidity and dogmatism; the analysis phase and the synthesis phase in thinking and perceiving; the overcoming of sets and the integration of sets; the separation of an item from a field and its reconstruction into new fields. Perhaps we are also dealing with the processes of deduction and induction.

Finally, we cannot overlook the fact that differences in the functioning of persons who are relatively open and closed extends not only to such cognitive activities as problem-solving, remembering and perceiving, but also to emotional experiences as well. In this connection, let us recall that we find differences in results between open and closed subjects not only in the extent to which they *enjoy* music, but also in extent to which they *enjoy* solving problems.

Part Four

The Study of Disbelief Systems

Our conceptual interests are not only in the open and closed character of belief systems but also in the general character of all belief systems; or, to put it more accurately (and clumsily), in the general character of all *belief-disbelief* systems. For example, in Chapter 7 we had little to say about the open-closed dimension of systems but a lot to say about belief congruence as a general principle governing the organization of all belief-disbelief systems.

In the following two chapters we propose to investigate more fully another general characteristic put forward earlier in Chapter 2; namely, the way in which a person's disbelief system is organized in relation to his belief system, regardless of how open or closed it may be. Recall that all cognitive systems are thought of as being organized into two interdependent parts, a belief system and a disbelief system. Further, the disbelief system is conceived to be composed of several subsystems arranged along a continuum of similarity to the belief system. We will now ask: Is it possible to demonstrate objectively the psychological existence of the several disbelief subsystems along such a continuum? To what extent is rejection of the several disbelief subsystems, and the adherents thereof, related to similarity-dissimilarity? Is the relation between similarity and rejection of disbelief subsystems the same in open and in closed persons? And what difference does all this make for everyday social behavior?

16

The Organization of
Disbelief Systems *

Consider for a moment the cognitive organization of a person who happens to be an Episcopalian. In line with our formulations we will say that his belief system is Episcopalianism and that his disbelief system is composed of several subsystems, such as Catholicism, Lutheranism, other Protestant denominations, and all the other religious systems of which he is aware. Each of his disbelief subsystems can be thought of as having an organization of its own, and can be described in terms of such properties as differentiation, isolation, comprehensiveness, and the like. At the same time, the several subsystems taken together can be thought of as being arranged in terms of similarity to Episcopalianism.

* In this chapter we will try to summarize succinctly large masses of data that were obtained and analyzed with the help of many students. We wish here to acknowledge our gratitude to Philip Jensen, Richard Bonier, James Davis (1958), Howard Ehrlich, Jacob Frankel, John J. Laffey, Jacques M. Levy, Joann S. Maryo (1958), Nancy Phares, Patricia W. Smith, Theodore S. Swanson, and Martin and Stephanie Zlotowski.

In everyday life our Episcopalian may do many things that touch on his belief-disbelief system. He may make friendly and derogatory remarks about persons belonging to various religious systems; he may worship regularly at a particular church, but on occasion, at another; he may selectively associate with and selectively avoid persons affiliated with one or another religious system; he may court, marry, and divorce someone who is or is not an Episcopalian; he may send his children to one or another denominational college.

What is the probability that our hypothetical Episcopalian will interact with, relate to, and feel differently toward others according to whether they belong to his own or to another religious system? If our conception of the organization of belief-disbelief systems is a fruitful one, we should expect similarity of disbelief subsystem to belief system to be one important determinant of such probabilities.

Actually, as we have already stated in Chapter 2, a person's belief-disbelief system is more than just a religious system. It also contains beliefs and disbeliefs that are political, scientific, philosophical, and esthetic, to name just a few. In the present research, however, we will deliberately restrict our analysis to the religious aspects of belief-disbelief systems. There are several reasons why we will do so: first, for the sake of simplicity; second, because it is relatively easy to find persons who identify themselves with religious systems; third, because such adherents are available for research in relatively large numbers; and fourth, because the range of differences in religious systems in America is greater than the range, say, in political systems. In the United States most people will identify themselves either as Democrats or Republicans; a few others will identify themselves as "Independents." Thus, our focus on religious groups is dictated primarily by reasons of methodological convenience rather than a concern with religion as such. Our main concern is really a theoretical one: to determine whether it is fruitful to explore the organization of a person's disbelief system as distinct from his belief system.

This chapter will deal with the general organization of disbelief systems along a similarity continuum, as determined for adherents to six major Christian religions. We will also investigate the general relation between similarity and rejection and whether this relation is the same among closed and open adherents to a particular faith. Finally, we will try to find out how stable these similarity continua are in different social contexts or frames of reference.

The Similarity Continua for Catholics, Episcopalians, Presbyterians, Lutherans, Methodists, and Baptists

First to be described is the procedure we developed for determining the similarity continuum. Subjects are presented with a mimeographed list of religions in alphabetical order, as follows:

Atheist
Baptist
Catholic
Episcopalian
Jewish
Lutheran
Methodist
Mohammedan
Presbyterian

A number of blank lines follow this list. The subject is simply asked to write the name of his own religion on the first line, the name of the religion most similar to his own on the second line, and so on. The least similar religion is written on the last line.*

We do not define what we mean by "similarity." Each subject decides this for himself.

The mean similarity rank assigned to each of the nine religions was determined separately for six groups of college students: Catholics, Episcopalians, Presbyterians, Lutherans, Methodists, and Baptists. The reason these six groups of subjects were used and no other is simply that they are the denominations most frequently found in our samples. Other Christian denominations, Jews, etc., were found too infrequently to warrant separate study.

Table 16.1 may be read as follows: The Catholics, on the average, judged the Episcopalians to be most similar to themselves,

---

* A tenth group, ex-Catholic, was also on the list. But this turned out to mean so many different things to different subjects that we dropped it from further study.

Table 16.1

The Similarity Matrix

		Rank Order of Similarity							
Group	Number	1	2	3	4	5	6	7	8
Catholic	120	Epis.	Luth.	Pres.	Meth.	Bapt.	Jew	Moham.	Ath.
Episcopalian	38	Cath.	Luth.	Pres.	Meth.	Bapt.	Jew	Moham.	Ath.
Lutheran	57	Pres.	Meth.	Epis.	Bapt.	Cath.	Jew	Moham.	Ath.
Presbyterian	100	Meth.	Bapt.	Luth.	Epis.	Cath.	Jew	Moham.	Ath.
Methodist	116	Pres.	Bapt.	Luth.	Epis.	Cath.	Jew	Moham.	Ath.
Baptist	26	Meth.	Pres.	Luth.	Epis.	Cath.	Jew	Moham.	Ath.

followed by the Lutheran, Presbyterian, Methodist, and Baptist denominations. Then follow the Jews, Mohammedans, and atheists.

Inspection of the similarity matrix shows the following:

1. All six Christian groups are unanimous in ranking as least similar to themselves Jews, then Mohammedans, then atheists.

2. If we stay within the Christian fold, we note that the rank order of similarity for Baptists is the exact reverse of that for Catholics.

3. The similarity continuum for Episcopalians is identical with that for Catholics, except that Catholics rank Episcopalians as most similar, and Episcopalians rank Catholics as most similar.

4. With the exception of the Episcopalians, all other Protestant denominations judge Catholics as the least similar of the Christian faiths to their own.

5. The similarity continua found cannot be attributed to similarities in social status, but to *cognitive* similarity of belief systems. For example, it is a widely known sociological fact (e.g., Barber, 1957) that Catholics are, generally speaking, relatively low in social status, while Episcopalians are relatively high. Despite this sociological fact, it is seen in Table 16.1 that Catholics judge Episcopalians, and Episcopalians judge Catholics, to be most similar to each other.

6. If we take the Catholic continuum as a point of departure, it becomes apparent that the similarity continua of the remaining groups are but variations of it, the variations arising from the fact that each denominational group views the continuum from its own position.

To determine more precisely whether the similarity matrix involving the Christian faiths is indeed reducible to one basic scale, we applied an "unfolding method" technique similar to that developed by Coombs (1950).[1] All six similarity continua can be reproduced from one scale, as shown in Figure 16.1.

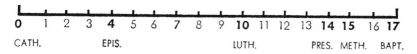

| 0 | 1 | 2 | 3 | 4 | 5 | 6 | 7 | 8 | 9 | 10 | 11 | 12 | 13 | 14 | 15 | 16 | 17 |

CATH.   EPIS.   LUTH.   PRES. METH. BAPT.

FIGURE 16.1. Scale positions of similarity for six Christian denominations.

How reliable is the similarity matrix shown in Table 16.1? Maryo (1958) has obtained data for additional samples of college students belonging to the same six Christian denominations. In her study Jews, Mohammedans, and atheists were not ranked for similarity. The similarity continua she obtained are identical to the ones shown here for Catholics, Lutherans, Presbyterians, Methodists, and Baptists. The continuum for Episcopalians shows some reversals, which may be due to the small number of Episcopalians in her study. Davis (1958) and Rokeach (1956b)[2] report similarity continua for Catholics and Methodists that are identical with those shown in Table 16.1.

Another problem that concerns us is whether there is an objective basis for the similarity continua that were obtained subjectively. A closely related question is the way in which college students come to learn the similarity continuum for their own denomination. One plausible hypothesis is that the similarity continuum is an institutionalized part of each denominational faith which is somehow transmitted to the adherent. We should therefore expect to find agreement between the similarity continua of priests and ministers, and lay members of each faith.

To find out if this is so, five ministers from each of the six Christian faiths were interviewed individually. Most of them came from the Lansing area, and a few from the New York area.*

* We wish to record here our gratitude to the following clergymen who participated in this study: Reverends R. R. Arthur, V. Baer, J. L. Barrett, P. T. Byrnes, A. C. Clarke, H. Date, N. F. Douty, H. A. Edwards, J. B. Everts, A. Finnegan, J. A. Gabriels, A. W. Goodhand, F. Grebe, D. L. Green, J. A. Gusweller, W. R.

Each clergyman was given a list of the six Christian denominations in alphabetical order and, starting with his own, was asked to rank the remaining five in terms of similarity to his own, in exactly the same way as described above. Many of the clergymen balked at the task put to them, pointing out that a particular denomination could be ranked as more similar or less similar to their own, depending upon whether one kept in mind doctrine, liturgy, church policy, current conflicts between denominations, etc. With some coaxing, however, all the clergymen completed the rankings, some more reluctantly than others.

In this way we obtained similarity continua for clergymen representing the six Christian denominations. Then we calculated the degree of correlation between the similarity ranks obtained for clergymen and for laymen. This was done separately for each of the six faiths.

The similarity rankings are perfectly correlated [3] for Episcopalian ministers and laymen (1.00). There is one reversal in rank for Catholics (.90) and for Baptists (.90). There are greater discrepancies in the case of Lutherans (.67) and still greater discrepancies in the case of Presbyterians (.47) and Methodists (.37).

The fact that the correlations are far from perfect is most likely due to the small sample of clergymen—five for each denomination—who served as judges. Nevertheless, when all six correlations are averaged [4] we get a correlation of .85. We thus have ground for concluding that there is in general substantial agreement between laymen and clergymen regarding the organization of disbelief systems in terms of similarity to a given belief system.

It would thus appear that the similarity continua perceived by college students may well have some objective validity, and it is our guess that these continua are somehow transmitted from priests and ministers, the "gatekeepers" of religion, to laymen. However, from informal interviews with some of our clergymen, we gained the impression that this transmission is probably not direct or deliberate. For one thing, the clergymen express great uncertainty about the accuracy of their rankings. For another, they state that they do not know of any theological or sacred

Hartman, G. M. Jones, Jr., C. T. Klinksick, F. X. Knapp, E. M. Love, R. P. Oldham, C. T. Mueller, J. A. Paul, J. Porter, J. F. Sefl, J. R. Sockman, E. L. Woldt, H. Wolf, K. Yates, and, finally, to a clergyman who remains anonymous.

writing that discusses explicitly the similarity continuum. This leaves open, pending further research, the question of the processes by which lay adherents come to learn the similarity continuum of their own denomination.

The Relation Between Similarity and Rejection

It is reasonable to hypothesize that the less the similarity of a particular disbelief subsystem, the greater will be its rejection. To test this hypothesis we also obtained information from each subject about the extent to which he accepts or rejects each of the nine religions. This was done with the aid of a five-item attitude scale repeated for each of the nine religions. This made a total of 45 items that were intermixed with the 40 items of the Dogmatism Scale. Subjects agreed or disagreed with each item on a —3 to +3 scale, with the zero point excluded. The five items are:

1. I would not hesitate to make friends with a ——.
2. I am willing to have a ——— marry into my family.
3. ——— are more public spirited than most other groups.
4. Most ——— live exceptionally moral lives.
5. I would like to have ——— in my fraternity or social club.

For each subject we first computed his acceptance score for each one of the nine religions. Then, using his own religion as a baseline, we obtained the difference between the score given to his own religion and that given to each of the other eight religions. The smaller the difference, the less the rejection; the larger the difference, the greater the rejection. We then plotted the relation between similarity and rejection for each of the six Christian faiths. The results for each of the six groups are shown graphically in Figure 16.2. The same results are also shown for closed and open subgroups. These subgroups were obtained by splitting the total group of subjects into roughly equal halves according to whether they scored above or below the median on the Dogmatism Scale.

Within the total continuum of disbelief systems, the results shown in Figure 16.2 reveal a clear-cut relationship [5] between similarity and rejection. Those systems perceived as most similar are, generally speaking, most accepted; those perceived to be least similar are most rejected. The results show that the rejection of a particular disbelief subsystem depends upon its position on the similarity continuum. At the same time, let us not overlook certain interesting exceptions to this generalization. These exceptions are probably important even though they are relatively small in size when seen in the context of the total relationship between similarity and rejection. But before we consider these in more detail, let us first note the shape of the relationship between similarity and rejection not only for the total group but also for the closed and open subgroups.

The curves for open and closed subgroups are seen to be remarkably parallel. This is the case in all six religious groups, suggesting that the particular relationship found in each religious group is generally quite stable. Despite this remarkably parallel set of findings there is nevertheless an important difference between open and closed subjects. With but few exceptions, the closed subjects reject each and every disbelief subsystem along the similarity continuum to a greater extent than do the open subjects. Within each of the six religions, there are eight comparisons that may be made between them, thus making 48 comparisons in all. In 46 out of the 48 comparisons the closed subjects are found to reject other faiths more than do open subjects.*

The results suggest, then, that not all phenomena of bigotry or rejection of outgroups are necessarily attributable to differences in personality organization and personality dynamics. The rejection of a particular outgroup is traceable to at least two independent sources. One is sheer similarity (and whatever gives rise to it). The other is openness-closedness of systems. Even if a person is quite open-minded he is likely to express different degrees of preference for disbelief subsystems according to their degree of perceived similarity to his own. In fact, cognitive similarity is clearly seen in Figure 16.2 to be a far more important determinant of acceptance or rejection.

* Similar results have been reported elsewhere by Rokeach (1956b) and have been obtained in other unpublished research by Rokeach and Jensen (1956f), Davis (1958), and Maryo (1958).

On the Mutual Rejection Between Factional Systems

Many observers have noted that we sometimes reject with great intensity those ideologies and groups that are most similar to our own. Some examples that come to mind are the Stalinist's rejection of the Trotskyist, the orthodox Freudian's rejection of the Adlerian, the vehement distrust of Roosevelt by the wealthy. Addressing himself to the problem of religious conflicts in the United States, sociologist Robin Williams writes:

> "Family quarrels" among religious groups are often intense —the just-noticeable differences seem under some conditions to evoke especially strong reactions (1956, p. 15). . . . It is necessary to note also the possibility that interreligious relations in some instances may be affected by strains and tensions with regard to value-orientations within a given religious grouping. The highly complicated processes set in motion by internal divergence in values constitute still another largely unexplored area that awaits scientific understanding. (1956, p. 20.)

Waelder, a psychoanalyst, has also shown an appreciation of this problem. He writes:

> While thus antagonism is readily understood where fundamental values differ, it is more surprising to find dislike in instances of small difference such as, e.g., the dislike between Spaniards and Portuguese, or the traditional mutual dislike between the Americans and the British. The latter has almost vanished in recent decades under the impact of historical necessity which has forced the reluctant relatives together.
>
> Freud called this the "narcissism of small differences." The fact that someone is close enough to us so that we feel called upon to compare ourselves with him, and is yet different, is conceived like a latent criticism of ourselves, an implied attack against the way we are, and an implicit invitation to mend our ways; and we resent it. (1949.)

With these comments in mind, let us now look again at Figure 16.2 and note particularly where we find divergences from the general relation between similarity and rejection. We believe that these divergences will make sense in the light of the remarks

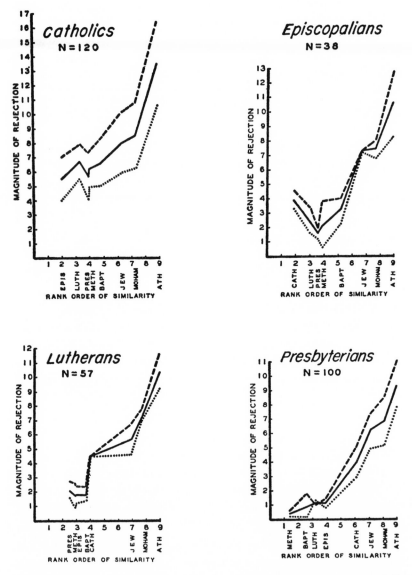

FIGURE 16.2. The relation between similarity and rejection of disbelief systems.

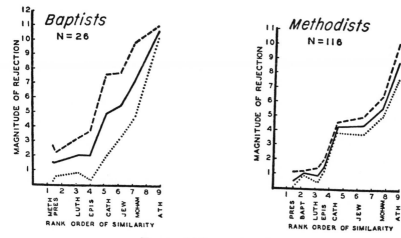

FIGURE 16.2, *continued*

made by Williams and Waelder about attitude toward the renegade, "family quarrels among religious groups," and Freud's
"narcissism of small differences." Note, for example, that the Episcopalians reject Catholics relatively more than any of the other
Christian groups, despite the fact that Catholics are seen to be
most similar. They also reject Lutherans to a relatively high degree, despite the fact that Lutherans are seen to be second most
similar. The Lutherans reject Presbyterians, Methodists, Episcopalians, and Baptists about equally, but to a lesser degree than
they reject Catholics. Note also that the Catholics reject *all* Protestant denominations at a consistently high level. But the Protestant groups likewise reject Catholics at a consistently high level.
The rejection seems to be mutual between Catholics and Protestants.

All these findings made good sense in the light of what is
known of the history of the Protestant Reformation, the special
role played by Martin Luther in the early part of the sixteenth
century when he challenged the authority of the Catholic
Church, and the breaking away of the Church of England from
the Catholic Church in 1531. They all seem to suggest that, regardless of perceived similarity, rejection is mutually high, relatively speaking, between "renegade" and "parent" systems,

probably because of the mutual threat they are seen to pose to each other's continued existence. To our mind, this "renegade" hypothesis does not contradict our major finding of an inverse relation between similarity and rejection over the *whole range* of the disbelief continuum. Our concern here has been to try to account for the several "bumps" in the curves shown in Figure 16.2, those found in that portion of the disbelief continuum that is relatively close in to the belief system.

The Effect of Frame of Reference

Another question we wondered about is the stability of these similarity continua from one social situation to another, and of the relationship between similarity and rejection. For example, do Methodists married to Catholics have a similarity continuum different from that of Methodists married to Methodists? Do Stalinists feel differently toward Trotskyists depending on whether the Trotskyist is evaluated in isolation, or in relation to Social Democrats, or in relation to Fascists? Do Catholics feel differently toward Lutherans depending on whether Lutherans are judged along with Baptists or along with Episcopalians? In other words, are the findings regarding the similarity continuum affected by the particular frame of reference or reference group or reference person operative in a given social situation?

First, we will cite some evidence obtained on the effect of varying reference persons on perceived similarity. In connection with a larger research on interfaith marriages,* rank orders of similarity were obtained for six groups of Methodists, each group married to persons of different Christian faiths, e.g., Methodist-Methodist, Methodist-Presbyterian, etc. We can thus compare the rank orders of similarity obtained for these different groups of Methodists in order to see to what extent they turn out to be the same or different. The more they are comparable to the previous data, the less the effect of spouse as reference person. The results are shown in Table 16.2.

* See Chapter 17 for a report on the findings. We are indebted to Stephanie and Martin Zlotowski for providing us with these additional data.

Table 16.2

Rank Orders of Similarity for Six Methodist Groups Married to Persons of Various Faiths

Religion Being Ranked	Rank Order Previously Found	Rank Order for Methodists Married to:					
		Meth.	Pres.	Bapt.	Luth.	Epis.	Cath.
Methodist	0	0	0	0	0	0	0
Presbyterian	1	1	1	1	1	1	1
Baptist	2	2	3	2	2	2.5	3
Lutheran	3	4	4	3	3	2.5	2
Episcopalian	4	3	2	4	4	4	4
Catholic	5	5	5	5	5	5	5
Correlation[a] between ranks		.94	.83	1.00	1.00	.99	.94

[a] As determined by *rho* correlation.

We observe that the similarity ranks are essentially the same for all Methodist groups, regardless of denomination of the spouse. All Methodists rank Presbyterians as most similar and Catholics as least similar. The rank orders of similarity for Methodists who are married to Baptists and for Methodists who are married to Lutherans are identical with those previously found for all other Methodist groups, who are for the most part unmarried. The rank orders for Methodists married to those of other faiths are also in close agreement with each other and with the rank order previously found. Thus, the Methodist similarity continuum seems to be a quite stable thing, uninfluenced by being single or married, and uninfluenced by the denominational affiliation of the marriage partner.

Another study by Davis (1958) concerns the effect of frame of reference on the perception of similarity and on the relation between similarity and rejection. Davis varied the frame of reference in two experiments, one with Catholics and one with Methodists. In Experiment I, three groups of Catholics were used, and in Experiment II, three groups of Methodists. Since the experiments are exactly the same in design let us describe only the Catholic one by way of illustration. We will call the three Catholic groups of Experiment I, A, B, and C. Group A was given a questionnaire that contained references to non-Catholic faiths occupying similarity positions 1, 2, 3, 4, and 5 (Episcopalians, Lutherans, Presbyterians, Methodists, and Baptists). In Group B's questionnaire mention was made only of 1, 3, and 5 (Episcopalians, Presbyterians, and Baptists), and Group C's questionnaire mentioned only 1, 2, and 3 (Episcopalians, Lutherans, and Presbyterians). In other words, three groups of Catholics are to report their perceptions of similarity and their feelings of rejection toward other non-Catholic faiths in different social contexts or frames of reference. The design of this experiment (and of the Methodist experiment) will perhaps be better grasped with the aid of the following formulation:

Group A responded to denominations: 1 2 3 4 5
Group B responded to denominations: 1   3   5
Group C responded to denominations: 1 2 3

Frame of reference B differs from frame of reference A in the number of faiths represented but not in range of faiths represented. Frame of reference C differs from B in range but not number; and it differs from A both in range and in number of faiths represented.

Limitations of space do not permit us to present here all the data thus obtained.* The main findings can be summarized as follows: In general the similarity rankings in the Catholic and Methodist experiments are in close agreement with those already reported and do not differ from one frame of reference to another. More important is the fact that frame of reference has no significant effect on the extent of rejection of a particular disbelief system. As can be seen graphically in Figure 16.3, the amount of rejection for any given disbelief subsystem is about the same under varying frames of reference. For example, the extent to which the Catholics reject the Episcopalians is approximately the same in the three experimental conditions. Likewise, the extent to which the Methodists reject any given faith is also approximately the same under the three frames of reference. Whatever differences there are turn out to be chance differences; they are not statistically significant.

* The interested reader who may wish to consult the full report of findings is referred to Davis (1958).

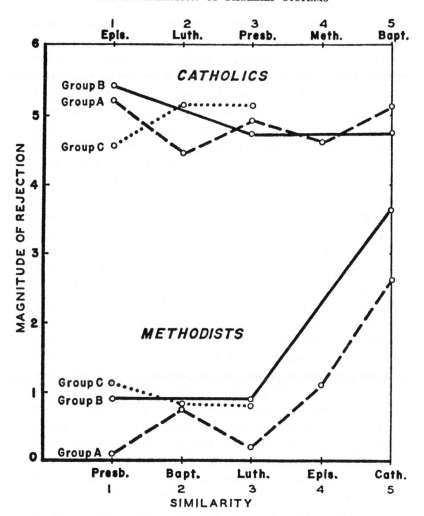

FIGURE 16.3. The relationship between smiliarity and rejection under varying frames of reference.

What are we to conclude from these results and from those obtained in the interfaith marriage study? Both sets of results suggest that disbelief systems are fairly stable and enduring cognitive organizations that resist being changed by the particular social situation in which the person may find himself. This is a quite surprising conclusion because it appears to violate a major tenet of contemporary psychological and sociological theory. This tenet is to the effect that attitudes and perceptions are to an important extent determined by such variables as membership groups, social norms, frames of reference, reference groups, reference persons, social roles, and levels of adaptation.[6] In the interfaith marriage study, it may reasonably be assumed that the group membership (the reference person, the frame of reference, or however else one might care to put it) of a Methodist should constantly shift according to the religious affiliation of the spouse. But the perceived similarity continua of Methodists married to Catholics is essentially the same as those of Methodists married to Methodists. In the Davis experiment, it is surprising for us to learn that Catholics and Methodists respond to the other faiths in stable ways regardless of experimental manipulations in the frame of reference.

One reasonable explanation is that the saliency of spouse as reference person is not great, and that the experimental attempt employed to manipulate frame of reference is not effective. But why not? Our theoretical emphasis on systems leads us to propose a possible answer. Perhaps single beliefs are more readily influenced than systems of beliefs by changes in the kinds of frames of reference or reference persons studied here. A Catholic married to a Jew, for example, might be more likely to change his beliefs about birth control and divorce than to change his cognitive organization about the nature of Catholicism and the way other faiths are arranged with respect to it. In other words, it should take a considerably bigger change in frame of reference and a change in a whole *system* of reference groups to influence behavior of the kind studied here: the organization of disbelief systems along a continuum of similarity to the belief system.

To return to the main focus of our inquiry: The results clearly point to the psychological reality of the organization of disbelief systems. We will next try to seek out some everyday behavioral manifestations of such disbelief systems.

Synopsis

Subjects belonging to six major Christian denominations were asked to rank Catholic, Episcopalian, Lutheran, Presbyterian, Methodist, and Baptist religions in order of perceived similarity to their own religion. They also judged the Jewish and Mohammedan religions and atheism for similarity. In this way a similarity-dissimilarity continuum was obtained for each of the six Christian groups. It was found that the six similarity continua are reducible to a single one, with each religious group merely judging the similarity continuum from its own position on it.

Similarity continua were also obtained from clergymen representing the same six Christian faiths. On the whole these were found to be in good agreement with those obtained with college students of different faiths.

We next determined the relation between similarity and amount of acceptance of each faith. In general, the more dissimilar a faith to one's own, the more it is rejected. The shape of the relationship is quite stable, being the same for closed and open subjects. But certain fluctuations in this relation are noted in the way Christians of various faiths reject each other. These are interpreted as arising out of historical and current conflict within the Christian fold.

A further finding emerges when the data are analyzed separately for persons of various faiths who score high and low on the Dogmatism Scale. Although the relation between similarity and rejection is the same in both groups, closed subjects consistently reject more than do open subjects all disbelief subsystems along the total range of the similarity continuum. Thus, bigotry or rejection of disbelief subsystems is seen to be a function of two variables: cognitive similarity and the degree to which one's system is open or closed, with cognitive similarity clearly being the more powerful determinant.

Finally, we studied the effect of frame of reference on perceived similarity and rejection. The similarity continua are essentially the same for married Methodists as for single ones, and the same for married Methodists no matter what the religion of their spouse may be. This suggests that a person's disbelief system is an enduring organization, uninfluenced by marital changes in frame of reference. A similar conclusion is reached in another study, wherein frame of reference was varied experimentally. The organization of disbelief systems in Catholics and in Methodists remain essentially unchanged by experimental variations in frame of reference.

Notes

1. We are indebted to Dr. Frank Restle for working out this scale. The scale shown in Figure 16.1 is derived from the similarity matrix shown in Table 16.1. The fact that Catholic and Baptist respondents give an exactly reversed ordering indicates that they are at the extreme ends, and their rankings set the order of the denominations. Information on the spaces between is given by the other four groups of respondents.

The rankings of similarity are taken as judgments of relative distance between perceived positions of denominations. For example, Episcopalians ranked Catholics as being more similar than Lutherans, and thus d_1, the distance from Episcopalians to Catholics, is less than d_2, the distance from Episcopalians to Lutherans. In much the same way, judgments by other groups enable us to make decisions about the relative sizes of the other distances: d_3 (Lutheran to Presbyterian), d_4 (Presbyterian to Methodist), and d_5 (Methodist to Baptist). These comparisons are then stated as a set of inequalities:

(1) $d_1 < d_2$
(2) $d_3 + d_4 < d_2$
(3) $d_2 < d_3 + d_4 + d_5$
(4) $d_3 + d_4 + d_5 < d_1 + d_2$
(5) $d_4 + d_5 < d_3$
(6) $d_4 < d_5$
(7) $d_5 < d_3 + d_4$

The first inequality was derived from the judgments of Episcopalians cited above. For another example, consider inequality (4), the most complex. The value $d_3 + d_4 + d_5$ is the distance from Lutheran to Baptist, and the value $d_1 + d_2$ is the distance from Lutheran to Catholic. Since Lutherans claimed Baptists were more similar to them than Catholics, the inequality follows.

It will be recognized that by adding the distances, in forming these inequalities, we are assuming that the denominations lie on a straight line. We now inquire whether this assumption of one-dimensionality is tenable or not.

If there exists a spacing of the six denominations on one dimension, which is entirely consistent with the ranking data, then one-dimensionality is a tenable hypothesis. The scale values in Figure 16.1 constitute such a spacing. Proof of this assertion is to reconstruct a table of ranked similarities, without errors or inversions, assuming that each group ranks its similarity to others according to the one common scale. The table so constructed is identical with the one obtained empirically. This proves that the inequalities are consistent. As is usually the case with a consistent system of inequalities, there are an infinite number of solutions. Strictly speaking, we have an "ordered metric" scale, that is, a ranking of the 15 distances between the 6 ordered denominations. But any other numerical scale satisfying the data would look very much like the one given above.

The scale points were determined by trial and error. Since a completely consistent solution was found, there was no need to employ more general computation methods, such as linear programming, for this particular application.

2. The data reported herein show what appears to be a reversal for the Methodist group. Baptists are ranked first and Presbyterians second. This reversal occurs because the continua reported are based upon a theologian's rankings rather than rankings by the subjects themselves. *Perceived* similarity ranks for Methodist subjects are identical with those reported here.

3. As determined by *rho* correlations.

4. Converting first to *z*.

310

5. More precisely, a positively accelerated, curvilinear relationship.

6. For an elaboration of these concepts, the reader is referred to Newcomb (1950), Charters and Newcomb (1958), Sherif (1958), and Helson (1948). See also Floyd Allport's discussion of adaptation-level in Chapter 10 of his book (1955).

17

Some Behavioral Manifestations
of Disbelief Systems

*Milton Rokeach, Gloria Cheek, Franz Geierhaas,
Figes Matheson, and Stephanie and Martin Zlotowski*

Through the investigations reported in the last chapter, we think a good deal of progress has been made in understanding the cognitive nature of disbelief systems. Disbelief systems do indeed seem to lead a "life" of their own which is not revealed by studying only belief systems. With the findings of Chapter 16 in mind it no longer seems meaningful to talk merely in terms of the classical dichotomy between ingroup and outgroup, or in terms of the dichotomy between positive and negative reference groups (Newcomb, 1950). We will henceforth be obliged to ask: *Which* outgroup? *Which* negative reference group? Where does it lie along the similarity continuum?

But it may be asked, what difference does it make? Can it be shown that these disbelief systems have important consequences for everyday behavior?

In this chapter we will report on three studies designed to explore such consequences. The first of these studies concerns the differential probability of movements into and out of Christian churches of various denominations. The second study concerns the differential rates of attendance at particular denominational colleges by persons of various denominations. The third involves the differential probability of interfaith marriages, and of premarital and marital conflict in such marriages.

Joining and Leaving a Church

Most churches keep membership records containing among other things the date of joining and a letter of transfer from the church of previous affiliation. Some churches also keep records on the date of termination of membership and a copy of the letter of transfer to the church joined subsequently. We selected for study two churches in Lansing, Michigan, from each of the following denominations: Episcopalian, Lutheran, Presbyterian, Methodist, and Baptist.*

Our major hypothesis is that the relative frequency of joining a particular church by persons of various faiths, and the relative frequency of leaving such a church to join churches of other faiths, is a function of the degree of similarity existing among the various Christian faiths.

The two churches selected from each denomination were those centrally located in Lansing and those having the largest parishes. Membership was predominantly white. In some cases we were permitted to look at the membership records ourselves; in other cases, the church secretary or minister obtained the data for us. All but two churches kept accurate records on where their new

* We wish to acknowledge gratefully the cooperation of the following clergymen in Lansing who provided us the data reported here: Reverends A. Archer, J. E. Breck, W. Brown, J. Fischbach, W. H. Halsted, J. F. W. Howell, W. Koepplin, K. F. Kraus, W. Kuhen, P. Morrison, C. M. Muilenburg, P. Proud, P. Schroeder, G. Selway, H. Sugden, and C. Taylor.

Comparable data from Catholic sources were not available, but we were able to obtain data on the frequency of Catholics' joining other churches from the churches they joined. These will also be considered here.

members came from, but only a few had adequate data on where departing members departed to. The data obtained covered three years (1953–1955).

Table 17.1

Total Estimated Church Membership in Greater Lansing Area for Six Christian Denominations

| Denomination | Total Membership in Greater Lansing [a] | | Weight |
	N	Percentage	
Catholic	20,032	42	1.0
Episcopalian	2,677	6	7.0
Lutheran	6,644	14	3.0
Presbyterian	4,203	9	4.7
Methodist	7,317	15	2.8
Baptist	6,540	14	3.0

[a] Obtained from the Lansing *State Journal* (January 1, 1956).

We first show, in Table 17.1, the total estimated membership for each of the six major Christian faiths in the Greater Lansing area. These figures are taken from the Lansing newspaper, the *State Journal*, as reported on January 1, 1956.[*] These population estimates are of interest primarily because they provide us with a base line for correcting the raw frequencies obtained for each faith so that they would not be affected by their uneven repre-

[*] These estimates were, in turn, obtained from the Lansing Council of Churches or from individual churches, if not represented in the Council. They include Lansing and East Lansing, and also include students attending churches in East Lansing. However, a check with the Lansing Council of Churches and with various clergymen revealed that the definition of "member" differs from one church to another. The Lutherans, Presbyterians, Methodists, and Baptists consider and count as members only those who are "received into membership," or become "communicant members" or "baptized believers." This occurs roughly between the ages of 11 and 15. The Episcopalian Church counts as members all those who are baptized, which takes place shortly after birth. The Catholic Church reports as members all persons from infancy on up. The estimates for Catholics and Episcopalians, as reported in the *State Journal*, are therefore not comparable with those for the remaining denominations. With the help of Father Meahm of the Lansing Diocese and Reverend Selway of St. Paul's Episcopal Church, whose help we gratefully acknowledge, we were able to correct these figures by subtracting from them the number of Catholics and Episcopalians estimated to be 12 years of age or under. Thus, the membership estimates reported in Table 17.1 are roughly comparable with each other.

sentation in the Greater Lansing population. For this reason we assigned weights to each group on the basis of its proportional representation in the total population. Taking the Catholic membership as a base line, it is seen in Table 17.1 that the number of Episcopalians is roughly one-seventh that of the Catholics. Accordingly, the raw frequencies on joining and leaving churches obtained for Episcopalians will be multiplied by seven. Similarly, the number of Lutherans is roughly one-third that of Catholics, so the raw frequencies obtained for Lutherans will be multiplied by three. The same procedure will be followed for all other faiths so that the corrected data will all be comparable to each other. In all the tables to be presented we have omitted data on persons having religious affiliations other than the six being studied here.* Also, all the tables that follow show the corrected frequencies, not the raw frequencies. To obtain the raw frequencies, simply divide the corrected frequencies by the appropriate weight shown in Table 17.1; that is, divide all Catholic frequencies by 1.0, all Episcopalian frequencies by 7.0, etc.

Table 17.2 shows the weighted frequencies of persons of various faiths joining and leaving various churches. To illustrate how the table may be read, let us take the Presbyterian data as an example. Presbyterian church records for 1953–1955 show that they gained a (weighted) total of 1968 new members. Of these, 1636 were Presbyterians, 230 were Methodists, and so on. The correlation [1] between similarity and frequency of joining the Presbyterian church is .94. Similarly, during the same period, the Presbyterian church reported losing 163 members. Of these, 132 joined another Presbyterian church, 28 joined a Methodist church, and so on. The correlation between similarity and frequency of leaving the Presbyterian church is .83.

A study of Table 17.2 shows that the vast majority of movement is within rather than between denominations. This is to be expected, of course. Only about 20 per cent of the gains and about 35 per cent of the losses in membership are across denominations. However, we are here primarily concerned with differential rates of movement in and out of denominations regardless of absolute numbers, in order to see if such rates of movement are related to, or are a function of, similarity.

* These are generally small and scattered in number.

Table 17.2

Relation Between Similarity and Weighted Frequencies of Church Members Gained from and Lost to Other Denominations (1953–55)

	Similarity Continuum						Total	Correlation
	0	1	2	3	4	5		
Episcopalian								
No. gained from:	(Epis.) 931	(Cath.) 42	(Luth.) 12	(Pres.) 42	(Meth.) 64	(Bapt.) 18	1,109	.39
No. lost to: [a]	—	—	—	—	—	—	—	—
Lutheran								
No. gained from:	(Luth.) 585	(Pres.) 33	(Meth.) 78	(Epis.) 14	(Bapt.) 24	(Cath.) 12	746	.89
No. lost to: [a]	—	—	—	—	—	—	—	—
Presbyterian								
No. gained from:	(Pres.) 1,636	(Meth.) 230	(Bapt.) 51	(Luth.) 24	(Epis.) 7	(Cath.) 20	1,968	.94
No. lost to:	132	28	0	3	0	0	163	.83
Methodist								
No. gained from:	(Meth.) 812	(Pres.) 56	(Bapt.) 18	(Luth.) 12	(Epis.) 28	(Cath.) 5	931	.83
No. lost to:	470	127	9	15	7	5	633	.94
Baptist								
No. gained from:	(Bapt.) 237	(Meth.) 25	(Pres.) 19	(Luth.) 6	(Epis.) 0	(Cath.) 1	288	.94
No. lost to:	135	64	71	9	14	2	295	.89
Total gained from:	4,201	386	178	98	123	56	5,042	.94
Total lost to:	737	219	80	27	21	7	1,091	1.00

[a] Data not available.

It is obvious from an inspection of the weighted frequencies and from the correlations that in general the greater the similarity of a given church to one's own, the greater the likelihood of gaining new members from it and losing old members to it. All the correlations are in the .80's and .90's, with but one exception. For Episcopalians, correlation between similarity and new members gained from other denominations is only .39. It is difficult to say why this correlation is lower than the rest. It could be due to sampling fluctuations or to lack of exactness of our weighing procedure.

It is desirable to get a single estimate for all denominations combined of the relationship between similarity and gain, and similarity and loss in members. The combined results are shown at the bottom of Table 17.2. Of 5,042 new members gained by all denominations, 4,201 are from the same denomination, 386 are from a denomination most similar, 178 are from a denomination next most similar, etc. The correlation between similarity and new members gained is .94. With respect to loss of members, all denominations considered together reported losing 1,091 old members. Of these, 737 rejoined another church of the same denomination, 219 rejoined a church most similar to it, etc. The rank order of frequency of loss to other denominations is identical with the rank order of similarity (1.00).

We feel justified in concluding from the analysis presented thus far that the two-way movements into and out of churches is generally a function of degree of similarity of disbelief subsystems to belief system.

Additional evidence on the relation between similarity and rate of leaving churches. The results shown in Table 17.2 with respect to persons of each faith were provided by churches of that faith. It is also possible to get information about members of one particular faith by collecting it from the new churches they join. This is especially helpful from a methodological standpoint when we desire information about a particular denomination but are not able to get it directly from the denominational source itself. For example, an inspection of Table 17.2 shows that there are scattered through it a total of 80 ex-Catholics who at the time under study had already joined one of the Protestant denominations: 42 became Episcopalians, 12 became Lutherans, and so on.

If our hypothesis is correct regarding the relation between similarity and rate of loss to other denominations, it should hold for these indirectly obtained data as well. Most especially, we will be interested in the Catholic group, but also in the Episcopalian and Lutheran groups since we have not been able to obtain this information from the churches themselves.

Table 17.3

Relation Between Similarity and Rate of Loss of Church Members to Other Denominations (Indirectly Obtained)

Church	Similarity Continuum						Total	Correlation
	0	1	2	3	4	5		
Catholic	(Cath.) —[a]	(Epis.) 42	(Luth.) 12	(Pres.) 20	(Meth.) 5	(Bapt.) 1	80	.90
Episcopalian	(Epis.) 931	(Cath.) —[a]	(Luth.) 14	(Pres.) 7	(Meth.) 28	(Bapt.) 0	980	.70
Lutheran	(Luth.) 585	(Pres.) 24	(Meth.) 12	(Epis.) 12	(Bapt.) 6	(Cath.) —[a]	639	.98
Presbyterian	(Pres.) 1,636	(Meth.) 56	(Bapt.) 19	(Luth.) 33	(Epis.) 42	(Cath.) —[a]	1,786	.60
Methodist	(Meth.) 812	(Pres.) 230	(Bapt.) 25	(Luth.) 78	(Epis.) 64	(Cath.) —[a]	1,209	.70
Baptist	(Bapt.) 237	(Meth.) 18	(Pres.) 51	(Luth.) 24	(Epis.) 18	(Cath.) —[a]	348	.58
Total lost to:	4,201	370	133	174	163	1[b]	5,042	.70

[a] Data not available from Catholic sources.
[b] The rank order correlation was calculated without this.

By rearranging the data shown in Table 17.2 we get Table 17.3. This shows the relation between similarity and frequency of loss of members suffered by a particular denomination, as obtained from reports by other denominations. Again we note positive relationships. For the Catholics the correlation between similarity and frequency of loss to other denominations is .90, indicating that defection from Catholicism is most likely to take place to religions perceived to be most similar to it and least likely to take place to religions perceived to be least similar to it. The other correlations range between .58 and .98, and the correlation for all groups combined is .70. These results agree pretty well with those shown in Table 17.2.

Choosing a Denominational College

In the summer of 1956, we obtained enrollment figures from the registrar of 18 denominational colleges in the Midwest for the two years 1951 and 1956. The hypothesis we wished to test was very similar to that tested in the study on movements into and out of churches; namely, that differential rates of attendance at a particular denominational college by persons of varying denominations is at least in part a function of the degree of similarity of disbelief subsystems to belief system.

Data were obtained for the following denominational colleges:

Catholic: Marygrove College (Michigan).

Lutheran: Augustana College (Illinois); Carthage College (Illinois); Valparaiso University (Indiana); Capital University (Ohio).

Presbyterian: Alma College (Michigan); Blackburn College (Illinois); Wooster College (Ohio).

Methodist: Albion College (Michigan); Greenville College (Illinois); Illinois Wesleyan University (Illinois); Baldwin-Wallace College (Ohio); Mt. Union College (Ohio); Ohio Wesleyan University (Ohio).

Baptist: Hillsdale College (Michigan); Kalamazoo College (Michigan); Franklin College (Indiana); Denison University (Ohio).

The raw frequencies obtained again have to be weighted in order to correct for the different proportions of each denomination in the population. Therefore, an attempt was made to secure population figures for the six major Christian denominations from various state and national religious bodies and from official religious publications. In this way we obtained various population estimates for the several denominations for the states we were interested in. Further research indicated, however, that the estimates thus obtained are almost useless since they are based on different criteria of membership. To take one example from esti-

Table 17.4

Relation Between Similarity and Weighted Frequencies of Students Enrolled in Various Denominational Colleges in Four States for 1951 and 1956

Religion	State	Year	Similarity Continuum						Total	Correlation
			0	1	2	3	4	5		
Catholic	Mich.	1956	(Cath.) 733	(Epis.) 7	(Luth.) 12	(Pres.) 0	(Meth.) 3	(Bapt.) 0	755	.84
Lutheran	Ill.	1951	(Luth.) 3,081	(Pres.) 395	(Meth.) 445	(Epis.) 161	(Bapt.) 189	(Cath.) 28	4,299	.89
	Ill.	1956	3,033	545	386	175	141	38	4,318	1.00
	Ind.	1951	3,954	197	207	77	45	72	4,552	.89
	Ind.	1956	4,869	179	182	112	36	71	5,449	.89
	Ohio	1951	1,974	188	238	77	78	17	2,572	.89
	Ohio	1956	2,364	150	277	56	69	20	2,936	.89
Presbyterian	Ill.	1951	(Pres.) 249	(Meth.) 196	(Bapt.) 57	(Luth.) 87	(Epis.) 56	(Cath.) 41	686	.94
	Ill.	1956	263	210	81	93	70	42	759	.94
	Mich.	1956	1,481	283	78	99	189	43	2,173	.77
	Ohio	1951	3,102	361	99	150	280	21	4,013	.77
	Ohio	1956	3,069	353	84	111	0	20	3,637	.89

Methodist

		(Meth.)	(Pres.)	(Bapt.)	(Luth.)	(Epis.)	(Cath.)	
Ill.	1951	1,781	470	150	156	147	72	.94
Ill.	1956	2,038	616	276	294	280	84	.80
Mich.	1951	1,596	701	162	150	672	70	.83
Mich.	1956	1,652	·851	108	213	637	42	.77
Ohio	1951	5,079	2,895	408	3,834	1,939	356	.71
Ohio	1956	4,292	2,712	381	3,777	1,554	345	.71

Baptist

		(Bapt.)	(Meth.)	(Pres.)	(Luth.)	(Epis.)	(Cath.)	
Ind.	1951	381	370	207	48	35	29	.94
Ind.	1956	543	339	240	39	49	32	.94
Mich.	1951	408	549	682	234	658	147	.31
Mich.	1956	588	507	686	231	595	134	.37
Ohio	1951	753	538	1,344	195	1,057	39	.37
Ohio	1956	453	566	1,560	183	1,421	66	.31

Total, 1951		22,358	6,860	3,999	5,169	5,156	892	.83
Total, 1956		25,378	7,318	4,351	5,383	5,044	937	.83

mates provided us for the state of Illinois for 1956: The number of Catholics is estimated by Catholic sources as 2.3 million, and the combined estimated total for Episcopalians, Lutherans, Presbyterians, Methodists, and Baptists is under a million. We will not enter here into a detailed consideration of all the sources of error which may have contributed to this estimate. Suffice it to say here that as far as we know there exist no accurate estimates on absolute number of members in the major religious denominations.*

We therefore proceeded on the assumption, admittedly unverified, that the relative proportion of persons belonging to the six major denominational groups under study are not too different from each other in Michigan, Illinois, Indiana, and Ohio. Furthermore, we proceeded on the additional assumption, equally unverified, that the relative proportions of these denominations in the four states is approximately the same as that obtained for the Greater Lansing area. Thus, we used the Lansing weights to correct the raw frequencies of enrollments in denominational colleges in four midwestern states. We are the first to admit that this is a crude procedure and our only reason for using it is that in the absence of more accurate information it represents our best guess of what the weights should be.

The results shown in Table 17.4 are the corrected frequencies of enrollments by students of different denominations in the various colleges for 1951 and 1956. It is seen that the correlations between similarity and the number of students enrolled are generally high. When the data are combined for all states and all denominations, the correlation between similarity and enrollment is .83 for both 1951 and 1956.

Is it possible to account for the relationships found on the basis of geographical proximity of students of varying denominations to the school they attend? To find out, we looked up the home address of all students enrolled at Alma College in Michigan. With Alma as the center, we drew five concentric circles on a map

---

* In this connection, Chein writes: "To begin with, we are sadly ignorant of a host of relevant actuarial facts. We have no accurate figures on the number of individuals who identify themselves, if only nominally, with each of the major religious groupings, to say nothing of the sectarian divisions within these. A fortiori, we have only the most approximate notions as to how these distribute themselves in absolute numbers within the various strata of the American population" (1956, p. 58).

of Michigan. Residence within the most central circle was scored 1, etc. In this way, the mean physical distance between home town and Alma was computed for each denominational group attending Alma College. The results showed that no one particular denominational group lived any closer to Alma than any other. We can thus conclude that proximity cannot account for the results found.

Interfaith Marriages

Our purpose in this study was twofold: To determine (1) whether the probability of interfaith marriages increases as interfaith similarity increases, and (2) whether degree of conflict—premarital and marital—decreases as interfaith similarity increases.

THE FREQUENCY OF INTERFAITH MARRIAGES

This research was conducted in the married housing area on the campus of Michigan State University. By knocking on many doors, raw frequencies of interfaith marriages were obtained for 632 couples, where one or both of the partners identified themselves as members of one of the six major Christian denominations. In 560 of these couples, both partners identified themselves as members of one or the other of the six major denominations, and these served as our source of data for this study.

The raw frequencies, however, must again be corrected so that they will be uninfluenced by the uneven representation of these denominations in the campus population. To arrive at the weights, we simply determined the relative proportion of times we encountered members of each of the six denominations in our total sample of 632 couples. The proportion of Catholics, Episcopalians, Lutherans, Presbyterians, Methodists, and Baptists are .31, .08, .15, .14, .19, and .12 respectively. On the basis of these proportions, the weights are 1.0, 3.9, 2.1, 2.2, 1.6, and 2.6 respectively. Raw data for each faith were again multiplied by these weights. The relation between similarity and weighted frequencies of interfaith marriages are shown in Table 17.5.

If we look at Table 17.5 and read across, it will be seen that 123 Catholics are married to Catholics, 31 to Episcopalians, and

Table 17.5

Relation Between Similarity and Weighted Frequencies of Interfaith Marriages

Religion	Similarity Continuum						Total	Correlation
	0	1	2	3	4	5		
Catholic	(Cath.) 123	(Epis.) 31	(Luth.) 13	(Pres.) 20	(Meth.) 19	(Bapt.) 13	219	.76
Episcopalian	(Epis.) 98	(Cath.) 8	(Luth.) 8	(Pres.) 11	(Meth.) 8	(Bapt.) 0	133	.71
Lutheran	(Luth.) 120	(Pres.) 9	(Meth.) 14	(Epis.) 16	(Bapt.) 13	(Cath.) 6	178	.60
Presbyterian	(Pres.) 103	(Meth.) 18	(Bapt.) 16	(Luth.) 8	(Epis.) 20	(Cath.) 9	174	.54
Methodist	(Meth.) 107	(Pres.) 24	(Bapt.) 26	(Luth.) 19	(Epis.) 20	(Cath.) 12	208	.89
Baptist	(Bapt.) 112	(Meth.) 16	(Pres.) 13	(Luth.) 11	(Epis.) 0	(Cath.) 5	157	.94
TOTAL	663	106	90	85	80	45	1,069	1.00

so on.* In the same way, the weighted frequency of Baptists married to Baptists is 112, Baptists married to Methodists is 16, and so on. Inspection of these frequencies in relation to the similarity continuum reveals once again that in general the frequency of interfaith marriages decreases as similarity decreases. The correlations between similarity and frequency of interfaith marriages range from .54 to .94. When the data are combined for all Christian denominations, the order of frequencies of marriage is identical with the order of similarity—a perfect correlation. These results clearly support the hypothesis that frequency of interfaith marriage varies directly with interfaith similarity.

PREMARITAL AND MARITAL CONFLICT IN INTERFAITH MARRIAGES

In order to obtain information on marital conflict, additional data were obtained for a small sample of couples selected from the larger group. The sample was composed only of couples in which at least one of the partners was a Methodist. Both husband and wife were asked to fill out a questionnaire aimed at measuring various aspects of premarital and marital relations thought to be indicative of conflict between the partners.

The questions directed toward the premarital period dealt with number of times the engagement was broken, the extent of parental resistance to the marriage, and whether the marriage was delayed as a result of religious disagreement. Questions designed to get at postmarital conflict were concerned with the frequency and nature of quarrels, quarrels about attending church, extent of compromise over religious issues, whether separation was contemplated, and actual separation from the marriage partner.

On the basis of responses to such questions, quantitative measures of conflict were obtained for the premarital period, the

---

* The reader is reminded that we are talking here of *weighted* frequencies. In the case of the 219 Catholic couples, one of the partners is always a Catholic, and is therefore a constant. In the case of 133 Episcopalian couples, one of the partners is always an Episcopalian and this is therefore a constant. Thus, the raw frequencies are corrected by multiplying them only by the weight assigned to the denomination of the *second* partner. For this reason, the number of Catholics married to Episcopalians is 31 but the number of Episcopalians married to Catholics is 8. In the first case, the raw frequency is 8, which when multiplied by a weight of 3.9 for Episcopalians, gives us 31. In the second case, the raw figure of 8 is multiplied by a weight of 1.0 for Catholics, which gives us 8.

marital period, and for both periods combined. The results are shown in Table 17.6. As can be seen by inspecting these results, the less the religious similarity between partners, the greater the conflict. This is true both for the premarital and marital periods and is especially evident in the combined conflict scores for both periods.

Table 17.6

Mean Premarital, Postmarital, and Total Conflict Scores for Methodists Married to People of Six Religious Denominations

Denomination of Couples (From most to least similar)	Number of Couples	Premar.	Postmar.	Total
Methodist-Methodist	7	0.0	2.0	2.0
Methodist-Presbyterian	7	1.0	3.9	4.9
Methodist-Baptist	10	.6	2.8	3.4
Methodist-Lutheran	7	.1	6.6	6.7
Methodist-Episcopalian	5	1.6	5.4	7.0
Methodist-Catholic	7	3.8	6.4	10.2

Interpretations and Implications

In discussing research needs in the study of religious conflict, Chein writes:

> We need to know far more than we do about the frequency and circumstances of contact between adherents of different faiths, about the degree to which and the ways in which religious identification and matters relevant to religious affiliation enter into contact situations; about the distribution of knowledge, beliefs, feelings, and policy orientations with regard to faiths and denominational affairs other than one's own (1956, pp. 58–59).

In a similar vein, Williams has this to say:

> . . . the problem for social science is that of specifying the variables that help to account for varying prevalence and intensity of conflict as a function of variations in religious value-orientations (1956, p. 13).

Naturally, we agree with these writers. The data presented in this chapter may be regarded as a beginning attempt to improve theory and knowledge in this area. But the data leave much to be desired by way of precision. For one thing, we have already pointed out that the estimates of the total number of members in each of the denominations are far from exact. Consequently, the weights employed are also inexact. Second, we used the Greater Lansing estimates of denominational populations and the weights based upon these as the basis for correcting the enrollment figures not only in the whole state of Michigan, but also in Illinois, Indiana, and Ohio. Third, we have no way of determining the accuracy of the data obtained from the various religious sources on gains and losses in membership, and on enrollment in denominational colleges. Fourth, we have no information on how clearly, actively, and devoutly identified our subjects are with the denomination with which they are affiliated.

These methodological difficulties notwithstanding, a large body of data has been reduced, at least in part, to understandable proportions. On the whole, data on joining and leaving a church, on choosing a denominational college, on choosing a marriage partner, and on conflict between partners, are remarkably stable and clear-cut. They all point to the fact that certain kinds of everyday behavior are systematically related to, and presumably some function of, the perceived similarity of various disbelief subsystems to one's own. It is also clear from these studies, as well as those reported in the last chapter, that perceived similarity has some basis in objective similarity among belief systems. For it would be impossible to account for the consistent findings obtained for one faith after another unless it is assumed that perceived similarity has a basis in objective similarity. It is not for us to specify what this objective basis is. This can best be accomplished by the specialist in comparative religion. We are content to say that the findings firmly establish the psychological validity and usefulness of the notion of disbelief systems as distinct from belief systems, and once again to reiterate our point that the organization of disbelief systems ought to be studied in its own right.

It should be pointed out that the correlations reported here include in every case the data on movements, enrollments, and marriages within denominations as well as between denominations. The reason we have included the within-denomination data in computing the correlations is that the within-denomination frequencies need not necessarily be higher than the between-denomination frequencies. It will be noticed in Table 17.4 that some denominational colleges have more students enrolled who are from other denominations than its own. But even if we were to exclude such data from the computations the relationships between similarity and frequency would still be consistently positive, although somewhat lower.

In need of further clarification, however, is the exact nature of the relationships found. The correlations tell us only that there is a relationship between two sets of ranks, but cannot tell us whether the relationship is curvilinear rather than linear. A casual inspection of the various results presented in this chapter suggests that the relationships are indeed curvilinear. Most of the persons under consideration seem to conform to the norm of attending a church and college of their own denomination, and marrying someone of their own denomination. As similarity between denominations decreases, the frequencies decrease, at first quickly, and then less quickly. The relation between similarity and frequency seems to follow the familiar J-curve of conformity.

These J-curves need not be thought of as solely psychological in nature. Our conceptualizations seem to have led us into a line of research that has uncovered meaningful correlations between a psychological variable—perceived similarity—and sociological variables. We may have only begun to scratch the surface in investigating this area. For example, future research may concern itself with a continuum of negative reference groups, with the relation between similarity of disbelief subsystems and sociometric choice, and with the relation between similarity and the formation of coalitions, mergers, or "united fronts" with one's political, religious, or scientific opponents. In France, for example, no one political party is normally strong enough to form a government by itself. The strongest party typically seeks a coalition with others to form a majority. Which others? It would be interesting to see whether the formation of such coalitions * is dependent upon perceived similarity.

---

* It should be pointed out that coalition behavior may be studied at both the individual and group level. Choosing a friend to be with on a particular evening

There are conceivably many stimulus objects that could be ranked in terms of similarity to a standard: stimuli varying in color, form, size, etc. In the present research, the stimuli perceived and responded to are far more complex than this: they are system variables, represented by such single words as *Methodist, Episcopalian, etc.* It is clear that humans are quite capable of responding to such "system stimuli." For example, our subjects show relatively little difficulty in deciding that Catholicism is such-and-such a distance away from their own belief system. The stimulus word *Catholicism* stands for a complex of beliefs and this is ordered in terms of similarity to other complexes of beliefs. Similarly, when a person is in the process of leaving one church to join another, or in the process of deciding which denominational college to attend, or which girl to marry, the decisions are apparently made, at least partly, at a molar * level in terms of "system variables." We are therefore led to suggest that the psychological analysis of stimulus and response per se is not necessarily indicative of an elementaristic approach to psychology. *The molarity or molecularity of the response depends upon the molarity or molecularity of the stimulus under scrutiny.* Thus, if what is desired is the study of molar behavior, then what seems necessary is to select molar system stimuli as independent variables.

A further implication of our notions regarding disbelief systems has been touched on earlier. The present findings suggest that, in the study of intergroup relations, it is not enough to talk merely in terms of ingroup and outgroup, or positive reference group and negative reference group. It will not do to assume a person or group has an undifferentiated conception, or attitude, or stance with respect to all outgroups, or all negative reference groups. A more valid model defining intergroup relations, and the decision-making processes that lead to such relations, is a series of outgroups or negative reference groups, arranged in terms of similarity to the ingroup or positive reference group.

---

is a form of temporary coalition; choosing a mate is a more permanent form. Our main point here is that the formation of coalitions among groups and among individuals may both be in part functions of similarity-dissimilarity of disbelief subsystems to belief systems.

 * Molar, as used here, is meant to be synonymous with holistic or global. For other distinctions between molar and molecular see Littman and Rosen (1950).

This is not to imply that similarity is the only property defining such organizations. We have mentioned in Chapter 2 several other properties of disbelief systems which are as yet still uninvestigated. One is the degree of isolation between belief and disbelief systems. A second is breadth of organization. A third is the degree of differentiation of the several disbelief subsystems with respect to the belief system, and with respect to each other.

Finally, we have not meant to imply that the correlation found between behavior and perceived similarity of the disbelief subsystems to the belief systems is necessarily a direct one or a causal one, or one that involves conscious awareness. Actually, our findings permit us to conclude only that concomitant relationships exist between perceived similarity on the one hand, and rates of joining and leaving a church, enrollment in a denominational college, interfaith marriage, and marital conflict, on the other. At this point, we can only speculate about the specific field conditions that actually produce such relationships. A task for future research is to study further the psychological processes and motivations that lead to decisions to leave one church and join another, decisions to attend one denominational college rather than another, etc. At this stage, we can only suggest the direction such further research should take. We may conceive of each disbelief subsystem in a person as somehow giving rise to a characteristic negative force of a certain strength. This determines the probability of the person's interaction with ideas, people, and authorities affiliated with systems other than his own. As the strength of the negative force associated with a given disbelief subsystem is increased, the probability of interaction is decreased, and the strength of a required opposing positive force, if there is to be interaction, is increased. In the study on movements in and out of churches, for example, informal interviews with several clergymen indicated that marriage is the most frequent explanation for leaving one's church to join a highly dissimilar church. Other reasons cited for interdenominational movement are moving from one neighborhood to another, the friendliness of the congregation, the social prestige, patterns of personal friendships, pressures arising from spouse, family, relatives, clergy, employers, and employees, the degree to which one favors a fundamentalist or liberal approach to religion, and the personality of the minister.

In the case of decisions to attend one denominational school rather than another, there are probably yet other motivational forces that are relevant. Although we have no specific information on this, we would guess that relevant here would be such things as the reputation of the school, willingness to admit a student with low grades, size of school, proximity to home, fundamentalist vs. liberal approach, influence of friends, relatives, teachers, or minister, preferential treatment to children of ministers and missionaries, major interest, and availability of scholarships.

As for interfaith marriages, again we have no specific information concerning the motivations that lead to a choice of a partner of another denomination. With further study, no doubt many motivational variables could be isolated.

Synopsis

In the present chapter we have presented evidence to the effect that the probability of movement in and out of the major Christian churches, the probability of enrollment at a particular denominational college by persons of various denominations, and the probability of interfaith marriages and of premarital and marital harmony increases as similarity between religions increases. These findings are interpreted as being behavioral expressions of the organization of disbelief subsystems along a continuum of similarity to the belief system.

Notes

1. All correlations reported in this chapter are rank-order (*rho*) correlations.

Part Five

On the Dynamics of Belief Systems

Up to now our main purpose has been to describe the structural ways in which a person's belief system is similar to and different from another's. In the course of doing so we have had occasion to investigate a variety of psychological phenomena involving relations to authority and to people and involving cognitive and emotional functioning, in order to determine whether a person's behavior in these diverse areas might be alternative yet interrelated expressions of his belief system. Up to now we have not been overly concerned with questions regarding the function or the psychodynamics of belief systems. For, as we have said earlier, it is necessary to describe a phenomenon under investigation before trying to explain it.

The four chapters in this section are, in one way or another, concerned with the functions served by belief systems, particularly open and closed belief systems. First to be explored, in Chapter 18, is the problem of changes in values in persons with open and closed belief systems over a period of six years and the meaning of such changes. Then, in the following two chapters, open and closed belief systems will be studied in relation to such personality variables as anxiety, reports on differences in childhood experiences, and time perspective. Finally, in the last chapter we will be concerned with some situational factors that might affect the extent to which a belief system becomes closed.

18

Changes in Values in Relation to Open-Closed Systems*

C. Gratton Kemp

The research to be reported here concerns a group of religious-minded persons who in 1950 were enrolled in a special training program in a denominational college in preparation for positions as Boy Scout executive or Y.M.C.A. or Y.W.C.A. secretary. At this time the subjects were given a number of psychological tests, including a test of their value orientations. Six years later these persons were contacted again and once more tested for their value orientation. At this time they also filled out the Dogmatism Scale. We wished to find out if these persons' values had changed over the six-year period

* Adapted from a doctoral dissertation submitted to the School for Advanced Graduate Studies at Michigan State University (1957).

and, if so, whether such changes were in any way related to the extent to which their belief systems were open or closed.

What may be reasonably predicted regarding changes in values? At first glance, it might appear from the theory of belief systems that those with relatively open systems should show greater changes than those with closed systems. Such a hypothesis would certainly be consistent with much current-day thinking about the nature of attitudes, and the role of attitudes and values in the personality structure. An attitude or value is seen to be a stubborn thing, rooted in irrational motives and extremely difficult to change. Many social ills are attributed to this fact, and researchers in this field will probably agree that changes in attitudes and values are extremely rare.

Closely related to the idea that attitudes and values are difficult to change is a widely prevailing value judgment that change is socially desirable, while non-change is socially undesirable. We note a widespread tendency in social science to label attitudes that resist change as rigid, authoritarian, reactionary, radical, absolute, intense, extreme, prejudiced, closed, fixated, dogmatic, or defensive. Thus, Hardy (1957) hypothesizes that persons who are authoritarian change their attitudes less frequently than persons who are anti-authoritarian; Goodstein (1953) and Taylor (1954) hypothesize that persons who hold extreme attitudes are more rigid or intolerant of ambiguity than those holding less extreme attitudes. Conversely, there is also the opposite tendency to characterize persons who do change their attitudes as progressive, mature, open-minded, tolerant, rational, reality-oriented, and so on. In short, attitude change and non-change are often seen to be behavioral (phenotypical) opposites, emanating from a parallel set of (genotypical) opposites conceived to underlie them in the personality.

To our mind, this way of thinking about the nature of change and non-change cannot be defended. It does not leave room for the additional possibility that both change and its absence may result from the same underlying motive. Two persons may both change a given attitude, but for opposing reasons: in one it may represent a "party-line" change in conformity to authority; in the other it may represent a more "genuine" change based on a deeper appreciation, or understanding, or maturity. Conversely, two persons may both refuse to change a given attitude: in one it may represent rigidity, and in the other, firmness or stability (Brownfain, 1952).

It is thus obvious that we must avoid associating the open mind with change and the closed mind with non-change. A more defensible view is that persons with relatively closed systems may sometimes manifest change and sometimes fixedness for basically the same reasons. These reasons have been variously described as conformity, other-directedness, identification with authority, ego defense, compartmentalization, isolation, opportunism, and expediency. Conversely, change and non-change in open systems may result equally from a correct appraisal of reality, from intellectual conviction rather than dogmatic conviction, and from independence rather than subservience to conformity pressures.

With these remarks we are now in a better position to state what to expect in a study of value change. It is not that open persons are expected to change their values and closed persons are not, but rather that both groups should change—but in different ways. Let us now describe in more detail how we went about determining the changes in values that take place over a six-year period in our religious-minded subjects. The initial study was conducted in 1950 with 129 students at Missouri Valley College, a Presbyterian coeducational college of liberal arts. Among other things the subjects filled out the Allport-Vernon Scale of Values. This test is a widely used one which, in the words of its authors:

> . . . aims to measure the relative prominence of six basic interests or motives in personality: the *theoretical, economic, aesthetic, social, political,* and *religious.* The classification is based directly upon Edward Spranger's *Types of Men,* a brilliant work which defends the view that the personalities of men are best known through a study of their values or evaluative attitudes (1931, p. 4).

To illustrate this test, let us cite two types of items taken from it. In parenthesis we give the value represented by each alternative the subject may select:

> If you were a university professor and had the necessary ability, would you prefer to teach: (a) poetry; *(aesthetic);* (b) chemistry and physics? *(theoretical).*

Do you think that a good government should aim chiefly at
   a. More aid for the poor, sick, and old *(social)*.
   b. the development of manufacturing and trade *(economic)*.
   c. introducing more ethical principles into its policies and diplomacy *(religious)*.
   d. establishing a position of prestige and respect among nations *(political)*.

All 129 subjects were contacted by mail in 1956 and their cooperation was solicited in filling out again the Allport-Vernon Scale, and also the Dogmatism Scale. One hundred and four replied. Of these, 90 were male and 14 female; 93 were between 29 and 31 years of age, and 11 between 32 and 34; 83 were Protestant, 20 were Catholic, and 1 was Jewish. All these subjects had been originally selected for a special reason: they had all majored in a special curriculum leading to an A.B. degree in Human Relations, in preparation for positions as Boy Scout executive or Y.M.C.A. or Y.W.C.A. secretary. The program was sponsored and financed by the American Humanics Foundation, whose aim was to "recruit, educate and develop men and women of character for the social movements of America, who shall be willing to dedicate their lives to the service of God and humanity in recognized and approved fields of social welfare" (1950). Thus the subjects selected were, in 1950, highly homogeneous with respect to occupational aspiration and the importance they placed on religious values.

Results and Discussion

The 104 subjects for whom data were collected in 1950 and 1956 were first divided into three groups, depending on the score they obtained on the Dogmatism Scale. Closed and open groups included those who scored in the upper and lower quarters of the distribution. The middle group consisted of the remaining half of the subjects. We will present first, in Table 18.1, value patterns of the three groups in 1950 and 1956. By value pattern we mean simply the rank order of mean scores obtained on the six values measured by the Allport-Vernon Scale.[1]

In 1950, the relative order of importance of the six values was: (1) *religious*, (2) *social*, (3) *political*, (4) *economic*, (5) *theo-*

Table 18.1

Rank Order of Importance of Six Values for the Total Group and for Open, Middle, and Closed Subgroups in 1950 and in 1956

	Num-ber	Reli-gious	Social	Politi-cal	Eco-nomic	Theo-retical	Es-thetic
			TEST, 1950				
Open	25	1	2	3	4	5	6
Middle	54	1	2	3	4	5	6
Closed	25	1	2	3	4	5	6
Total group	104	1	2	3	4	5	6
			RETEST, 1956				
Open	25	1	2	4	6	3	5
Middle	54	1	2	3	4	5	6
Closed	25	1	5	2	3	4	6
Total group	104	1	2.5	2.5	5	4	6

retical, and (6) *esthetic.* This pattern is identical for the total group, and for all three subgroups. Note, too, that all groups are highest on *religious* values. In terms of religious orientation and in terms of total value pattern, then, the groups are remarkably homogeneous.

These findings may now be compared with those found on the 1956 retest:

1. The rank order of values for the total group is virtually unchanged from 1950 to 1956, with the exception that *economic* and *theoretical* values, originally ranked fourth and fifth, are now reversed.

2. All groups still rank highest on *religious* values.

3. The middle group retains the same pattern in 1956 as it had in 1950.

4. The patterns of the open and closed groups, however, show interesting changes. For the open group, *religious* and *social* values still rank first and second. *Theoretical* values shift from fifth to third place, *esthetic* from sixth to fifth, *political* drops from third to fourth, and *economic* drops from fourth to sixth. For the closed group, *religious* is again first, but *social* drops from second

to fifth, *political* moves up from third to second, *economic* from fourth to third, *theoretical* from fifth to fourth, and *esthetic* remains in sixth place.

To what extent are these changes in patterns significant? Statistical analysis [2] reveals that the combined group (as well as the subgroups) are significantly in agreement or homogeneous in value patterns in 1950. But this is not so in 1956; the total group is no longer found to be homogeneous, according to statistical tests. Instead of the single pattern that could be said to characterize the total group in 1950, there are in 1956 three value patterns, one for each group, and each apparently different from the other two.

Further insight into the changes that have taken place over the six-year period may be obtained by comparing for each of the six values separately the mean scores obtained in 1950 and in 1956. The results are shown in Table 18.2. *Religious* values do not change significantly for any group. *Social* values decrease significantly for the total group and this is attributable to the fact that it is primarily the closed group that decreases significantly on this value. Concerning *political* values, no significant differences are found for any group. On *economic* values, it is the open group that changes significantly, being less economically oriented in 1956 than in 1950. At the same time, the open group scores significantly higher on *theoretical* values in 1956 than in 1950. Finally, there is a significant increase in *esthetic* values for the total group, but this increase is not significant for any of the subgroups considered separately.

To summarize the major value changes shown in Table 18.2: (1) The closed group becomes significantly less concerned with *social* values over a six-year period following graduation. (2) The open group becomes significantly less interested in *economic* values and significantly more interested in *theoretical* values. (3) The middle group shows no significant changes in any of the six values from test to retest.

What is the psychological significance of the changes in value and value patterns, as shown in Tables 18.1 and 18.2? It is clear that all three groups start out with identical value patterns when first tested in 1950. In 1956, they are all still highest on *religious* values. But *religious* values are now imbedded in a different value

Table 18.2

Mean Value Scores Obtained on Test, and Retest after Six Years for Open, Middle, and Closed Groups and for Total Group

Value	Group	1950 Mean	1956 Mean	Dif-ference [a]
Religious	Open	44.1	44.4	.3
	Middle	42.7	42.7	.0
	Closed	39.1	41.1	2.0
	Total group	42.2	42.7	.5
Social	Open	32.5	30.9	−1.6
	Middle	31.6	30.6	−1.0
	Closed	33.2	28.4	−4.8 [b]
	Total group	32.2	30.1	−2.1 [b]
Political	Open	29.1	27.8	−1.3
	Middle	29.1	29.1	.0
	Closed	30.4	30.9	.5
	Total group	29.4	29.2	−.2
Economic	Open	27.0	23.4	−3.6 [c]
	Middle	28.7	27.8	−.9
	Closed	29.0	29.1	.1
	Total group	28.4	27.1	−1.3
Theoretical	Open	25.4	29.4	4.0 [b]
	Middle	26.0	27.6	1.6
	Closed	27.7	28.6	.9
	Total group	26.3	28.3	2.0 [c]
Esthetic	Open	21.6	23.9	2.3
	Middle	21.7	23.6	1.9
	Closed	20.5	22.3	1.8
	Total group	21.4	23.4	2.0 [c]

[a] Significances of differences in means were determined by two-tailed t-tests.
[b] Very significant, $p = .01$.
[c] Significant, $p = .05$.

configuration in each of the three groups. In 1950, the closed group is first on *religious*, second on *social*, third on *political;* in 1956, this group is still highest on *religious*, but second in importance is *political* and third in importance is *economic. Social*, second in importance in 1950, is down to fifth in 1956. We would thus say that the *religious* values of the closed group have become more motivated by power drives and by materialistic considerations. Our interpretation is that the closed group, after six years, still clings most to *religious* values, but in a more opportunistic way.

In 1950, the open group is also first on *religious* values, second on *social*, and third on *political* values. By 1956, *religious* values are still uppermost and *social* values are still second in importance, but *theoretical* values replace *political* values as third in importance. *Political* values drop from third to fourth; *economic* values drop from fourth to sixth; and *esthetic* values move up one notch from sixth to fifth place. These changes suggest that the open group has become more religious in a deeper sense, in contrast to the closed group, which seems to have become more "superficial," as if giving "lip service" to religious values.

We have calculated correlations between the obtained dogmatism score and sheer amount of change. These correlations are, of course, close to zero. They range from —.12 to +.10 for the six values, showing, contrary to common-sense assumption, that change is not associated with open systems, or non-change with closed systems. Both open and closed groups are found to change over time, but in different ways. And it is the middle group that shows no change in value pattern after six years. These results become understandable in the light of our discussion at the beginning of this chapter on the nature of change and non-change.

The results just considered on value change are paralleled in an interesting way by additional findings on the vocational

Table 18.3

Change and Non-change of Choice in Boy Scout Profession by Open, Middle, and Closed Groups

Vocational Choice	Open	Middle	Closed	Total
In Boy Scout profession in 1956	2 (8%)	30 (56%)	5 (20%)	37 (36%)
Not in Boy Scout profession in 1956	23 (92%)	24 (44%)	20 (80%)	67 (64%)
TOTAL	25	54	25	104

choices of the subjects. As has already been pointed out, the subjects who took part in the present study were selected because of their interest in the vocations of professional scouting, Y.M.C.A., or Y.W.C.A. work. Only 2 of the 104 reported being in Y.M.C.A. or Y.W.C.A. work in 1956, but 37 out of the 104 entered and remained in the scouting profession. Let us see how many of the 37 come from each of our three groups. As Table 18.3 shows, a disproportionately large percentage of middle subjects (56 per cent) are Boy Scout executives while this is true for only a relatively small percentage of open subjects (8 per cent) and closed subjects (20 per cent). These results are very significant.[3] Thus, parallel to the finding that middle subjects do not change their values over a six-year period is the additional finding that they also do not change their vocational choice nearly as much as the open and closed groups.

Of further interest is a fuller breakdown of the jobs held by open, middle, and closed groups in 1956. This is shown in Table

Table 18.4

Present Positions (1956) of Open, Middle, and Closed Groups

Open		Middle		Closed	
Boy Scout executive	2	Boy Scout executive	30	Boy Scout executive	5
Housewife	8	Interviewing	3	Army (career)	5
Occupational		Secretary	2	Banking	3
therapy	1	Dir. community serv.	2	Air Force (career)	2
Medicine	1	Salvation Army exec.	1	Managerial, business	3
Minister	8	Radio announcer	1	Navy (career)	2
Printer	1	Supt. of recreation	2	Engineer	2
Psychologist	1	Teacher	2	Probation officer	2
Social worker	1	Y.M.C.A. secretary	1	Printer	1
Teacher	2	Y.W.C.A. secretary	1		
		Boys' counselor	1		
		Clerical	4		
		Salesmen	4		
TOTALS	25		54		25

18.4. Considering first the data for the middle group, we confirm even more strongly the fact that they change least in vocational choice. In addition to the 30 who are employed as Boy Scout

343

executives in 1956, at least 7 or 8 others are engaged in social welfare work. This makes a total of about 37 or 38 out of 54 (70 per cent) whose vocation six years later is roughly the same as the one they chose while still in college.

On the other hand, the patterns of vocational choice among the open and closed groups diverge sharply from that found for the middle group, and also from each other. On the whole, open subjects move toward professions requiring more advanced professional training in vocations that involve dealings with people in need of help: occupational therapy, medicine, the ministry, psychology, social work, and teaching. Over half of the open group—14 out of 25—change their original vocational preferences in a direction that seems to be more demanding from an intellectual standpoint, without giving up their original interest in social welfare.*

As for the closed group, their occupational interests are seen to go in yet a different direction. There is a greater leaning toward military careers (9 out of 25), a greater emphasis on commercial pursuits (6 out of 25), and in general a greater concentration in the administrative field. They clearly involve *political* and *economic* values above all else, which is consistent with the increases shown on these values from test to retest.†

It is again reasonable to inquire whether the differences found among the three groups on values and on vocational choice could be attributable to differences in intelligence. In 1950, all the subjects took the Otis Intelligence Test, Form A. The means for the open, middle, and closed groups are 118, 114, and 118, respectively, the differences not being statistically significant. These

---

* To be noted, however, is that 9 of the 25 subjects in the open group are women (8 housewives, 1 social worker). Since there were 14 women in the total sample of 104, there is the possibility that the 9 women in the open group serve to bias the results shown in Tables 18.1 and 18.2. To find out if this is the case, comparisons were made between the men and women in the open group to find out if they differ in any important respect. The value patterns between men and women were identical in 1950, and also in 1956. There were no significant differences between them on any of the six values, either in 1950 or in 1956. The mean IQ on the Otis Test of Intelligence, Form A, was 118 for the men, 117 for the women. Finally, the two subgroups do not differ on half a dozen other personality measures.

† Needless to say, no cause-effect relationship is suggested. It is impossible to state from the data available whether values change because of change in vocation, or vice versa.

findings show once again that intelligence is unrelated to open-ness-closedness of belief systems and therefore cannot account for the differences found among open, middle, and closed groups.

In conclusion, then, it could be said that the results of this study are consistent with formulations regarding the nature of open and closed belief systems. Although it was not possible to predict on theoretical grounds the exact changes in values to be expected, it is seen that both open and closed persons change their values over time. But the basic difference in the quality of such changes seems to lie in diametrically opposed directions as far as personality integration is concerned.

Synopsis

We have reported here on value changes that took place over a six-year period in persons varying in degree of open or closed belief systems. The subjects were religiously oriented persons attending a denominational college and were all in a special curriculum designed to prepare them for a career as Boy Scout executives or in Y.M.C.A. or Y.W.C.A. work. Subjects were tested with the Allport-Vernon Scale of Values in 1950 and again in 1956, at which time they were also given the Dogmatism Scale. There is no correlation between scores on the Dogmatism Scale and change in values, nor should any correlation be expected. The reason for this becomes clear when the data are analyzed. Closed, middle, and open groups all had identical value patterns in 1950, the rank order of importance of the six Allport-Vernon values being: *religious, social, political, economic, theoretical,* and *esthetic*. In 1956, the rank order of these values was the same for the middle group, but changed for the closed and open groups. Although *religious* values were still predominant in all groups, the closed group increased in *political* and *economic* values and decreased markedly in *social* values. The open group remained unchanged in its *religious* and *social* values but increased in *theoretical* values and decreased in *economic* and *political* values. Thus adherence to *religious* values seems to become more opportunistic in the closed group after six years; in the open group *religious* values seem to become less superficial.

The vocational choices of the closed, middle, and open groups follow closely these changes or non-changes in value patterns. Roughly 70 per cent of the middle group became Boy Scout executives as planned, or entered closely related professions. But most of the open and closed subjects changed their vocational choice after leaving college; the open subjects more frequently entered vocations requiring more advanced professional training in careers involving social welfare, and the closed subjects more frequently entered military and commercial careers of an administrative nature.

The results found on changes in value patterns and in vocational choice do not seem to be attributable to intelligence since closed, middle, and open subjects are not found to differ in this respect.

Notes

1. As far as we know, despite the fact that the Allport-Vernon Scale is clinically evaluated in terms of *profiles,* it is not typically analyzed quantitatively in terms of value patterns and changes in such patterns. For another study that compares value patterns of persons scoring high and low on anti-Semitism, see Evans (1952).

2. The coefficient of concordance, W (Edwards, 1954), was employed to determine the extent of agreement in value patterns among subjects within the total group and within the subgroups from test to retest. The results are shown in Table 18.5 below. Note that in 1956 the total group is no longer significantly homogeneous ($W = .03$) but the three subgroups are.

Table 18.5

Coefficient of Concordance for Open, Middle, and Closed Groups and for Combined Group on the Test and Retest

	Test, 1950		Retest, 1956	
	W	p	W	p
Open	.50	.01	.39	.01
Middle	.42	.01	.36	.01
Closed	.48	.01	.35	.01
Total group	.48	.01	.03	N.S.

3. Chi-square $= 20.4$.

19

Open and Closed Systems in Relation to Anxiety and Childhood Experience

Milton Rokeach and C. Gratton Kemp

We have already suggested in Chapter 3 that to the extent a belief-disbelief system is closed, it represents a cognitive network of defenses against anxiety. This leads us to the simple hypothesis that those with relatively closed systems should manifest more anxiety than those with relatively open systems. Another hypothesis which follows is that religious and political groups that are shown to be relatively more closed in their systems, namely, Catholic and Communist groups, should score higher on measures of anxiety than other political and religious groups. A third hypothesis to be tested is that differences in

347

openness-closedness and anxiety should be traceable to differences in childhood experience.

We have obtained data for a variety of groups in the United States and England bearing on these hypotheses. In all cases the measure of anxiety employed was the 30 items from the Minnesota Multiphasic Personality Inventory (M.M.P.I.) used by Welch (1952). Subjects respond to each of these items on a 7-point agree-disagree scale, identical with that used with the Dogmatism Scale. Many of these items are the same as those appearing in the better-known Taylor Scale (1953). Some typical items are: "I work under a great deal of tension"; "I have nightmares every few nights"; "My sleep is fitful and disturbed"; "I frequently notice my hand shakes when I try to do something."

Correlational Data

Table 19.1 shows the correlations obtained between dogmatism and anxiety. The groups are the same as those under consideration in Chapters 4 and 6. All the correlations obtained in the United States and in England with college and worker samples are positive. They range from .36 to .64, and all are very significant.

Table 19.1

Correlations Between Dogmatism and Anxiety Scales

Group	Number	Correlation [a]
Mich. State U. I	202	.44
New York colleges	207	.58
Mich. State U. II	153	.64
Mich. State U. III	186	.57
English colleges I	137	.52
English colleges II	80	.47
English workers	60	.36

[a] The correlations are product-moment correlations, and are all very significant, $p = .01$.

Also illuminating in this connection are the results of two studies by Rokeach and Fruchter (1956d), and by Fruchter, Rokeach, and Novak (1958). The first analysis was conducted with the

New York colleges group, the second with the Michigan State University III group.[1] In both of these studies, dogmatism and anxiety are clearly shown to emerge together as part of a single psychological factor. This factor also includes self-rejection and paranoid tendencies. *Not* included in this factor are liberalism-conservatism, ethnocentrism, rigidity, and the F Scale.

Dogmatism and Anxiety
Among Various Political and Religious Groups

Do the religious and political groups that score relatively high on the Dogmatism Scale also score relatively high on the Anxiety Scale? To find out, we will inspect side by side the mean dogmatism and anxiety scores obtained for various religious and political groups. Such inspection should give us invaluable clues as to the functions served by different political and religious groups.

With this in mind, we analyzed the data for the Michigan State University subjects and the New York college subjects, categorized in terms of their religious affiliation; also the English colleges I group, categorized in terms of their political affiliation. The results are shown in Tables 19.2, 19.3, and 19.4.[2]

Table 19.2

*Mean Dogmatism and Anxiety Scores for Michigan State University
I Group*

Group	Number	Dogmatism		Anxiety	
		Mean	*S.D.*	*Mean*	*S.D.*
1. Catholics	42	191.1	27.1	83.1	19.2
2. Protestants	145	180.1	25.4	83.6	25.2
3. Nonbelievers	15	174.6	21.1	71.9	18.9

DIFFERENCES BETWEEN MEANS

1 vs. 2	11.0[b]	.5
1 vs. 3	16.5[b]	11.2[a]
2 vs. 3	5.5	11.7[a]

[a] Significant, $p = .05$.
[b] Very significant, $p = .01$.

Table 19.3

Mean Dogmatism and Anxiety Scores for New York Colleges Group

		Dogmatism		Anxiety	
Group	Number	Mean	S.D.	Mean	S.D.
1. Catholics	46	147.4	30.0	85.0	28.6
2. Protestants	24	138.3	32.2	71.5	24.7
3. Jews	131	139.5	24.5	79.9	25.4
4. Nonbelievers	6	147.2	30.6	69.5	9.8

DIFFERENCE BETWEEN MEANS [a]		
1 vs. 2	9.1	13.5[c]
1 vs. 3	7.9[b]	5.1
1 vs. 4	.2	15.5[c]
2 vs. 3	− 1.2	8.4
2 vs. 4	− 8.9	2.0
3 vs. 4	− 7.7	10.4[c]

[a] Difference in means involving the nonbelievers were corrected by the Cochran-Cox approximation when variances differed significantly.
[b] Nearly significant, $p = .10$.
[c] Significant, $p = .05$.

Table 19.4

Mean Dogmatism and Anxiety Scores for English Colleges I

		Dogmatism		Anxiety	
Group	Number	Mean	S.D.	Mean	S.D.
1. Conservatives	54	258.8	49.7	81.0	25.7
2. Liberals	22	242.9	29.2	81.3	20.4
3. Attleeites	27	252.7	36.6	80.2	24.2
4. Bevanites	19	255.2	37.9	90.4	21.4
5. Communists	13	261.6	32.6	73.5	22.0

DIFFERENCE BETWEEN MEANS		
1 vs. 5	2.8	7.5
2 vs. 5	18.7[a]	7.8
3 vs. 5	8.9	6.7
4 vs. 5	6.4	16.9

[a] Nearly significant, $p = .06$.

In some ways the results are in accord with expectations, and in other ways they are surprisingly contrary. Consider first the results for the Michigan State University I Group (Table 19.2). The mean dogmatism score is highest for Catholics, next highest for Protestants, and lowest for those who express no religious preference. As for anxiety, both Catholic and Protestant groups are equally high, and the nonbeliever group is relatively low. The difference in anxiety between Catholic and nonbeliever groups is very significant, as is also the difference between Protestant and the nonbeliever groups. Considering these results as a whole, it may be said that the groups scoring high in dogmatism tend also to score high in anxiety, and that the group scoring lowest in dogmatism also scores lowest in anxiety.

These results may now be compared with those found for the New York colleges groups (Table 19.3). Consistent with the Michigan State University I findings, the Catholic group again scores relatively high, and the nonbeliever group scores relatively low on anxiety. This difference is significant. But note that *both* the Catholic and nonbeliever groups have relatively high dogmatism means. This is certainly not consistent with the findings for the Michigan State University I group. In the Michigan State University I group, the Catholics score high on both dogmatism and anxiety, and the nonbelievers score low on both. In the New York group, the Catholics score high on both variables, but the nonbeliever group scores high on dogmatism and low on anxiety.

Turning now to the English data, shown in Table 19.4, it is seen that the pattern for the Communists is similar to that for the New York nonbelievers, who, as has been pointed out in Chapter 6, are probably strongly leftist in orientation. Here also we see that the Communist group scores highest on dogmatism but *lowest* on anxiety. This is of course exactly opposite to theoretical expectations and to the empirical findings of *positive* relations between dogmatism and anxiety.

Considering the results of Tables 19.2, 19.3, and 19.4 all together, we gain two major impressions: (1) the Catholic group scores relatively high in dogmatism and relatively high in anxiety; (2) Communists and other leftists (New York nonbelievers) whose exact political affiliations are unknown also score relatively high on dogmatism but relatively low on anxiety. Thus, we are confronted with a rather paradoxical set of results: Political and religious groups that score relatively high on the Dogmatism

Scale may manifest either a good deal or relatively little anxiety. This is despite the fact that dogmatism and anxiety are always positively correlated and are found in two factor-analytic studies to emerge together as a single psychological factor.

Of particular interest is the finding that the English Communists are lowest in anxiety even though they score higher than any of the other political groups on dogmatism. Before we try to speculate any further about possible explanations for this finding, which is against theoretical expectations, let us present here some additional data that are relevant. It will be recalled from Chapter 6 that the Dogmatism Scale used with the Communists was Form D, containing 66 items. We have analyzed the responses to each of these 66 items for all English political groups. The results are presented in full in Appendix A, and the student of the psychology of politics may find these of intrinsic interest. Our immediate interest is to find out what light these results might throw upon the specific issue at hand. Since the Communists score higher than the other political groups on the Dogmatism Scale considered as a whole, it is reasonable to expect that they will generally score higher than the other groups on each of the 66 statements in the Dogmatism Scale. However, what we find instead is that Communists score generally higher on statements that tap primarily the structural and formal aspects but not the dynamic or functional aspects of belief systems. More specifically, we unexpectedly find that the Communists score lowest [3] of all the groups (disagree most) on the following 22 statements, most of which are concerned with functional aspects:

1. The United States and Russia have just about nothing in common.
2. The highest form of government is a democracy and the highest form of a democracy is a government run by those who are most intelligent.
3. Even though I have a lot of faith in the intelligence and wisdom of the common man I must say that the masses behave very stupidly at times.
4. Fundamentally, the world we live in is a pretty lonesome place.
5. It is only natural for a person to be rather fearful of the future.

6. There is so much to be done and so little time to do it in.
7. Once I get wound up in a heated discussion I just can't stop.
8. In a discussion I sometimes interrupt others too much in my eagerness to put across my own point of view.
9. My hardest battles are with myself.
10. At times I think I am no good at all.
11. If I had to choose between happiness and greatness, I'd choose greatness.
12. I have often felt that strangers were looking at me critically.
13. People say insulting and vulgar things about me.
14. I am sure I am being talked about.
15. In times like these it is often necessary to be more on guard against ideas put out by people or groups in one's own camp than by those in the opposing camp.
16. My blood boils whenever a person stubbornly refuses to admit he's wrong.
17. I sometimes have a tendency to be too critical of the ideas of others.
18. It is by returning to our glorious and forgotten past that real social progress can be achieved.
19. To achieve the happiness of mankind in the future it is sometimes necessary to put up with injustices in the present.
20. If a man is to accomplish his mission in life it is sometimes necessary to gamble "all or nothing at all."
21. Unfortunately, a good many people with whom I have discussed important social and moral problems don't really understand what's going on.
22. There is nothing new under the sun.

In contrast, the Communists endorse the following 24 statements more strongly than any of the other political groups. Most of these concern structural and formal aspects of belief systems.

1. Communism and Catholicism have nothing in common.
2. The principles I have come to believe in are quite different from those believed in by most people.
3. In a heated discussion people have a way of bringing up irrelevant issues rather than sticking to the main issue.

4. It is sometimes necessary to resort to force to advance an ideal one strongly believes in.

5. It is better to be a dead hero than to be a live coward.

6. The main thing in life is for a person to want to do something important.

7. Most people are failures and it is the system which is responsible for this.

8. It is only natural for a person to have a guilty conscience.

9. There are a number of people I have come to hate because of the things they stand for.

10. A man who does not believe in some great cause has not really lived.

11. It is only when a person devotes himself to an ideal or cause that life becomes meaningful.

12. Of all the different philosophies which exist in this world there is probably only one which is correct.

13. A person who gets enthusiastic about too many causes is likely to be a pretty "wishy-washy" sort of person.

14. To compromise with our political opponents is dangerous because it usually leads to the betrayal of our own side.

15. When it comes to differences of opinion in religion we must be careful not to compromise with those who believe differently from the way we do.

16. To compromise with our political opponents is to be guilty of appeasement.

17. In times like these a person must be pretty selfish if he considers primarily his own happiness.

18. The worst crime a person could commit is to attack publicly the people who believe in the same thing he does.

19. A group which tolerates too much differences of opinion among its own members cannot exist for long.

20. There are two kinds of people in this world: those who are for the truth and those who are against the truth.

21. A person who thinks primarily of his own happiness is beneath contempt.

22. The present is all too often full of unhappiness. It is only the future that counts.

23. To one who really takes the trouble to understand the

world he lives in, it's an easy matter to predict future events.

24. While the use of force is wrong by and large, it is sometimes the only way possible to advance a noble ideal.

It is clear from the preceding that the statements endorsed most by Communists differ strikingly from those they reject most. As already stated, the Communists endorse most strongly those items on the Dogmatism Scale that are concerned with the structural and formal aspects of belief systems; they reject most those items concerned with the dynamic aspects. More than any other political group, they deny admissions of personal weakness, feelings of self-deprecation, anxiety, aloneness and isolation, fear of the future, feelings of urgency, or a paranoid outlook on life. They score higher than any other group on the total Dogmatism Scale by virtue of their greater endorsement of the former type of item, and despite their greater rejection of the latter type of item.

These findings are of course consistent with the fact that the English Communists and the New York nonbelievers also score low on the Anxiety Scale. The problem confronting us now is to try to reconcile these unexpected findings with those showing that dogmatism and anxiety generally correlate positively with each other, and with the finding that Catholics score generally higher on both.

One possibility that suggests itself is that the English Communists and the New York nonbelievers are manifestly less anxious than the other groups because they are low in latent anxiety. It may well be that, theoretically, dogmatism is a defense against anxiety, and some of our other findings are indeed consistent with this hypothesis. But, as we have noted, the Communist subjects score lowest in anxiety. From this it could be argued that they are not high in dogmatism, but are merely expressing genuine intellectual convictions.

This explanation is hard to accept for two reasons. First, the Communist group and the New York nonbelievers score higher than other groups on opinionation as well as on dogmatism. People who express intellectual rather than dogmatic conviction probably do not have to be so opinionated about their convictions. Second, if Communists are indeed lower in anxiety than the other groups, it implies that there is a selective factor operating in recruitment to communism; that is, persons low in anxiety are more likely than persons of average or high anxiety to be recruited to the Communist party. We cannot think of any evidence from our own observations, from Almond's research on Communist defectors (1954), or from Communist sources which would point to the operation of such a selective factor. Why should persons of low anxiety be more likely recruits to communism? If anything, those most exploited and, hence, most anxious should more likely be recruited to it.

This leads us to another possibility that might account for the obtained results. It is widely believed that one way to reduce feelings of anxiety is to become active, to participate in absorbing daily affairs. The Communist party, more than most other political groups, provides precisely such an opportunity. It expects from its members a good deal of activity to serve its political ends —party meetings, participation in trade unions and other organizations, week-end activities such as selling the *Daily Worker*, reading current and classic Marxist literature, and so on. Not to be ignored, furthermore, is the comradeship provided in carrying out its group activities. Is it not possible, therefore, that frequent participation in such group activities serves the function of reducing anxiety, or at the very least, reducing external manifestations of anxiety? If one is constantly busy, tired, and in need of sleep, there is no time to be anxiously preoccupied with oneself and with apprehension of the future.

On the other hand, there is considerably less demand for active participation from those who are good Catholics. Attending Mass and going to confession are about all that is formally required by way of activity. This is a far cry from the all-out, urgent activity expected from a good Communist. What we are suggesting, then, is the possibility that communism, by virtue of such greater demands made on its adherents, may be more effective than Catholicism as an anxiety-reducing agent. This could account for the fact that even though Catholics and Communists both score relatively high on the Dogmatism Scale, Catholics score relatively high ($M = 85$ and 83) and Communists relatively low ($M = 74$) on the Anxiety Scale.

The above, of course, are merely *ad hoc* speculations. They are presented here because our findings regarding dogmatism and anxiety in political and religious groups do not conform to a priori expectations. The only justification for such speculations is that they suggest the direction further research may profitably take. For example, one possible way to test the validity of the interpretation just offered is, first, to determine the level of manifest anxiety for persons when they first join a particular religious, or political, or social group. One can then keep track of the degree and kind of activity for individual members within groups and between groups for specified periods of time, after which time they may again be tested for manifest anxiety. Such a line of research should tell us something about the effects of degree and kind of group activity on the reduction of anxiety and, more generally, about the functions served by various political and religious groups.

Some Early Experiences Related to Dogmatism and Anxiety

Let us now turn to inspect some data we have available on childhood experience which may throw further light on the dynamics of open and closed systems. To investigate the role of childhood experiences systematically is a formidable research task in itself, and something we have not been able to do thus far. But a limited amount of such data, which are quite illuminating, were obtained in connection with the research reported in the preceding chapter on value change in religious-minded persons, and will be presented here. In this research, the subjects' responses were obtained to several questions concerning their attitudes toward father and mother, anxiety symptoms they had manifested in childhood, and the nature of the identifications they had formed in childhood.

The first two questions they were asked are: "What sort of a person was your father?" and, "What sort of a person was your mother?" Following the work of Adorno *et al.*, three judges independently categorized the responses into three types: ambivalence, mild ambivalence, and glorification of parent. Average agreement among these judges was approximately 90 per cent. The following are some typical comments made by the subjects which may serve as examples of each category:

AMBIVALENCE TOWARD PARENT

Father: "Stubborn, quick-tempered, but at times good na-
tured, and just a nice guy." . . . "A quiet person who has
done for me what I wanted if he thought it was O.K.
However, he has never been a pal to whom I could take
my troubles. We had a lot of fun though, and heed each
other's advice."

Mother: "Some of the time she was a reserved autocrat in
the home; other times she was different and more like-
able, almost lovable." . . . "Was good to me over minor
things, but didn't handle the hard things too well. She
had her good and bad points."

MILD AMBIVALENCE

Father: "A pretty good dad most of the time, but comes
down hard on things that count, which may be good."
. . . "Very strict at times but on the whole not too hard
to get along with, and understanding at all times."

Mother: "Made you toe the mark, but when you were in
trouble she was real understanding. You could count on
her being fair." . . . "She gave you the feeling you could
do things. Sometimes she was hard on you when you
didn't quite make the grade, but most times she was en-
couraging and kind."

GLORIFICATION OF PARENT

Father: "A very fine person who tries to uphold the Christian virtues of life." . . . "Friendly, intelligent, frank,
generous, likes to spend time with his family and do
things for us."

Mother: "The best, no limit in any way." . . . "Very wonder-
ful and understanding, kindhearted toward her children."
. . . "Unselfish, loving, tireless."

Shown in Table 19.5 are the frequencies of ambivalent, mildly
ambivalent, and glorification responses to fathers and mothers
given by the open, middle, and closed groups, the same groups
discussed in the preceding chapter. Notice first the similarity of
the data obtained on attitudes toward father and mother. Sixty-

Table 19.5

*Frequency of Responses to "What Sort of Person Was Your Father?"
and "What Sort of Person Was Your Mother?" by Open,
Middle, and Closed Groups*

Type of Response	Open	Middle	Closed
		To Fathers	
Ambivalence toward father	16 (64%)	4 (7%)	3 (12%)
Mild ambivalence	6 (24%)	12 (22%)	15 (60%)
Glorification of father	3 (12%)	38 (70%)	7 (28%)
		To Mothers	
Ambivalence toward mother	17 (68%)	4 (7%)	3 (12%)
Mild ambivalence	5 (20%)	10 (19%)	14 (56%)
Glorification of mother	3 (12%)	40 (74%)	8 (32%)

four per cent of the open group report an ambivalent attitude toward father, and 68 per cent, toward mother. This is to be
compared with 7 per cent of the middle group and 12 per cent
of the closed group, who express ambivalence toward father and
mother. As for mild ambivalence, it is the closed group that is
highest in this respect, 60 per cent of the subjects expressing
mild ambivalence to father and 56 per cent to mother. The comparable figures for the open group are 24 and 20 per cent, and
for the middle group, 22 and 19 per cent. Finally, it is the middle
group that is highest with respect to glorification of father and
mother (70 and 74 per cent, respectively). The comparable percentages for the open group are 12 and 12 per cent, and for the
closed group it is 28 and 32 per cent.

These results are very significant from a statistical standpoint.
When we compare these results with those reported in *The Authoritarian Personality* (1950), there is agreement insofar as the
open subjects express ambivalence toward parents. There is also
agreement insofar as the closed subjects are less able to express
ambivalence, and generally glorify their parent more.

These results are on the whole consistent with the notions put
forward by Frenkel-Brunswik (1949) that the inability to express
emotional ambivalence toward parents predisposes one to form
an authoritarian outlook on life.

However, we must note that it is the middle-scoring subjects who most often idealize their parents, considerably more than the closed subjects. It is difficult to account for this finding since there is little theory or empirical research to guide us. The research on *The Authoritarian Personality* was also conducted with extreme high and low scorers, and this is also generally true in the present work. At the moment, we can only draw explicit attention to these unexpected findings and go on to see if they are encountered again in other comparisons that follow.

Let us now turn to the next question that was put to the subjects: "What other people (relations, guardians, friends, etc.) influenced your development?" The reason for asking this was to find out about the extent or breadth of influence and identifications outside the immediate family. It is reasonable to assume that those who are characteristically more open in their belief systems will report that in childhood they were more influenced by persons beyond the confines of the immediate family. Conversely, it is reasonable to expect that those with relatively closed systems will report a constriction of extrafamily influences and identifications.

The responses to this question were categorized into three degrees of breadth of identification with others. First were those who reported that they identified only with the local clergyman and/or Boy Scout leader. The second category included a somewhat broader set of identifications. Several people were mentioned rather than just one or two, such as clergymen, Boy Scout leader, friends with whom one had shared a sport or hobby, teacher, a farmer on whose farm one had spent part of a summer vacation, etc. The third category is a general response, the subject saying that he was influenced by a number of people, with no reference to any one particular person or group.

Three judges, working independently, agreed in their categorization on 95 per cent of the responses. The relative frequencies of each of these categorizations was then determined for the open, middle, and closed groups, and the results are shown in Table 19.6.

Seventy-two per cent of the open subjects respond to this question in a general way, with no pinpointing of particular persons or groups outside the family as being especially influential in

Table 19.6

Frequency of Responses to, "What Other People (Relatives, Guardians, Friends, etc.) Influenced Your Development?" by Open, Middle, and Closed Groups

Type of Response	Open	Middle	Closed
Clergyman and/or Boy Scout leader	2 (8%)	38 (70%)	15 (60%)
Several people specifically mentioned	5 (20%)	10 (19%)	8 (32%)
A general response with no reference to any one person or group	18 (72%)	6 (11%)	2 (8%)

their development. The comparable percentages for the middle and closed groups are only 11 and 8 per cent. On the other hand, 70 per cent of the middle group and 60 per cent of the closed group specify the local clergyman and/or Boy Scout leader as the ones who had been influential in their development. The over-all results are again very significant. Note further that this time the results for the middle and closed groups are very similar to each other and that both are about equally different from those found for the open group.

When we consider these results in relation to those shown in Table 19.5 on attitudes toward parents, a fairly clear pattern emerges. Most of the subjects in the open group express ambivalence toward father and mother and also report being generally influenced by others outside the family. Most of the middle and closed subjects, on the other hand, express mild ambivalence or glorification of parents and report being influenced by relatively few persons outside the family. These findings suggest that the development of closed belief systems may be a function of breadth or narrowness of identification with others which, in turn, may be a function of the extent to which ambivalent feelings toward parents are permitted within the family atmosphere.

The pattern of findings just considered receives yet further support when we compare the responses of the three groups on questions concerning the presence of various neurotic symptoms in childhood. As Frenkel-Brunswik has pointed out (1949), the inability to express emotional ambivalence toward parents necessitates the repression of hostility. This should be anxiety-provoking. Since open-minded subjects are more able to express ambivalence, we should expect them to show fewer symptoms of anxiety as compared with closed-minded subjects. The results are shown in Tables 19.7 and 19.8.

Table 19.7

Number of Subjects in Open, Middle, and Closed Groups Reporting Presence of Anxiety Symptoms

Questions	Open	Middle	Closed
Did you ever:			
suck your thumb?	6 (24%)	21 (39%)	5 (20%)
bite your nails?	2 (8%)	27 (50%)	16 (64%)
have temper tantrums?	1 (4%)	14 (26%)	14 (56%)
have nightmares?	1 (4%)	20 (37%)	10 (40%)
walk in your sleep?	0 (0%)	14 (26%)	9 (36%)
talk in your sleep?	0 (0%)	28 (52%)	8 (32%)
Mean number of symptoms	.4	2.3	2.5

Again we find striking differences between the open group on the one hand, and the middle and closed groups on the other. The open subjects report far fewer symptoms of anxiety. Only 6 out of the 25 subjects in this group report having sucked their thumbs, 2 report having bitten their nails, 1 reports having had temper tantrums, and another one, nightmares. Not one of this group reports having walked or talked in his sleep. The findings for the middle and closed groups far exceed these frequencies, as will be immediately evident from an inspection of Table 19.7. The mean number of symptoms reported by open, middle, and closed groups are .4, 2.3, and 2.5, respectively.

Similar results are obtained with respect to age at which bed-wetting stopped, as shown in Table 19.8. Twenty-one out of the 25 open-minded subjects replied "I don't remember" to this question, but not a single one of the middle and closed subjects replied in this way. Assuming "I don't remember" responses to be two years of age or less, the mean age at which bed-wetting stopped are 2.2, 8.5, and 6.2, respectively, for the three groups under consideration.

Table 19.8

Comparison of Open, Middle, and Closed Groups on the Replies to the Question, "At What Age Approximately Did You Stop Wetting the Bed?"

Age	Open	Middle	Closed
X [a]	21	0	0
3	3	2	2
4	1	3	7
5		3	3
6		5	2
7		6	1
8		7	4
9		8	6
10		7	
11		6	
12		4	
13		2	
14		1	
Mean age	2.2	8.5	6.2

[a] X, "I don't remember," assumed as 2 years for purposes of establishing mean age.

When we consider all the results presented in this section as a whole, it is safe to say that the middle and closed groups do not turn out to differ strikingly from each other as might have been expected from the results on attitudes toward parents. Rather, both middle and closed groups are found to differ markedly from the open group. Why the middle and closed groups do not differ much from each other is a problem that will merit further investigation. We are presently at a loss to explain it. One possibility is that there may be little psychological difference between a middle and high score on the Dogmatism Scale—that both may represent equally high degrees of closedness. Another possibility is that the nature of the sample may possibly have something to do with it. It will be recalled that the subjects were all students at a Presbyterian college, all high in religious values, all enrolled in a sponsored program of training for social welfare with youth. Thus, they may be atypical with respect to the meaning to be assigned to a particular score on the Dogmatism Scale, or with respect to parent-child relationships, or with respect to neurotic symptoms. It is hard to say.

Whatever the reason may be for the similarity between middle and closed groups, we should not lose sight of certain major conclusions to which the findings point. First, the results provide additional confirmation for the hypothesis that closed cognitive systems may represent a defense against anxiety; second, that persons differing in degree of openness-closedness are different in their attitudes toward parents and, presumably, in parent-child relationships; and third, that the extent to which a child's belief system develops into an open or closed one may in part be a function of the breadth or narrowness of identifications with persons outside the immediate family.

Synopsis

In this chapter we have reported data from a variety of sources regarding the functional aspects of belief systems. The findings are as follows:

1. Scores on dogmatism and anxiety correlate from .36 to .64 in various groups tested in the United States and England. Two factor-analysis studies show that dogmatism and anxiety are factorially similar.

2. American Catholics score relatively high on measures of dogmatism and anxiety. English Communists and a small group of New York college students, identifying themselves as being without religious affiliation, also score relatively high on dogmatism. But, contrary to expectation, they both score relatively low on anxiety.

3. Analysis of the responses given by English Communists to each of 66 items of the Dogmatism Scale reveals that they endorse, significantly more than other political groups, those statements that generally have to do with structural, formal aspects of belief systems. But they generally reject most those statements having to do with the functional aspects of belief systems. These results are in accord with the finding that English Communists score lower than any of the other political groups on a scale measuring manifest anxiety. Two alternative explanations are of-

fered to account for these unexpected findings. The one favored is that Communist political activity serves as a successful therapeutic device in reducing manifest anxiety, thus possibly accounting for the results obtained.

4. Further light is shed on the functional aspects of belief systems by relating differences in openness-closedness to earlier experience. Low scorers on the Dogmatism Scale, as compared with middle or high scorers, express more ambivalence toward their fathers and mothers, report being more widely influenced by persons outside the immediate family, and report having had relatively fewer anxiety symptoms in childhood. On the other hand, the reports of middle and closed subjects are on the whole similar and, compared with open subjects, they reveal more glorification of parents, a more restricted influence by persons outside the family, and a greater incidence in childhood of thumb-sucking, nail-biting, temper tantrums, nightmares, walking and talking while asleep, and bed-wetting.

All of the preceding suggest the hypothesis that when ambivalence toward parents is not permitted expression it leads both to anxiety and to a narrowing of possibilities for identification with persons outside the family. Both, in turn, are interpreted as leading to the development of closed belief systems.

Notes

1. The interested reader may wish to inspect the rotated factor loadings which are reproduced in Appendix D.

2. All differences in means in Tables 19.2, 19.3, and 19.4 are tested for significance by one-tailed t tests.

3. This does not mean, of course, that the Communists are always significantly lowest. See Appendix A for t's.

20

Time Perspective, Dogmatism, and Anxiety

Milton Rokeach and Richard Bonier

As we have already stated in Chapter 2, the more closed the belief-disbelief system, the more narrow is the time perspective and the less are the psychological past, present, and future adequately represented in one's behavior. A person may be said to have a broad time perspective if what he does is influenced not only by his conception of the present situation, but also by his appreciation of past events leading up to the present, and by his anticipation of future outcomes. On the other hand, a person may be said to have a narrow time perspective if he is too greatly oriented in the past, or the present, or the future. A number of investigations show that certain groups have narrow time perspectives and that age and present circumstances will determine whether narrowness of time perspective is typically past-, present-, or future-oriented. Fink (1953), for example, found in his investigation of aged persons that those who are institutionalized are considerably more past-oriented than those who are not institutionalized. Barndt and Johnson (1955) found that delinquent boys are more present-oriented than a comparable group of nondelinquents; Wallace (1956) found a group of schizophrenics to be more present-oriented than a control group. Farber,* studying prison inmates, concludes that extent of pain and suffering increases as a function of future-orientation.

In ideological movements, time perspectives appear to be typically future-oriented. The past hardly exists, and the present is unimportant in its own right. The present is a vestibule to the future rather than something to be enjoyed and appreciated in its own right; it is a means to a future end rather than an end in itself. It is the future that counts and the suffering and injustice existing in the present is sometimes condoned, even glorified, for the sake of securing some future heaven, Utopia, promised land, Platonic or classless society.

We have already put forward the hypothesis, and some data consistent with this hypothesis, that the major function served by closed systems is to defend the self or the group against anxiety. The central feature of anxiety, as distinguished from fear, is a dread of the future (May, 1950), for the future is the most ambiguous and unknowable medium in man's cognitive world. It follows that attempts to cope with anxiety should involve a de-emphasis of the present and a preoccupation with the future. It also follows that persons characterized as having relatively closed systems should manifest not only more anxiety but also more future-orientation than those with relatively open systems.

Subjects and Procedure

To measure time perspective, subjects were asked to tell stories about five TAT † cards: Card 2 shows two women and a man;

---

* Cited by Lewin (1951).

† *Note to the general reader*: TAT stands for the Thematic Apperception Test, developed by H. A. Murray (1938). It consists of a series of pictures to each of which the subject is invited to respond by telling a story. The story told is assumed

Card 4, a man and woman; Card 7BM, two men; Card 9BM, four men; Card 12BG, an outdoor scene.[1] The subjects were 30 students selected from a larger pool of 225 introductory psychology students who had filled out the Dogmatism Scale. Fifteen had scored highest and the other 15 lowest on this scale. Each subject was seen individually and was asked to tell stories about the five TAT cards, which were presented in random order. All stories were tape recorded and later analyzed for frequency of use of the past, present, and future *tense*, the assumption being that the relative frequency of tense used is an index of time perspective.[2]

After the subject had completed telling all five stories, he was asked to indicate how much time had elapsed in the action of each story. He was shown a printed line six inches long, intersected at the middle, and was asked to mark off two points, one representing where he felt the story began, the other where it ended. In this way two additional measures of time orientation were obtained: (1) degree of *extension* [3] into the future, measured by length of line marked off to the right of the midpoint; and (2) *time span* [4] covered, regardless of past, present, or future, measured by total length of line marked off, representing the beginning and end of the story.

In addition to the above procedures, three judges independently evaluated the TAT stories and rated each subject on five-point rating scales for the degree of future orientation, and for the degree of anxiety manifested in the story.

Results

We first computed the percentage of past, present, and future tenses used by each subject. A number of the protocols were scored independently by two persons to estimate reliability. This was found to be close to perfect, which is to be expected in view of the objective nature of the variable being considered. Table 20.1 shows the proportions of past, present, and future responses given by open and closed groups to each of the five TAT cards. Inspection of this table reveals a remarkable consistency in the

---

to be a projection of the story-teller's needs onto the picture. Psychological analysis of the major needs expressed is the primary purpose of this test.

Table 20.1

Mean Proportion of Past, Present, and Future Responses to Five TAT Cards by Closed and Open Groups

TAT card	Group	Per cent Past	Per cent Present	Per cent Future	Total
9BM	Closed	29	47	24	100
	Open	25	71	4	100
12BG	Closed	30	44	26	100
	Open	27	68	5	100
7BM	Closed	15	54	31	100
	Open	13	82	5	100
4	Closed	6	46	48	100
	Open	11	71	18	100
2	Closed	7	62	31	100
	Open	10	84	6	100
Mean Per cent	Closed	17	51	32	100
	Open	17	75	8	100

responses of the closed and open groups to each of the five TAT cards. These results are decisively in accord with expectations. There are no differences between closed and open groups in the frequency of past responses. But the open group consistently gives more present responses, and the closed group consistently gives more future responses. These findings show up without exception to all five TAT cards. Considering the results for all five TAT cards taken together, 17 per cent of the responses of both groups are past-oriented. Half the responses of the closed group are present-oriented as against three-fourths of those of the open group. About 30 per cent of all the responses of the closed group are future-oriented as compared with only 8 per cent for the open group. The differences between groups are very significant.[5]

In addition to these group comparisons, the percentage of past, present, and future responses for each individual was also determined. The distribution of scores is shown in Table 20.2. It is immediately obvious from a glance at these distributions that open and closed groups do not differ in percentage of past responses. However, the difference between the two groups on

Table 20.2

*Distribution of Past, Present, and Future Responses
for Closed and Open Groups*

Percentage Score	Past		Present		Future	
	Closed	Open	Closed	Open	Closed	Open
86–90				1		
81–85				5		
76–80				2		
71–75				2		
66–70			1	4		
61–65						
56–60			4			
51–55			2	1		
46–50			1		1	
41–45			5		2	
36–40		1	2		2	
31–35					4	
26–30	1	1			4	
21–25	4	3			2	
16–20	1	3				1
11–15	7	2				1
6–10	2	3				9
1–5		2				4
TOTALS	15	15	15	15	15	15

present responses is quite striking; with but one exception,* there is no overlapping of scores between closed and open groups. Even more striking are the distributions of scores on future tense. The range of future responses for the closed group is from 21 to 48 per cent. For the open group the range is from 3 to 17 per cent. There is no overlapping whatsoever, a result rarely found in psychological research. We are thus tempted to say that the tense in which a story is told on the Thematic Apperception Test neatly separates the open mind from the closed mind.

These results are so unusually clear-cut that we ourselves would have suspected them were it not for the fact that we obtained highly similar and clear-cut results on a preliminary study. Because these data are repetitious we omit them here.[6]

In contrast to these results are the findings obtained with the

* The highest score obtained by the closed group is 66; the lowest score obtained by the open group is 54, and the next lowest is 67.

six-inch lines the subjects marked off in order to provide us with a measure of extension into the future and of the time span covered by the story. No differences are found between closed and open groups with respect to extension into the future; in each group, about 50 per cent of the stories take place in the future. As for time span covered, the results are also negative and, in fact, quite opposite to what we would have expected: the mean time span is substantially higher for closed than for open subjects. We will discuss these negative findings shortly.

Let us now consider the results obtained from the judges' ratings of the TAT stories for future orientation and anxiety. Three judges listened independently to each of the tape-recorded stories, without knowing whether the subject who had related the story scored high or low on the Dogmatism Scale, and rated these stories on five-point scales. The combined reliability for all three judges on future orientation is .85. The mean ratings on future orientation for the closed and open groups are 4.3 and 2.1, respectively, the higher scores representing greater future orientation. This difference is very significant. The 7 highest scores are obtained by closed subjects; the 11 lowest scores are obtained by open subjects.

The same three judges also rated the degree of anxiety expressed in each of the TAT stories under the same conditions. Two criteria were used: (1) the behavior of the subject while telling the story suggesting that he found the situation anxiety-provoking, such as excessive hesitation, coughing, voice tremor, etc., and (2) anxiety expressed in the story told. The ratings were again on a five-point scale. The pooled inter-rater reliability is .82. The mean ratings on anxiety for closed and open groups are 3.3 and 2.3, respectively, and this difference is significant.

To supplement the quantitative analyses of time perspective and anxiety, a qualitative content analysis of each of the TAT stories was made for 20 of the 30 subjects, 10 from each group. In general, the majority of the subjects in both groups tell rather bland stories that are difficult to distinguish from each other in terms of story content. However, four closed subjects repeatedly told stories depicting threatening situations. Some examples of these stories are: "criminals on the lam" (Card 2); "sinister old man advising anxious young man," "student in trouble," "corrupt boss" (Card 4); "murder story," "unreal, bizarre situation" (Card 7BM).

A better idea of the kinds of threatening stories told by these closed subjects may be gained from the following:

> *Card 2.* "There are possibly three Negroes and one white. And they look like they were of a low class of people. They are ex-cons and they've escaped. They were walking in a wilderness and they're resting. A couple of them could be—a couple look like they were on the watch and the other two are hiding their faces. They will probably run into the police and get caught, but not before one of them is killed in a gun battle."

> *Card 7BM.* "A man who expresses anger—a temperamental sort of anger—he's pulling away from her. She went out with another man. She's trying to explain to him but he won't listen to her. He's going to leave and kill the other man. She's trying to hold him back, but he's full of hatred. He's going to go out and fight, and very likely kill the other man."

> *Card 9BM.* "Two men. They look very sinister. The older one is a corrupt city boss, and he's instructing the younger man to go out and take care of an old lady who's got the goods on him. The young man is holding out for some more money. He goes finally to the old lady's house but she's not there. She's left for the State Capitol to tell the authorities about the boss. She'll get there and tell her story, only to discover that the state officials are on the city boss's side."

Of the 50 stories given by the closed subjects, a total of 16 dealt with fearful situations similar to those described above. These were contributed by four of the ten closed-minded subjects. In contrast, not one of the 50 TAT stories given by open-minded subjects was of this nature. These subjects generally concerned themselves with fairly bland, banal themes.

As would be expected from the time-perspective hypothesis proposed earlier, the two groups end their stories in characteristically different ways. For example, a common response to Card 2 was: "These are men (laborers, soldiers) who are tired and resting." The open subjects generally stop at this point. In contrast, closed subjects generally are not content to let the matter rest here. They add such statements as: "They will return to their job after a break"; "They will go on to the battlefront"; and "They won't be caught by the boss." Such story endings may be interpreted in terms of a greater intolerance of ambiguity and a greater need for closure in closed persons. The story must be tied up in a neat package with no loose ends. Being more anxious about the future, they feel more compelled to project into the future the outcome of events taking place in the present. Perhaps it is for this reason that their relative frequency of the use of the future tense is greater, and of the present tense, less, than is the case for open subjects.

Interpretations

There seems to be little doubt that subjects differing in openness or closedness, as measured by the Dogmatism Scale, also differ markedly in their orientation to present and future, and that such differences are associated with differences in anxiety. These conclusions are drawn from a simple analysis of tenses employed, from the judges' ratings of the stories for future orientation and anxiety, and from content analysis of story endings and threatening themes. At the same time, it may be asked why our measures of extension into the future do not also differentiate closed from open groups. A reasonable explanation is that this measure does not get at the same aspect of future orientation as the tense analysis. D. J. van Lennep (1957) comments that there are at least two forms of future orientation, ". . . one of which is connected with the concept of expectation and which is a negation of the present,* and another one, which is, on the contrary, specific to creative men: a form which means being open to the future and must be specifically valued. The latter form is found especially in people who are not dogmatic." Van Lennep finds that good and poor report writing by scientists is a function of the ability to view past, present, and future in proper perspective. In line with van Lennep's distinction between the two kinds of future orientation, it becomes more understandable why no dif-

---

* This is the kind we have studied here.

ferences are found between the two groups with respect to extension into the future and time span covered. Sheer extension into the future and time span do not necessarily indicate an orientation toward the future at the expense of the present. They may reflect instead creative anticipations of the future. Future orientation is a healthy thing in many walks of life—in scientific work, in the business world, in planning a career, a family, a vacation, and so on. It is a necessary ingredient of healthy ambition and the achievement motive, as studied by McClelland, *et al.* (1953). It includes the ability to hope and plan, and to substitute the reality principle for the more infantile pleasure principle. Future orientation is essential for adequate adjustment and in itself is not necessarily narrow. It is only when a person is future-oriented to the point of sacrificing an appreciation of the past and present that we may say that his future orientation is narrow. The open-minded subjects are not lacking in future orientation as such, and thus hold their own with respect to the measures of extension into the future and time span. But they are not preoccupied with it, as are the closed subjects. As has been shown in Table 20.1, only 8 per cent of the open persons' responses to the TAT stories are in the future as against 32 per cent of the responses of the closed persons.

We have already mentioned that, contrary to expectation, the closed subjects generally report a broader time span than the open subjects. This reversal with respect to subjects' perception of temporal scope may not necessarily be in conflict with the other findings reported. What is actually being measured here is what the subject himself considers to be the time scope of his stories. It is the subject's estimate of time span when he is asked to go back to the story, rather than a direct measure of the actual time span. In retrospect, it seems more reasonable to expect closed subjects to see their stories as spanning more time. It is a convenient self-delusion when one is anxious about the future to feel that one actually has a comprehensive grasp of past, present, and future, even if one does not. The feeling that one is master of one's fate is thus enhanced.

Synopsis

The main purpose of the present study was to test the hypothesis that the more closed a person's belief system, the more oriented will he be toward the future, and the less concerned will he be with the present. A second purpose was to test the hypothesis that closed belief systems, future-oriented time perspectives, and the relation between the two can perhaps be best understood as defenses against anxiety.

Analysis of TAT stories showed that closed and open groups did not differ in frequency of use of the past tense. The closed group used the future tense significantly more and the present tense significantly less than the open group. There was little or no overlapping of results with respect to use of present and future tense. Judges' ratings of future orientation confirmed these findings and, moreover, revealed more anxiety in the stories told by the closed group. Content analysis further revealed a greater existence of threat themes and a greater need for closure in the stories told by the closed subjects. Measures of extension and time scope showed no differences between groups and some of the possible reasons for these negative findings were discussed.

Notes

1. These cards are the ones used by Fink (1953) in his research on time perspective in the aged. Thus, the interested reader may wish to compare directly the two sets of results.

2. In this respect we are following the work of Eson (1951) and Fink (1953).

3. This measure is equivalent to that employed by Wallace (1956).

4. Le Shan (1952) and Barndt and Johnson (1955) used roughly similar measures of time span but considered time span to be synonymous with *future orientation*.

5. As determined by analysis of variance.

6. The interested reader is referred to Bonier (1957).

21

The Effect of Threat on the Dogmatization of Catholicism

Milton Rokeach, Hans H. Toch, and Theodore Rottman

We feel quite justified in concluding from the evidence presented thus far that to a large extent the shape of a person's belief-disbelief system is relatively enduring, "carried around" within his personality from one situation to another and accounting for many of the uniformities we can observe in his actions. But this does not mean that the situation itself cannot influence a person's behavior. Nor does it mean that a person's belief system is open or closed to the same degree at different times. We think of a person's belief system as possessing not only enduring properties, but also the property of expanding and contracting, of becoming more open, or more closed, in response to a specific situation in which the person finds himself.

We assume that the more threatening a situation is to a person, the more closed his belief system will tend to become. Just as threat or anxiety built into the personality as a result of early experiences can lead to closed systems that endure, so should situational threats lead to similar effects that should last at least as long as the person experiences threat.

What holds true of people considered in isolation should also apply to people who hold beliefs in common and form groups, movements, or institutions. Here we would expect that if a threat to the collective belief system occurs, the people who hold it should develop a closed system. And we might predict that the degree to which this occurs should also vary with the extent of the threat.

In this chapter we will report on an investigation designed to test the broad hypothesis that situational threat will lead to more closed belief systems. There are no doubt many ways in which this hypothesis can be tested. The way we have chosen to do this is somewhat unusual because our analysis is at the institutional rather than at the individual level, and our method is historical rather than experimental. One motive for doing so is to try to extend the application of our formulations to institutional as well as individual behavior; a second motive is to extend the use of quantitative methods to the analysis of events long past.

The object of our attention is the Catholic Church as an institution. Throughout its history the Church appears to have weathered innumerable crises, some temporary and minor, others that shook the very foundations of the institution. Some of these crises originated in the Church itself, others in the secular world. Some were of short duration, while others lasted in one form or another for centuries. There were disputes among those high within the hierarchy concerning basic points of doctrine, disputes that affected adherents located throughout immense geographical areas. There were secular rulers intent on gaining control of the Church or limiting its authority. There were epidemics of personal misconduct and slackening of discipline involving sizable proportions of the Church's vast organization. Finally, there developed spontaneous movements among peoples under the jurisdiction of the Church, advocating new practices and beliefs and condemning current ones. A series of such movements culminated in the

Protestant Reformation in the sixteenth century, ending the Church's spiritual monopoly over the Western world.

Whenever major crises occurred in the history of the Church, assemblies of ecclesiastical dignitaries and theological experts were convened to discuss the situation and to take appropriate action. Thus, only recently (January, 1959) Pope John XXIII announced his intent to convoke the twenty-first ecumenical council of the Catholic Church. The Vatican communiqué publicizing this news reported that the Pope "underlined the daily increasing perils threatening the spiritual lives of the faithful, notably errors which are infiltrating their ranks at various points and the immoderate attraction of material goods, which have increased more than ever with the advent of technical progress." The council, according to the communiqué, "aims . . . at the edification of Christian peoples" as well as representing "an invitation to the separated communities in quest of unity." According to the *Catholic Encyclopedia* (1908), ecumenical councils represent "a common effort of the church, or part of the church, for self-preservation and self-defense. They appear . . . whenever faith or morals or discipline are seriously threatened" (p. 424). It is at these Church councils, convened during times of crisis, that official Church doctrines, or dogmas, are formulated. A "dogma," in the Catholic sense of the word, is an authoritative religious truth enacted by an ecclesiastical assembly.

The official proceedings of Church councils may thus be taken as the institutionalized responses of the Catholic Church to the historical events preceding the councils. By analyzing these historical events we propose to gauge, at least in a rough way, the amount of threat to the Church. And by analysis of the content of council proceedings, we propose to ascertain the amount of dogmatization in the Church. In line with our hypothesis, we should expect to find that the degree to which the institutionalized belief system becomes closed should be a direct function of situational threat.

The most important councils are undoubtedly the Ecumenical Councils, which constitute the main landmarks in the history of the Church since the days of Constantine. "Oecumen" means "empire," and Ecumenical Councils originally represented the Graeco-Roman Empire, the known inhabited world of that day.

The Ecumenical Councils were composed of ecclesiastics convoked from all over the world, meeting under the presidency of the Pope or his legates. They were assumed to speak for the Church. In the words of the *Catholic Encyclopedia,* they represented "the mind of the Church in action," and its "highest expression of authority."

The decrees of the Ecumenical Councils are official doctrine. Several of these decrees, in fact, constitute cornerstones of the belief system of the Church. One such basic tenet is the Nicene Creed, formulated by the First Council of Nicea, which was convened by Emperor Constantine in A.D. 325. The crisis prompting this council was a dispute over whether Christ was "coequal" with God. This dispute—the Arian controversy—had formed two enemy camps in the Eastern Church, and constituted a serious threat to its unity. Recognizing this threat, Constantine brought several hundred bishops and other ecclesiastics to Nicea at his expense. The Emperor himself took an active part in the Council, despite the fact that he was not a member of the Church hierarchy. He prompted the adoption of the Nicene Creed, which declared the equality of Christ with God, and the immortality of Christ. Arius and others of the losing faction (two bishops who refused to sign the Creed) were banished, and unity was temporarily restored.

This very brief account is introduced here to illustrate the function of councils and the origin of dogmas. A threatening historical situation leads to the convocation of a council; the council formulates doctrines or disciplinary measures which are designed to remove the threat.

Before proceeding to our study, it is relevant to mention briefly the nineteen other councils and to outline their main concerns. The Second Council (First Constantinople, 381) dealt with the question of the divinity of the Holy Ghost and amended the Nicene Creed to include relevant references. The next four councils (Ephesus, 431; Chalcedon, 451; Second Constantinople, 553; and Third Constantinople, 680–681) concerned themselves mainly with the identity of Christ. The controversies on this question were quite violent. For example, each of the opposing parties in the Council of Ephesus brought armed escorts to the proceedings. The Seventh Council (Second Nicea, 787) decreed that images should be "revered" but not "worshipped." The Eighth Council (Fourth Constantinople, 869) was mainly concerned with a jurisdictional dispute. The Ninth through the Fourteenth Councils (First, Second, Third, and Fourth Lateran, and First and Second Lyons) took place in the twelfth and thirteenth centuries. They dealt with various matters ranging from heresies (such as those of the Albigenses and Waldenses), Church discipline, Church-state relations, to the crusades and rules for the election of the Pope. The Fifteenth Council (Vienne, 1311–1313) considered complaints against the Knights Templar, but also took up such issues as Church reform, a new crusade, and the teaching of oriental languages at universities. Then followed two controversial "reforming councils" in the fifteenth century (Constance and Basle) which, among other things, condemned Jan Hus and attempted to pacify Bohemia. The Eighteenth Council (Fifth Lateran, 1518–1519) issued mainly disciplinary decrees. The next council was the famous Council of Trent, precipitated by Martin Luther and the German Reformation, which covered three two-year periods between 1545 and 1563. The Twentieth Council, the Vatican Council, convened in 1869, and in 1870 affirmed the doctrine of papal infallibility by a vote of 533 to 2.

Our study includes only twelve of these twenty councils. Three of the twenty—the First and Second Constantinople and the Vatican Council—had to be excluded because they did not enact any disciplinary decrees. In the case of five others, there are historical indications which suggest that the proceedings are incomplete or that their records may have been altered. These are the Second Nicea, the Fourth Constantinople, the First Lateran, the Vienne, and the Fifth Lateran Councils.

All the canons to be considered in this study have been translated and compiled by Schroeder (1937, 1950). Since there is no reason to assume systematic distortions in translation, our material may be said to derive from primary sources.

In the case of institutional threat, the best source of material would be statements by Church officials of the period. These would be preferable to retrospective historical accounts because our primary concern is with the extent to which a given event is perceived to be threatening, rather than with the extent to which it is objectively threatening. The point has already been made by Znaniecki (1952) that "a transgression has to be viewed by the investigator as it is defined by participants in the system, for its disorganizing effect upon the system depends upon the importance which they ascribe to it" (p. 343). Since it did not prove possible to obtain contemporary Catholic statements, Catholic historical accounts seemed the best second choice. Fortunately, Schroeder's volume on the General Councils (1937) contains a running commentary of historical events leading up to each council. In the case of the Council of Trent, which is not included among those covered in Schroeder's book, we consulted Mourret and Thompson (1947), Wright (1926), and the Bull of Convocation to the Council of Trent, quoted in Schroeder (1950). All these works are written from a Catholic viewpoint, and carry the Imprimatur.

With these historical accounts before us, we proceeded to break them down into separate events. Some of these were judged to be events precipitating the convening of the council and others to be merely contributing to it. The total number of events we ended up with ranged from 4 for the Third Lateran Council to 40 for the Council of Trent. All these were then rated for degree of situational threat. This was accomplished with the aid of a seven-point rating scale, with +3 representing events posing dire threat to the continued existence of the Church, and —3 representing events ensuring the continued existence of the Church.

Schisms were rated +3. By way of example, we may cite the following event taken from Wright (1926): "In 1517, a German monk named Martin Luther . . . began by attacking the sale of indulgences, and ended by tearing down in North Germany the entire Catholic edifice of sacraments, priests, bishops, and papal supremacy" (p. 174). Another illustration of an event rated +3 concerns the Second Lateran Council: "The day that witnessed the election of Innocent II to the highest honor of Christendom, saw also a few hours later the election of Cardinal Pietro Pierleone as anti-pope" (p. 195).*

Ratings of +2 were assigned to events that seemed to imply less serious threat. One example, relating to the Council of Trent, is from Mourret and Thompson (1947): "While the preliminaries

---

* Page references for all historical statements, except those pertaining to the Council of Trent, are to Schroeder (1937).

were dragging on, Maurice of Saxony . . . threatened the city of Trent at close range" (p. 560). Another example concerns the Council of Lyons: "In the Pope's mind, the chief purpose of the Council was the liberation of the Holy Land by means of a Crusade" (p. 324). Ratings of +1.5 or +1 were given to such items as: "The Council [First Nicea] dealt also with the controversy regarding the time of celebrating Easter" (p. 17), and "Philip . . . had been robbing the Church of France" (p. 365), the latter relating to the Council of Vienne.

In general, there were relatively few negative ratings assigned. Rated —1, for example, was: "The Pope was highly enthusiastic

Table 21.1

Ratings on Situational Threat for Twelve Catholic Councils

Council	Precipitating Events		Contributing Events		
	No. of Events	Avg. per Event	No. of Events	Avg. per Event	Combined Average
First Nicea (325)	1	3.00	6	2.00	2.50
First Constantinople (381)	4	1.75	5	0.50	1.13
Ephesus (431)	2	3.00	3	3.00	3.00
Chalcedon (451)	1	1.00	11	0.64	0.82
Second Lateran (1139)	3	1.83	3	1.66	1.75
Third Lateran (1179)	3	1.83	1	2.00	1.92
Fourth Lateran (1215)	2	2.00	6	1.08	1.54
First Lyons (1245)	3	2.33	6	1.58	1.96
Second Lyons (1274)	1	2.00	4	0.88	1.44
Constance (1414–1418)	1	2.50	6	0.67	1.59
Basle (1431–1449)	4	2.33	29	1.38	1.86
Trent (1545–1563)	6	3.00	34	2.85	2.93

over the idea of a general council [Second Nicea] and promised his whole-hearted cooperation" (p. 142). Rated —2 is the following event relating to the First Council of Constantinople: "With the death of the Emperor in 378, a period of toleration set in. . . . Arianism in all its forms came practically to an end" (p. 61). The following item (from the Council of Basle) was rated —3: "The Greeks conceded to the Pope all the rights and privileges that he enjoyed before the schism" (p. 470).

Table 21.1 shows the mean ratings for situational threat for the precipitating and contributing events of each council. It may be helpful if we illustrate the distinction between these two kinds of events. Referring to the Council of Nicea, Schroeder (1937) states that the precipitating occasion for its assembly "was Arianism . . . by its warfare against the divinity of Christ." Arius preached "the heresy that would shake the church to its foundations" (p. 8). This precipitating event was judged to pose a maximum threat and, accordingly, is assigned a value of +3.

To assess the historical conditions more fully, we next take into account other events that contributed to the convening of the Council of Nicea. These include such occurrences as the Meletian Schism brought about by Bishop Meletius who attempted to form an alliance with the followers of Arius (+3), a general conflict between the Roman Church and the Eastern Church (+1.5), and Constantine's attempt to reconcile Arius and the bishop of Alexandria (+1).

Each of the contributing events were rated separately and averaged. This average was then combined with the average rating for the precipitating events. The final rating of situational threat is the mean of these two averages. For the Council of Nicea, then, the mean rating for the precipitating events is +3.00, and for contributing events, +2.00. The final rating is thus +2.50.

As seen in Table 21.1, the two councils that score highest with respect to the situational threat preceding them are Ephesus and Trent. The latter was convened to counter the threat of the Reformation. The Council of Ephesus was the culmination of controversy over the question of Christ's human attributes. This dispute, known as the Nestorian Controversy, became extremely bitter. Anathemas and counteranathemas were the order of the day, and the Pope (Celestine) as well as the Emperor (Theodosius II) and his family became embroiled. Scoring lowest on situational threat is Chalcedon.

To what extent are these ratings reliable? To answer this question, two judges independently rated the same events. The rank order correlation between the two judges was .95.

We will now describe how we went about assessing the degree of dogmatism reflected in the proceedings of the twelve councils. In all, over 400 canons were enacted by these councils, ranging from 4 for the First Council of Constantinople to 137 for the Council of Trent. Each of these canons was rated twice: once to gauge the amount of punishment prescribed for violators of the canon, and once to assess the amount of absolute authority implied in it. Both variables were rated on a three-point scale, and the ratings for each council were averaged separately.

It may help to cite two short canons, to demonstrate how they were rated on these two variables. The first illustration is Canon 8 of the First Lateran Council. It is directed against the Normans who once had invaded the city of Benevento and held Pope Leo prisoner for a time:

> Desiring with the grace of God to protect the recognized possessions of the Holy Roman Church, we forbid under penalty of anathema any military person to invade or forcibly hold Benevento, the city of St. Peter. If anyone act contrary to this, let him be anathematized (p. 184).

This canon was given a high rating on both dimensions. It was rated high on punitiveness because it directed that infractors be anathematized. It was rated high on absolutism because it invoked the grace of God and the Holy Roman Church. By contrast, Canon 11 of the Council of Chalcedon was rated low on both punitiveness and absolutism. It reads:

> All the poor and those in need of help when traveling shall after an examination be provided with ecclesiastical letters of peace only and not with commendatory letters, because commendatory letters ought to be granted to those persons only who are in high estimation (p. 102).

However, a canon need not be necessarily high or low on both variables. The rank-order correlation between punitiveness and absolutism for the twelve councils is only .46.

Table 21.2

Mean Punitiveness and Absolutism Ratings of Canons for Twelve Councils

Council	No. of Canons	Mean Punitiveness Score	Mean Absolutism Score	Combined Mean
First Nicea	20	1.85	2.08	1.97
First Constantinople	4	1.75	1.75	1.75
Ephesus	6	2.83	2.33	2.58
Chalcedon	28	1.89	1.70	1.80
Second Lateran	30	2.38	2.05	2.22
Third Lateran	27	2.17	1.72	1.95
Fourth Lateran	70	2.16	1.55	1.86
First Lyons	27	1.93	1.63	1.78
Second Lyons	32	2.11	1.55	1.83
Constance	7	2.14	1.92	2.03
Basle	15	2.27	1.83	2.05
Trent	137	2.32	2.18	2.25

Table 21.2 gives the mean punitiveness and absolutism ratings of one judge for each council and also shows the combined means. To check on the reliability of these ratings, thirty-six canons were selected to be independently rated by a second judge. This sample consisted of the first, middle, and last canon of each council. The rank-order correlation between the two sets of ratings on punitiveness was .81, and on absolutism, .65. These reliabilities are reasonably satisfactory.

We come now to the major question of this research. Is there any relation between degree of situational threat and the degree to which the Catholic belief system becomes closed, as reflected in the council proceedings? The results are shown in Table 21.3. Looking first at the rank order of ratings, which are obtained from Tables 21.1 and 21.2, certain facts become readily apparent. The Council of Ephesus ranks highest on situational threat and also highest on punitiveness and absolutism. The Council of Trent ranks second highest on threat, third highest on punitiveness, and second highest on absolutism. The First Council of Constantinople ranks next to the lowest on threat, lowest on punitiveness, and seventh on absolutism. The Council of Chalcedon, which

Table 21.3

*Rank-Order Correlations Between Situational Threat
and Institutional Dogmatism*

Council	A Situational Threat	B Punitiveness	C Absolutism	D B and C Combined
First Nicea	3	11	3	6
First Constantinople	11	12	7	12
Ephesus	1	1	1	1
Chalcedon	12	10	9	10
Second Lateran	7	2	4	3
Third Lateran	5	5	8	7
Fourth Lateran	9	6	11.5	8
First Lyons	4	9	10	11
Second Lyons	10	8	11.5	9
Constance	8	7	5	5
Basle	6	4	6	4
Trent	2	3	2	2

ranks lowest on situational threat, ranks tenth on punitiveness and ninth on absolutism.

A more global picture is obtained from the rank-order correlations among these variables. The correlation between situational threat and punitiveness is .52, and between situational threat and absolutism, .66. Both these correlations are statistically significant. When the punitiveness and absolutism ranks are combined, their average correlates .66 with situational threat. This is also statistically significant. We thus find good empirical support for the hypothesis that as situational threat increases there is a corresponding increase in institutional dogmatism.

Undoubtedly, the continued existence of an institution depends upon appropriate responses by its leaders to new situations. An important change in circumstances calls for corresponding changes in the institution. On the other hand, groups also have to protect themselves against *too much* change, because beyond a certain point the group would change itself out of existence. With too much modification, an Anabaptist is transformed into a Mennonite, and a Mennonite into an Amish. As Sorokin (1947) puts it, "If the component of meanings of the United States is replaced by that of the Buddhist Church, or that of Harvard University by that of the United Steel Corporation, the United States and Harvard University cease to exist, even if all their vehicles and personnel remain the same" (p. 381).

What are these "component meanings" that have to be preserved? Are the issues doctrinal, or is there something else at stake? There is an anonymous little poem that goes:

> The cheese-mites asked how the cheese got there,
> And warmly debated the matter;
> The orthodox said it came from the air,
> And the heretics said from the platter.

Actually, as far as the real point at issue is concerned, the positions in this memorable debate could just as easily have been reversed. For beyond the question of how the cheese got there, and beyond the question of who are the orthodox and who the heretics lies another issue—the issue of the legitimacy of the authority on which the belief system rests.

Speaking of the Inquisition, the Catholic historian Knox explains: "The head and chief offense, in their eyes, was the defiance of spiritual authority of which their other doctrines were merely the corollaries" (1926, p. xiv). In American Inquisitors (1928), Walter Lippman's fundamentalist tells Socrates: "You know and I know that the issue is not whether Adam was created at nine o'clock in the morning or whether he descended from an ape. The issue is whether there exists a book which, because it is divinely inspired, can be regarded by men as 'the infallible rule of faith and practice' or whether men must rely upon human reason alone and henceforth do without an infallible rule of faith and practice" (p. 63). In a letter published in Boston by Towgood (1748) a "dissenting gentleman" proclaims: "The Controversy betwixt us, Sir, I apprehend, may easily be brought to a plain and short Issue . . . It turns upon the single Point . . . That the Church hath Power to decree Rites and Ceremonies and Authority in Matters of Faith" (p. 6). The more concerted or widespread the attacks on authority or the authority's belief system (which amounts to the same thing), the more closed or dogmatic the reaction to be expected. Our results are consistent with this expectation.

A final word may be in order concerning the nature of our study. To our minds, the study suffers from certain methodological inadequacies. Our definition of what is an historical event was somewhat arbitrary; the canons might have been rated on other dimensions; the rating scale might have been more rigorously defined. What appears to us to make up for these possible methodological weaknesses is that this study represents a quantitative attempt to test a psychological hypothesis with historical material. As far as we know, it is one of the first attempts to apply quantitative methods to the analysis of a religious movement.

Synopsis

We have investigated the effects of situational threat on the dogmatization of Catholicism. Positive correlations are found between independent measures of the amount of situational threat that preceded the convening of a dozen ecumenical councils of the Catholic Church, and the degree of absolutism and punitiveness expressed in the canons enacted by these ecumenical councils.

Part Six

Summing Up

The report of our research effort to date is more or less complete. We now pause to look behind in order to sum up, and to peer ahead in order to see how far we have yet to go. What exactly have we learned about the role of belief systems in the total organization of the person? To what extent have we succeeded in grasping the essence of the open and closed mind? In what way are personality, ideology, and the cognitive processes all related to each other? And where do we go from here?

Our most general aim has been to develop a way of thinking, to seek out a set of concepts in terms of which it would be possible to describe and to measure the organization of all belief systems, and to describe individual differences in such organization. We have persisted in this aim on the faith that a reasonably adequate description of the way in which belief systems are organized would also turn out to be reasonably adequate for the description of personality, ideology, cognitive functioning, and their interconnections. In the course of our research we have had occasion to look into many issues—the way we relate ourselves to people (individually and collectively), to authority, to ideas, and to systems of ideas; our stance with respect to the past, present, and future; the broad outlines of the way we perceive, think, remember, and feel. Basic to all these kinds of functioning are certain structural properties which bind them together. These activities are seen to be but different behavioral manifestations of the same belief structure, but different phenotypic expressions of similar genotypes.

22

Personality, Ideology, and Cognitive Functioning

Consider first the findings which suggest that we categorize people and groups of people in terms of the extent to which their beliefs are congruent or incongruent with our own. We generally seem to prefer, to one degree or another, those with belief systems that are more congruent with our own.* Our findings suggest that this organizing principle is far more important than other kinds of categorizations, such as race or ethnic grouping, in determining our relations with others. If race or ethnic categorizations are important it is primarily because they are convenient symbols that stand for complexes of beliefs which to one degree or another are seen to be similar to and different from our own. We find this organizing principle to

* Other research which seems to support this generalization is that of Izard (1959), Lott and Rosell (1959), Lundy (1958), and Rosenfeld and Jackson (1959).

hold for southerners as well as northerners, for those high in prejudice as well as those low in prejudice, and for younger as well as older Jewish children.

It is therefore not surprising to learn that, with belief held constant, the greater the rejection of Negroes, the greater also the rejection of whites; the greater the rejection of gentiles (by Jewish children), the greater also the rejection of Jews. Prejudice toward a specific outgroup takes on a new significance when it is seen to be but a special case of a more general misanthropy, which often includes one's own group. However, the misanthropy is not necessarily expressed indiscriminately and in a negative way toward all. It takes the external form of rejection only in the case of those who disagree with the misanthropist; in the case of those who agree, there is acceptance, but with a "string attached."

However, the general tendency to organize people in terms of belief does not mean that we are all equally misanthropic. There are individual differences among us in the *absolute* extent to which we are willing to accept and reject others on this basis, and there are *relative* degrees of preference for those with similar versus opposed beliefs. The reason Christ-like figures such as Gandhi and Schweitzer are idealized is that they have the capacity to love those who disagree with them no less than those who agree with them, and to love all to a far greater extent than most men are capable of. In this connection, our findings on northerners versus southerners are quite illuminating. Southerners as compared with northerners seem to reject all people more in absolute terms—whites as well as Negroes, those who agree with them as well as those who disagree with them. Southerners also show a greater discrepancy in preference for whites over Negroes, but this discrepancy is overshadowed by an even greater discrepancy in their preference for those who agree with them over those who disagree with them.

Another thing we learn about the nature of belief systems is that for all individuals, even those whose systems are relatively closed, the categorization of people and groups is continuous rather than dichotomous. From the literature on prejudice and authoritarianism, one would expect that those who are intolerant, or authoritarian, or closed, characteristically show either-or, black-white categorizations of people. But the data we have presented on disbelief systems show that this is not so. Disbeliefs are seen to be arranged by virtually everyone in terms of a continuum of similarity. For persons holding religious beliefs, for instance, atheism is generally seen to be at the tail end of this continuum, and is rejected more than other "isms." Other religious systems are accepted more and more, the more similar they are to their own. This conclusion seems warranted from the various kinds of data we have presented—on attitudinal rejection, on movements in and out of various churches, on enrollment in denominational colleges by students of varying denominations, on interfaith marriages, and on the extent of conflict in such marriages. When we find minor deviations from the more or less linear relation between similarity and preference, they are readily explained in terms of "the renegade hypothesis."

There is no reason to think that these generalizations apply only to the religious realm. They probably apply to other realms as well—political, philosophical, scientific, and so on. It would be interesting to see if similar results would be obtained in France where there is a diversity of political viewpoints, or if similar results could be found in the academic world, where there is also diversity in viewpoints. But the organization of disbelief systems is probably far more complicated than we have been able to show. As suggested earlier in this work, a person's belief system is not just a religious one or a political one, or a scientific one. However fruitful such categories may be from a sociological standpoint, we doubt that the mind can be profitably broken down into such compartments. We regard the findings on religious disbelief systems merely a crude approximation of yet more complex psychological organizations, which because of their very complexity are difficult to study.

The view we have taken here about the way we organize the social world in terms of the principle of belief congruence leads us to view man's intolerance to man in a way that differs in certain important respects from those currently held. In order to state what these differences are as clearly as possible, we present them here in tabular form:

Table 22.1

Contrasting Characteristics of Prejudice as Conventionally Conceived and as Conceived Here

As Conceived Here	As Conventionally Conceived
1. The basic criterion of categorization is a belief criterion: how much we like and dislike those whose belief-disbelief systems are similar to or different from our own.	1. The basic criterion of categorization is an ethnic or racial criterion: how much we like and dislike Jews, Negroes, foreigners, etc.
2. The definition is a psychological one, the exact cleavages of groups shifting according to the specific issue under consideration, and shifting according to the specific belief system under consideration.	2. The definition is a sociological one, the criterion for prejudice being external to individuals, applying primarily or solely to institutionalized forms of prejudice, forever fixed in its lines, and allegedly applicable to all persons within a culture regardless of differences in the content of their belief systems.
3. The definition is a general one, being equally applicable to phenomena of intolerance in the world of politics, religion, art, and science; to different historical eras; to past, present, and future forms of intolerance regardless of specific manifestations.	3. The definition is primarily concerned with a form of intolerance typical of the political right. It is not generally applicable.
4. The definition is a structural one, cutting across specific ideological content. In the Opinionation Scale this is achieved by having two parts, a left opinionation and right opinionation subscale, so that no matter whether one's ideology is left or right of center, individual differences in degree of intolerance may be measured.	4. The definition is a substantive one, being applicable only to groups specifically mentioned. Intolerance toward individuals and groups not mentioned may still exist but are not measured.
5. Acceptance of those who agree (opinionated acceptance) is as much a manifestation of intolerance as is rejection of those who disagree (opinionated rejection). Conversely, tolerance is defined as the extent to which others are accepted regardless of whether they agree or disagree with us.	5. Acceptance of minority group is a manifestation of tolerance, rejection a manifestation of intolerance.
6. Extent of acceptance-rejection of in-group is equal in importance to extent of acceptance-rejection of out-group.	6. The primary focus is on the acceptance-rejection of minority groups. There is less concern with acceptance-rejection of majority groups.

7. Outgroups are seen to be arranged along a continuum of similarity to the ingroup.	7. The ingroup-outgroup distinction is more or less a dichotomous one.
8. Cognitive similarity of outgroup to ingroup is perhaps a more important determinant of social discrimination than individual differences in personality dynamics.	8. There is great emphasis on personality dynamics as a determinant of social discrimination. Sheer cognitive dissimilarity as a determinant of social discrimination is overlooked.

The principle of belief congruence governing the organization of belief systems helps us to organize not only the world of people, but also the world of ideas and authority in relation to each other. Recall that in the music experiment, for example, the subjects responded to the composer in essentially the same way they responded to the composer's music. Recall also that disbelief systems are arranged in terms of congruence to the belief system. These facts suggest that each person is somehow motivated to arrange the world of ideas, of people, and of authority in harmonious relations with each other. Recently, a number of others have proposed similar views. Festinger (1957) talks about cognitive dissonance between two elements in a system and the ways people try to reduce such dissonance. Heider (1958) talks about structural imbalance that motivates the individual to strive toward structural balance. Newcomb (1956) expresses similar ideas, and so do Osgood et al. (1957) when they talk about attitudinal congruity and incongruity.*

The major conclusions to which we have drawn attention thus far are those that emerge from our findings about the nature of all belief systems, regardless of the degree to which they are open or closed. They are independent of personality. In summary, we organize the world of ideas, people, and authority basically along lines of belief congruence. What is not congruent is further organized in terms of similarity to what is congruent. Much of our behavior with respect to diverse belief systems, and with respect to persons and authorities identified with such systems, seems, at least in part, to be determined by such cognitive organizations.

The major portion of our research effort, however, concerns the

---

* It would be a worthwhile task to examine more closely the extent to which these various concepts overlap each other, the respective ranges of their application, and how they may be more integrated with each other.

ways in which belief systems differ from each other. In this connection, we have talked of such things as individual differences in isolation, differentiation, time perspective, the specific content of primitive beliefs, the formal content of beliefs about authority and people, and the structure of peripheral beliefs. We have tried to show that all these properties may have something in common that ties them together and justifies our considering them as but different expressions of a yet more fundamental variable. We are referring to the capacity to distinguish information from source of information and to evaluate each on its own merits. This variable, in the extreme, describes the essence of the open and closed mind and, with its diverse manifestations, is at the cornerstone of our attempts to understand whatever relationships may exist among personality, ideology, and cognitive functioning. These considerations have served to guide us in our attempts to define and to measure individual differences in general authoritarianism and intolerance; they have led us to see that the interrelations that exist among the acceptance and rejection of authority, of people, and of ideas have a common structural basis and also a common functional basis; they have permitted us to proceed from the study of the properties of single beliefs to the study of the properties of systems of belief; and we can now see better than before that the experiencing and enjoying of something new is enhanced to the degree that the "significant other" is thrown off when we are encountering the new.

In discussing further the way in which belief systems differ from each other, let us first comment on our two main instruments—the Dogmatism and Opinionation Scales. Our results strongly support the view that these scales represent more general measures of authoritarianism and intolerance than others currently in use. They are shown to be negligibly related to liberalism-conservatism. But more impressive in this respect are the findings for English Communists. Of all political groups tested in England, the Communists score lowest on the F Scale and the Ethnocentrism Scale, but highest on the Dogmatism and Opinionation Scales. These results make sense only if we assume that the F and E Scales represent measures of right authoritarianism and intolerance, while the Dogmatism and Opinionation Scales represent more general measures.* The reason the latter two scales represent general measures is that the theory guiding their construction is structure- rather than content-oriented. In the case of the Dogmatism Scale, specific ideological content is avoided because the items are designed to tap various structural and formal aspects of openness and closedness. In the case of the Opinionation Scale, a structure-oriented test is achieved by balancing an equal number of left-of-center and right-of-center items.

But the Dogmatism Scale, on which we have relied most heavily, would seem to be more than just a measure of individual differences in authoritarianism. As has already been said earlier in this work, we consider it to be first and foremost a measure of the extent to which the total mind is an open mind or a closed one. The reason we think of it in this way is that the theory guiding its construction involves many defining characteristics of open and closed systems; of which belief about the nature of authority is but one.

There is no need here to go into great detail regarding the evidence bearing on the validity of the Dogmatism Scale as a measure of the open and closed mind. We have already done so at the end of Part Three. It will perhaps suffice to say here that those who score extremely high on this scale are shown to differ consistently from those who score extremely low in the ability to form new belief systems, whether these new systems are conceptual, perceptual, or esthetic in nature. In the course of finding this out we have also been able to make further theoretical elaborations of our conceptual scheme by distinguishing between rigid thinking and dogmatic thinking and, in parallel ways, between the ability to analyze and synthesize, between breaking down a system and building it up again. In the course of our research, we have also succeeded in making contact with the work of Witkin and his associates (1954) by specifying in what way their work ties in and does not tie in with ours. It turns out that their conception of "field-dependence" and "field-independence" involves good and poor analytic abilities that help or hinder the breaking down of items from fields. Their distinction between the two does not ad-

* This conclusion has been independently confirmed in a recent study by Barker (1958).

dress itself to the synthesizing ability to build up items into new fields.

Furthermore, we can point to a number of variables that determine the ability to form new systems. These may be briefly reiterated as follows:

1. The ability to remember or to keep in mind all the new parts to be integrated;

2. A willingness to "play along" or to entertain new systems;

3. Past experience, which determines whether a particular system is, psychologically speaking, new or not new;

4. Presenting new beliefs to be formed into new systems all at once or gradually. In closed persons the formation of new systems is facilitated when the new beliefs are presented all at once, in which case the new beliefs do not have to be reconciled with old ones. In open persons, it makes no difference whether the new beliefs are presented gradually or all at once; the subjects work them through cognitively in either case.

5. The degree to which there is isolation within the belief system. The greater the isolation—that is, the less the intercommunication between individual beliefs—the more is the formation of new systems retarded.

In our recapitulation at the end of Part Three we have also pointed to a number of implications of these findings which may again be briefly restated:

1. The psychological processes involved in ideological functioning can be studied by analogy in the laboratory.

2. Many important aspects of intellectual functioning in particular and cognitive functioning in general can be attributed to personality rather than to intelligence, as presently conceived and measured. If intelligence does exert an influence on the ability to analyze and to synthesize, it probably does so in interaction with personality.

3. It is possible to investigate many spheres of activity—ideological, conceptual, perceptual, and esthetic—via the common structural bond that ties them all together in the person's belief system.

4. In dealing with the formation of new systems in open and closed persons the essence of the difference between them is in the ability to synthesize rather than analyze. This suggests that the

ability to synthesize is far more important to creativity than the ability to analyze. Although we have not been directly concerned here with the problem of creativity as such, our investigations of open and closed systems may be seen as a contribution to the study of creativity.

5. A person's cognitive functioning is not a thing apart from his affective or emotional functioning. They are seen to be different facets of a person's total behavior. This point merits further elaboration. What is the relation between the cognitive and the affective and in what way does our theory, which is a cognitive theory, address itself to affective as well as cognitive aspects of behavior?

Let us begin by saying that, to our minds, analysis in terms of beliefs and systems of beliefs does not necessarily restrict us only to the study of cognitive behavior. We assume that every affective state also has its representation as a cognitive state in the form of some belief or some structural relation among beliefs within a system. With respect to the enjoyment of music, for example, we all build up through past experience a set of beliefs or expectancies about what constitutes "good" and "bad" music. It is in terms of such expectancies, which are more often implicit than explicit, that we enjoy a particular composition. Thus, a person who is exposed to a particular piece of classical music or jazz may enjoy it, even though it may be totally unfamiliar to him, because it is congruent with an already-existing set of beliefs he has built up over time. Depending on the extent to which he is prepared to entertain new systems, he may or may not enjoy Schönberg or other music perceived as incompatible with his own beliefs about what constitutes good music. The situation with respect to the *enjoyment* of strange music is not much different from the *enjoyment* some of our subjects express in working on the Doodlebug Problem, or indeed, the *enjoyment* some of them may derive from meeting a total stranger whose belief system is radically at variance with their own. In all cases, enjoyment or its opposite is the affective counterpart of a belief organization and can be thought of as being in one-to-one relation (isomorphic) with it. Thus, our cognitive approach is as much concerned with affection as with cognition.

In much the same way, *authoritarianism* as an affective personality state can also be conceived in terms of cognitive beliefs about the nature of authority; a *fear* of aloneness and isolation can be represented as a cognitive belief that "Man on his own is a helpless and miserable creature" (one of the items on the Dogmatism Scale); *anxiety* can be represented as a cognitive belief that "It is only natural for a person to be fearful of the future" (another item from the Dogmatism Scale). In precisely the same way such affective states as self-hate, a need for self-aggrandizement, and a paranoid outlook on life can all be seen as having their cognitive counterparts within the belief-disbelief system.

Thus the traditional distinction between what is cognitive and what is affective may be a convenient one but not a necessary one. Our conceptual and research strategy has been to translate the affective to the cognitive. This in no way denies the reality of the affective states of man nor implies that our cognitive approach has ignored it. Indeed, a way is paved for the study of a person's emotions through an examination of his cognitions. For all the things a person feels and wants must surely be represented by what he believes and knows. A psychoanalyst cannot know of a patient's repressions unless their traces are somehow present in his patient's belief-disbelief system. If there were no cognitive traces whatsoever in the patient there would be no way for the psychoanalyst to know that something has been repressed.

The relation between the cognitive and the affective brings us to the problem of functional aspects of belief systems. As stated earlier, such systems are seen to serve two opposing sets of functions. On the one hand, they represent Everyman's theory for understanding the world he lives in.* On the other hand, they represent Everyman's defense network through which information is filtered, in order to render harmless that which threatens the ego. The beautiful thing about a belief system is that it seems to be constructed to serve both masters at once: to understand the world insofar as possible, and to defend against it insofar as necessary. We do not agree with those who hold that people selectively distort their cognitive functioning so that they will see, remember, and think only what they want to. Instead, we hold

---

* A similar view has recently been expressed by Kelly (1955) when he implies that every man is his own theorist, employing his own system of concepts to interpret and understand himself and his world.

to the view that people will do so only to the extent that they have to, and no more. For we are all motivated by the desire, which is sometimes strong and sometimes weak, to see reality as it actually is, even if it hurts.

A great deal of further work will be required to explore fully the ramifications of this view. In our research to date, we have not been overly preoccupied with the exploration of the functional or dynamic aspects of belief systems. This is deliberate. For, as we have already said, prior to the problem of function and explanation are the problems of definition and description. The analysis of the structural properties of belief and cognition, the measurement of such properties, and the extent to which they are interrelated seem to be logically and scientifically prior to the analysis of the motivational variables underlying them. Once this descriptive task has been satisfactorily accomplished, attention can then be more fruitfully and selectively directed to the issue of psychodynamic determinants. A given motivation may then be seen to affect simultaneously a whole class of structural properties rather than just a single one. It is somewhat inefficient to ask separately for each and every belief, or opinion, or attitude, or act: "What function does this serve in the total economy of the person?" For all we know, we might be asking the same question a thousand times over. It is more economical to see what structural interrelations first exist and then ask a single question at the end about the functions served by all the variables that turn out to go together within a belief system.

This brings us to a closely related question. Have we not stressed personality too much at the expense of situational determinants of social behavior? A field-theoretical position requires a consideration of both personal and situational conditions, and their interactions, as determinants of behavior. A sole concern with personality ignores the role of the present context; a sole concern with the present context leaves us with the embarassment of individual differences.* In recent years, there has been a good deal of criticism from both social psychologists and sociolo-

* A parallel point has been made a few years ago by J. B. S. Haldane who, in discussing his position on the Lysenko controversy, stated: "Genes exhibit a good deal of stability in their reproduction, otherwise heredity would be impossible. They do not exhibit complete stability, or evolution would be impossible."

gists regarding the one-sidedness of personality approaches to social issues. This criticism is to some extent justified. But equally one-sided and un-"field-theoretical" is a focus on situational aspects to the exclusion of personality. For example, much experimental work in social psychology might well be criticized on the ground that it typically ignores the role of personality and concentrates instead, as experimenters of all persuasions will, on the effects on behavior arising from the experimental manipulation of variables.

Studies of the structure of a person can teach as much about what consistencies we may expect of him in different situations, for it is what the person brings to the situation that gives meaning to it. Conversely, studies of the structure of the situation can teach us much about what variations we may expect of persons in different situations. It is often very difficult to study both sets of determinants within the confines of a single piece of research. But it should not be difficult in a research program such as the present one to keep a general eye out on both sets of determinants even though the individual studies, considered separately, are sometimes slanted to one side or to the other.

Our research program proceeded on the assumption that while a person's belief-disbelief system is a relatively enduring structure, the extent to which it influences behavior, and the extent to which it is open or closed at any particular moment, is jointly influenced by situational conditions interacting with personality. A person's belief-disbelief system is never totally activated or engaged at any one time. Each situation, according to its structure and according to the motivational forces it gives rise to, activates only certain beliefs relevant to that situation. George and Handlon make a similar point when they distinguish between a *belief* and an *expectancy*. They write:

> Beliefs are considered to be relatively permanent states of the central nervous system. In everyday terms, they are those stored memories whose contents specify for the organism what may be expected to happen . . . if certain behavior . . . is performed under certain stimulating circumstances. Since at any given moment the organism's behavior is a function of a relatively few of the totality of its stored beliefs, we shall call those beliefs which are actually influ-

encing behavior at any given instant of time *expectancies* . . . Beliefs may be converted into expectancies through the action of the activating stimulus state (1957, p. 14).

For example, when we look at a particular painting only those beliefs directly concerned with or in communication with the realm of painting are aroused; when we interact with an employer only that part of the belief-disbelief system is activated that is directly concerned with or in communication with beliefs about employers. In this connection let us also point again to the research on belief versus race as determinants of discrimination. Although a person may align himself with others primarily in terms of belief, such alignments may be assumed to be continually changing as situations change, as each situation involves different issues, thus activating endless kaleidoscopes of beliefs relevant to each situation.

In some of our research we have stressed primarily personality determinants, in others situational determinants, and in yet others the interaction between the two. The many findings we have reported in this volume regarding differences between persons who are open and closed in their belief systems can be accounted for by assuming that an enduring state of threat in the personality is one condition giving rise to closed belief systems. With the exception of our English Communist sample, about which we have already commented in Chapter 19, the correlations between closed belief systems and anxiety are always positive and, from the standpoint of factor analysis, factorially the same. This position is bolstered by some additional data presented in Chapter 19, admittedly fragmentary, which suggest at least partly that threat and its effects on the closing up of belief systems has its origin in childhood experience. Our guess is that a fuller account of the nature of childhood determinants would not turn out to be very different from that put forward by Frenkel-Brunswik (1948b) in her study of prejudice in children.

As for situational effects on belief systems, the data that are relevant here are those on the effects of situational threat on the dogmatization of Catholicism. These results are consistent with the view that threat emanating from the contemporary situation, as well as threat built into the personality, may both lead to similar effects on behavior. Although none of these studies considered separately can be regarded as field-theoretical because they deal either with situational or personality determinants, considered together they supplement each other and help to round out the picture.

We have said that some of our research is also concerned with the interaction between personality and the situation. We are referring to the experiments reported in Chapters 10 and 12, wherein both personality and situational determinants are studied within the confines of a single experiment. These are concerned with the effects of the experimental manipulation of selected variables on open and closed persons. In one experiment (Chapter 10), we see that the effects are the same on both open and closed groups. By-passing memory by putting the new beliefs within the person's visual field produces facilitative effects in both groups which speed up the formation of new conceptual systems. In the second experiment (Chapter 12), which is concerned with transfer effects and with the effects of immediate versus gradual presentation of beliefs, we note differential rather than similar effects on open and closed persons. The interpretation of these results has already been discussed and need not be repeated. But what is to be emphasized here is that the interaction between personality and the situation is an enormously complicated affair, sometimes leading to similarities and sometimes to differences in behavior. Such complications can sometimes be predicted in advance by a personality approach to behavior, providing its concepts are so formulated that, in their application, they are sensitive to situational variations.

Some Methodological and Theoretical Issues Meriting Further Research

In our research program, we have chosen to focus our attention primarily on substantive rather than methodological issues. There are, however, certain methodological issues that must be considered in order to assess adequately the validity of our findings and to guide further research.

Let us consider first the conventions employed in the behavioral sciences regarding statistical significance. It seems to us that the major contribution of statistical theory lies in the fact that it helps us to assess the probability with which chance is or is not operating to produce a particular set of results in a particular research. Conventions regarding statistical significance at the 5-per cent and 1-per cent levels rest upon the assumption that the results of each study are to be evaluated separately for statistical significance, independently from the results obtained in all other relevant studies. Suppose all the differences reported herein turned out to be significant at the 15-per cent instead of at the usual 5-per cent level? What we are driving at is that in evaluating the outcome of our research effort from a statistical standpoint, the trend of results is a more important consideration than the precise level of significance achieved by a particular set of differences.

Another issue concerns response set. It is apparent that both the Dogmatism and Opinionation Scales are so constructed that agreement with the items leads to a high score, and disagreement to a low score. We have been generally unsuccessful in our attempts to construct statements worded in the opposite direction. One question that may therefore be raised is this: To what extent are responses to the Dogmatism and Opinionation Scales determined by the content of the items or by a consistent tendency on the part of the subject to agree with the items regardless of their content (response set)? A second question is even more important: Can response set account for the many differences reported herein between open and closed subjects, and can it account for the other findings in which the Dogmatism and Opinionation Scales are used? This issue merits serious consideration in view of the fact that in the past few years a great deal of attention has been directed toward the role of response set, acquiescence, and social desirability as determinants of responses to personality scales. There is no need to enter here into a detailed review of the work on response set since Christie, Havel, and Seidenberg (1958) have recently done so, particularly as it relates to the F Scale. It may be assumed that whatever objections have been raised with respect to response set in the F Scale may also be raised with respect to the present scales.

Christie *et al.* conclude from their analysis, which seems well supported by their data, that the F Scale measures response set only to a minor degree. This of course does not preclude its presence in the Dogmatism and Opinionation Scales. Although we have no direct data bearing on this issue, let us tentatively assume that response set is present to at least some degree in the present scales. This brings us to the second question, which we regard as a far more important one: Is it possible to account for the many findings of the present research on the basis of response set?

There are four indirect lines of evidence that lead us to reject this as a serious possibility:

1. It will be remembered that systematic differences in results were obtained between the Dogmatism and Opinionation Scales on the one hand and the F and E Scales on the other. In view of the fact that all these scales are consistently worded in a negative manner, it is unlikely that response set can account for the *differences* in the results obtained with these two sets of scales.

2. In drawing the distinction between dogmatic and rigid thinking, we used the Dogmatism and Rigidity Scales. Most of the items in the latter scale are also worded in a negative direction, so that agreement indicates rigidity. If response set were a significant determinant of scores on the Dogmatism and Rigidity Scales, it is again hardly likely that we would have been able to get the differential results we actually obtained on problem-solving between high and low rigid groups, on the one hand, and high and low dogmatic groups on the other.

3. With respect to the Opinionation Scale, if response set were an important determinant we should expect to find that those who agree with left-opinionation items should also agree with right-opinionation items, and vice versa. But we never find this to be the case. Those groups that we have good reason to believe are right-oriented agree more wtih right-opinionation items and less with left-opinionation items. Thus, most of our American samples score high on right opinionation, but low on left opinionation. Conversely, Communists score high on left opinionation but low on right opinionation. Also, the correlations between left and right opinionation are either close to zero or negative rather than positive, which also argues against the response-set hypothesis.

4. Consider finally the rich variety of differences we have obtained between high and low scorers on the Dogmatism Scale. To mention a few, we have obtained differences between them

with respect to conceptual and perceptual synthesis but not with respect to analysis, differences on party-line thinking and loyalty to a system, differences on positive transfer effects from one problem to another, differences on the enjoyment of new music but not on the enjoyment of more traditional music, and differences with respect to the tense in which TAT stories are told.

It would be extremely difficult and strained to try to account for such differences and others not mentioned above on such a simple basis as response set. But, these considerations notwithstanding, it would be most desirable to ascertain *directly* how much variance of scores on the Dogmatism and Opinionation Scales are attributable to response set. This would require an analysis very similar to that made for the F Scale by Christie, Havel, and Seidenberg (1958). Until such an analysis is forthcoming, we will not be able to tell for sure what role response set has played in our research.

Another methodological issue that we have already considered many times is whether the differences obtained between high and low scorers on the Dogmatism Scale, particularly with respect to cognitive functioning, can be explained away as being due to intelligence. As we have shown, however, the correlation between scores on the Dogmatism Scale and intelligence is typically close to zero, when intelligence is measured by such tests as the American Council on Education Test, the Ohio State Psychological Examination Test, and the Wonderlic Test. Similarly, extreme scorers on the Dogmatism Scale typically do not differ from each other in intelligence. It would therefore be hard to account for our findings on this basis.

This leads us to question what intelligence tests do measure. With the tests and samples we have employed, intelligence is negligibly related to open-mindedness, to conceptual and perceptual analysis and synthesis, and to the ability to enjoy new musical systems. It seems to us that we *are* dealing here with intelligence, although not with the kind of intelligence measured by current intelligence tests. Apparently, intelligence tests do not tap the kinds of cognitive functioning we have been describing in this work. This seems paradoxical. For the current work is concerned with the very same cognitive processes with which intelligence tests are allegedly concerned. This suggests the need for a systematic reappraisal of current concepts of the nature of intelligence, a task which is large in scope and which, we hope, will receive attention in the near future.

Another problem that merits further research involves a more effective utilization of scaling methods than has been employed here. Further work is needed to find out to what extent the Dogmatism and Opinionation Scales are unidimensional, or can be made so. Also, in our eagerness to forge ahead on substantive issues, we have for the large part by-passed the scaling problems inherent in the continua of similarity seen by different religious groups, and the fact that the psychological distance separating one disbelief subsystem from another is not equal. We have treated our data as if the units are equal and, consequently, our analysis of the behavioral manifestations of the organization of disbelief systems is probably more crude than it ought to be.

Turning our attention now to other issues that merit further theoretical and empirical research, we wish to single out especially the following:

1. Our theory regarding the organization of belief systems is by no means complete. There are probably other properties of belief systems that have been overlooked in the present work. And a good deal needs yet to be learned about the internal structure of belief systems, a problem we have thus far by-passed. For example, it would be desirable to know to what extent the various defining characteristics of open and closed systems are interrelated and indeed characteristics of open and closed persons.* For example, will a person with an isolated belief system also show isolation in the disbelief system, isolation between belief and disbelief systems, and isolation among peripheral beliefs? Similar questions could be asked about the state of differentiation in various parts of the system.

2. Another variable we have not studied thus far is the breadth or scope of the belief-disbelief system. People will obviously dif-

---

* Some of these problems have recently been investigated by Alson (1958) and Vidulich (1958). Alson uses methods that are modifications of those first developed by Zajonc (1954) for the analysis of cognitive structure, and Vidulich uses interview methods that attempt to get at similar variables. Unfortunately, the results of both investigations, which yield partly positive and partly negative findings, are difficult to evaluate because of methodological complications in their research which are too involved to discuss here.

fer in this respect. A person may know a lot (or a little) about the total spectrum of possible belief systems or he may know a lot (or a little) about a narrow band of the spectrum "close in." We cannot assume that an open-minded person is necessarily broad, or that a closed-minded person is necessarily narrow. We can think of some persons we have known who have struck us as extremely erudite as far as breadth is concerned but closed-minded about what they know. Despite this, some of them have struck us as highly creative in their own fields and we tentatively hypothesize from this that closed-minded persons may be creative providing their belief systems are broad and providing that they are their own authority, and thus not dependent upon external authority.

3. Another problem worthy of investigation is how belief-disbelief systems are formed in childhood and the conditions under which they change.

4. We have made much of the notion of *system* variables, such as forming a system, enjoying a system, and defecting from a system. It would be fruitful to try to isolate other system variables and study behavior with respect to them.

5. We need to know more about pre-ideological beliefs and their relation to ideological beliefs. We have called the former "primitive beliefs." We suspect that if we knew more about the nature of such primitive beliefs, their organization, and how to modify them, we would know more about the conditions leading to the formation and modification of belief systems. This should have important implications for the psychology of politics, personality, mental health, psychotherapy, and education.

6. In a similar way, we need to study also the nature of the "meta-beliefs" we build up about authority. As has already been pointed out, all persons must necessarily rely on authority as a "liaison system" in their efforts to cognize the world they live in. This "liaison system" may be thought of as having a structure of its own. How it develops and changes, and how it is related to primitive beliefs on the one hand and to peripheral beliefs on the other are problems that merit further study.

7. Since the Dogmatism and Opinionation Scales are structure-rather than content-oriented, it is now more feasible to study such phenomena as authoritarianism and intolerance in other

cultures and to compare such results with those we have obtained in the United States and England. Most interesting in this connection would be the study of closed and open orientations in the Soviet Union and in other eastern European countries.

8. The structural properties that define the organization of belief-disbelief systems may be merely the cognitive representation of parallel structural properties existing in social organizations. A systematic attempt to explore such possible parallelism might lead to an integration of psychology and sociology.

9. What are the conditions that lead to temporary and enduring modifications of various aspects of the belief system, particularly with respect to its open and closed dimension? Relevant here is the informal observation that in the immediate academic setting in which we have pursued our research there has been a marked reduction in the frequency of use of opinionated language, probably as a result of an awareness of its psychological significance. This suggests that everyday interpersonal relations may sometimes be changed without too much effort. It also has implications for propaganda. Perhaps the use of opinionated language on the "Voice of America" or "Radio Moscow" has effects opposite to that intended.

The preceding are not meant to be exhaustive. They supplement other methodological and theoretical issues that have already been raised in the various chapters of this book. The reader will perhaps raise yet other issues and see yet other implications arising from the present work. There is no reason to think, as we end here, that the study of the organization of belief systems has been completed. More likely, it has just begun.

APPENDICES

Appendix A

Comparison Between Communist and Other Political Groups in England on Means of 66 Items of the Dogmatism Scale

Items from Dogmatism Scale	Commu- nists N = 13	Bevan- ites N = 19	Atlee- ites N = 27	Liber- als N = 22	Conser- vatives N = 54	t [a]
°1. U.S. and Russia have nothing in common.	2.2	2.6	3.0	2.5	3.1	1.8
2. Communism and Catholicism have nothing in common.	4.2	3.7	3.7	3.2	3.4	1.4
3. My principles are different from most others.	4.0	4.0	3.7	2.9	3.2	1.6
4. People bring up irrelevant issues.	6.4	6.0	6.3	5.6	6.0	2.2
°5. Best government is democracy run by most intelligent.	3.8	4.3	4.7	4.5	5.4	2.1
°6. Belief in free speech, but not for all.	3.9	3.7	4.0	3.7	4.5	—.8
7. Force is wrong, but sometimes necessary.	5.5	3.5	3.6	4.1	3.8	3.0
8. Masses are intelligent, but also stupid.	3.7	5.8	5.8	5.6	5.7	3.3
°9. Better knowledge of beliefs than disbeliefs.	5.2	5.2	4.9	4.8	4.9	.5
10. Certain "isms" really the same, not different.	4.6	4.4	4.5	4.2	4.9	.6
°11. Man on his own is helpless and miserable.	2.9	2.1	3.4	3.8	3.9	1.4
°12. World we live in a lonesome place.	1.9	3.6	3.0	3.0	3.5	3.0
°13. Most people don't give a "damn" for others.	3.4	3.2	3.7	3.6	3.9	.8
°14. I want to find someone to solve my problems.	4.1	4.5	3.4	3.2	3.6	1.0
°15. It's natural to fear future.	2.6	4.4	3.9	4.0	3.6	3.4
°16. So much to do, so little time to do it in.	5.4	6.0	5.7	6.1	5.7	1.1
°17. Once I get wound up, I can't stop.	2.9	4.2	4.0	3.8	2.9	1.9
°18. I repeat myself to make sure I'm understood.	4.0	3.7	4.2	3.4	3.1	1.4
°19. I don't listen.	3.0	4.4	3.3	2.9	3.4	2.2

413

Items from Dogmatism Scale	Commu- nists N = 13	Bevan- ites N = 19	Atlee- ites N = 27	Liber- als N = 22	Conser- vatives N = 54	t [a]
20. I interrupt others to put across my own views.	3.9	5.0	4.6	4.6	4.3	1.9
°21. Better be dead hero than live coward.	4.6	2.8	2.7	3.3	3.6	1.9
22. Hardest battles are with myself.	3.6	4.9	4.7	5.2	4.5	2.2
23. I'm no good.	3.1	5.3	4.6	4.6	4.5	3.0
24. I'm afraid people will find out what I'm really like.	2.3	3.3	2.9	2.1	3.1	1.3
°25. Secret ambition is to become a great man.	4.9	5.8	5.1	4.1	5.2	1.2
°26. Main thing in life is to do something important.	5.0	4.4	3.6	4.3	4.4	1.8
°27. If given chance I'd benefit world.	5.9	5.5	6.1	4.6	5.7	2.0
28. Greatness more important than happiness.	1.7	2.2	1.9	1.9	2.2	.8
29. People won't practice what they preach.	5.5	5.1	5.5	5.6	5.7	.8
30. Most people failures and the system is responsible.	5.2	4.0	3.3	3.0	2.9	3.2
31. Strangers look at me critically.	2.6	4.2	3.7	4.5	4.3	2.8
32. Only natural to have guilty conscience.	3.9	3.4	3.1	3.4	3.5	1.1
33. People say insulting things about me.	2.3	3.2	2.4	2.5	2.6	1.5
34. I'm talked about.	2.5	4.2	2.8	3.1	3.2	2.4
°35. There are just a handful of great thinkers.	4.7	5.3	5.4	4.7	4.5	1.0
°36. I hate some people because of what they stand for.	4.2	3.6	3.2	2.9	2.7	1.9
°37. A man without a cause hasn't lived.	5.9	4.5	4.0	5.1	4.5	2.4
°38. Life meaningful when there is devotion to cause.	6.3	5.3	5.1	5.6	5.3	2.3
°39. There is only one correct philosophy.	5.2	2.1	2.2	2.3	3.0	4.0
°40. Person believing in too many causes is "wishy-washy."	3.5	2.8	3.1	3.1	3.5	1.1
°41. To compromise is to betray own side.	4.2	3.3	2.5	2.2	2.9	3.0
°42. In religion, we should not compromise.	3.2	2.2	2.9	1.9	2.8	2.1
°43. To consider only one's own happiness is selfish.	5.3	3.4	4.2	4.6	4.3	2.7
44. To compromise is to appease.	3.9	2.1	1.7	1.8	2.6	3.3
°45. Worse crime is to attack those of similar beliefs.	3.9	2.6	2.3	2.5	3.0	2.2

Items from Dogmatism Scale	Commu-nists N = 13	Bevan-ites N = 19	Atlee-ites N = 27	Liber-als N = 22	Conser-vatives N = 54	t [a]
*46. Guard against subversion from within.	3.3	3.3	4.3	3.9	4.1	1.3
*47. Groups tolerating diverse opinions can't exist.	3.5	3.3	3.3	3.1	3.4	.5
*48. Two kinds of people: those for, those against truth.	3.4	2.1	2.4	2.2	2.9	1.7
*49. My blood boils when others won't admit they're wrong.	4.4	4.4	4.9	4.6	4.9	.8
*50. One who thinks of own happiness beneath contempt.	5.2	3.2	4.1	4.3	4.4	2.5
*51. Most printed ideas aren't worth paper printed on.	4.2	3.3	4.2	3.1	3.3	1.7
52. I'm too critical of others' ideas.	4.5	5.4	5.2	4.7	4.8	1.6
*53. To know what's going on, rely on leaders.	3.5	2.7	4.1	3.1	4.5	1.4
*54. Reserve judgment until you hear leaders' opinions.	5.2	5.2	5.5	4.9	5.3	.5
*55. Pick friends who believe as you do.	4.2	4.2	4.3	3.0	4.2	1.7
56. Don't waste money on reading opposing views.	3.7	3.4	3.7	3.2	3.3	.5
57. Keep young people away from confusing books.	3.1	2.3	3.2	3.1	3.4	1.1
*58. Present unhappy. Future is what counts.	4.3	3.0	2.8	2.9	3.4	2.0
59. To progress, return to glorious past.	1.3	1.5	1.4	1.5	1.9	1.7
60. For happiness in future, present injustice necessary.	3.7	4.6	4.5	4.2	4.8	1.5
*61. To accomplish mission, gamble all or nothing.	3.9	5.3	4.4	5.6	5.1	2.6
*62. Most people don't understand what's going on.	4.5	5.3	4.7	4.6	4.6	1.6
*63. Most people don't know what's good for them.	4.3	4.0	4.4	4.0	3.9	.5
64. Nothing new under the sun.	2.0	3.2	2.9	3.1	3.4	2.3
65. If you understand, it's easy to predict the future.	4.5	2.6	2.6	2.1	2.9	3.5
66. Force necessary to advance ideal.	4.9	3.5	3.7	3.6	3.3	2.0

* Items retained in final 40-item Dogmatism Scale, Form E.

[a] In each case t ratios were computed between the mean for Communists and the mean of whichever political group was most different from the Communist mean. These two means are italicized in all cases.

Appendix B

The California F Scale

1. Obedience and respect for authority are the most important virtues children should learn.
2. A person who has bad manners, habits, and breeding can hardly expect to get along with decent people.
3. If people would talk less and work more, everybody would be better off.
4. The businessman and the manufacturer are much more important to society than the artist and the professor.
5. Science has its place, but there are many important things that can never possibly be understood by the human mind.
6. Young people sometimes get rebellious ideas, but as they grow up they ought to get over them and settle down.
7. What this country needs most, more than laws and political programs, is a few courageous, tireless, devoted leaders in whom the people can put their faith.
8. No sane, normal, decent person could ever think of hurting a close friend or relative.
9. Nobody ever learned anything really important except through suffering.
10. What the youth needs is strict discipline, rugged determination, and the will to work and fight for family and country.
11. An insult to our honor should always be punished.
12. Sex crimes, such as rape and attacks on children, deserve more than mere imprisonment; such criminals ought to be publicly whipped, or worse.
13. There is hardly anything lower than a person who does not feel a great love, gratitude, and respect for his parents.
14. Most of our social problems would be solved if we could somehow get rid of the immoral, crooked, and feeble-minded people.

15. Homosexuals are hardly better than criminals and ought to be severely punished.
16. When a person has a problem or worry, it is best for him not to think about it, but to keep busy with more cheerful things.
17. Every person should have complete faith in some supernatural power whose decisions he obeys without question.
18. Some people are born with an urge to jump from high places.
19. People can be divided into two distinct classes: the weak and the strong.
20. Some day it will probably be shown that astrology can explain a lot of things.
21. Wars and social troubles may someday be ended by an earthquake or flood that will destroy the whole world.
22. No weakness or difficulty can hold us back if we have enough will power.
23. It is best to use some prewar authorities in Germany to keep order and prevent chaos.
24. Most people don't realize how much our lives are controlled by plots hatched in secret places.
25. Human nature being what it is, there will always be war and conflict.
26. Familiarity breeds contempt.
27. Nowadays when so many different kinds of people move around and mix together so much, a person has to protect himself especially carefully against catching an infection or disease from them.
28. Nowadays more and more people are prying into matters that should remain personal and private.
29. The wild sex life of the old Greeks and Romans was tame compared to some of the goings-on in this country, even in places where people might least expect it.

Appendix C

The Gough-Sanford Rigidity Scale

1. I am often the last one to give up trying to do a thing.
2. There is usually only one best way to solve most problems.
3. I prefer work that requires a great deal of attention to detail.
4. I often become so wrapped up in something I am doing that I find it difficult to turn my attention to other matters.
5. I dislike to change my plans in the midst of an undertaking.
6. I never miss going to church.
7. I usually maintain my own opinions even though many other people may have a different point of view.
8. I find it easy to stick to a certain schedule, once I have started it.
9. I do not enjoy having to adapt myself to new and unusual situations.
10. I prefer to stop and think before I act even on trifling matters.
11. I try to follow a program of life based on duty.
12. I usually find that my own way of attacking a problem is best, even though it doesn't always seem to work in the beginning.
13. I am a methodical person in whatever I do.
14. I think it is usually wise to do things in a conventional way.
15. I always finish tasks I start, even if they are not very important.
16. I often find myself thinking of the same tunes or phrases for days at a time.

* This scale is now included in the California Psychological Inventory, where it is labeled F_x (Flexibility). In the CPI, the items are scored in a reverse direction from that used in this book, so that a high score denotes a nonrigid or flexible individual. Permission to reproduce this scale has been granted by the Consulting Psychologists Press.

17. I have a work and study schedule which I follow carefully.
18. I usually check more than once to be sure that I have locked a door, put out the light, or something of the sort.
19. I have never done anything dangerous for the thrill of it.
20. I believe that promptness is a very important personality characteristic.
21. I am always careful about my manner of dress.
22. I always put on and take off my clothes in the same order.

Appendix D

Rotated Factor Loadings for Dogmatism and Related Concepts

A. Michigan State University II Group (N = 207) °

Variable	I	II	III	h²
1. Anxiety	.77	−.25	.27	.727
2. Paranoia	.72	−.14	.26	.597
3. Self-rejection	.69	−.29	.37	.698
4. Dogmatism	.46	.21	.62	.637
5. Authoritarianism (F scale)	.27	.48	.66	.737
6. Rigidity	.23	.32	.71	.652
7. Ethnocentrism (E scale)	.21	.59	.47	.614
8. Conservatism (P.E.C.)	−.07	.69	.19	.523
9. Left opinionation	.17	−.63	.26	.498
10. Right opinionation	.03	.85	.19	.765

° From Rokeach and Fruchter (1956d).

B. New York College's Group (N = 153) °

Scale	I	II	III	h²
1. Dogmatism	.68	.10	.48	.707
2. F Scale	.38	.37	.70	.771
3. Anxiety	.72	.03	.27	.588
4. Rigidity	.28	.32	.54	.472
5. Ethnocentrism	.12	.53	.39	.446
6. Political-economic Conservatism	.01	.44	.22	.245
7. Intellectual rejection	.29	.49	.63	.717
8. Intellectual acceptance	−.02	.60	.10	.373
9. Opinionation	.35	.53	.13	.426
10. Right-left score	.12	.61	.11	.402

° From Fruchter, Rokeach, and Novak (1958).

REFERENCES

ABELSON, R. P., and ROSENBERG, M. J. (1958). Symbolic psycho-logic: A model of attitudinal cognition. *Behavioral Science, 3:* 1-13.

ADELSON, J. (1953). A study of minority group authoritarianism. *J. abnorm. soc. Psychol., 48:* 477-485.

ADORNO, T. W., Frenkel-Brunswik, Else, Levinson, D. J., and Sanford, R. N. (1950). *The authoritarian personality.* New York: Harper.

AIKEN, H. D. (1951). The aesthetic relevance of belief. *J. Aesthet., 9:* 301-315.

ALLPORT, F. H. (1955). *Theories of perception and the concept of structure.* New York: Wiley.

ALLPORT, G. W., and VERNON, P. E. (1931). *A study of values.* Boston: Houghton Mifflin.

ALLPORT, G. W. (1954). *The nature of prejudice.* Cambridge: Addison-Wesley.

ALLPORT, G. W. (1955). *Becoming: basic considerations for a psychology of personality.* New Haven: Yale University Press.

ALMOND, G. (1954). *The appeals of communism.* Princeton: Princeton University Press.

ALSON, E. (1958). Cognitive structure and dogmatism. Unpublished Ph.D. Dissertation. University of Buffalo.

AMERICAN HUMANICS FOUNDATION (1950). *The Doings.* Marshall, Missouri: Missouri Valley College.

ASCH, S. E. (1952). *Social psychology.* New York: Prentice-Hall.

BARBER, B. (1957). *Social stratification.* New York: Harcourt, Brace.

BARKER, E. N. (1958). Authoritarianism of the political right, center, and left. Unpublished Ph.D. Dissertation. Teachers College, Columbia University.

BARNDT, R. J., and JOHNSON, D. M. (1955). Time orientation in delinquents. *J. abnorm. soc. Psychol., 51:* 343-345.

BARRON, F. (1953). Complexity-simplicity as a personality dimension. *J. abnorm. soc. Psychol., 48:* 163-172.

BECKER, W. C. (1954). Perceptual rigidity as measured by aniseikonic lenses. *J. abnorm. soc. Psychol., 49:* 419-422.

BERGER, E. M. (1952). The relation between expressed acceptance of self and expressed acceptance of others. *J. abnorm. soc. Psychol.,* 47: 778-782.

BLACK, M. (1946). *Critical thinking.* New York: Prentice-Hall.

BLANSHARD, P. (1951). *Communism, democracy and Catholic power.* Boston: Beacon Press.

BLOCK, J., and BLOCK, JEANNE (1951). An investigation of the relationship between intolerance of ambiguity and ethnocentrism. *J. Personality, 19:* 303-311.

BONIER, R. J. (1957). A study of the relationship between time perspective and open-closed belief systems. Unpublished M.A. Thesis, Michigan State University Library.

BROWN, R. W. (1953). A determinant of the relationship between rigidity and authoritarianism. *J. abnorm. soc. Psychol., 48:* 469-476.

BROWNFAIN, J. J. (1952). Stability of the self-concept as a dimension of personality. *J. abnorm. soc. Psychol., 47:* 597-606.

BRUNER, J. S. (1951). Personality dynamics and the process of perceiving. In R. R. Blake and G. V. Ramsey (Eds.), *Perception: An approach to personality.* New York: Ronald.

BRUNER, J. S., MATTER, JEAN, and PAPANEK, MIRIAM L. (1955). Breadth of learning as a function of drive level and mechanization. *Psychol. Rev., 62:* 1-10.

CAMPBELL, D. T., and McCANDLESS, B. R. (1951). Ethnocentrism, xenophobia, and personality. *Hum. Relat., 4:* 185-192.

CASSERLY, J. V. L. (1953). *The retreat from Christianity in the modern world.* New York: Longmans, Green.

Catholic Encyclopedia (1908). New York: Gilmary Society, Vol. IV.

CATTELL, R. B., and TINER, L. G. (1949). The varieties of structural rigidity. *J. Personality, 17:* 321-341.

CHARTERS, W. W., and NEWCOMB, T. M. (1958). Some attitudinal effects of experimentally increased salience of a membership group. In Eleanor E. Maccoby, T. M. Newcomb, and E. L. Hartley (Eds.), *Readings in social psychology.* New York: Holt, 276-281.

CHEIN, I. (1956). Research needs. *J. soc. Issues, 12:* 57-66.

CHRISTIE, R., and JAHODA, MARIE (Eds.) (1954). *Studies in the scope and method of "The Authoritarian Personality."* Glencoe, Illinois: Free Press.

CHRISTIE, R. (1956a). Eysenck's treatment of the personality of communists. *Psychol. Bull., 53:* 411-430.

CHRISTIE, R. (1956b). Some abuses of psychology. *Psychol. Bull., 53:* 439-451.

CHRISTIE, R., and COOK, PEGGY (1958). A guide to published literature relating to the authoritarian personality through 1956. *J. Psychol.*, 45: 171-199.

CHRISTIE, R., HAVEL, JOAN, and SEIDENBERG, B. (1958). Is the F Scale irreversible? *J. abnorm. soc. Psychol.*, 56: 143-159.

COOK, S. (1957). Desegregation: A psychological analysis. *Amer. Psychologist*, 12: 1-13.

COOMBS, C. H. (1950). Psychological scaling without a unit of measurement. *Psychol. Rev.*, 57: 145-158.

CRONBACH, L. J., and MEEHL, P. E. (1955). Construct validity in psychological tests. *Psychol. Bull.*, 52: 281-302.

CROSSMAN, R. (Ed.) (1949). *The god that failed.* New York: Harper.

DAVIS, J. H. (1958). The disbelief gradient and frame of reference. Unpublished M.A. Thesis. Michigan State University Library.

DEUTSCH, M., and COLLINS, MARY E. (1951). *Interracial housing: A psychological evaluation of a social experiment.* Minneapolis: University of Minnesota Press.

DUNCKER, K. (1945). On problem-solving. *Psychol. Monogr.*, 58, No. 5 (Whole No. 270).

EDWARDS, A. L. (1954). *Statistical methods for the behavioral sciences.* New York: Rinehart.

EHRLICH, H. J. (1955). Dogmatism and intellectual change. Unpublished M.A. Thesis. Ohio State University Library.

ERNST, M. L., and LOTH, D. (1952). *Report on the American communist.* New York: Holt.

ESON, M. E. (1951). Analysis of time perspective at five age levels. Unpublished Ph.D. Dissertation. University of Chicago Library.

EVANS, R. I. (1952). Personal values as factors in anti-Semitism. *J. abnorm. soc. Psychol.*, 47: 749-756.

EYSENCK, H. J. (1954). *The psychology of politics.* London: Routledge & Kegan Paul.

EYSENCK, H. J. (1956a). The psychology of politics: A reply. *Psychol. Bull.*, 53: 177-182.

EYSENCK, H. J. (1956b). The psychology of politics and the personality similarities between fascists and communists. *Psychol. Bull.*, 53: 431-438.

FESTINGER, L. (1943). A statistical test for means of samples from skew populations. *Psychometrika*, 8: 205-210.

FESTINGER, L. (1957). *A theory of cognitive dissonance.* Evanston, Illinois: Row, Peterson.

FINK, H. (1953). The relationship of time perspective to age, institutionalization and activity. Unpublished Ph.D. Dissertation. Michigan State University Library.

FISHER, J. (1951). The memory process and certain psychosocial attitudes, with special reference to the law of prägnanz. I. Study of nonverbal content. *J. Personality, 19:* 406-420.

FISHMAN, J. (1957). New directions in College Board research. *College Board Review,* No. 33, 9-12.

FORD, L. I. (1956). The relationship between prejudice and dogmatism in opinion change. Unpublished Ph.D. Dissertation. Purdue University Library.

FRANK, L. K. (1939). Time perspectives. *J. soc. Philosophy, 4:* 293-312.

FRENKEL-BRUNSWIK, ELSE, and SANFORD, R. N. (1945). Some personality factors in anti-Semitism. *J. Psychol., 20:* 271-291.

FRENKEL-BRUNSWIK, ELSE (1948a). Dynamic and cognitive categorization of qualitative material: II. Application to interviews with the ethnically prejudiced. *J. Psychol., 25:* 261-277.

FRENKEL-BRUNSWIK, ELSE (1948b). A study of prejudice in children. *Hum. Relat., 1:* 295-306.

FRENKEL-BRUNSWIK, ELSE (1949). Intolerance of ambiguity as an emotional and perceptual personality variable. *J. Personality, 18:* 108-143.

FRENKEL-BRUNSWIK, ELSE (1951). Personality theory and perception. In R. R. Blake and G. V. Ramsey (Eds.), *Perception: An approach to personality.* New York: Ronald.

FRENKEL-BRUNSWIK, ELSE (1954). Further explorations by a contributor to "The Authoritarian Personality." In R. Christie and M. Jahoda (Eds.), *Studies in the scope and method of "The Authoritarian Personality."* Glencoe, Illinois: Free Press, 226-275.

FROMM, E. (1941). *Escape from freedom.* New York: Farrar and Rinehart.

FROMM, E. (1947). *Man for himself.* New York: Rinehart.

FRUCHTER, B., ROKEACH, M., and NOVAK, E. G. (1958). A factorial study of dogmatism, opinionation, and related scales. *Psychol. Reports, 4:* 19-22.

GEORGE, F. H., and HANDLON, J. H. (1957). A language for perceptual analysis. *Psychol. Rev., 64:* 14-25.

GLAZER, N. (1954). New light on "The Authoritarian Personality." *Commentary, 17:* 289-297.

GOLDSTEIN, K., and SCHEERER, M. (1941). Abstract and concrete behavior: An experimental study with special tests. *Psychol. Monogr., 53,* No. 2 (Whole No. 239).

GOODSTEIN, L. D. (1953). Intellectual rigidity and social attitudes. *J. abnorm. soc. Psychol., 48:* 345-353.

GOUGH, H. G., and SANFORD, R. N. (1952). Rigidity as a psychological variable. Unpublished manuscript. University of California, Institute of Personality Assessment and Research.

GUNTHER, J. (1955). *Inside Africa*. New York: Harper.

HANLEY, C., and ROKEACH, M. (1956). Care and carelessness in psychology. *Psychol. Bull.*, 53: 183-186.

HARDY, K. R. (1957). Determinants of conformity and attitude change. *J. abnorm. soc. Psychol.*, 54: 289-294.

HARTLEY, E. (1946). *Problems in prejudice*. New York: Kings Crown.

HATHAWAY, S. R., and McKINLEY, J. C. (1943). *The Minnesota Multiphasic Personality Inventory*. New York: Psychological Corporation.

HEIDER, F. (1958). *The psychology of interpersonal relations*. New York: Wiley.

HELSON, H. (1948). Adaptation-level as a basis for a quantitative theory of frames of reference. *Psychol. Rev.*, 55: 297-313.

HILGARD, E. R. (1956). *Theories of learning*. New York: Appleton-Century-Crofts.

HOFFER, E. (1951). *The true believer*. New York: Harper.

HYMAN, H. H., and SHEATSLEY, P. B. (1954). "The Authoritarian Personality"—a methodological critique. In R. Christie and M. Jahoda (Eds.), *Studies in the scope and method of "The Authoritarian Personality."* Glencoe, Illinois: Free Press, 50-122.

INKELES, A., and LEVINSON, D. J. (1954). National character: The study of modal personality and sociocultural systems. In G. Lindzey, (Ed.), *Handbook of social psychology*. Cambridge: Addison-Wesley, 977-1020.

IZARD, C. E. (1959). Personality similarity and friendship. *Amer. Psychologist, 14:* 366 (Abstract).

JACKSON, D. N. (1956). A short form of Witkin's embedded-figures test. *J. abnorm. soc. Psychol.*, 53: 254-255.

JACKSON, D. N. (1957). Intellectual ability and mode of perception. *J. consult. Psychol., 21:* 458.

JAHODA, M. (1956). Psychological issues in civil liberties. *Amer. Psychologist, 11:* 234-240.

JOHNSON, D. M. (1955). *The psychology of thought and judgment*. New York: Harper.

KATONA, G. (1940). *Organizing and memorizing*. New York: Columbia University Press.

KATZ, D., and BRALY, K. W. (1952). Verbal stereotypes and racial prejudice. In G. E. Swanson, T. M. Newcomb, and E. L. Hartley (Eds.), *Readings in social psychology*. New York: Holt, 67-73.

KELLY, G. A. (1955). *The psychology of personal constructs*. New York: Norton.

KEMP, C. G. (1957). Changes in patterns of personal values in relation to open-closed belief systems. Unpublished Ph.D. Dissertation. Michigan State University Library.

KLEIN, G. (1958). Cognitive control and motivation. In G. Lindzey (Ed.), *Assessment of human motives*. New York: Rinehart, 87-118.

KNOX, FATHER R. (1926). Introduction to Maycock, A. L., *The Inquisition*. London: Constable.

KÖHLER, W. (1938). *The place of value in a world of facts*. New York: Liveright.

KOHS, S. C. (1923). *Intelligence measurement*. New York: Macmillan.

KOUNIN, J. S. (1941). Experimental studies of rigidity. I and II. *Character and Personality, 9:* 251-272, 273-282.

KOUNIN, J. S. (1948). The meaning of rigidity: A reply to Heinz Werner. *Psychol. Rev., 55:* 157-166.

KRECH, D., and CRUTCHFIELD, R. S. (1948). *Theory and problems of social psychology*. New York: McGraw-Hill.

KRECH, D. (1949). Notes toward a psychological theory. *J. Personality, 18:* 66-87.

KUTNER, B. (1958). Patterns of mental functioning associated with prejudice in children. *Psychol. Monogr., 72,* No. 7 (Whole No. 460).

LAFFEY, J. L. (1957). A theoretical and empirical analysis of loyalty to and defection from a belief system. Unpublished M.A. Thesis. Michigan State University Library.

LESHAN, L. L. (1952). Time orientation and social class. *J. abnorm. soc. Psychol., 47:* 589-592.

LEVINSON, D. J., and SANFORD, R. N. (1944). A scale for the measurement of anti-Semitism. *J. Psychol., 17:* 339-370.

LEVINSON, D. J. (1949). An approach to the theory and measurement of ethnocentric ideology. *J. Psychol., 28:* 19-39.

LEVITT, E., and ZELEN, S. (1953). The validity of the Einstellung test as a measure of rigidity. *J. abnorm. soc. Psychol., 48:* 573-580.

LEVITT, E. (1956). The water-jar Einstellung tests as a measure of rigidity. *Psychol. Bull., 53:* 347-370.

LEWIN, K. (1936). *Principles of topological psychology*. New York: McGraw-Hill.

LEWIN, K. (1942). Time perspective and morale. In G. B. Watson (Ed.), *Civilian Morale*. Boston: Houghton Mifflin.

LEWIN, K. (1951). *Field theory in social science*. New York: Harper.

LINDNER, R. M. (1953). Political creed and character. *Psychoanalysis, 2:* 10-33.

LIPPMAN, W. (1928). *American inquisitors*. New York: Macmillan.

LITTMAN, R. A., and ROSEN, E. (1950). Molar and molecular. *Psychol. Rev.*, 57: 58-65.

LOTT, A. J., and ROSELL, J. (1959). Race, sex, and assumed similarity. *Amer. Psychologist, 14:* 367 (Abstract).

LUCHINS, A. S. (1942). Mechanization in problem solving—the effect of "Einstellung." *Psychol. Monogr.*, 54, No. 6 (Whole No. 248).

LUCHINS, A. S. (1949). Rigidity and ethnocentrism: A critique. *J. Personality, 17:* 449-466.

LUNDY, R. M. (1958). Self-perceptions regarding masculinity-femininity and descriptions of same and opposite sociometric choices. *Sociometry, 21:* 238-246.

McCLELLAND, D. C., ATKINSON, J. W., CLARK, R. A., and LOWELL, E. L. (1953). *The achievement motive.* New York: Appleton-Century-Crofts.

McGOVNEY, W. C. (1953). Dogmatism and rigidity as determinants of cognition. Unpublished M.A. Thesis. Michigan State University Library.

MACKINNON, D. W. (1944). The structure of personality. In J. McV. Hunt (Ed.), *Personality and the behavior disorders.* New York: Ronald, 3-48.

MAIER, N. R. F. (1930). Reasoning in humans. I. On direction. *J. comp. Psychol., 10:* 115-143.

MANNHEIM, K. (1946). *Ideology and utopia.* London: Routledge & Kegan Paul.

MARYO, JOANN S. (1958). Factors related to similarity, rejection and religious affiliation. Unpublished M.A. Thesis. Michigan State University Library.

MASLOW, A. H. (1943). The authoritarian character structure. *J. soc. Psychol., 18:* 401-411.

MASLOW, A. H. (1948). Cognition of the particular and of the generic. *Psychol. Rev., 55:* 22-40.

MASLOW, A. H. (1951). Resistance to acculturation. *J. soc. Issues, 7:* 26-29.

MASLOW, A. H. (1954). *Motivation and personality.* New York: Harper.

MAY, R. (1950). *The meaning of anxiety.* New York: Ronald.

MEAD, G. H. (1952). Language and the development of the self. In G. E. Swanson, T. M. Newcomb, and E. L. Hartley (Eds.), *Readings in social psychology.* New York: Holt, 44-54.

MEYER, L. (1956). *Emotion and meaning in music.* Chicago: University of Chicago Press.

MIKOL, B. (1958). Open and closed belief systems as correlates of the

427

acceptance of new music and its composers. Unpublished Ph.D. Dissertation. Michigan State University Library.

MILLER, J. G. (1955). Toward a general theory for the behavioral sciences. *Amer. Psychologist, 10:*513-531.

MILLS, C. W. (1951). *White collar.* New York: Oxford University Press.

MORRIS, C. (1956). *Varieties of human value.* Chicago: University of Chicago Press.

MOURRET, F., and THOMPSON, N. (1947). *History of the Catholic Church.* Vol. 5, St. Louis: Herder.

MURRAY, H. A. (1938). *Explorations in personality.* New York: Oxford University Press.

NEWCOMB, T. M. (1950). *Social psychology.* New York: Dryden.

NEWCOMB, T. M. (1956). The prediction of interpersonal attraction. *Amer. Psychologist, 11:* 575-586.

ORAM, A. (1957). Some determinants of the formation and modification of new belief systems. Unpublished M.A. Thesis. Michigan State University Library.

ORWELL, G. (1951). *1984.* New York: New American Library.

OSGOOD, C. E., SUCI, G. J., and TANNENBAUM, P. H. (1957). *The measurement of meaning.* Urbana, Illinois: University of Illinois Press.

PETTIGREW, T. F. (1958). The measurement and correlates of category width as a cognitive variable. *J. Personality, 26:* 532-544.

PIAGET, J. (1954). *The construction of reality in the child.* New York: Basic.

POSTMAN, L. (1951). Toward a general theory of cognition. In J. H. Rohrer and M. Sherif (Eds.), *Social psychology at the crossroads.* New York: Harper, 242-272.

RIEMANN, H. (1956). Catechism of musical aesthetics. In Meyer, L., *Emotion and meaning in music.* Chicago: University of Chicago Press.

RIGG, M. G. (1948). Favorable versus unfavorable propaganda in the enjoyment of music. *J. exp. Psychol., 38:* 78-81.

ROGERS, C. (1951). *Client-centered therapy.* Boston: Houghton Mifflin.

ROKEACH, M. (1948). Generalized mental rigidity as a factor in ethnocentrism. *J. abnorm. soc. Psychol., 43:* 259-278.

ROKEACH, M. (1951a). A method for studying individual differences in "narrow-mindedness." *J. Personality, 20:* 219-233.

ROKEACH, M. (1951b). "Narrow-mindedness" and personality. *J. Personality, 20:* 234-251.

ROKEACH, M. (1951c). Prejudice, concreteness of thinking, and reification of thinking. *J. abnorm. soc. Psychol., 46:* 83-91.

ROKEACH, M. (1952). Attitude as a determinant of distortions in recall. *J. abnorm. soc. Psychol., 47:* 482-488.

ROKEACH, M. (1954). The nature and meaning of dogmatism. *Psychol. Rev., 61:* 194-204.

ROKEACH, M., McGOVNEY, W. C., and DENNY, M. R. (1955). A distinction between dogmatic and rigid thinking. *J. abnorm. soc. Psychol., 51:* 87-93.

ROKEACH, M. (1956a). Political and religious dogmatism: An alternative to the authoritarian personality. *Psychol. Monogr., 70,* No. 18 (Whole No. 425).

ROKEACH, M. (1956b). On the unity of thought and belief. *J. Personality, 25:* 224-250.

ROKEACH, M., and EGLASH, A. (1956c). A scale for measuring intellectual conviction. *J. soc. Psychol., 44:* 135-141.

ROKEACH, M., and FRUCHTER, B. (1956d). A factorial study of dogmatism and related concepts. *J. abnorm. soc. Psychol., 53:* 356-360.

ROKEACH, M., and HANLEY, C. (1956e). Eysenck's tender-mindedness dimension: A critique. *Psychol. Bull., 53:* 169-176.

ROKEACH, M., and JENSEN, P. K. (1956f). The disbelief gradients of religious conviction measured by rejection: A comparison of high and low dogmatics. Unpublished manuscript.

ROKEACH, M., ORAM, A., and MARR, J. (1959). The effects of meprobamate on analysis and synthesis in thinking. *J. Psychol., 48:* 359-366.

ROSENFELD, H., and JACKSON, J. (1959). Effect of similarity of personalities on interpersonal attraction. *Amer. Psychologist, 14:* 366-367 (Abstract).

SALOMON, A. (1949). Prophets, priests and social scientists. *Commentary, 7:* 594-600.

SANFORD, R. N. (1956). The approach to the authoritarian personality. In McCary, J. L. (Ed.), *Psychology of personality.* New York: Logos Press.

SARNOFF, I., and KATZ, D. (1954). The motivational bases of attitude change. *J. abnorm. soc. Psychol., 49:* 115-124.

SCHROEDER, H. J. (1937). *Disciplinary decrees of the general councils.* St. Louis: Herder.

SCHROEDER, H. J. (1950). *Canons and decrees of the Council of Trent.* St. Louis: Herder.

SCODEL, A., and MUSSEN, P. (1953). Social perceptions of authoritarians and nonauthoritarians. *J. abnorm. soc. Psychol., 48:* 181-184.

SHERIF, M. (1958). Group influences upon the formation of norms and attitudes. In Eleanor E. Maccoby, T. M. Newcomb, and E. L. Hartley (Eds.), *Readings in social psychology.* New York: Holt, 219-232.

SHILS, E. A. (1954). Authoritarianism: "right" and "left." In R. Christie, and M. Jahoda (Eds.,) *Studies in the scope and method of "The Authoritarian Personality."* Glencoe, Illinois: Free Press, 24-49.

SIEGEL, S. (1956). *Nonparametric statistics.* New York: McGraw-Hill.

SMITH, F. T. (1943). *An experiment in modifying attitudes toward the Negro.* New York: Teachers College, Columbia University.

SMITH, M. B., BRUNER, J. S., and WHITE, R. W. (1956). *Opinions and personality.* New York: Wiley.

SMITH, PATRICIA W. (1957). Race and belief as determinants of discrimination. Unpublished M.A. Thesis. Michigan State University Library.

SOLOMON, M. D. (1952a). Studies in mental rigidity and the scientific method. I. Rigidity and abilities implied in scientific method. *Science Education, 36:* 240-247.

SOLOMON, M. D. (1952b). Studies in mental rigidity and the scientific method. II. Mental rigidity and comprehensiveness. *Science Education, 36:* 263-269.

SOLOMON, M. D. (1953). Studies in mental rigidity and the scientific method. III. Rigidity and comprehensiveness in the normal classroom situation. *Science Education, 37:* 121-131.

SOROKIN, P. A. (1947). *Society, culture and personality.* New York: Harper.

SULLIVAN, P. L., and ADELSON, J. (1954). Ethnocentrism and misanthropy. *J. abnorm. soc. Psychol., 49:* 246-250.

SWANSON, T. S. (1958). Problem solving as related to dogmatism, depersonalization, and familiarity with chess. Unpublished M.A. Thesis. Michigan State University Library.

TAYLOR, I. A. (1954). Perceptual closure and extreme social attitudes. *Amer. Psychologist, 9:* 482. (Abstract).

TAYLOR, JANET A. (1953). A personality scale of manifest anxiety. *J. abnorm. soc. Psychol., 48:* 285-290.

THURSTONE, L. L. (1944). *A factorial study of perception.* Chicago: University of Chicago Press.

TOCH, H. H. (1955). Crisis situations and ideological revaluations. *Publ. Opin. Quart., 19:* 53-67.

TOLMAN,.E. C. (1948). Cognitive maps in rats and men. *Psychol. Rev., 55:* 189-208.

TOLMAN, E. C. (1954). Freedom and the cognitive need. *Amer. Psychologist, 9:* 536-538.

TOWGOOD, M. (1748). *The dissenting gentleman's answer to the Rev. Mr. White's three letters.* Boston: Rogers and Fowle.

TRUEBLOOD, D. E. (1942). *The logic of belief.* New York: Harper.

VAN LENNUP, D. J. (1957). Personal communication.

VIDULICH, R. N. (1956). The integration of multiple sets into a new belief system. Unpublished M.A. Thesis. Michigan State University Library.

VIDULICH, R. N. (1958). An empirical analysis of the belief referents of persons with open and closed cognitive systems. Unpublished Ph.D. Thesis. Michigan State University Library.

WAELDER, R. (1949). Notes on prejudice. *Vassar Alumnae Magazine.*

WALLACE, M. (1956). Future time perspective in schizophrenia. *J. abnorm. soc. Psychol., 52:* 240-245.

WECHSLER, D. (1955). *The Wechsler adult intelligence scale.* New York: Psychological Corporation.

WEISSKOPF-JOELSON, EDITH. (1953). Some suggestions concerning Weltanschauung and psychotherapy. *J. abnorm. soc. Psychol., 48:* 601-604.

WELCH, G. S. (1952). An anxiety index and an internalization ratio for the MMPI. *J. consult. Psychol., 16:* 65-72.

WERNER, H. (1946). Abnormal and subnormal rigidity. *J. abnorm. soc. Psychol., 41:* 15-24.

WERTHEIMER, M. (1945). *Productive thinking.* New York: Harper.

WESTIE, F. R. (1952). Negro-white status differentials and social distance. *Amer. sociol. Rev., 17:* 550-558.

WHALLEY, ELSA A. (1955). Individual life-philosophies in relation to personality and to systematic philosophy: An experimental study. Unpublished Ph.D. Dissertation. The University of Chicago Library.

WHITE, C. (1952). The use of ranks in a test of significance for comparing two treatments. *Biometrics, 8:* 33-41.

WHITE, R. W. (1959). Motivation reconsidered: the concept of competence. *Psychol. Rev., 66:* 297-333.

WILLIAMS, GENEVA D. (1943). The effect of program notes on the enjoyment of musical selections. *J. gen. Psychol., 29:* 261-279.

WILLIAMS, R. M. (1956). Religion, value-orientations, and intergroup conflict. *J. soc. Issues, 12:* 12-20.

WITKIN, H. A. (1950). Individual differences in ease of perception of embedded-figures. *J. Personality, 19:* 1-15.

WITKIN, H. A., LEWIS, HELEN B., HERTZMAN, M., MACHOVER, KAREN, MEISSNER, PEARL BRETNALL, and WAPNER, S. (1954). *Personality through perception.* New York: Harper.

REFERENCES

Wonderlic, E. F. (1945). *Wonderlic personnel manual.* P.O. Box 7, Northfield, Illinois.

Wright, C. (1926). *The story of the Catholic Church.* New York: Boni.

Zajonc, R. B. (1954). Cognitive structure and cognitive tuning. Unpublished Ph.D. Thesis. University of Michigan Library.

Znaniecki, F. (1952). *Cultural sciences, their origin and development.* Urbana, Illinois: University of Illinois Press.

INDEX